T0245104

## Probabilistic Forecasting and Bayesian Data Assimilation

In this book the authors describe the principles and methods behind probabilistic forecasting and Bayesian data assimilation. Instead of focusing on particular application areas, the authors adopt a general dynamical systems approach, with a selection of low-dimensional, discrete time numerical examples designed to build intuition about the subject.

Part I explains the mathematical framework of ensemble-based probabilistic forecasting and uncertainty quantification. Part II is devoted to Bayesian filtering algorithms, from classical data assimilation algorithms such as the Kalman filter, variational techniques, and sequential Monte Carlo methods, through to more recent developments such as the ensemble Kalman filter and ensemble transform filters. The McKean approach to sequential filtering in combination with coupling of measures serves as a unifying mathematical framework throughout Part II.

The prerequisites are few. Some basic familiarity with probability is assumed, but concepts are explained when needed, making this an ideal introduction for graduate students in applied mathematics, computer science, engineering, geoscience and other emerging application areas of Bayesian data assimilation.

# Probabilistic Forecasting and Bayesian Data Assimilation

SEBASTIAN REICH

University of Potsdam and University of Reading

COLIN COTTER

Imperial College London

# CAMBRIDGE
## UNIVERSITY PRESS

University Printing House, Cambridge CB2 8BS, United Kingdom

Cambridge University Press is part of the University of Cambridge.

It furthers the University's mission by disseminating knowledge in the pursuit of education, learning and research at the highest international levels of excellence.

www.cambridge.org
Information on this title: www.cambridge.org/9781107663916

© Sebastian Reich and Colin Cotter 2015

First published 2015

*A catalogue record for this publication is available from the British Library*

*Library of Congress Cataloguing in Publication data*

ISBN 978-1-107-66391-6 Paperback

# Contents

# Preface

Classical mechanics is built upon the concept of *determinism*. Determinism means that knowledge of the current state of a mechanical system completely determines its future (as well as its past). During the nineteenth century, determinism became a guiding principle for advancing our understanding of natural phenomena, from empirical evidence to first principles and natural laws. In order to formalise the concept of determinism, the French mathematician Pierre Simon Laplace postulated an *intellect* now referred to as *Laplace's demon*:

We may regard the present state of the universe as the effect of its past and the cause of its future. An intellect which at a certain moment would know all forces that set nature in motion, and all positions of all its items of which nature is composed, if this intellect were also vast enough to submit these data to analysis, it would embrace in a single formula the movements of the greatest bodies of the universe and those of the tiniest atoms; for such an intellect nothing would be uncertain and the future just like the past would be present before its eyes.[1]

Laplace's demon has three properties: (i) exact knowledge of the laws of nature; (ii) complete knowledge of the state of the universe at a particular point in time (of course, Laplace was writing in the days before knowledge of quantum mechanics and relativity); and (iii) the ability to solve any form of mathematical equation exactly. Except for extremely rare cases, none of these three conditions is met in practice. First, mathematical models generally provide a much simplified representation of nature. In the words of the statistician George Box: "All models are wrong, some are useful". Second, reality can only be assessed through measurements which are prone to measurement errors and which can only provide a very limited representation of the current state of nature. Third, most mathematical models cannot be solved analytically; we need to approximate them and then implement their solution on a computer, leading to further errors. At the end of the day, we might end up with a perfectly deterministic piece of computer code with relatively little correspondence to the evolution of the natural phenomena of interest to us.

---

[1] We have found this quote in the *Very Short Introduction to Chaos* by Smith (2007*b*), which has also stimulated a number of philosophical discussions on imperfect model forecasts, chaos, and data assimilation throughout this book. The original publication is *Essai philosophique sur les probabilités* (1814) by Pierre Simon Laplace.

Despite all these limitations, computational models have proved extremely useful, in producing ever more skilful *weather predictions*, for example. This has been made possible by an iterated process combining *forecasting*, using highly sophisticated computational models, with *analysis* of model outputs using observational data. In other words, we can think of a computational weather prediction code as an extremely complicated and sophisticated device for extrapolating our (limited) knowledge of the present state of the atmosphere into the future. This extrapolation procedure is guided by a constant comparison of computer generated forecasts with actual weather conditions as they arrive, leading to subsequent adjustments of the model state in the weather forecasting system. Since both the extrapolation process and the data driven model adjustments are prone to errors which can often be treated as *random*, one is forced to address the implied inherent *forecast uncertainties*. The two main computational tools developed within the meteorology community in order to deal with these uncertainties are *ensemble prediction* and *data assimilation*.

In ensemble prediction, forecast uncertainties are treated mathematically as random variables; instead of just producing a single forecast, ensemble prediction produces large sets of forecasts which are viewed as realisations of these random variables. This has become a major tool for quantifying uncertainty in forecasts, and is a major theme in this book. Meanwhile, the term *data assimilation* was coined in the computational geoscience community to describe methodologies for improving forecasting skill by combining measured data with computer generated forecasts. More specifically, data assimilation algorithms meld computational models with sets of observations in order to, for example, reduce uncertainties in the model forecasts or to adjust model parameters. Since all models are approximate and all data sets are partial snapshots of nature and are limited by measurement errors, the purpose of data assimilation is to provide estimates that are better than those obtained by using either computational models or observational data alone. While meteorology has served as a stimulus for many current data assimilation algorithms, the subject of uncertainty quantification and data assimilation has found widespread applications ranging from cognitive science to engineering.

This book focuses on the *Bayesian* approach to data assimilation and gives an overview of the subject by fleshing out key ideas and concepts, as well as explaining how to implement specific data assimilation algorithms. Instead of focusing on particular application areas, we adopt a general dynamical systems approach. More to the point, the book brings together two major strands of data assimilation: on the one hand, algorithms based on *Kalman's formulas* for Gaussian distributions together with their extension to nonlinear systems; and on the other, *sequential Monte Carlo methods* (also called *particle filters*). The common feature of all of these algorithms is that they use *ensemble prediction* to represent forecast uncertainties. Our discussion of ensemble-based data assimilation algorithms relies heavily on the *McKean approach* to filtering and the concept of *coupling of measures*, a well-established subject in probability which has not yet found widespread applications to Bayesian inference and data assimilation. Furthermore, while data assimilation can formally be treated as a special instance of the mathematical subject of filtering and smoothing, applications from the geosciences have highlighted that data assimilation algorithms are needed for very high-dimensional and highly nonlinear scientific models where the classical large sample size limits of statistics cannot be obtained in practice. Finally, in contrast with the assumptions of the *perfect model scenario* (which are central to most of mathematical filtering theory), applications from geoscience and other areas require data assimilation algorithms which can cope with systematic model errors. Hence robustness of data assimilation algorithms under finite ensemble/sample sizes and systematic model errors becomes of crucial importance. These aspects will also be discussed in this book.

It should have become clear by now that understanding data assimilation algorithms and quantification of uncertainty requires a broad array of mathematical tools. Therefore, the material in this book has to build upon a multidisciplinary approach synthesising topics from analysis, statistics, probability, and scientific computing. To cope with this demand we have divided the book into two parts. While most of the necessary mathematical background material on uncertainty quantification and probabilistic forecasting is summarised in Part I, Part II is entirely devoted to data assimilation algorithms. As well as classical data assimilation algorithms such as the Kalman filter, variational techniques, and sequential Monte Carlo methods, the book also covers newer developments such as the ensemble Kalman filter and ensemble transform filters. The *McKean approach* to sequential filtering in combination with coupling of measures serves as a unifying mathematical framework throughout Part II.

The book is written at an introductory level suitable for graduate students in applied mathematics, computer science, engineering, geoscience and other emerging application areas of Bayesian data assimilation. Although some familiarity with random variables and dynamical systems is helpful, necessary mathematical concepts are introduced when they are required. A large number of numerical experiments are provided to help to illustrate theoretical findings; these are mostly presented in a semi-rigorous manner. Matlab code for many of these is available via the book's webpage. Since we focus on ideas and concepts, we avoid proofs of technical mathematical aspects such as existence, convergence etc.; in particular, this is achieved by concentrating on finite-dimensional discrete time processes where results can be sketched out using finite difference techniques, avoiding discussion of Itô integrals, for example. Some more technical aspects are collected in appendices at the end of each chapter, together with descriptions of alternative algorithms that are useful but not key to the main story. At the end of each chapter we also provide exercises, together with a brief guide to related literature.

With probabilistic forecasting and data assimilation representing such rich and diverse fields, it is unavoidable that the authors had to make choices about the material to include in the book. In particular, it was necessary to omit many interesting recent developments in *uncertainty quantification* which are covered by Smith (2014). A very approachable introduction to data assimilation is provided by Tarantola (2005). In order to gain a broader mathematical perspective, the reader is referred to the monograph by Jazwinski (1970), which still provides an excellent introduction to the mathematical foundation of filtering and smoothing. A recent, in-depth mathematical account of filtering is given by Bain & Crisan (2009). The monograph by del Moral (2004) provides a very general mathematical framework for the filtering problem within the setting of Feynman–Kac formulas and their McKean models. Theoretical and practical aspects of sequential Monte Carlo methods and particle filters can, for example, be found in Doucet, de Freitas & Gordon (2001). The popular family of *ensemble Kalman filters* is covered by Evensen (2006). The monograph by Majda & Harlim (2012) develops further extensions of the classic Kalman filter to imperfect models in the context of turbulent flows. We also mention the excellent monograph on optimal transportation and coupling of measures by Villani (2003).

We would like to thank: our colleagues Uri Ascher, Gilles Blanchard, Jochen Bröcker, Dan Crisan, Georg Gottwald, Greg Pavliotis, Andrew Stuart and Peter Jan van Leeuwen for the many stimulating discussions centred around various subjects covered in this book; our students Yuan Cheng, Nawinda Chutsagulprom, Maurilio Gutzeit, Tobias Machewitz, Matthias Theves, James Tull, Richard Willis and Alexandra Wolff for their careful reading of earlier drafts of this book; Jason Frank, who provided us with detailed and very valuable feedback; Dan and Kate Daniels who provided childcare whilst much of Colin's work on the book was taking place; and David Tranah from Cambridge University Press who provided guidance throughout the whole process of writing this book.

Finally, we would like to thank our families: Winnie, Kasimir, Nepomuk, Rebecca, Matilda and Evan, for their patience and encouragement.

# 1 Prologue: how to produce forecasts

This chapter sets out a simplified mathematical framework that allows us to discuss the concept of forecasting and, more generally, prediction. Two key ingredients of prediction are: (i) we have a computational model which we use to simulate the future evolution of the physical process of interest given its current state;[1] and (ii) we have some measurement procedure providing partially observed data on the current and past states of the system. These two ingredients include three different types of error which we need to take into account when making predictions: (i) *precision errors* in our knowledge of the current state of the physical system; (ii) differences between the evolution of the computational model and the physical system, known as *model errors*; and (iii) *measurement errors* in the data that must occur since all measurement procedures are imperfect. Precision and model errors will both lead to a growing divergence between the predicted state and the system state over time, which we attempt to correct with data which have been polluted with measurement errors. This leads to the key question of data assimilation: *how can we best combine the data with the model to minimise the impact of these errors, and obtain predictions (and quantify errors in our predictions) of the past, present and future state of the system?*

## 1.1 Physical processes and observations

In this book we shall introduce *data assimilation algorithms*, and we shall want to discuss and evaluate their *accuracy* and *performance*. We shall illustrate this by choosing examples where the physical dynamical system can be represented mathematically. This places us in a somewhat artificial situation where we must generate data from some mathematical model and then pretend that we have only observed part of it. However, this will allow us to assess the performance of data assimilation algorithms by comparing our forecasts with the "true evolution" of the system. Once we have demonstrated the performance of such algorithms in this setting, we are ready to apply them to actual data assimilation problems

---

[1] It is often the case, in ocean modelling for example, that only partial observations are available and it is already challenging to predict the *current state* of the system (nowcasting). It is also often useful to reconstruct past events when more data become available (hindcasting).

where the true system state is unknown. This methodology is standard in the data assimilation community.

We shall use the term *surrogate physical process* to describe the model that we use to generate the true physical dynamical system trajectory for the purpose of these investigations. Since we are building the surrogate physical process purely to test out data assimilation algorithms, we are completely free to choose a model for this. To challenge these algorithms, the surrogate physical process should exhibit some complex dynamical phenomena. On the other hand, it should allow for numerically reproducible results so that we can make comparisons and compute errors. For example, we could consider a surrogate physical process described in terms of a finite-dimensional state variable $z \in \mathbb{R}^{N_z}$ of dimension $N_z \geq 1$, that has time dependence governed by an *ordinary differential equation* (ODE) of the form

$$\frac{\mathrm{d}z}{\mathrm{d}t} = f(z) + g(t), \quad z(0) = z_0, \tag{1.1}$$

with a chosen vector field $f : \mathbb{R}^{N_z} \to \mathbb{R}^{N_z}$ and a time-dependent function $g(t) \in \mathbb{R}^{N_z}$ for $t \geq 0$ such that solutions of (1.1) exist for all $t \geq 0$ and are unique. While such an ODE model can certainly lead to complex dynamic phenomena, such as *chaos*, the results are not easily reproducible since closed form analytic solutions rarely exist. Instead, we choose to replace (1.1) by a *numerical approximation* such as the *forward Euler scheme*

$$z^{n+1} = z^n + \delta t \left( f(z^n) + g(t_n) \right), \quad t_n = n\, \delta t, \tag{1.2}$$

with iteration index $n \geq 0$, step-size $\delta t > 0$, and initial value $z^0 = z_0$.[2] Usually, (1.2) is used to approximate (1.1). However, here we will choose (1.2) to be our actual surrogate physical process with some specified value of $\delta t$ (chosen sufficiently small for stability). This is then completely reproducible (assuming exact arithmetic, or a particular choice of rounding mode) since there is an explicit formula to obtain the sequence $z^0$, $z^1$, $z^2$, etc.

We shall often want to discuss time-continuous systems, and therefore we choose to use linear interpolation in between discrete time points $t_n$ and $t_{n+1}$,

$$z(t) = z^n + (t - t_n)\frac{z^{n+1} - z^n}{\delta t}, \quad t \in [t_n, t_{n+1}], \tag{1.3}$$

to obtain a completely reproducible time-continuous representation of a surrogate physical process. In other words, once the vector field $f$, together with the step-size $\delta t$, the initial condition $z_0$, and the forcing $\{g(t_n)\}_{n \geq 0}$, have been specified in (1.2), a unique function $z(t)$ can be obtained for $t \geq 0$, which we will denote by $z_{\mathrm{ref}}(t)$ for the rest of this chapter. It should be emphasised at this point that we need to pretend that $z_{\mathrm{ref}}(t)$ is not directly accessible to us during the data assimilation process. Our goal is to estimate $z_{\mathrm{ref}}(t)$ from partial

---

[2]  Throughout this book we use superscript indices to denote a temporal iteration index, for example $z^n$ in (1.2). Such an index should not be confused with the $n$th power of $z$. The interpretation of $z^n$ should hopefully be clear from the circumstances of its use.

measurements of $z_{ref}(t)$, using imperfect mathematical models of the dynamical system. We will return to these issues later in the chapter.

To clarify the setting, we next discuss a specific example for producing surrogate physical processes in the form of a reference solution $z_{ref}(t)$.

---

**Example 1.1**   The *Lorenz-63 model* (Lorenz 1963) has a three-dimensional state variable $z := (x, y, z)^T \in \mathbb{R}^{N_z}$, for scalar variables $x, y, z$, with $N_z = 3$. The variable $z$ satisfies an equation that can be written in the form (1.2) with vector field $f$ given by

$$f(z) := \begin{pmatrix} \sigma(y - x) \\ x(\rho - z) - y \\ xy - \beta z \end{pmatrix}, \tag{1.4}$$

and parameter values $\sigma = 10$, $\rho = 28$, and $\beta = 8/3$. We will use this vector field in the discrete system (1.2) to build a surrogate physical process with step-size $\delta t = 0.001$ and initial conditions

$$x_0 = -0.587, \quad y_0 = -0.563, \quad z_0 = 16.870. \tag{1.5}$$

As we develop this example throughout this chapter, we will discuss model errors, defined as differences between the surrogate physical process and the imperfect model that we will use to make predictions. For that reason we include a non-autonomous forcing term $g$ in (1.2), which will have different definitions in the two models. We shall define the forcing $g(t_n) = g^n = (g_1^n, g_2^n, g_3^n)^T \in \mathbb{R}^3$ for the surrogate physical process as follows: set $a = 1/\sqrt{\delta t}$ and, for $n \geq 0$, define recursively

$$g_i^{n+1} = \begin{cases} 2g_i^n + a/2 & \text{if } g_i^n \in [-a/2, 0), \\ -2g_i^n + a/2 & \text{otherwise,} \end{cases} \tag{1.6}$$

for $i = 1, 2, 3$ with initial values

$$g_1^0 = a(2^{-1/2} - 1/2), \quad g_2^0 = a(3^{-1/2} - 1/2), \quad g_3^0 = a(5^{-1/2} - 1/2).$$

It should be noted that $g_i^n \in [-a/2, a/2]$ for all $n \geq 0$. In order to avoid an undesired accumulation of round-off errors in floating point arithmetic, we need to slightly modify the iteration defined by (1.6). A precise description of the necessary modification can be found in the appendix at the end of this chapter. A reader familiar with examples from the dynamical systems literature might have noticed that the iteration (1.6) reduces to the *tent map iteration* with $a = 1$ and the interval $[-1/2, 1/2]$ shifted to $[0, 1]$. The factor $a > 0$ controls the amplitude of the forcing and the interval has been shifted such that the forcing is centred about zero. We choose this for the surrogate physical process since it is completely reproducible in exact arithmetic, but has very complicated dynamics that can appear random.

The numerical solutions obtained from an application of (1.2) for $n = 0, \ldots,$ $N - 1$ with $N = 2 \times 10^5$ lead to a time-continuous reference solution $z_{ref}(t)$

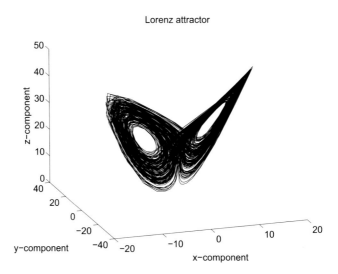

**Figure 1.1** Trajectory of the modified Lorenz-63 model as described in Example 1.1. This trajectory provides us with the desired surrogate physical process. The cloud of solution points is part of what is called the model attractor.

according to the interpolation formula (1.3) for time $t \in [0, 200]$, which is used for all experiments conducted in this chapter. See Figure 1.1 for a phase portrait of the time series. Solutions asymptotically fill a subset of phase space $\mathbb{R}^3$ called the model *attractor*.

Next, we turn our attention to the second ingredient in the prediction problem, namely the measurement procedure. In this setting, neither $z_{\mathrm{ref}}(t)$ nor (1.2) will be explicitly available to us. Instead, we will receive "observations" or "measurements" of $z_{\mathrm{ref}}(t)$ at various times, in the form of measured data containing partial information about the underlying physical process, combined with measurement errors. Hence we need to introduce a mathematical framework for describing such partial observations of physical processes through measurements.

We first consider the case of an error-free measurement at a time $t$, which we describe by a *forward map* (or operator) $h : \mathbb{R}^{N_z} \to \mathbb{R}^{N_y}$

$$y_{\mathrm{obs}}(t) = h(z_{\mathrm{ref}}(t)), \tag{1.7}$$

where we typically have $N_y < N_z$ (corresponding to a partial observation of the system state $z_{\mathrm{ref}}$). For simplicity, we shall only consider $N_y = 1$ in this chapter. Since $h$ is non-invertible, we cannot deduce $z_{\mathrm{ref}}(t)$ from simple inversion, even if the measurements are free from errors.

More realistically, a measurement device will lead to measurement errors, which may arise as the linear superposition of many individual errors $\eta_i \in \mathbb{R}$, $i = 1, \ldots, I$. Based on this assumption, we arrive at a mathematical model of

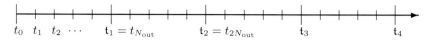

**Figure 1.2** Diagram illustrating model timesteps $t_0$, $t_1$, etc. and observation times $t_1 = t_{N_{\text{out}}}$, $t_2$, etc. Here, $N_{\text{out}} = 5$.

type

$$y_{\text{obs}}(t) = h(z_{\text{ref}}(t)) + \sum_{i=1}^{I} \eta_i(t). \tag{1.8}$$

The quality of a measurement is now determined by the magnitude of the individual error terms $\eta_i$ and the number $I$ of contributing error sources. Measurements will only be taken at discrete points in time, separated by intervals of length $\Delta t_{\text{out}} > 0$. To distinguish the discrete model time $t_n = n\,\delta t$ from instances at which measurements are taken, we use Gothic script to denote measurement points, i.e.,

$$t_k = k\,\Delta t_{\text{out}}, \qquad k \geq 1,$$

and $\Delta t_{\text{out}} = \delta t N_{\text{out}}$ for given integer $N_{\text{out}} \geq 1$. This is illustrated in Figure 1.2.

We again consider a specific example to illustrate our "measurement procedure" (1.8).

---

**Example 1.2** We consider the time series generated in Example 1.1 and assume that we can observe the x-component of

$$z_{\text{ref}}(t) = (x_{\text{ref}}(t), y_{\text{ref}}(t), z_{\text{ref}}(t))^{\mathrm{T}} \in \mathbb{R}^3.$$

This leads to a linear forward operator of the form

$$h(z_{\text{ref}}(t)) = x_{\text{ref}}(t).$$

In this example, we shall use a modified tent map of type (1.6) to model measurement errors. More specifically, we use the iteration

$$\xi_{k+1} = \begin{cases} 2\xi_k + a/2 & \text{if } \xi_k \in [-a/2, 0), \\ -2\xi_k + a/2 & \text{otherwise,} \end{cases} \tag{1.9}$$

with $a = 4$ and starting value $\xi_0 - a(2^{-1/2} - 1/2)$ for $k \geq 0$. From this sequence we store every tenth iterate in an array $\{\Xi_i\}_{i \geq 1}$, i.e.,

$$\Xi_i = \xi_{k=10i}, \qquad i = 1, 2, \dots . \tag{1.10}$$

An observation $x_{\text{obs}}$ at time $t_1 = \Delta t_{\text{out}} = 0.05$ is now obtained as follows:

$$x_{\text{obs}}(t_1) := x_{\text{ref}}(t_1) + \frac{1}{20} \sum_{i=1}^{20} \Xi_i.$$

This procedure fits into the framework of (1.8) with $I = 20$ and $\eta_i(t_1) = \Xi_i/20$, $i = 1, \dots, 20$.

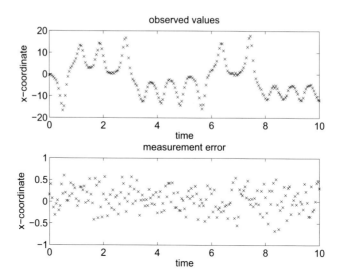

**Figure 1.3** Observed values for the x-component and their measurement errors over the time interval $[0, 10]$ with observations taken every $\Delta t_{\text{out}} = 0.05$ time units.

For the next observation at $t_2 = 2\Delta t_{\text{out}} = 0.1$ we use

$$x_{\text{obs}}(t_2) = x_{\text{ref}}(t_2) + \frac{1}{20} \sum_{i=21}^{40} \Xi_i,$$

and this process is repeated for all available data points from the reference trajectory generated in Example 1.1. Numerical results are displayed for the first 200 data points in Figure 1.3. Our procedure of defining the measurement errors might appear unduly complicated, but we will find later in Chapter 2 that it mimics important aspects of typical measurement errors. In particular, the measurement errors can be treated as *random* even though a perfectly deterministic procedure has defined them.

## 1.2    Data driven forecasting

We now assume that $N_{\text{obs}}$ scalar observations $y_{\text{obs}}(t_k) \in \mathbb{R}$ at $t_k = k\,\Delta t_{\text{out}}$, $k = 1, 2, \ldots, N_{\text{obs}}$, have been made at time intervals of $\Delta t_{\text{out}}$. To define what we understand by a *forecast* or a *prediction*, we select a point in time $t_{k_*}$ that we denote the *present*. Relative to $t_{k_*}$, we can define the *past* $t < t_{k_*}$ and the *future* $t > t_{k_*}$. A possible forecasting (or prediction) problem would be to produce an *estimate* for

$$y_{\text{ref}}(t) := h(z_{\text{ref}}(t))$$

with $t > t_{k_*}$ and only observations from the past and present available. Such statements can be *verified* as soon as a future moment becomes the present and a new measurement becomes available. More generally, we would, of course, like to make predictions about the complete surrogate process $z_{\mathrm{ref}}(t)$ for $t > t_{k_*}$ and not only about the quantity we can actually observe. We will come back to this more challenging task later in this chapter.

Returning to the problem of predicting future observations, we first utilise the concept of *polynomial interpolation*. Recall that there is a unique polynomial

$$q(t) = b_0 + b_1 t + b_2 t^2 + \cdots + b_p t^p \tag{1.11}$$

of order $p$ with coefficients $b_l$ through any $p + 1$ data points. We would like to find a polynomial that interpolates observations at $p + 1$ present and past observation times $\{t_{k_*}, t_{k_*-1}, \ldots, t_{k_*-p}\}$ with the aim of using it to predict future observations. This leads to the interpolation conditions

$$q(t_k) = y_{\mathrm{obs}}(t_k), \qquad t_k \in \{t_{k_*}, t_{k_*-1}, \ldots, t_{k_*-p}\},$$

which determine the $p+1$ coefficients $b_l$ in (1.11) uniquely. A predicted observation at $t > t_{k_*}$ is then simply provided by $q(t)$. Since $t$ is outside the interval of the observed data points, the prediction is an *extrapolation* from the data. For the linear case $p = 1$ we obtain

$$q(t) = y_{\mathrm{obs}}(t_{k_*}) + (t - t_{k_*}) \frac{y_{\mathrm{obs}}(t_{k_*}) - y_{\mathrm{obs}}(t_{k_*-1})}{t_{k_*} - t_{k_*-1}}$$

$$= y_{\mathrm{obs}}(t_{k_*}) + (t - t_{k_*}) \frac{y_{\mathrm{obs}}(t_{k_*}) - y_{\mathrm{obs}}(t_{k_*} - \Delta t_{\mathrm{out}})}{\Delta t_{\mathrm{out}}}.$$

Upon setting $t = t_{k_*+1}$ we obtain the extrapolation formula

$$y_{\mathrm{predict}}(t_{k_*+1}) := q(t_{k_*+1}) = 2y_{\mathrm{obs}}(t_{k_*}) - y_{\mathrm{obs}}(t_{k_*-1}). \tag{1.12}$$

As soon as $y_{\mathrm{obs}}(t_{k_*+1})$ becomes available, we can compare this prediction with the observed value. Furthermore, we can use this new observation point (and discard the oldest one from $t_{k_*-1}$) and a correspondingly updated linear extrapolation formula to obtain $y_{\mathrm{predict}}(t_{k_*+2})$. This can be iterated over several time intervals, repeatedly using data to predict the new observation. To assess the accuracy of this procedure we introduce the following measure.

**Definition 1.3** (Root mean square error)   For a set of predictions and observations at times $\{t_1, t_2, \ldots, t_N\}$ the root mean square error (RMSE) is given by

$$\text{time averaged RMSE} = \sqrt{\frac{1}{N} \sum_{k=1}^{N} |y_{\mathrm{obs}}(t_k) - y_{\mathrm{predict}}(t_k)|^2}. \tag{1.13}$$

In the case of linear interpolation, if there are $N_{\mathrm{obs}}$ observations then $N = N_{\mathrm{obs}} - 2$ since we cannot make predictions using linear interpolation for the first two observations.

We illustrate the linear interpolation prediction strategy by our next example.

---

**Example 1.4**   We utilise the observations generated in Example 1.2 for the first solution component of the Lorenz-63 system, i.e., $y_{\text{obs}}(t_k) = x_{\text{obs}}(t_k)$. Recall that the observation interval is $\Delta t_{\text{out}} = 0.05$. We set the first $t_{k_*}$ equal to $t_{k_*} = 100$, and make a total of 2000 verifiable predictions until we reach $t = 200$. The linear extrapolation formula (1.12) is used for making predictions of observations, and the quality of these predictions is assessed using the time averaged RMSE (1.13) with $N = 2000$. A snapshot of the computational results over a short time-window can be found in Figure 1.4. The time averaged RMSE over the whole interval is approximately 1.2951.

It is usually desirable to "extend the prediction window" by making predictions further into the future. In view of this, we modify the procedure so that at each time $t_{k_*}$, we attempt to predict the observation at time $t_{k_*+2}$ instead of $t_{k_*+1}$. The associated linear extrapolation formula becomes

$$y_{\text{predict}}(t_{k_*+2}) := q(t_{k_*+2}) = 3y_{\text{obs}}(t_{k_*}) - 2y_{\text{obs}}(t_{k_*-1}).$$

The results can also be found in Figure 1.4; the quality of the predictions is clearly worse over this larger window. This is confirmed by the time averaged RMSE which increases to approximately 3.3654.

---

The results of Example 1.4 show that linear interpolation does not provide good predictions over longer times. This suggests the accuracy of forecasts can be improved by extending the extrapolation formula (1.12) to use a linear combination of the present data point plus several previous data points of the form

$$y_{\text{predict}}(t_{k_*+1}) = \sum_{l=0}^{p} a_l\, y_{\text{obs}}(t_{k_*-l}). \tag{1.14}$$

We have already seen that linear extrapolation fits into this framework with $p = 1$ and coefficients $a_0 = 2$, $a_1 = -1$. We recall that the linear extrapolation formula (1.12) was based on first deriving the linear interpolation formula. Hence, as a first attempt at deriving coefficients $a_l$ for (1.14) with $p > 1$, we shall use higher-order interpolation formulas. Interpolation formulas of order $p$ can be conveniently based on the Lagrange polynomials (Süli & Mayers 2006) of order $p$

$$l_j(t) = \frac{\prod_{i \neq j}(t - t_i)}{\prod_{i \neq j}(t_j - t_i)},$$

where the indices $i$ and $j$ run over the integers

$$\{k_*, k_* - 1, \ldots, k_* - p\}.$$

These polynomials have the useful property that

$$l_j(t_i) = \begin{cases} 1 & \text{if } j = i, \\ 0 & \text{otherwise,} \end{cases}$$

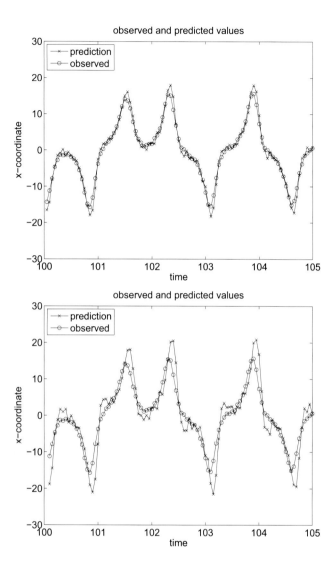

**Figure 1.4** Observed values for the x-component and its predicted values using linear extrapolation. The figure at the top shows the results from linear extrapolation over a single observation interval $\Delta t_{\text{out}} = 0.05$, while the figure beneath shows results when doubling the prediction interval to $0.1$ time units.

which leads to the interpolation formula

$$q(t) = l_{k_*}(t)\, y_{\text{obs}}(\mathsf{t}_{k_*}) + l_{k_*-1}(t)\, y_{\text{obs}}(\mathsf{t}_{k_*-1}) + \cdots + l_{k_*-p}(t)\, y_{\text{obs}}(\mathsf{t}_{k_*-p}). \quad (1.15)$$

The coefficients $a_l$ in (1.14) are obtained by setting $t = \mathsf{t}_{k_*+1}$ in (1.15), i.e.

$$a_l = l_{k_*-l}(\mathsf{t}_{k_*+1}), \qquad l = 0, 1, \ldots, p.$$

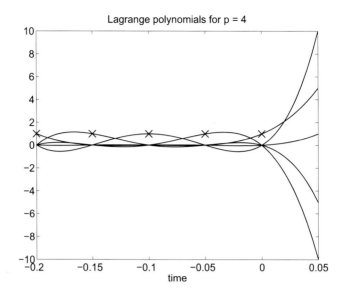

**Figure 1.5** Lagrange polynomials $l_j(t)$ of order four corresponding to observations at $t_i = 0, -0.05, -0.1, -0.15, -0.2$. The coefficients $a_l$ in (1.14) are equal to the values of the Lagrangian polynomials at $t = 0.05$. Crosses mark the points where each polynomial takes the value one. Note that the other polynomials are zero at those interpolation points, and note the steep increase in magnitude outside the interpolation interval $t \in [-0.2, 0]$.

---

**Example 1.5**   We consider extrapolation based on polynomial interpolation of order $p = 4$. The associated extrapolation coefficients in (1.14) are

$$a_0 = 5, \ a_1 = -10, \ a_2 = 10, \ a_3 = -5, \ a_4 = 1,$$

and the associated Lagrange polynomials are shown in Figure 1.5, taking $t_{k_*} = 0$ for simplicity. The values of the extrapolation coefficients can be obtained by inspecting the intersection of the Lagrange polynomials with the vertical line at $t = 0.05$.

The results of applying the fourth-order extrapolation formula to the data set from Example 1.2 are shown in Figure 1.6; the time averaged RMSE was 4.2707. This error is much larger than that observed for linear extrapolation (compare Example 1.4). The reason for this discrepancy can be found in the strong separation of the Lagrange polynomials outside the interpolation interval (compare Figure 1.5), which results in relatively large coefficients $a_l$ in (1.14). Hence even relatively small measurement errors can be severely amplified and do not necessarily cancel out. This effect becomes even more pronounced when the prediction interval is doubled to $2\Delta t_{\text{out}}$. The associated extrapolation coefficients are now given by

$$a_0 = 15, \ a_1 = -40, \ a_2 = 45, \ a_3 = -24, \ a_4 = 5.$$

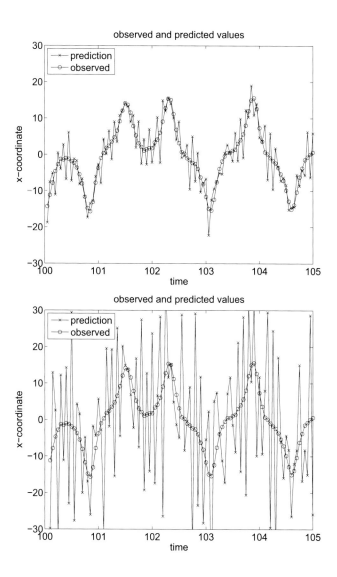

**Figure 1.6** Observed values for the x-component and its predicted values using fourth-order extrapolation. The figure at the top shows the results from extrapolation over a single observation interval $\Delta t_{\mathrm{out}} = 0.05$ while the figure beneath shows results for doubling the prediction interval to $0.1$ time units. Compare these results to those displayed in Figure 1.4 for linear extrapolation.

See Figure 1.6 for numerical results.

We now discuss an entirely different approach for determining the coefficients $a_l$ in (1.14). Instead of using polynomial interpolation, we shall seek the coefficients that optimise the prediction errors for a chosen subset of the observations, which we call the *training set*. These extrapolation coefficients are then fixed, and can be used to predict future observations. We shall assess the performance of our extrapolation coefficients on the remaining observation points, which we shall call the *test set*. For simplicity, let us assume that the training set consists of the first $N_T < N_{obs}$ observations $\{y_{obs}(t_1), \ldots, y_{obs}(t_{N_T})\}$, and use the remaining data points as the test set.

Given a chosen set of coefficients $a_l \in \mathbb{R}$, $l = 0, \ldots, p$, we can obtain a prediction of $y_{obs}(t_{j+p+1})$ for $0 < j \le N_T - p - 1$ by using (1.14). The quality of the predictions is measured by the residuals

$$r_j = y_{obs}(t_{j+p+1}) - y_{predict}(t_{j+p+1})$$

$$= y_{obs}(t_{j+p+1}) - \sum_{l=0}^{p} a_l y_{obs}(t_{j+p-l}) \tag{1.16}$$

for $j = 1, 2, \ldots, J$ with $J = N_T - p - 1$. We now seek the coefficients $a_l$ in (1.14) such that the resulting time averaged RMSE is minimised over the training set. This is equivalent to minimising the functional

$$L(\{a_l\}) = \frac{1}{2} \sum_{j=1}^{J} r_j^2;$$

we have recovered the *method of least squares*. The minimum of $L(\{a_l\})$ is attained when the partial derivatives of $L$ with respect to the coefficients $a_l$ vanish, i.e.,

$$\frac{\partial L}{\partial a_l} = -\sum_{j=1}^{J} y_{obs}(t_{j+p-l}) \, r_j = 0 \tag{1.17}$$

for $l = 0, \ldots, p$. These conditions lead to $p + 1$ linear equations which may be solved for the $p + 1$ unknown coefficients $a_l$.

Once an optimal set of coefficients $a_l$ has been found, these coefficients can be used in (1.14) to make predictions over the test set. The underlying assumption is that the training and test sets display a similar behaviour. Mathematically speaking, this relies on the assumption of *stationarity* of the time series of observations. See Chorin & Hald (2009) for more details.

We mention in passing that (1.14) with coefficients $a_l$ determined by the method of least squares may be considered as a particular instance of an *autoregressive model* of order $p + 1$. The class of autoregressive models provides an example of purely data driven models.

---

**Example 1.6**   We return again to the setting from Example 1.4. We replace the linear extrapolation procedure by predictions using (1.14) with the coefficients $a_l$ determined by the method of least squares. We find that setting $p = 4$ in (1.14) and a training set with $N_T = N_{obs}/2 = 2000$ leads to a time averaged RMSE of

0.9718 with coefficients

$$a_0 = 2.0503, \ a_1 = -1.2248, \ a_2 = -0.2165, \ a_3 = 0.4952, \ a_4 = -0.1397.$$

Note that these values fluctuate much less about the observed values than those obtained from fourth-order interpolation (compare Example 1.5) and that the values for $a_0$ and $a_1$ are relatively close to those obtained from linear extrapolation (compare (1.12)). Hence we may argue that the method of least squares leads to a modified linear extrapolation procedure with a slight reduction in the time averaged RMSE.

We also apply the same methodology to predict $y$ at $t_{k_*+2}$ (prediction over $2\Delta t_{\text{out}} = 0.01$) and find that the averaged RMSE increases to 2.3039. See Figure 1.7 for some numerical results.

---

The mathematical structure of the least squares approach becomes more transparent when put into matrix notation. We first collect the unknown coefficients $a_l$ into a vector

$$x = \begin{pmatrix} a_0 \\ a_1 \\ \vdots \\ a_p \end{pmatrix} \in \mathbb{R}^{p+1}$$

and the residuals $r_j$ into a vector

$$r = \begin{pmatrix} r_1 \\ r_2 \\ \vdots \\ r_J \end{pmatrix} \in \mathbb{R}^J.$$

Next we write (1.14) as

$$r = b - Ax,$$

where $b \in \mathbb{R}^J$ is defined by

$$b = \begin{pmatrix} y_{\text{obs}}(t_{p+2}) \\ y_{\text{obs}}(t_{p+3}) \\ \vdots \\ y_{\text{obs}}(t_{p+J+1}) \end{pmatrix} \in \mathbb{R}^J$$

and the matrix $A \in \mathbb{R}^{J \times (p+1)}$ by

$$A = \begin{pmatrix} y_{\text{obs}}(t_{p+1}) & y_{\text{obs}}(t_p) & \cdots & y_{\text{obs}}(t_1) \\ y_{\text{obs}}(t_{p+2}) & y_{\text{obs}}(t_{p+1}) & \cdots & y_{\text{obs}}(t_2) \\ \vdots & \vdots & & \vdots \\ y_{\text{obs}}(t_{p+J}) & y_{\text{obs}}(t_{p+J-1}) & \cdots & y_{\text{obs}}(t_J) \end{pmatrix}.$$

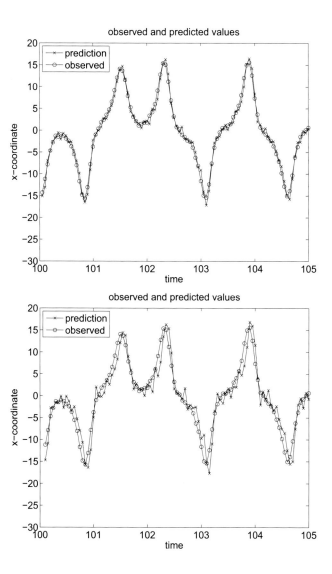

**Figure 1.7** Observed values of the x-component and corresponding predicted values using the method of least squares with $p = 4$ in (1.14). The figure on the top shows the results from predictions over a single observation interval $\Delta t_{\text{out}} = 0.05$, and the figure beneath shows results when doubling the prediction interval to $0.1$ time units. The results should be compared to those in Figures 1.4 and 1.6 obtained from extrapolation.

For square matrices $A$ (i.e., $J = p + 1$) with $\det(A) \neq 0$ we recall that $x$ can be determined such that $r = 0$ and

$$x = A^{-1}b.$$

However, in practice we are usually dealing with the case of overdetermined systems of equations for which $J \gg p + 1$ and for which there is in general no $x$

such that $r = 0$. The method of least squares determines $x_* \in \mathbb{R}^{p+1}$ such that the norm of the vector $r$ is minimised, i.e.,

$$x_* = \arg\min \|r\|^2 = \arg\min \|Ax - b\|^2.$$

We find that the gradient of the functional $L(x) = \|Ax - b\|^2$ with respect to $x$ is given by

$$\nabla_x L(x) = 2A^{\mathrm{T}}(Ax - b) \in \mathbb{R}^{p+1}.$$

Here $A^{\mathrm{T}} \in \mathbb{R}^{(p+1) \times J}$ denotes the transpose of $A$. Furthermore, the Hessian (matrix of second derivatives) of $L(x)$ is

$$H = 2A^{\mathrm{T}}A \in \mathbb{R}^{(p+1) \times (p+1)},$$

which is positive definite when $A$ has maximum column rank $p + 1$. If this is the case, then setting $\nabla L(x_*) = 0$ leads to the following equation for $x_*$,

$$A^{\mathrm{T}}Ax_* = A^{\mathrm{T}}b.$$

We can confirm that we have a minimiser of $L(x)$ since

$$
\begin{aligned}
L(x_* + \delta x) &= L(x_*) + \nabla_x L(x_*)^{\mathrm{T}} \delta x + \delta x^{\mathrm{T}} A^{\mathrm{T}} A \delta x \\
&= L(x_*) + \delta x^{\mathrm{T}} A^{\mathrm{T}} A \delta x \\
&> L(x_*),
\end{aligned}
$$

for all vectors $\delta x \neq 0$.

## 1.3 Model driven forecasting and data assimilation

So far in this chapter, we have used observations and elementary mathematical tools to design *linear models* for predicting future outcomes in the observable variable $y = h(z)$. More precisely, we have considered mathematical tools that rely on the observed quantities alone, without any reference to our surrogate physical process from which they were generated. The predictions were constrained by the assumption of a polynomial form in time, or by optimising the coefficients over a training set. These models are often described as *empirical* or *bottom-up*. We now introduce our third ingredient, the use of *mechanistic* or *top-down* models of the physical process that are derived from *first principles*, a process well established in the context of classical mechanics (Arnold 1989), for example. In practice such first principles might be provided by conservation of mass and/or energy or by Newton's laws of motion, or other analogues in e.g. biology, sociology or economics. Given an estimate of the system state $z(t_0)$ at time $t_0$, a model allows us to obtain estimates of the system state $z(t)$ for $t > t_0$. In almost all cases the model is imperfect, and model errors lead to increased errors in the state estimate over time, unless it is corrected by introducing more data at later times.

In the somewhat artificial setting of this chapter, we imagine that understanding of the surrogate physical process has allowed us to derive a model from first principles, in the form of the difference equation

$$z^{n+1} = z^n + \delta t f(z^n), \qquad t_{n+1} = t_n + \delta t. \qquad (1.18)$$

In this case, we have chosen a scenario where the difference between the surrogate physical process, as provided by (1.2), and our mechanistic model, as given by (1.18), is simply in the inclusion or omission of the time-dependent driving term $g(t)$. This allows us to easily quantify the impact of the error. In practice, when data are obtained from an observed physical process, quantifying this error is a much more difficult problem. In our case, provided that we have exact knowledge of the state $z_{ref}^n$ of our surrogate physical process at time $t_n$ and provided we use this information in order to set $z_{model}^n = z_{ref}^n$ in our mechanistic model, the one step ahead *prediction error* $e^{n+1} = z_{model}^{n+1} - z_{ref}^{n+1}$ is given by

$$e^{n+1} = -\delta t \, g(t_n), \qquad t_n = n \, \delta t. \qquad (1.19)$$

We will also call $e^n$ the *model error* since $e^n$ reflects the difference between (1.2), our surrogate physical process, and (1.18), our mechanistic model for this process. One specific type of model errors are *discretisation errors* that arise when mechanistic models are approximated numerically. We will return to the issue of discretisation errors in Chapter 4.

At this point two major challenges arise. First, we wish to predict over time intervals much larger than $\delta t$. Second, we can only partially observe the present states of the underlying physical process in intervals of $\Delta t_{out}$; we do not have access to the full state vector $z_{ref}(t)$ at any moment in time. The first difficulty requires us to assess the propagation and accumulation of model errors over several timesteps, under the hypothetical assumption that both the physical process and the mechanistic model start from the same initial state $z^0$ at $t_0 = 0$. We explore this in the next example.

---

**Example 1.7**   We return to Example 1.1 and simulate (1.18) with the vector field $f(z)$ given by (1.4). We then compare the surrogate physical process as simulated in Example 1.1.

The numerical solution obtained from an application of (1.18) is stored over a time interval $t_0 = 0$ to $t_{end} = 200$ in intervals of $\Delta t_{out} = 0.05$. These $3 \times 4001$ data points provide us with the model output $z_{model}(t_k)$ at $t_k = k \Delta t_{out}$, which can be compared to the reference trajectory $z_{ref}(t_k)$ from Example 1.1. We plot the phase portrait of the time series from our mechanistic model in Figure 1.8. The result looks rather similar to the phase portrait displayed in Figure 1.1, which indicates that our mechanistic model is able to capture qualitative aspects of the surrogate physical process.

We next check whether this property carries over to specific predictions. In order to assess this aspect of our mechanistic model, both the mechanistic model and physical process are started from the same initial condition (1.5) at time $t_0 =$

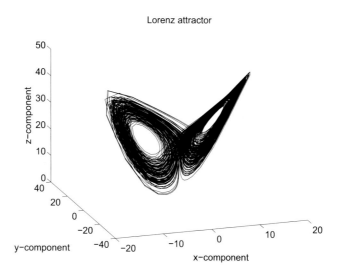

Lorenz attractor

**Figure 1.8** Long trajectory from our mechanistic model which traces the Lorenz attractor of our model. The shape of the attractor is nearly identical to that displayed in Figure 1.1.

0. We display the results in all three state variables over a time interval $[0, 10]$ in Figure 1.9. A difference in the solutions becomes noticeable at about $t = 2$; this is much longer than the prediction intervals obtained for linear interpolation and/or an autoregressive model obtained from the method of least squares. However, this comparison is unrealistic as we require the precise knowledge of the initial state in order to make predictions based on our mechanistic model. Indeed, the exact initial or present state is unavailable in most practical applications.

The previous example has demonstrated that the use of mechanistic models can lead to skilful predictions over relatively long time intervals, provided the model state from which we start our prediction is sufficiently close to the state of the physical process under consideration at the initial time. It should also be obvious that the quality of model-based predictions will depend on the relative magnitude of the modelling errors $e^n$ and the subsequent systematic contributions from $\delta t f(z^n)$ in (1.18).

From these findings we conclude that (i) we need methods for estimating appropriate initial conditions for our mechanistic model from the available observations; and that (ii) we should strive to improve our mechanistic models by making the unaccounted contributions from $g(t)$ as small as possible. Both tasks can be addressed by clever combinations of mechanistic models with observational data. Associated computational techniques are often referred to as *data assimilation* in the geosciences and *filtering/smoothing* in the engineering community. Throughout this book we will primarily use the term data assimilation,

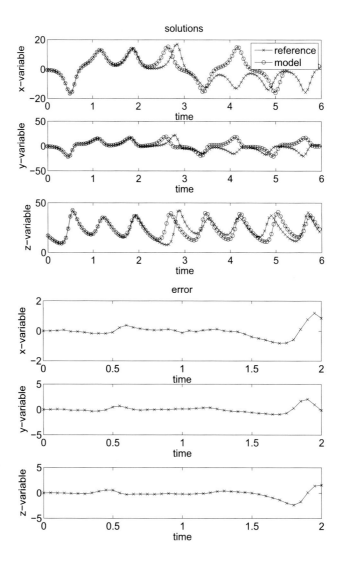

**Figure 1.9** We compare the behaviour of our mechanistic model to the reference trajectory under the assumption that both start from the same initial condition at time $t = 0$. The differences between the model and nature are caused by the non-autonomous driving terms $g^n = g(t_n)$ in (1.2) and their accumulative effect. These differences become significant at about $t = 2$ as can be seen from the bottom panel, which displays the differences in all three solution components as a function of time.

which, broadly speaking, covers the task of combining mechanistic models with partial observations in order to produce skilful forecasts.

To give a flavour of what is to come in Part II of this book, we present an application of the method of least squares to the state estimation of a mechanistic model (1.18). Let us assume that observations $y_{\mathrm{obs}}(t_k)$ are available at time instances

$$t_k = k\,\Delta t_{\text{out}}, \qquad k = 1, \dots, N_{\text{A}},$$

where $\Delta t_{\text{out}} = N_{\text{out}}\delta t$ for given integer $N_{\text{out}} \geq 1$. Starting from the initial condition $z^0$ at $t = 0$, $kN_{\text{out}}$ applications of (1.18) produces a model solution $z_{\text{model}}(t_k)$ and a simulated observation $y_{\text{model}}(t_k) = h(z_{\text{model}}(t_k))$, which can be compared to the observed value $y_{\text{obs}}(t_k)$. The differences between simulated and true observations is measured in a residual

$$r_k = y_{\text{model}}(t_k) - y_{\text{obs}}(t_k) = h(z_{\text{model}}(t_k)) - y_{\text{obs}}(t_k), \qquad k = 1, \dots, N_{\text{A}}.$$

The residual implicitly depends on the model initial condition $z^0$, since this changes the entire model trajectory and therefore the simulated observations $y_{\text{model}}(t_k)$. To simplify the discussion, we will assume that the forward operator $h$ is linear and is represented by a row vector $H \in \mathbb{R}^{1 \times N_z}$, i.e.,

$$h(z) = Hz.$$

Adopting the method of least squares, we seek the initial condition $z^0$ that minimises the residual sum

$$L(z^0) = \frac{1}{2} \sum_{k=1}^{N_{\text{A}}} r_k^2. \tag{1.20}$$

We denote a minimiser by $z_*^0$, and recall from elementary calculus that $z_*^0$ has to be a critical point of $L$ to be a candidate for a minimum, i.e., the gradient $\nabla_{z^0} L(z^0) \in \mathbb{R}^{N_z}$ has to vanish at $z^0 = z_*^0$. In contrast with the linear least squares method considered previously, we now must solve systems of nonlinear equations to find critical points of $L$. These critical points may correspond to local minima or even maxima. The main complication arises from the nonlinear dependence of $z_{\text{model}}(t_k)$ on $z^0$. In order to make this dependence explicit, we introduce the map $\psi$ as a shorthand for the $N_{\text{out}}$-fold application of (1.18), i.e. if we define

$$z_{\text{model}}(t_{k+1}) = \psi(z_{\text{model}}(t_k)), \qquad k \geq 0,$$

then

$$z_{\text{model}}(t_k) = \psi^k(z^0) := \underbrace{\psi(\psi(\cdots\psi(z^0)))}_{k\text{-fold application of }\psi}. \tag{1.21}$$

Computing the gradient of $L(z^0)$ requires the Jacobian matrix of first derivatives of $z_{\text{model}}(t_k) \in \mathbb{R}^{N_z}$ with respect to the initial condition $z^0 \in \mathbb{R}^{N_z}$, given by

$$Dz_{\text{model}}(t_k) := D\psi^k(z^0) \in \mathbb{R}^{N_z \times N_z}.$$

The Jacobian can be computed from (1.21) directly or using the following recursive approach. First we note that a single application of (1.18) leads to

$$Dz^1 := D(z^0 + \delta t f(z^0)) = I + \delta t Df(z^0),$$

since $Dz^0 = I$ and $Df(z) \in \mathbb{R}^{N_z \times N_z}$ denotes the Jacobian matrix of partial derivatives of $f(z)$. The calculation of $Dz^2$ can now be decomposed into

$$Dz^2 := D(z^1 + \delta t f(z^1)) = (I + \delta t Df(z^1))\, Dz^1,$$

using the chain rule of differentiation. More generally, one finds the recursion

$$Dz^{n+1} = (I + \delta t Df(z^n))\, Dz^n \tag{1.22}$$

for $n \geq 0$ with $Dz^0$ equal to the identity matrix. Upon setting $n = kN_{\text{out}}$, we obtain the desired expression for the Jacobian $D\psi^k(z^0)$ and the gradient of $L$ is given by

$$\nabla_{z^0} L(z^0) = \sum_{k=1}^{N_A} (D\psi^k(z^0))^{\mathrm{T}} H^{\mathrm{T}} r_k. \tag{1.23}$$

The minimiser $z_*^0$ must satisfy

$$\nabla_{z^0} L(z_*^0) = 0.$$

Later in this book we will show that an explicit calculation of the Jacobian $Dz_{\text{model}}(t_k)$ *via* the recursion (1.22) is not necessary for determining (1.23). We emphasise again that, in contrast with the linear method of least squares, the existence and uniqueness of a critical point of $L$ is often not guaranteed *a priori*. In addition, critical points may correspond to local maxima or saddle points instead of minima.

A (local) minimum of $L$ can be searched for by the *gradient* or *steepest decent method*, which is an iteration of the form

$$z^{(l+1)} = z^{(l)} - \alpha \nabla_{z^0} L(z^{(l)}) \tag{1.24}$$

for $l \geq 0$ and an appropriate initial guess $z^{(0)}$. The coefficient $\alpha > 0$ needs to be chosen sufficiently small in order to guarantee

$$L(z^{(l+1)}) \leq L(z^{(l)})$$

throughout the iteration process. More refined gradient methods would choose the coefficient $\alpha$ adaptively (see Nocedal & Wright (2006), for example).

Let us assume that we have obtained a reasonable estimate for the initial state $z^0$ of our mechanistic model and that a series of $N_A$ observations within the assimilation window become available at $t_1, \ldots, t_{N_A}$. Then we can iterate (1.24) with starting value $z^{(0)} = z^0$ until

$$\|\nabla_{z^0} L(z^{(l_*)})\| \leq \varepsilon, \tag{1.25}$$

where $\varepsilon > 0$ is a desired tolerance. The resulting $z_*^0 = z^{(l_*)}$ is often called the *analysis* at $t = 0$ and we have completed what is often called a *variational data assimilation* cycle.

Once the analysis $z_*^0$ has been obtained, we can use the mechanistic model (1.18) with adjusted initial condition $z^0 = z_*^0$ to obtain *forecasts* $z_{\text{model}}(t)$ for $t > t_{N_A}$. In due course, a new sequence of observations $y_{\text{obs}}(t_{N_A+k})$, $k = 1, \ldots, N_A$,

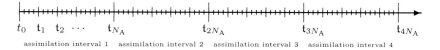

assimilation interval 1    assimilation interval 2    assimilation interval 3    assimilation interval 4

**Figure 1.10** Diagram illustrating model time-steps, observation times, and assimilation intervals. At the end of each assimilation window, a new trajectory is computed that uses the observations made during that window.

becomes available. At this point a new data assimilation cycle can be initiated. More specifically, we can repeat the above nonlinear least squares method by minimising the cost functional $L(z^0)$ with residuals $r_k$, $k = 1, \ldots, N_A$, now given by

$$r_k = H\psi^k(z^0) - y_{\text{obs}}(t_{N_A+k})$$

and starting value $z^{(0)} = z_{\text{model}}(t_{N_A})$ in (1.24).[3] The information from the previous sequence of observations feeds in via the choice of initial condition for the steepest descent calculation, which may select a particular local minimum; this may also speed up the calculation by starting closer to the minimum. It is often also desirable to make better use of this information by including a penalty term in the functional that becomes large if $z^0$ gets too far from this initial guess, encoding our belief that the previous data assimilation cycle gave us a good guess for the current system state. This presents a difficulty: we must then decide how much weight in the functional to give the previous forecast relative to the new observational data. We leave this problem for now, but it is a central topic for the rest of the book.

In contrast with the forecasted values $z_{\text{model}}(t)$, $t > t_{N_A}$, which do not make use of the observations $y_{\text{obs}}(t_{N_A+k})$, $k \geq 1$, the minimiser $z_*^0$ of $L$ now provides an improved approximation $z_{\text{model}}(t)$, called the *analysis*, using the mechanistic model (1.18) with adjusted initial condition $z_{\text{model}}(t_{N_A}) = z_*^0$. In order to distinguish the forecast from the analysis we introduce the notation $z_{\text{model}}^f(t_k)$ for the forecast at time $t_k$, $k = N_A + 1, \ldots, 2N_A$, and $z_{\text{model}}^a(t_k)$ for the analysis arising from the adjusted initial condition at $t_{N_A}$.

Once time $t$ is increased beyond $t = t_{2N_A}$ the analysis $z_{\text{model}}^a(t)$ becomes a forecast and, as soon as all necessary observations have become available, $z_{\text{model}}^a(t_{2N_A})$ is taken as the starting value $z^{(0)}$ for the next assimilation cycle covering the interval $[t_{2N_A}, t_{3N_A}]$. The process of producing forecasts with the mechanistic model and correcting them by assimilating available observations over finite time intervals can now be repeated as often as desired, as illustrated in Figure 1.10.

Each data assimilation cycle effectively leads to a nudging of the model output towards observations. In other words, the sequence of data assimilation cycles

---

[3] The simplification of always minimising with respect to $z^0$ and only changing the observations in the definition of the residuals $r_k$ is possible since our mechanistic model (1.18) is assumed to be time independent.

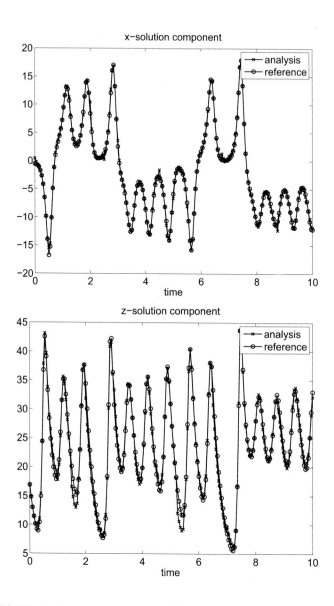

**Figure 1.11** We display the results from 40 data assimilation cycles each over a window of length $5\,\Delta t_{\mathrm{out}} = 0.25$. Only the x-variable is observed in intervals of $\Delta t_{\mathrm{out}} = 0.05$. The synchronising effect of the nonlinear least squares approach can be clearly seen both in the x variable and the unobserved z variable, while the model output without adjustments from the data assimilation cycles loses track of the underlying physical process at about $t = 2$. Compare Figure 1.9.

should ideally synchronise the model (1.18) with the physical process via partial observations and corresponding adjustments in model forecasts $z^{\mathrm{f}}_{\mathrm{model}}(\mathrm{t}_{mN_{\mathrm{A}}})$,

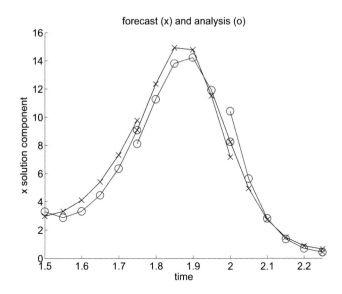

**Figure 1.12** We display the forecast (which does not take the observations into account) and the analysis (which has assimilated the observations) for three data assimilation cycles. The forecast is in blue and marked with crosses, and the analysis is in red and marked with circles. At the beginning of each assimilation window, the previous forecast terminates, the most recent analysis turns into a forecast and eventually provides the starting value for the next assimilation cycle. This can be best seen at $t = 1.75$, where the upper cross marks the last step of the forecast starting at $t = 1.5$. The circles between $t = 1.5$ and $t = 1.75$ represent the subsequent analysis using the data available from that interval. The next forecast (crosses) starts from the last analysis (circle) at $t = 1.75$. This forecast window ranges from $t = 1.75$ to $t = 2.0$. The process then repeats, and this new forecast is modified by the data available from the interval $[1.75, 2.0]$. This data assimilation step provides the second, lower circle at $t = 2.0$ as well as the starting value of a new forecast over the interval $[2.0, 2.25]$.

$m \geq 1$. The most recently adjusted model state is then used as an initial condition for model-based forecasts further into the future.

We now demonstrate this synchronising effect with our "mechanistic" Lorenz-63 model from Example 1.7.

---

**Example 1.8**   We implement the nonlinear least squares method for the Lorenz-63 model already investigated in Example 1.7. Recall that the model output deviates from the surrogate physical process after a relatively short time interval even if both the mechanistic model (1.18) and the reference model (1.2) are started from identical initial conditions at $t_0 = 0$. We now consider sequences of $N_A = 5$ observations with observation interval $\Delta t_{\text{out}} = 0.05$ in order to adjust the model's initial states over each data assimilation window $[t_{mN_A}, t_{(m+1)N_A}]$ with $m = 0, 1, 2, \ldots, 39$. See Figure 1.11 for a comparison between the reference trajectory $z_{\text{ref}}(t)$ and the analysis $z^{\text{a}}_{\text{model}}(t)$ over all 40 assimilation cycles, and

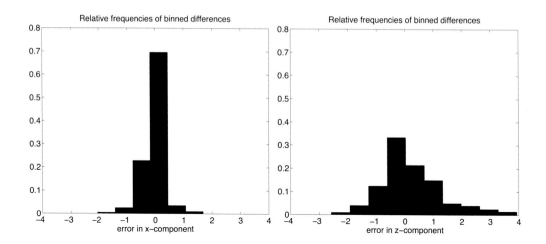

**Figure 1.13** Relative frequencies of binned differences between the reference solution and the analysis, in both x and z. It is tempting to view these relative frequencies as arising from finite samples of an underlying random variable with unknown specifications. We could then discuss the probability of an analysis falling within a certain range of the (generally unavailable explicitly) true system state. It is a task of uncertainty quantification to characterise such probabilities.

Figure 1.12 for a zoomed region displaying the difference between model forecasts $z_{\text{model}}^{\text{f}}(t)$ and their analysis $z_{\text{model}}^{\text{a}}(t)$. The nonlinear method of least squares is implemented with step-length $\alpha = 0.025$ in the gradient method (1.24) and $\varepsilon = 0.01$ in (1.25). This small value of $\alpha$ is necessary in order to avoid a divergence of (1.24). More efficient minimisation methods could be implemented but are outside the scope of this book.

In practical applications, such as weather forecasting, it is desirable to obtain *a priori* estimates of the likelihood of an analysis being within a certain range of the (generally not explicitly available) true system state. This gives an indication of how seriously to take the forecast; this is crucial when using forecasts in decision-making and planning. We display a histogram of the resulting differences between the reference solution $z_{\text{ref}}(t)$ and the analysis $z_{\text{model}}^{\text{a}}(t)$ in Figure 1.13. Note, for example, that the errors in the z-component have a much broader distribution than those in the x-component. More abstractly, we will view histograms, such as the ones displayed in Figure 1.13, as resulting from finite samples of underlying *random variables* with generally unknown distribution. It is a task of *uncertainty quantification* to provide as much information about these random variables as possible.

We have already mentioned that the analysis can be used to generate forecasts over time intervals where observations have not yet been obtained. In order to illustrate this aspect of data assimilation we use the analysis $z_{\text{model}}^{\text{a}}(t)$ at time $t = 10$ as the initial condition for our model (1.18) at $t = 10$. We then run this

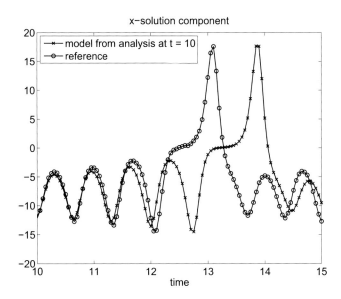

**Figure 1.14** Forecast started from the analysis at time $t = 10$ and reference solution from the surrogate physical process. It can be seen that the forecast stays close to the reference solution for about two time units after which its starts diverging due to errors in the analysis and model errors.

model over the time interval $[10,15]$ in order to produce a forecast which can be compared to the reference solution $z_{\text{ref}}(t)$ of our surrogate physical process over the same time interval. The result is displayed in Figure 1.14, where it can be seen that the forecast stays close to the reference solution up to time $t \approx 12$. It is a task of uncertainty quantification to quantify the actual forecast uncertainties without explicit knowledge of the reference solution. In addition to analysis errors, forecast errors will be also treated as random variables. We will learn about computational methods for estimating their distributions later in this book.

We conclude this example by emphasising that the nonlinear least squares method is sensitive to the length of the assimilation window. If the window is chosen too large, then the data assimilation procedure leads to a divergence of the gradient method (1.24) due to the increasingly nonlinear behaviour of the functional $L$. We also found that a shorter window of $2\Delta t_{\text{out}}$ (i.e. two observations per assimilation cycle) leads to results similar to those displayed in Figure 1.11 for five observations per assimilation cycle. This is surprising, since with $N_A = 2$ we cannot expect that $L$ has a unique (local) minimum. In particular, the computed minimiser $z_*^0$ will depend on the initial guess for the steepest decent method. As we will see in later chapters, such a dependence is not necessarily a disadvantage.

The previous example has demonstrated the effectiveness of using observations to estimate the state of a mechanistic model, then using the model with adjusted initial conditions to generate forecasts. The nonlinear method of least squares provides us with the first example of a data assimilation algorithm, which also goes under the name of *variational data assimilation* or *maximum likelihood estimation*. While the results are encouraging, we will learn about even more sophisticated data assimilation methods later in this book. These methods rely on a probabilistic interpretation of model forecasts as well as measurement errors. The necessary mathematical tools will be provided in subsequent chapters. In particular, we will need to introduce the concept of a *random variable*, together with methods for performing computer experiments with random variables (*Monte Carlo methods*). We will then apply these tools to mechanistic models of type (1.18) to describe *stochastic processes* and *forecast uncertainties*. We also need to introduce *Bayesian inference* as a probabilistic framework for inferring information on random variables from (partial) observations and available prior knowledge about the random variable under consideration. Once these mathematical foundations have been established, the second part of this book on data assimilation algorithms can be entered.

We end this introductory chapter with some general comments on the process of building mathematical models for making predictions and the role of data assimilation within this process. We can use well-established theories, such as Newton's laws of motion, to build mathematical models in the form of evolution equations/dynamical systems as encountered in this chapter in Equation (1.18). These models can be discretised and programmed on a computer, allowing mathematical experiments to be performed. The analysis of such computational models falls, broadly speaking, into the world of *applied computational mathematics*. When making predictions, this is one side of the coin; the other side is the world of measured data and their mathematical structure. This area is traditionally investigated from a mathematical perspective by *statisticians*. While the two sides of the same coin have largely been developed independently over the years, there is an increasing awareness that they belong together and that maximal benefit can be gained by combining them within the framework of *data assimilation*. Data assimilation can be used for state estimation, for adapting models through parameter estimation, and for intercomparison of models. The Bayesian formalism has emerged as a particularly fruitful approach to data assimilation and is primarily the approach that we will follow in this book. See Figure 1.15 for a graphical illustration of this discussion.

## Problems

**1.1**  Implement the numerical model from Example 1.1 and store the resulting reference trajectory in time intervals of $\Delta t_{\text{out}} = 0.05$ in a file for later use in other examples. Do not store the system state from every single time-step as this becomes very inefficient, even for low-dimensional problems; it is much better to overwrite the state vector on each time-step, and take a copy of the vector when

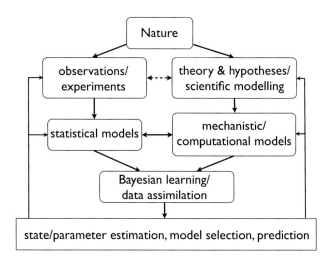

**Figure 1.15** A schematic presentation of the complex process of building and using mathematical models. An essential building block is data assimilation which is a mathematical technique for combining mechanistic models with statistical models based on data. Here a statistical model refers to a set of probability distributions describing observed data, while a mechanistic model consists of evolution equations which give rise to deterministic and/or stochastic processes. Mechanistic models depend on parameters (including the state of the model), which we treat as random variables. Finally, a computational model is typically an algorithm that allows us to produce process realisations of the mechanistic model. Among the possible outcomes of data assimilation are improved predictions through parameter and state estimation as well as model selection.

you need to store it. The resulting data set should be stored in a matrix of size $3 \times 4001$. Do not forget to replace (1.6) by (1.27) and check that your numerical results reproduce the model attractor from Figure 1.1.

**1.2** Implement the numerical observation process as defined in Example 1.2 using the reference trajectory generated in Problem 1.1. Store the numerically generated observation values $y_{\mathrm{obs}}(t_k)$ for $k = 1, \ldots, N_{\mathrm{obs}} = 4000$, in a file for later use. Investigate the difference between using the two recursions (1.28) and (1.9) for generating measurement errors. Hint: You might obtain a trajectory different from the one displayed in Figure 1.3. Differences can arise even for mathematically identical implementations due to round-off errors.

**1.3** Follow Example 1.4 and use linear extrapolation in order to produce forecasts from the observations produced in Problem 1.2. Compute the time averaged RMSE and compare to the values produced in Problem 1.4.

**1.4** Implement the method of least squares in the setting laid out in Example 1.6. Compare your coefficients $a_l$, $l = 1, \ldots, 4$, to the one stated in Example 1.6. Also, compare the resulting time averaged RMSEs.

**1.5** Implement the mechanistic model for our surrogate physical process as described in Example 1.7. Use (1.5) as initial conditions at $t_0 = 0$. Your results should reproduce the phase portrait displayed in Figure 1.8. Now compare the model trajectory to the reference trajectory $z_{\mathrm{ref}}(t)$ computed in Exercise 1.1. Next, vary the initial conditions $(x_0, y_0, z_0)$ for the mechanistic model by adding arbitrary perturbations $(\delta_x, \delta_y, \delta_y) \in [-1, 1]^3$ and study the impact of these perturbations on the forecast quality with respect to the reference trajectory $z_{\mathrm{ref}}(t)$.

## 1.4      Guide to literature

A thought-provoking introduction to many of the topics raised in this chapter can be found in Smith (2007b). Another book from the same series by Hand (2008) discusses some of the data related issues in more detail. The Lorenz-63 model was introduced by Lorenz (1963) and provides a widely studied chaotic dynamical system. Polynomial interpolation and the method of least squares are covered in Süli & Mayers (2006). A broad overview of minimisation techniques including the nonlinear method of least squares is given in Nocedal & Wright (2006). The importance of uncertainty quantification and data assimilation for numerical weather forecasting is demonstrated in Kalnay (2002). In fact, numerical weather forecasting provides an ideal motivation as well as an application area for most of the material covered in this book.

## 1.5      Appendix: Numerical implementation of tent map iteration

In this appendix, we discuss the implementation on a computer of the tent map iteration

$$g^{n+1} = \begin{cases} 2g^n & \text{if } g^n \in [0, 1/2), \\ 2(g^n - 1) & \text{otherwise,} \end{cases} \tag{1.26}$$

for given initial $g^0 \in [0, 1]$ and $n \geq 0$. We consider the case where this iteration is approximated by a binary floating point representation of the non-negative real numbers $g^n$ in the form of

$$g^n = m \times 2^l,$$

where

$$m = 0.m_1 m_2 m_3 \cdots ,$$

is called the *mantissa* and $m_i \in \{0, 1\}$ are the mantissa *bits*. The integer $l$ is called the *exponent* of the representation. For efficient storage, the exponent $l$ is chosen such that $m_1 = 1$ unless $m = 0$. If the mantissa has only finitely many non-zero bits, then $i^*$ denotes the largest $i$ such that $m_i = 1$. We call $i^*$ the *mantissa length*. As an example, consider

$$g^n = 0.1101 \times 2^2,$$

with mantissa length $i^* = 4$, which corresponds to

$$g^n = 1 \times 2^1 + 1 \times 2^0 + 0 \times 2^{-1} + 1 \times 2^{-2} = 3.25$$

in our standard decimal representation. We also find that $g^n = 1$ corresponds to $0.1 \times 2^1$ in our binary representation. Furthermore, $g^n \in [0, 1/2)$ implies that the associated exponent $l$ satisfies $l \leq -1$. Similarly, we find that $g^n \in [0, 1]$ implies $l \leq 1$.

Now consider the tent map iteration written in this representation. Straightforwardly, $2g^n$ leaves the mantissa of $g^n$ unaltered while its exponent is increased by one. Understanding the impact of $2 - 2g^n$ on $g^n \in [1/2, 1)$ is more delicate. We obtain

$$0.1 \times 2^2 - 0.1m_2m_3 \cdots \times 2^1 = (0.1 - 0.01m_2m_3 \cdots) \times 2^2$$
$$= 0.00\overline{m}_2\overline{m}_3 \cdots \times 2^2$$
$$= 0.\overline{m}_2\overline{m}_3 \cdots \times 2^0,$$

where $\overline{m}_i = m_i + 1$ modulo 2 for all $i = 1, \ldots, i^* - 1$. If $i^*$ is finite, then we obtain $\overline{m}_{i^*} = m_{i^*} = 1$. In this case, the mantissa length of $g^{n+1}$ is reduced by at least one (it is exactly one in the case in which $\overline{m}_2 = 1$). Consequently, if the initial $g^0$ is chosen such that its mantissa $m$ has finite length, then the tent map will ultimately lead to $g^n = 0$ after sufficiently many iterations of the tent map. Of course, a number with infinite mantissa length will lead to zero for any number of tent map iterations.

Since digital computers rely on a binary representation of real numbers with a mantissa of necessarily finite length, any computer implementation of the tent map iteration will ultimately result in $g^n = 0$, after sufficiently many iterations. This is in stark contrast to the "true" tent map, which generically produces infinite, non-repetitive sequences $\{g_n\}_{n=0}^{\infty}$. This example should serve as a warning not to identify a mathematical model with a computer implementation of it.

The following modification mimics the desired asymptotic behaviour of the tent map iteration when implemented in finite floating point arithmetic:

$$g^{n+1} = \begin{cases} 1.99999g^n & \text{if } g^n \in [0, 1/2), \\ 1.99999(g^n - 1) & \text{otherwise.} \end{cases}$$

Similarly, the following modifications were applied to the iterations (1.6) and (1.9), respectively:

$$g_i^{n+1} = \begin{cases} 1.99999g_i^n + a/2 & \text{if } g_i^n \in [-a/2, 0), \\ -1.99999g_i^n + a/2 & \text{otherwise,} \end{cases} \tag{1.27}$$

$$\xi_{k+1} = \begin{cases} 1.99999\xi_k + a/2 & \text{if } \xi_k \in [-a/2, 0), \\ -1.99999\xi_k + a/2 & \text{otherwise.} \end{cases} \tag{1.28}$$

# Part I

# Quantifying Uncertainty

# 2 Introduction to probability

In the previous chapter we discussed how models can be used to interpolate data from observations, and to make predictions about future states of physical systems. Since predictions are often used to make decisions, it is crucial to be able to estimate their uncertainty. The main theme of this book is prediction algorithms that provide uncertainty quantification for forecasts, expressed in the language of probability. Hence, in this chapter we recall some basic material from probability theory. In particular, we will introduce the concept of a *random variable* as a useful mathematical abstraction for the description of computational (and, more generally, scientific) experiments such as the ones conducted in Chapter 1.

A familiar example is that of a coin flip, in which case the measureable output consists of two elements: heads or tails. The associated random variable is formally written as $X : \Omega \to \{\text{heads}, \text{tails}\}$, where the *sample space* $\Omega$ mathematically represents the set of all possible physical processes that go into flipping a coin. An actual coin flip amounts to selecting a specific realisation $\omega \in \Omega$ of such a physical process which assigns the outcome (heads or tails) to $X(\omega)$. For an idealised coin, the probability of heads or of tails should both be equal to one half. Putting oneself in the position of Laplace's demon, there is, of course, nothing random about flipping a coin: the outcome of a coin flip is determined by all of the forces acting on the coin in motion, together with the starting configuration of the coin. This knowledge is inaccessible in practice and the dynamic processes involved are so complex that flipping a coin constitutes an experiment with unpredictable (or random) outcome.

In a similar vein, we will find later in this chapter that the non-autonomous forcing $\{\Xi_i\}_{i=1}^{\infty}$ generated by the simple recursion (1.10) can also be considered as the outcome of random experiments, even though these numbers are produced by an entirely deterministic procedure. This observation will also allow us to treat measurement errors such as (1.8) as realisations of an appropriate random variable.

While probability theory deals with the formal mathematical rules of how to manipulate and process probabilities, there remains the separate issue of how to actually assign probabilities to events or outcomes of experiments in the first place. There are several different methodologies for achieving this including:

(i) Conducting a large number of identical experiments and recording the *rel-*

*ative frequency* of an event $A$ to occur. The probability of an event is then the large sample limit of this relative frequency.

(ii) Identifying equally likely alternatives and assigning equal probabilities to each of these alternatives.

(iii) Estimating probabilities based on perceived knowledge and previous experience of similar systems (this is necessarily subjective, and requires us to revise these estimates when new information is received).

Returning to the coin flipping experiment, we find that probabilities of possible outcomes (heads or tails) can be assigned by either method (i) or (ii). When assigning probabilities to outcomes of computer experiments, method (i) is suitable. On the other hand, method (iii) is often necessary in more complex situations when repeated experimentation is infeasible, and/or when possible events cannot *a priori* be categorised as equally likely.

This chapter puts this discussion aside, and focuses on the mathematical rules of how to manipulate and process probabilities. We start with a formal definition of a random variable. This formal language places our intuitive understanding of probability in a mathematical framework required for rigorous work; we include it for completeness. Given a sample space $\Omega$, an *event* is a subset $E \subset \Omega$. We assume that the set $\mathcal{F}$ of all events forms a $\sigma$-*algebra* (i.e., $\mathcal{F}$ is non-empty, and closed over complementation and countable unions).

---

**Example 2.1**   If $\Omega = \{1, 2, 3\}$, then an associated $\sigma$-algebra of possible events is defined by

$$\mathcal{F} = \{\Omega, \emptyset, \{1\}, \{2\}, \{3\}, \{1, 2\}, \{1, 3\}, \{2, 3\}\}.$$

---

**Example 2.2**   If $\Omega = [0, 1] \subset \mathbb{R}$, then the associated set $\mathcal{F}$ of all events can be taken as the smallest $\sigma$-algebra containing all open intervals $(a, b) \subset \Omega$; this $\mathcal{F}$ is also known as a $\sigma$-algebra of *Borel sets*, or just Borel $\sigma$-algebra. We mention that the concept of a $\sigma$-algebra of Borel sets can be generalised from the unit interval to the whole real line.

---

Having defined a sample space $\Omega$ with associated $\sigma$-algebra $\mathcal{F}$ of all possible events, each event $A \in \mathcal{F}$ is assigned a *probability* $\mathbb{P}(A) \in [0, 1]$. If $\mathbb{P}(A) = 0$, this means that the event will (almost) never occur, while probability one implies that the event will (almost) always occur. A probability of one half implies that chances of the event occurring are the same as the chances of the event not occurring etc. Probabilities of events should satisfy certain properties in order to be mathematically self-consistent.

**Definition 2.3** (Probability measure)   A *probability measure* is a function $\mathbb{P} : \mathcal{F} \to [0, 1]$ with the following properties:

(i) total probability equals one, $\mathbb{P}(\Omega) = 1$, and

(ii) probability is additive for disjoint events, so if $A_1, A_2, \ldots, A_n, \ldots$ is a finite or countable collection of events $A_i \in \mathcal{F}$ and $A_i \cap A_j = \emptyset$ for $i \neq j$, then

$$\mathbb{P}\left(\bigcup_i A_i\right) = \sum_i \mathbb{P}(A_i).$$

The triple $(\Omega, \mathcal{F}, \mathbb{P})$ is called a *probability space*.

---

**Example 2.4**   We return to the $\sigma$-algebra from Example 2.1 and postulate that

$$\mathbb{P}(\{i\}) = 1/3,$$

for $i = 1, 2, 3$. Following the properties of a probability measure, we may also quickly conclude that, for example,

$$\mathbb{P}(\{1, 3\}) = 1/3 + 1/3 = 2/3.$$

Hence we can extend the probability measure $\mathbb{P}$ to the complete $\sigma$-algebra $\mathcal{F}$.

---

---

**Example 2.5**   In the case of $\Omega = [0, 1]$, a probability measure can be introduced by first saying that each interval $(a, b) \subset [0, 1]$ is assigned the probability

$$\mathbb{P}((a, b)) = b - a.$$

This definition is then extended to the associated Borel $\sigma$-algebra $\mathcal{F}$ using the probability measure properties (i) and (ii), and we obtain the *uniform probability measure* on the unit interval $[0, 1]$.

---

## 2.1   Random variables

Formally, when we consider random processes in this book there will be an underlying abstract probability space $(\Omega, \mathcal{F}, \mathbb{P})$ representing all sources of uncertainty (as already discussed in the context of coin flipping). However, in practice we are usually only interested in the impact of these uncertainties on observables (such as heads or tails in the case of coin flipping). This means that most of the time we can focus on the concept of a *random variable*, which relates the underlying probability space $(\Omega, \mathcal{F}, \mathbb{P})$ to induced uncertainties/probabilities in an observable (or measureable) quantity of interest.

Let us simplify things for the moment by assuming that any such quantity will take values in the space of real numbers. This leads us to the following formal definition of a univariate random variable.

**Definition 2.6** (Univariate random variable)    A function $X : \Omega \to \mathbb{R}$ is called a (univariate) *random variable* if the sets $A_x$, defined by

$$A_x = \{\omega \in \Omega : X(\omega) \leq x\},$$

are elements of the set of all events $\mathcal{F}$, i.e., $A_x \in \mathcal{F}$ for all $x \in \mathbb{R}$. The (cumulative) *probability distribution function* of $X$ is given by

$$F_X(x) = \mathbb{P}(A_x).$$

If $X$ only takes finitely many values in $\mathbb{R}$, then we call $X$ a *discrete random variable*, otherwise it is called a *continuous random variable*.

For a given random variable $X$ on $\mathbb{R}$, we define an *induced probability measure* $\mu_X$ on $\mathbb{R}$ (not $\Omega$) *via*

$$\mu_X(B) = \mathbb{P}(\{\omega \in \Omega : X(\omega) \in B\})$$

for all intervals $B$ in $\mathbb{R}$ (more precisely for all sets $B$ in the Borel $\sigma$-algebra on $\mathbb{R}$).

Often, when working with a random variable $X$, the underlying probability space $(\Omega, \mathcal{F}, \mathbb{P})$ is not emphasised. Typically, only the *target space* $\mathcal{X}$ (currently $\mathbb{R}$) and the probability distribution or *measure* $\mu_X$ on $\mathcal{X}$ are specified. We then say that $\mu_X$ is the *law* of $X$ and write $X \sim \mu_X$ or $\mathrm{law}(X) = \mu_X$. However, the underlying probability space is important when discussing several random variables and their mutual relations. We will come back to this issue later in this chapter.

What makes random variables $X(\omega)$ different from regular functions $f(t)$ is that they are mappings from a probability space. Usually, we choose the input $t$ for a function $f$, and observe the output $f(t)$. For random variables, the input $\omega$ is determined at random according to the laws of the probability space, and we just observe the output $X(\omega)$, which we refer to as a "realisation" of the random variable $X$.

---

**Example 2.7**    We return to the coin flipping experiment with the associated random variable defined by $X : \Omega \to \{\mathrm{heads}, \mathrm{tails}\}$. Generally speaking, we do not know anything about $\Omega$ and the associated probability space. We only wish to predict whether we will obtain heads or tails, and so our interest is focused on the induced probability measure $\mu_X(\mathrm{heads}) = \mu_X(\mathrm{tails}) = 1/2$. This situation will arise repeatedly throughout this book and the emphasis will therefore be on probability measures induced by random variables rather than on the underlying probability space $(\Omega, \mathcal{F}, \mathbb{P})$ itself.

---

The following definition of expectation provides an important tool for obtaining descriptive numbers, which we call statistics, about probability measures.

**Definition 2.8** (Expectation)   A probability measure $\mu_X$ on $\mathcal{X}$ induces an associated (Lebesgue) integral over $\mathcal{X}$ and

$$\mathbb{E}[f(X)] = \int_{\mathcal{X}} f(x)\mu_X(\mathrm{d}x)$$

is called the *expectation* of a function $f : \mathcal{X} \to \mathbb{R}$. Two important choices for $f$ are $f(x) = x$, which leads to the mean $\bar{x} = \mathbb{E}[X]$ of $X$, and $f(x) = (x - \bar{x})^2$, which leads to the variance $\sigma^2 = \mathbb{E}[(X - \bar{x})^2]$ of $X$.

The integral is formally defined by first considering functions $f$ which only take finitely many distinct values $f_i$ in which case

$$\mathbb{E}[f(X)] = \sum_i f_i\, \mu_X(\{x \in \mathcal{X} : f(x) = f_i\}).$$

Such simple functions are then used to approximate general functions $f$ and their expectation values. More details can be found in standard textbooks on measure theory.

**Definition 2.9** (Absolute continuity)   A probability measure $\mu_X$ on $\mathcal{X} = \mathbb{R}$ is called *absolutely continuous* (with respect to the standard Lebesgue integral $\mathrm{d}x$ on $\mathbb{R}$) if there exists a *probability density function* (PDF) $\pi_X : \mathcal{X} \to \mathbb{R}$ with $\pi_X(x) \geq 0$, and

$$\int_{\mathbb{R}} f(x)\mu_X(\mathrm{d}x) = \int_{\mathbb{R}} f(x)\pi_X(x)\mathrm{d}x.$$

The shorthand $\mu_X(\mathrm{d}x) = \pi_X(x)\mathrm{d}x$ is often adopted.

An immediate consequence is that $\int_{\mathcal{X}} \pi_X(x)\mathrm{d}x = 1$, which follows from the particular choice $f(x) = 1$. We also obtain

$$F_X(x) = \int_{-\infty}^{x} \pi_X(x')\mathrm{d}x'.$$

If a probability measure $\mu_X$ is absolutely continuous then for all practical purposes we can work within the classical Riemann integral framework without needing Lebesgue integration. Furthermore, any function $\pi_X(x)$ such that $\pi_X(x) \geq 0$ and

$$\int_{\mathbb{R}} \pi_X(x)\mathrm{d}x = 1,$$

can serve as the PDF of a random variable.

Univariate random variables naturally extend to the *multivariate* case, for example, $\mathcal{X} = \mathbb{R}^{N_x}$, $N_x > 1$. Consider, for example, a bivariate random variable $X : \Omega \to \mathbb{R}^2$ with components $X_1 : \Omega \to \mathbb{R}$ and $X_2 : \Omega \to \mathbb{R}$. Definition 2.6 is generalised as follows. The sets

$$A_x = \{\omega \in \Omega : X_1(\omega) \leq x_1,\ X_2(\omega) \leq x_2\},$$

$x = (x_1, x_2) \in \mathbb{R}^2$, are assumed to be elements of the set of all events $\mathcal{F}$. The (cumulative) *probability distribution function* of $X = (X_1, X_2)$ is defined by

$$F_X(x) = \mathbb{P}(A_x),$$

and the induced probability measure on $\mathbb{R}^2$ is denoted by $\mu_X$. In particular, the definition $\mu_X(B_x) := F_X(x)$ for $B_x = (-\infty, x_1] \times (-\infty, x_2]$ can be extended to all sets $B$ in the Borel $\sigma$-algebra on $\mathbb{R}^2$. If $\mu_X$ is absolutely continuous with respect to the Lebesgue measure on $\mathbb{R}^2$, then it has a PDF $\pi_X(x)$, which satisfies

$$F_X(x_1, x_2) = \int_{-\infty}^{x_1} \int_{-\infty}^{x_2} \pi_X(x_1', x_2') \mathrm{d}x_1' \mathrm{d}x_2'.$$

We shall now discuss a few examples of random variables with well-known probability distributions.

---

**Example 2.10**   We use the notation $X \sim \mathrm{N}(\overline{x}, \sigma^2)$ to denote a univariate *Gaussian random variable* with mean $\overline{x}$ and variance $\sigma^2$. Its PDF is given by

$$\pi_X(x) = \frac{1}{\sqrt{2\pi}\sigma} e^{-\frac{1}{2\sigma^2}(x-\overline{x})^2},$$

$x \in \mathbb{R}$, which is often referred to as a normal distribution. In the multivariate case, we use the notation $X \sim \mathrm{N}(\overline{x}, P)$ to denote a Gaussian random variable with PDF given by

$$\pi_X(x) = \frac{1}{(2\pi)^{N_x/2}|P|^{1/2}} \exp\left(-\frac{1}{2}(x-\overline{x})^{\mathrm{T}} P^{-1}(x-\overline{x})\right),$$

for $x \in \mathbb{R}^{N_x}$. Here $\overline{x} \in \mathbb{R}^{N_x}$ denotes the mean, defined by

$$\overline{x} = \mathbb{E}[X] = \int_{\mathbb{R}^{N_x}} x \pi_X(x) \mathrm{d}x,$$

and $P \in \mathbb{R}^{N_x \times N_x}$ denotes the covariance matrix, defined by

$$P = \mathbb{E}[(X-\overline{x})(X-\overline{x})^{\mathrm{T}}] = \int_{\mathbb{R}^{N_x}} (x-\overline{x})(x-\overline{x})^{\mathrm{T}} \pi_X(x) \mathrm{d}x,$$

and where we adopt the shorthand notation $|P| = |\det P|$ is the absolute value of the determinant of $P$. The PDF $\pi_X(x)$ of a Gaussian random variable $X \sim \mathrm{N}(\overline{x}, P)$ is denoted by $\mathrm{n}(x; \overline{x}, P)$.

---

**Example 2.11**   The univariate *Laplace distribution* has PDF

$$\pi_X(x) = \frac{\lambda}{2} e^{-\lambda|x|}, \tag{2.1}$$

$x \in \mathbb{R}$. This may be rewritten as

$$\pi_X(x) = \int_0^\infty \frac{1}{\sqrt{2\pi}\sigma} e^{-x^2/(2\sigma^2)} \frac{\lambda^2}{2} e^{-\lambda^2\sigma/2} \mathrm{d}\sigma.$$

Here, the integrand is the product of a Gaussian PDF with mean zero and variance $\sigma^2$ and a $\sigma$-dependent weight factor. Replacing the integral by a Riemann sum over a sequence of quadrature points $\{\sigma_j\}_{j=1}^J$, we obtain

$$\pi_X(x) \approx \sum_{j=1}^J \alpha_j \frac{1}{\sqrt{2\pi}\sigma_j} e^{-x^2/(2\sigma_j^2)}, \qquad \alpha_j \propto \frac{\lambda^2}{2} e^{-\lambda^2 \sigma_j/2} (\sigma_j - \sigma_{j-1}),$$

and the constant of proportionality is chosen such that the weights $\alpha_j$ sum to one. This finite sum approximation provides an example of a *Gaussian mixture* distribution, i.e. a weighted sum of Gaussians. In this particular example, the Gaussians are all centred about zero. The most general form of a Gaussian mixture is

$$\pi_X(x) = \sum_{j=1}^J \alpha_j \frac{1}{\sqrt{2\pi}\sigma_j} e^{-(x-m_j)^2/(2\sigma_j^2)},$$

with weights $\alpha_j > 0$ subject to $\sum_{j=1}^J \alpha_j = 1$, and locations $-\infty < m_j < \infty$. Univariate Gaussian mixtures generalise to mixtures of multivariate Gaussians.

---

**Example 2.12**   As a third example, we consider the *point measure* $\mu_{x_0}$ defined by

$$\int_{\mathcal{X}} f(x)\mu_{x_0}(\mathrm{d}x) = f(x_0).$$

The associated random variable $X$ has the outcome $X(\omega) = x_0$ with probability 1. We call such a random variable *deterministic*, writing $X = x_0$ for short. Note that the point measure is not absolutely continuous with respect to the Lebesgue measure, i.e., there is no corresponding PDF. Using the *Dirac delta* notation $\delta(\cdot)$, we shall nevertheless often formally write $\mu_{x_0}(\mathrm{d}x) = \delta(x-x_0)\mathrm{d}x$ or $\pi_X(x) = \delta(x-x_0)$. Following the formal definition of a random variable, we find

$$F_{x_0}(x) = \mathbb{P}(\{\omega \in \Omega : X(\omega) \le x\})$$
$$= \int_{-\infty}^x \mu_{x_0}(\mathrm{d}x)$$
$$= \begin{cases} 1 & \text{if } x \ge x_0, \\ 0 & \text{otherwise,} \end{cases} \tag{2.2}$$

for the cumulative distribution function of the point measure $\mu_{x_0}$.

---

   Throughout this book we will repeatedly encounter transformations of random variables. Therefore, it is of utmost importance to understand how probability distributions of random variables transform under diffeomorphisms.

**Lemma 2.13** (Invertible transformations of random variables)   Let $X : \Omega \to \mathbb{R}^{N_x}$ be a random variable with PDF $\pi_X$, and let $Y : \Omega \to \mathbb{R}^{N_x}$ be a random variable defined by $Y = \Phi(X)$ for smooth and invertible $\Phi : \mathbb{R}^{N_x} \to \mathbb{R}^{N_x}$ (i.e., $\Phi$ is a diffeomorphism). Then, $Y$ has PDF $\pi_Y$ given by

$$\pi_Y(y) = \pi_X(\Phi^{-1}(y))|J(y)|,$$

where $\Phi^{-1}$ denotes the inverse of $\Phi$,

$$J(y) = D\Phi^{-1}(y) \in \mathbb{R}^{N_x \times N_x}$$

the Jacobian matrix of partial derivatives, and $|J|$ the absolute value of the determinant of $J$, i.e., $|J| = |\det J|$.

*Proof*  By conservation of probability,

$$\begin{aligned}
\mu_Y(A) &= \mathbb{P}(\{\omega \in \Omega : Y(\omega) \in A\}) \\
&= \mathbb{P}(\{\omega \in \Omega : \Phi(X(\omega)) \in A\}) \\
&= \mathbb{P}(\{\omega \in \Omega : X(\omega) \in \Phi^{-1}(A)\}) \\
&= \mu_X(\Phi^{-1}(A)),
\end{aligned}$$

for any Borel set $A \subset \mathbb{R}^{N_x}$, where $\Phi^{-1}(A)$ denotes the preimage of $A$ under $\Phi$. Hence

$$\int_A \pi_Y(y)\,\mathrm{d}y = \int_{\Phi^{-1}(A)} \pi_X(x)\mathrm{d}x,$$

and a change of variables $x = \Phi^{-1}(y)$ gives

$$\int_A \pi_Y(y)\,\mathrm{d}y = \int_A \pi_X(\Phi^{-1}(y))|J(y)|\,\mathrm{d}y.$$

Since this is true for all Borel sets $A \in \mathbb{R}^{N_x}$, we obtain the desired result.  □

We now discuss several mathematical concepts relating to pairs of random variables $X_1 : \Omega \to \mathcal{X}$ and $X_2 : \Omega \to \mathcal{X}$. We may treat $X_1$ and $X_2$ as components of a single multivariate random variable $Z = (X_1, X_2)$ over $\mathcal{Z} = \mathcal{X} \times \mathcal{X}$, which then has some *joint distribution* $\mu_Z(z) = \mu_{X_1 X_2}(x_1, x_2)$.

**Definition 2.14** (Marginals, independence, conditional probability distributions) Let $X_1$ and $X_2$ denote two random variables on $\mathcal{X}$ with joint PDF $\pi_{X_1 X_2}(x_1, x_2)$. The two PDFs,

$$\pi_{X_1}(x_1) = \int_{\mathcal{X}} \pi_{X_1 X_2}(x_1, x_2)\mathrm{d}x_2$$

and

$$\pi_{X_2}(x_2) = \int_{\mathcal{X}} \pi_{X_1 X_2}(x_1, x_2)\mathrm{d}x_1,$$

are called the *marginal PDFs*, i.e. $X_1 \sim \pi_{X_1}$ and $X_2 \sim \pi_{X_2}$. The two random variables are called *independent* if

$$\pi_{X_1 X_2}(x_1, x_2) = \pi_{X_1}(x_1)\,\pi_{X_2}(x_2).$$

We also introduce the *conditional PDFs*

$$\pi_{X_1}(x_1|x_2) = \frac{\pi_{X_1X_2}(x_1,x_2)}{\pi_{X_2}(x_2)}$$

and

$$\pi_{X_2}(x_2|x_1) = \frac{\pi_{X_1X_2}(x_1,x_2)}{\pi_{X_1}(x_1)}.$$

The conditional PDF $\pi_{X_1}(x_1|x_2)$ is the PDF for $X_1$ under the assumption that $X_2(\omega)$ takes the value $x_2$. For independent random variables we obviously have $\pi_{X_1}(x_1|x_2) = \pi_{X_1}(x_1)$. These formulas lead to the following important definition which we shall use for iteratively constructing joint distributions from conditional probabilities.

**Definition 2.15** (Disintegration)   The two equivalent representations

$$\pi_{X_1X_2}(x_1,x_2) = \pi_{X_1}(x_1|x_2)\pi_{X_2}(x_2) = \pi_{X_2}(x_2|x_1)\pi_{X_1}(x_1) \qquad (2.3)$$

are called *disintegrations* of the joint PDF $\pi_{X_1X_2}$. In the case of several random variables $X_1, X_2, \ldots, X_n$, this becomes, for example,

$$\pi_{X_1\cdots X_n}(x_1,\ldots,x_n) = \pi_{X_1}(x_1|x_2,\ldots,x_n)\pi_{X_2}(x_2|x_3,\ldots,x_n)\cdots\pi_{X_n}(x_n). \quad (2.4)$$

We can also use these formulas to deduce the following formula for the marginal distributions.

**Lemma 2.16** (Marginals as expectation of conditional PDFs)   Let $X_1$ and $X_2$ be two random variables with joint PDF $\pi_{X_1X_2}$ as above. Then

$$\pi_{X_1}(x_1) = \mathbb{E}\left[\pi_{X_1}(x_1|X_2)\right], \qquad (2.5)$$

where the expectation is taken with respect to the random variable $X_2$.

*Proof*

$$\pi_{X_1}(x_1) = \int_{\mathcal{X}} \pi_{X_1X_2}(x_1,x_2)\mathrm{d}x_2$$

$$= \int \pi_{X_1}(x_1|x_2)\pi_{X_2}(x_2)\mathrm{d}x_2$$

$$= \mathbb{E}\left[\pi_{X_1}(x_1|X_2)\right],$$

as required.   □

If we have a pair of random variables, we would like to quantify how they are related. Correlation is a useful tool for measuring the dependence between two variables.

**Definition 2.17** (Correlation)   The *correlation* between two univariate random variables $X$ and $Y$ is given by

$$\mathrm{corr}(X,Y) = \frac{\mathbb{E}[(X-\bar{x})(Y-\bar{y})]}{\sqrt{\mathbb{E}[(X-\bar{x})^2]\mathbb{E}[(Y-\bar{y})^2]}},$$

with $\bar{x} = \mathbb{E}[X]$ and $\bar{y} = \mathbb{E}[Y]$.

The normalisation factor is chosen so that $|\operatorname{corr}(X,Y)| \leq 1$ and $|\operatorname{corr}(X,Y)| \approx 1$ indicates a high degree of correlation.[1]

---

**Example 2.18**   A joint Gaussian distribution $\pi_{X_1 X_2}(x_1, x_2)$, $x_1, x_2 \in \mathbb{R}$, with mean $(\overline{x}_1, \overline{x}_2)$, covariance matrix

$$P = \begin{bmatrix} \sigma_{11}^2 & \sigma_{12}^2 \\ \sigma_{21}^2 & \sigma_{22}^2 \end{bmatrix}, \tag{2.6}$$

and $\sigma_{12} = \sigma_{21}$ leads to a Gaussian conditional distribution

$$\pi_{X_1}(x_1|x_2) = \frac{1}{\sqrt{2\pi}\sigma_c} e^{-(x_1 - \overline{x}_c)^2 / (2\sigma_c^2)}, \tag{2.7}$$

with conditional mean

$$\overline{x}_c = \overline{x}_1 + \sigma_{12}^2 \sigma_{22}^{-2}(x_2 - \overline{x}_2)$$

and conditional variance

$$\sigma_c^2 = \sigma_{11}^2 - \sigma_{12}^2 \sigma_{22}^{-2} \sigma_{21}^2.$$

Note that

$$P^{-1} = \frac{1}{\sigma_{11}^2 \sigma_{22}^2 - \sigma_{12}^2 \sigma_{21}^2} \begin{bmatrix} \sigma_{22}^2 & -\sigma_{12}^2 \\ -\sigma_{12}^2 & \sigma_{11}^2 \end{bmatrix} = \begin{bmatrix} \sigma_c^{-2} & \sigma_c^{-2}\frac{\sigma_{12}^2}{\sigma_{22}^2} \\ \sigma_c^{-2}\frac{\sigma_{12}^2}{\sigma_{22}^2} & \sigma_c^{-2}\frac{\sigma_{11}^2}{\sigma_{22}^2} \end{bmatrix}$$

and

$$\pi_{X_1 X_2}(x_1, x_2) = \frac{1}{\sqrt{2\pi}\sigma_c} \exp\left( -\frac{1}{2\sigma_c^2}(x_1 - \overline{x}_c)^2 \right)$$
$$\times \frac{1}{\sqrt{2\pi}\sigma_{22}} \exp\left( -\frac{1}{2\sigma_{22}^2}(x_2 - \overline{x}_2)^2 \right),$$

which can be verified by direct calculations. See Problem 2.5. The correlation between $X_1$ and $X_2$ is given by $\operatorname{corr}(X_1, X_2) = \sigma_{12}^2/(\sigma_{11}\sigma_{22})$. Since $|\operatorname{corr}(X_1, X_2)| \leq 1$, we find that $|\sigma_{12}^2| \leq \sigma_{11}\sigma_{22}$.

The PDF $\pi_{X_i}(x)$ of a Gaussian random variable $X_i \sim \mathrm{N}(\overline{x}_i, \sigma_{ii}^2)$ is denoted by $\mathrm{n}(x; \overline{x}_i, \sigma_{ii}^2)$. For given $x_2$, we define $X_1|x_2$ as the random variable with conditional probability distribution $\pi_{X_1}(x_1|x_2)$. From the previous calculations we then obtain $X_1|x_2 \sim \mathrm{N}(\overline{x}_c, \sigma_c^2)$ and

$$\pi_{X_1 X_2}(x_1, x_2) = \mathrm{n}(x_1; \overline{x}_c, \sigma_c^2)\,\mathrm{n}(x_2; \overline{x}_2, \sigma_{22}^2). \tag{2.8}$$

---

The concept of independence can be extended to sequences of random variables, as follows.

---

[1] However, it is important to note that high correlation between two variables does not indicate that there is a causal link. For example, the price of wheat in Angola may be highly correlated with the sales of laptops in Dakar, but this does not mean that more people in Dakar are buying laptops because the price of wheat in Angola has increased.

**Definition 2.19** (Independent and identically distributed)   Let $X$ be a random variable with distribution $\pi_X$. A sequence of random variables $\{X_i\}_{i=1}^M$ with joint PDF $\pi_{X_1,\ldots,X_M}$ is called *independent and identically distributed* (i.i.d.) with distribution $\pi_X$ if

(i) the variables are mutually independent, i.e.,

$$\pi_{X_1,\ldots,X_M}(x_1,\ldots,x_M) = \pi_{X_1}(x_1)\pi_{X_2}(x_2)\cdots\pi_{X_M}(x_M),$$

where $\pi_{X_i}$ is the marginal distribution for $X_i$, $i = 1,\ldots,M$, and

(ii) the marginal distributions are all the same, i.e., $\pi_{X_i}(x) = \pi_X(x)$.

A particular realisation of an i.i.d. sequence of random variables of size $M$ with distribution $\pi_X$, i.e.,

$$(x_1,\ldots,x_M) = (X_1(\omega),\ldots,X_M(\omega)),$$

is referred to as "$M$ independent samples from the random variable $X$".

The values of a sequence of $M$ samples represent outcomes of an experiment where $X$ is repeatedly measured. There are many numerical algorithms for simulating random variables on a computer, and in this book we shall often discuss algorithms where we "draw" or "generate" $M$ samples of a random variable $X$.

Simple random variables are often used to model complex deterministic behaviour, since they are cheap to simulate on a computer, and facilitate mathematical analysis. In the following example, we return to the sequence $\{\Xi_i\}$ defined by (1.10) in Example 1.2 of Chapter 1, and consider how the entries of this sequence might be approximated as independent samples of a random variable.

---

**Example 2.20**   We investigate the properties of the sequence $\{\Xi_i\}_{i=1}^I$ defined by (1.10) and (1.9) with $I = 10^4$ and $I = 10^7$, respectively. Figure 2.1 displays relative frequencies of the $\Xi_i$ values in ten bins from the interval $[-a/2, a/2] = [-2, 2]$. The relative frequencies become essentially equal for $I = 10^7$. This shows that the $\Xi_i$ values are uniformly distributed over the interval $[-2, 2]$. Although the sequences $\{\Xi_i\}$ are generated in an entirely deterministic manner, these relative frequencies suggest that they behave like an identically distributed sequence of random variables with uniform distribution in $[-2, 2]$. We observe that they appear to have mean $\overline{\xi}_i = 0$, for example.

An important aspect of the coin flipping experiment is that outcomes of successive flips are independent of each other. This clearly cannot be the case for the tent map process since successive $\Xi_i$ values are, by definition, dependent. Since the dependence of a sequence of samples is difficult to assess numerically we instead compute the empirical (normalised) autocorrelations

$$C(\tau) = \frac{\sum_{i=1}^{I-\tau} \Xi_i \Xi_{i+\tau}}{\sum_{i=1}^{I-\tau} \Xi_i \Xi_i}, \qquad \tau \geq 0.$$

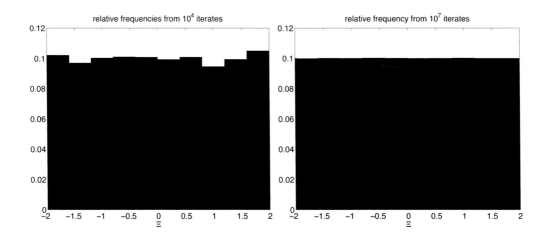

**Figure 2.1** Relative frequencies of the samples $\Xi_i$ in ten bins from the interval $[-2, 2]$ for sample sizes $I = 10^4$ (left) and $I = 10^7$ (right), respectively. It can be concluded that the distribution of samples converges to a uniform distribution over the interval $[-2, 2]$ for sample sizes sufficiently large.

The variables $\Xi_i$ and $\Xi_{i+\tau}$ are uncorrelated if $C(\tau) = 0$ for $\tau > 0$ and $I \to \infty$. For sample size $I = 10^7$, we find $C(0) = 1$ by definition and

$$C(1) = 0.1228 \times 10^{-3}, \quad C(2) = -0.1172 \times 10^{-3}, \quad C(3) = -0.1705 \times 10^{-3}.$$

Hence we may conclude that, for all practical purposes, the samples $\Xi_i$ are uncorrelated.[2] We have already briefly mentioned in Chapter 1 that (1.9) is a scaled and shifted version of the tent map iteration (1.26), which is known to display *chaotic* solution behaviour and which has the uniform distribution on $[0, 1]$ as the stationary distribution (recall that it is necessary to replace the factor 2.0 by 1.99999 in order to avoid an undesirable accumulation of round-off errors in computer implementations). This suggests that we might approximate the $\Xi_i$ values by independent samples from a uniform random variable $U : \Omega \to [-a/2, a/2]$.

Next we consider the accumulated measurement error

$$\delta = \sum_{i=1}^{20} \eta_i = \frac{1}{20} \sum_{i=1}^{20} \Xi_i. \tag{2.9}$$

We can generate a total of $5 \times 10^5$ samples of $\delta$ by using appropriate patches from the sequence of $\Xi_i$ values. We denote these samples by $\delta_j$ and display their relative frequencies in Figure 2.2. For comparison we also display the relative frequencies of an equal number of samples from a Gaussian distribution with mean zero and variance $\sigma^2 = 1/15$.

The results from Figure 2.2 suggest that we may safely approximate the mea-

---

[2] Recall that although independence implies zero correlation, the reverse is not generally true.

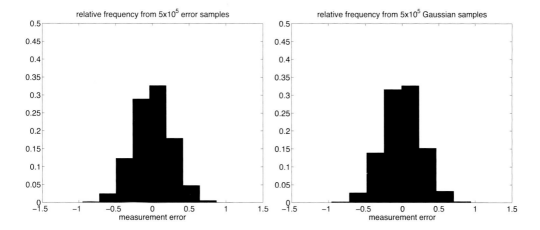

**Figure 2.2** The relative frequencies on the left represent the spatial distribution of the measurement error samples $\delta_j$. For comparison we also generated the same number of samples from a Gaussian distribution with mean zero and variance $\sigma^2 = 1/15$ and display the resulting relative frequencies over bins of the same size.

surement errors $\delta_j$ by realisations from a Gaussian random variable with mean zero and variance $\sigma^2 = 1/15$. This leads to a simplified observation model which we will discuss in more detail later in Chapter 5.

We now reconsider another example from Chapter 1 and put it into the context of random variables.

**Example 2.21**    We considered the method of least squares in Chapter 1 in order to estimate the coefficients $a_l$ in the autoregressive model 1.14 of order five. We now use the data from Example 1.6 and analyse the resulting residuals $r_j$, defined by (1.16). The relative frequencies in Figure 2.3 display a bell-shaped distribution similar to the data presented in Figure 2.2.

Figure 2.3 suggests that the residuals follow a Gaussian distribution and that we may treat the residuals as realisations of a Gaussian random variable $R$. We verify this hypothesis by computing the empirical estimates for the mean $\bar{r} = \mathbb{E}[R]$, the variance $\sigma^2 = \mathbb{E}[(R - \bar{r})^2]$,

$$\text{skewness} = \frac{\mathbb{E}[(R - \bar{r})^3]}{\sigma^3}$$

and

$$\text{kurtosis} = \frac{\mathbb{E}[(R - \bar{r})^4]}{\sigma^4} - 3.$$

The skewness and kurtosis are zero for Gaussian random variables. Empirical estimators for the mean and the variance from samples $\{r_j\}_{j=1}^J$ of size $J$ are

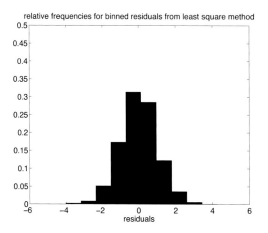

**Figure 2.3** Relative frequencies of the binned residuals (1.16) obtained from the method of least squares applied to the data used in Example 1.6 from Chapter 1. The relative frequencies again resemble those of a Gaussian random sample.

provided by

$$\bar{r}_J := \frac{1}{J}\sum_{j=1}^{J} r_j, \quad \sigma_J^2 := \frac{1}{J-1}\sum_{j=1}^{J}(r_j - \bar{r}_J)^2$$

and by

$$\text{skewness}_J = \frac{1}{J\sigma_J^3}\sum_{j=1}^{J}(r_j - \bar{r}_J)^3, \quad \text{kurtosis}_J = \frac{1}{J\sigma_J^4}\sum_{j=1}^{J}(r_j - \bar{r}_J)^4 - 3$$

for the skewness and kurtosis, respectively. With $J = 2000$ data points we obtain the values $\bar{r}_J \approx 0.0060$, $\sigma_J^2 \approx 1.0184$, skewness$_J \approx 0.0031$, kurtosis$_J \approx 0.3177$. While the data are therefore not perfectly Gaussian, a Gaussian approximation with mean zero and variance one seems nevertheless justifiable.

## 2.2      Coupling of measures and optimal transportation

We now consider the reverse situation, in which two marginal distributions are given and we wish to find an appropriate joint distribution with associated random variables. This leads us to the concept of *coupling*.

**Definition 2.22** (Coupling)   Let $\mu_{X_1}$ and $\mu_{X_2}$ denote two probability measures on a space $\mathcal{X}$. A *coupling* of $\mu_{X_1}$ and $\mu_{X_2}$ consists of a pair $Z = (X_1, X_2)$ of random variables such that $X_1 \sim \mu_{X_1}$, $X_2 \sim \mu_{X_2}$, and $Z \sim \mu_Z$. The joint measure $\mu_Z$ on the product space $\mathcal{Z} = \mathcal{X} \times \mathcal{X}$, is called the *transference plan* for this coupling. The set of all transference plans is denoted by $\Pi(\mu_{X_1}, \mu_{X_2})$.

Since the involved measures will generally be assumed to be absolutely continuous throughout this book, the discussion of couplings will be mostly restricted to the less abstract case of $\mathcal{X} = \mathbb{R}^{N_x}$ and $\mu_{X_1}(\mathrm{d}x) = \pi_{X_1}(x)\mathrm{d}x$, $\mu_{X_2}(\mathrm{d}x) = \pi_{X_2}(x)\mathrm{d}x$. In other words, we generally assume that the marginal measures are

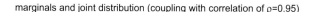

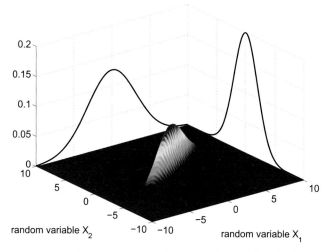

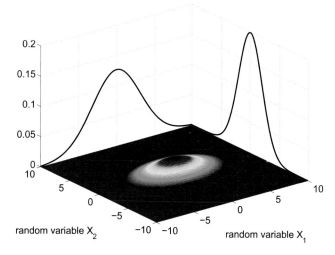

**Figure 2.4** The figure shows possible couplings (joint distributions) between two univariate Gaussian random variables $X_1$ and $X_2$. The top panel is for a correlation of $\rho = 0.95$ while the bottom panel is for $\rho = 0.1$. The marginal distributions are also shown in both cases. The marginal distribution for $X_2$ has smaller variance, and thus is more "concentrated" around the mean.

absolutely continuous. We will find, however, that couplings are often not absolutely continuous on $\mathcal{Z} = \mathcal{X} \times \mathcal{X} = \mathbb{R}^{N_x} \times \mathbb{R}^{N_x}$. Clearly, couplings always exist since we can use the trivial product coupling

$$\pi_Z(x_1, x_2) = \pi_{X_1}(x_1)\pi_{X_2}(x_2),$$

in which case the associated random variables $X_1$ and $X_2$ are independent.

---

**Example 2.23**  We set $N_x = 1$ and consider a pair of univariate Gaussian PDFs $\pi_{X_i}(x_i) = \mathrm{n}(x_i; \overline{x}_i, \sigma_{ii}^2)$, $i = 1, 2$. We seek a coupling in $z = (x_1, x_2)$ of the form $\pi_Z(z) = \mathrm{n}(z; \overline{z}, P)$. We quickly find from the given marginals that $\overline{z} = (\overline{x}_1, \overline{x}_2)^{\mathrm{T}}$ and the covariance matrix $P$ must be of the form

$$P = \begin{pmatrix} \sigma_{11}^2 & \rho\,\sigma_{11}\sigma_{22} \\ \rho\,\sigma_{11}\sigma_{22} & \sigma_{22}^2 \end{pmatrix}.$$

Since $P$ has to be positive definite, the correlation

$$\rho = \frac{\sigma_{12}^2}{|\sigma_{11}||\sigma_{22}|} = \frac{\sigma_{21}^2}{|\sigma_{11}||\sigma_{22}|}$$

between $X_1$ and $X_2$ has to satisfy

$$\rho^2 \le 1. \tag{2.10}$$

We now investigate the conditional PDF $\pi_{X_2}(x_2|x_1)$ further. Making use of the formulas in Example 2.18, we obtain

$$\pi_{X_2}(x_2|x_1) = \mathrm{n}(x_2; \overline{x}_c, \sigma_c^2)$$

with

$$\overline{x}_c = \overline{x}_2 - \frac{\sigma_{21}^2}{\sigma_{11}^2}(\overline{x}_1 - x_1) = \overline{x}_2 - \rho\frac{\sigma_{22}}{\sigma_{11}}(\overline{x}_1 - x_1)$$

and

$$\sigma_c^2 = \sigma_{22}^2 - \sigma_{12}^4\sigma_{11}^{-2} = (1 - \rho^2)\sigma_{22}^2.$$

We find that the limit $\rho \to 1$ leads to $\sigma_c \to 0$, which implies that the conditional probability density becomes a Dirac delta distribution centred about

$$\overline{x}_c = \overline{x}_2 - \frac{\sigma_{22}}{\sigma_{11}}(\overline{x}_1 - x_1).$$

Hence optimising the correlation between $X_1$ and $X_2$ has led us to a deterministic coupling

$$X_2 = \overline{x}_2 + \frac{\sigma_{22}}{\sigma_{11}}(X_1 - \overline{x}_1). \tag{2.11}$$

Such a coupling is commonly used in order to transform random numbers from a $N(0,1)$ random number generator into Gaussian random numbers with mean $\overline{x}$ and variance $\sigma^2$. This particular case leads to $\overline{x}_1 = 0$, $\overline{x}_2 = \overline{x}$, $\sigma_{11} = 1$ and $\sigma_{22} = \sigma$ in (2.11). We will find later that this coupling is optimal in the sense that it maximises the correlation between $X_1$ and $X_2$. Joint distributions in $z$ are shown in Figure 2.4 for a small correlation $\rho = 0.1$ and a nearly optimal correlation $\rho = 0.95$.

---

Motivated by the previous example, we now discuss deterministic couplings in a more general setting. The reader might also want to recall Lemma 2.13.

**Definition 2.24** (Deterministic coupling)  Assume that we have a random variable $X_1$ with law $\mu_{X_1}$ and a probability measure $\mu_{X_2}$. A diffeomorphism $T : \mathcal{X} \to \mathcal{X}$ is called a *transport map* if the induced random variable $X_2 = T(X_1)$ satisfies

$$\mathbb{E}[f(X_2)] = \int_{\mathcal{X}} f(x_2)\mu_{X_2}(\mathrm{d}x_2) = \int_{\mathcal{X}} f(T(x_1))\mu_{X_1}(\mathrm{d}x_1) = \mathbb{E}[f(T(X_1))] \quad (2.12)$$

for all suitable functions $f : \mathcal{X} \to \mathbb{R}$. The associated coupling

$$\mu_Z(\mathrm{d}x_1, \mathrm{d}x_2) = \delta(x_2 - T(x_1))\mu_{X_1}(\mathrm{d}x_1)\mathrm{d}x_2, \quad (2.13)$$

where $\delta(\cdot)$ is the standard Dirac distribution, is called a *deterministic coupling*. Note that $\mu_Z$ is not absolutely continuous, even if both $\mu_{X_1}$ and $\mu_{X_2}$ are.

Using

$$\int_{\mathcal{X}} f(x_2)\delta(x_2 - T(x_1))\mathrm{d}x_2 = f(T(x_1)),$$

it indeed follows from the above definition of $\mu_Z$ that

$$\int_{\mathcal{X}} f(x_2)\mu_{X_2}(\mathrm{d}x_2) = \int_{Z} f(x_2)\mu_Z(\mathrm{d}x_1, \mathrm{d}x_2) = \int_{\mathcal{X}} f(T(x_1))\mu_{X_1}(\mathrm{d}x_1)$$

and $X_2$ has marginal distribution $\mu_{X_2}$.

We now discuss a simple example.

---

**Example 2.25**  Let $\pi_{X_1}(x)$ and $\pi_{X_2}(x)$ denote two PDFs on $\mathcal{X} = \mathbb{R}$. The associated cumulative distribution functions are defined by

$$F_{X_1}(x) = \int_{-\infty}^{x} \pi_{X_1}(x')\mathrm{d}x', \qquad F_{X_2}(x) = \int_{-\infty}^{x} \pi_{X_2}(x')\mathrm{d}x'.$$

The right inverse of $F_{X_2}$ is given by

$$F_{X_2}^{-1}(p) = \inf\{x \in \mathbb{R} : F_{X_2}(x) \geq p\}$$

for $p \in [0, 1]$. The inverse may be used to define a transport map that transforms $X_1$ into $X_2$ as follows,

$$X_2 = T(X_1) = F_{X_2}^{-1}(F_{X_1}(X_1)).$$

For example, consider the case where $X_1$ is a random variable with uniform distribution $\mathrm{U}[0, 1]$, and $X_2 \sim \mathrm{N}(0, 1)$ is a standard Gaussian random variable. Then the transport map between $X_1$ and $X_2$ is simply the inverse of the cumulative distribution function

$$F_{X_2}(x) = \frac{1}{\sqrt{2\pi}} \int_{-\infty}^{x} e^{-(x')^2/2}\mathrm{d}x'.$$

This provides a standard tool for converting uniformly distributed random variables into Gaussian random variables. The construction generalises to univariate measures $\mu_{X_2}$ which are not absolutely continuous. Consider, for example, the point measure $\mu_{x_0}$ with cumulative distribution function (2.2). Its right-continuous inverse is defined by

$$F_{x_0}^{-1}(p) = \inf\{x \in \mathbb{R} : F_{x_0}(x) \geq p\} = x_0$$

for all $p \in [0, 1]$.

We can extend the transform method of Example 2.25 to random variables in $\mathbb{R}^{N_x}$ with $N_x \geq 2$ by applying the disintegration formula (2.4) to the $N_x$ components of $x$, and obtaining subsequent recursive one-dimensional couplings along each dimension. The resulting deterministic coupling is called the *Knothe–Rosenblatt rearrangement* (Villani 2009), also well-known to statisticians as the *conditional quantile transform*. While the Knothe–Rosenblatt rearrangement can be used in quite general situations, it has the undesirable property that the map depends on the order in which the $N_x$ dimensions of $\mathcal{X}$ are processed.

We now generalise the deterministic couplings for univariate Gaussians from Example 2.23 to the multivariate case.

**Example 2.26**  Consider two Gaussian distributions $\mathrm{N}(\bar{x}_1, P_1)$ and $\mathrm{N}(\bar{x}_2, P_2)$ in $\mathbb{R}^{N_x}$ with means $\bar{x}_1$ and $\bar{x}_2$ and covariance matrices $P_1$ and $P_2$, respectively. We first define the *square root* $P^{1/2}$ of a symmetric positive definite matrix $P$ as the unique symmetric matrix which satisfies $P^{1/2}P^{1/2} = P$. Then the affine transformation

$$x_2 = T(x_1) = \bar{x}_2 + P_2^{1/2}P_1^{-1/2}(x_1 - \bar{x}_1) \tag{2.14}$$

provides a deterministic coupling. Indeed, we find that

$$(x_2 - \bar{x}_2)^{\mathrm{T}}P_2^{-1}(x_2 - \bar{x}_2) = (x_1 - \bar{x}_1)^{\mathrm{T}}P_1^{-1}(x_1 - \bar{x}_1)$$

under the suggested coupling. In contrast with the univariate case, deterministic couplings are not uniquely defined since

$$x_2 = T(x_1) = \bar{x}_2 + P_2^{1/2}QP_1^{-1/2}(x_1 - \bar{x}_1),$$

where $Q$ is any orthogonal matrix, also provides a coupling.

Deterministic couplings can be viewed as a special case of an integral transform defined by

$$\pi_{X_2}(x_2) = \int_{\mathcal{X}_1} \pi_{X_2}(x_2|x_1)\pi_{X_1}(x_1)\mathrm{d}x_1,$$

where $\pi_{X_2}(x_2|x_1)$ denotes the conditional PDF for the random variable $X_2$ given $X_1 = x_1$ induced by the coupling $\pi_{X_1X_2}(x_1, x_2)$ via

$$\pi_{X_2}(x_2|x_1) = \frac{\pi_{X_1X_2}(x_1, x_2)}{\pi_{X_1}(x_1)}.$$

Furthermore, we formally have

$$\pi_{X_2}(x_2|x_1) = \delta(x_2 - T(x_1))$$

for deterministic couplings. The trivial coupling $\pi_Z(x_1, x_2) = \pi_{X_1}(x_1)\pi_{X_2}(x_2)$ leads to $\pi_{X_2}(x_2|x_1) = \pi_{X_2}(x_2)$ and we conclude that $X_2$ is independent of $X_1$. A transport map $x_2 = T(x_1)$ leads instead to dependent random variables and a *covariance matrix*

$$\text{cov}(X_1, X_2) := \mathbb{E}[X_1 X_2^{\mathrm{T}}] - \mathbb{E}[X_1](\mathbb{E}[X_2])^{\mathrm{T}} = \mathbb{E}[X_1 T(X_1)^{\mathrm{T}}] - \bar{x}_1 \bar{x}_2^{\mathrm{T}},$$

which is non-zero in general. One way to select a particular coupling is to choose the one that maximises the covariance. In fact, in many applications (including the ones we will consider later in this book) it is desirable to maximise the covariance or correlation between $X_1$ and $X_2$ subject to the desired marginal distributions. In addition, maximising the covariance for given marginals also has an important geometric interpretation. For simplicity, consider univariate random variables $X_1$ and $X_2$. Then we have

$$\begin{aligned}
\mathbb{E}[(X_2 - X_1)^2] &= \mathbb{E}[X_1^2] + \mathbb{E}[X_2^2] - 2\mathbb{E}[X_1 X_2] \\
&= \mathbb{E}[X_1^2] + \mathbb{E}[X_2^2] - 2\mathbb{E}[(X_1 - \bar{x}_1)(X_2 - \bar{x}_2)] - 2\bar{x}_1 \bar{x}_2 \\
&= \mathbb{E}[X_1^2] + \mathbb{E}[X_2^2] - 2\bar{x}_1 \bar{x}_2 - 2\text{cov}(X_1, X_2).
\end{aligned}$$

Hence, finding a joint measure $\mu_Z$ that minimises the expectation of $(X_1 - X_2)^2$ simultaneously maximises the covariance between univariate random variables $X_1$ and $X_2$. This geometric interpretation extends to multivariate random variables and leads to the celebrated *Monge–Kantorovitch problem*.

**Definition 2.27** (Monge–Kantorovitch problem)  A transference plan $\mu_Z^* \in \Pi(\mu_{X_1}, \mu_{X_2})$ is called the solution to the *Monge–Kantorovitch problem* with cost function $c(x_1, x_2) = \|x_1 - x_2\|^2$ if

$$\mu_Z^* = \arg\inf_{\mu_Z \in \Pi(\mu_{X_1}, \mu_{X_2})} \mathbb{E}[\|X_1 - X_2\|^2], \qquad \text{law}(Z = (X_1, X_2)) = \mu_Z, \quad (2.15)$$

where $\Pi(\mu_{X_1}, \mu_{X_2})$ denotes the set of all possible couplings between $\mu_{X_1}$ and $\mu_{X_2}$. The associated functional

$$W(\mu_{X_1}, \mu_{X_2}) = \sqrt{\inf \mathbb{E}[\|X_1 - X_2\|^2]} \qquad (2.16)$$

is called the $L^2$-*Wasserstein distance* between $\mu_{X_1}$ and $\mu_{X_2}$.

---

**Example 2.28**  In this example we consider couplings between two discrete random variables $X_1$, $X_2$ with domain given by the discrete set

$$\mathcal{X} = \{a_1, a_2, \ldots, a_M\}, \qquad a_i \in \mathbb{R}, \qquad (2.17)$$

and probability distributions

$$\mathbb{P}(X_1 = a_i) = 1/M, \quad \mathbb{P}(X_2 = a_i) = w_i,$$

respectively, with $w_i \geq 0$, $i = 1, \ldots, M$, and $\sum_i w_i = 1$. Any coupling between these two probability distributions is characterised by a matrix $T \in \mathbb{R}^{M \times M}$ such that its entries $t_{ij} = (T)_{ij}$ satisfy $t_{ij} \geq 0$ and

$$\sum_{i=1}^{M} t_{ij} = 1/M, \qquad \sum_{j=1}^{M} t_{ij} = w_i. \tag{2.18}$$

These matrices characterise the set of all couplings $\Pi$ in the definition of the Monge–Kantorovitch problem. The joint measures of $X_1$ and $X_2$ are of the form

$$\mu_{X_1 X_2}(\mathrm{d}x_1, \mathrm{d}x_2) = \sum_{i,j=1}^{M} t_{ij} \delta(x_1 - a_j) \delta(x_2 - a_i) \mathrm{d}x_1 \mathrm{d}x_2. \tag{2.19}$$

Given a coupling $T$ and the mean values

$$\overline{x}_1 = \frac{1}{M} \sum_{i=1}^{M} a_i, \qquad \overline{x}_2 = \sum_{i=1}^{M} w_i a_i,$$

the covariance between the associated discrete random variables $X_1$ and $X_2$ is defined by

$$\mathrm{cov}(X_1, X_2) = \sum_{i,j=1}^{M} (a_i - \overline{x}_2) t_{ij} (a_j - \overline{x}_1). \tag{2.20}$$

The particular coupling defined by $t_{ij} = w_i/M$ leads to zero correlation between $X_1$ and $X_2$. On the other hand, maximising the correlation leads to a linear transport problem in the $M^2$ unknowns $\{t_{ij}\}$. More precisely, the unknowns $t_{ij}$ have to satisfy the inequality constraints $t_{ij} \geq 0$, the equality constraints (2.18), and should minimise

$$J(\{t_{ij}\}) = \sum_{i,j=1}^{M} t_{ij} (a_i - a_j)^2$$

which, following our previous discussion, is equivalent to maximising (2.20). An algorithm for solving the minimisation problem, which relies on the coefficients $a_i$ being real numbers, is given in Appendix 5.8. The basic idea of this algorithm is demonstrated in the following example. The more general coupling problem, also called a *linear transport problem*, for $a_i \in \mathbb{R}^{N_x}$, $N_x > 1$, is much harder to solve. See Appendix 7.4 and the textbook by Strang (1986).

---

**Example 2.29**  In this example we demonstrate how to obtain the optimal coupling for the (sorted) discrete target set $\mathcal{X}$ given by

$$a_i = \frac{1}{2M} + \frac{i-1}{M} \in [0,1]$$

with $M = 10$. The weights $w_i$ are determined by

$$w_i = \frac{e^{-(a_i - 0.1)^2/0.2}}{\sum_{j=1}^{M} e^{-(a_j - 0.1)^2/0.2}}.$$

The optimal coupling matrix is

$$T^* \approx \begin{pmatrix}
0.1 & 0.1 & 0.0002 & 0 & 0 & 0 & 0 & 0 & 0 & 0 \\
0 & 0 & 0.0998 & 0.1 & 0.0003 & 0 & 0 & 0 & 0 & 0 \\
0 & 0 & 0 & 0 & 0.0997 & 0.081 & 0 & 0 & 0 & 0 \\
0 & 0 & 0 & 0 & 0 & 0.019 & 0.1 & 0.03 & 0 & 0 \\
0 & 0 & 0 & 0 & 0 & 0 & 0 & 0.07 & 0.04 & 0 \\
0 & 0 & 0 & 0 & 0 & 0 & 0 & 0 & 0.06 & 0.013 \\
0 & 0 & 0 & 0 & 0 & 0 & 0 & 0 & 0 & 0.045 \\
0 & 0 & 0 & 0 & 0 & 0 & 0 & 0 & 0 & 0.025 \\
0 & 0 & 0 & 0 & 0 & 0 & 0 & 0 & 0 & 0.012 \\
0 & 0 & 0 & 0 & 0 & 0 & 0 & 0 & 0 & 0.005
\end{pmatrix}.$$

This matrix can be obtained through the following considerations. We start with the smallest $a_1 = 1/2M = 0.05$ and its probability weight $w_1 \approx 0.200157$. Since a diagonal entry in $T$ does not contribute to the transport cost $J(T)$, we set $t_{11}^*$ to its maximal possible value which is $t_{11}^* = 1/M = 0.1$. The next cheapest transport cost is achieved through the $t_{12}^*$ entry which couples $a_1 = 0.05$ with $a_2 = 0.15$. Hence we again set $t_{12}^*$ to its maximal possible value $t_{12}^* = 0.1$. This leaves us with $t_{13}^* \approx 0.000157 \approx 0.0002$ and $t_{1j}^* = 0$ for all $j \geq 4$. We now continue to distribute the probability weight $w_2 = 0.200157$ across the second row of $T^*$. Since the columns must sum to $1/M$, we are required to set $t_{2,1}^*$ and $t_{2,2}^*$ equal to zero and $t_{23}^* \approx 0.1 - 0.000157 \approx 0.0998$. The remaining probability weight is distributed then according to $t_{24}^* = 0.1$ and $t_{25}^* \approx 0.000314 \approx 0.0003$. Again all entries $t_{2j}^*$, $j \geq 6$, are set equal to zero. The remaining rows are now filled in exactly the same manner and we obtain the complete coupling matrix $T^*$. The algorithm in Appendix 5.8 is a formalisation of this construction. Note that the fact that the set $\mathcal{X}$ has been sorted is crucial.

Another special case of a linear transport problem occurs when two probability distributions with discrete sets $\mathcal{X}_1 = \{a_1, \ldots, a_M\}$ and $\mathcal{X}_2 = \{b_1, \ldots, b_M\}$ and uniform probabilities $\mathbb{P}(a_i) = \mathbb{P}(b_i) = 1/M$ are to be coupled. This is called an *assignment problem*.

We now return to continuous random variables and state the following remarkable result.

**Theorem 2.30** (Optimal transference plan)  If the measures $\mu_{X_1}$, $\mu_{X_2}$ on $\mathcal{X} = \mathbb{R}^{N_x}$ are absolutely continuous and have bounded second-order moments, then the optimal transference plan that solves the Monge–Kantorovitch problem corresponds to a deterministic coupling with transfer map

$$X_2 = T(X_1) = \nabla_x \psi(X_1),$$

for some convex potential $\psi : \mathbb{R}^{N_x} \to \mathbb{R}$.

*Proof*  We assume that the infimum in (2.15) is attained by deterministic couplings. This assumption will be justified later in this section. Here we only demonstrate that the optimal transfer map is generated by a potential $\psi$.[3]

We denote the associated PDFs by $\pi_{X_i}$, $i = 1, 2$. To obtain the optimal transfer map, we seek extrema of the following functional,

$$\mathcal{K}[T, \Psi] = \frac{1}{2} \int_{\mathbb{R}^{N_x}} \|T^{-1}(x) - x\|^2 \pi_{X_2}(x) \mathrm{d}x$$

$$+ \int_{\mathbb{R}^{N_x}} \Psi(x) \left[\pi_{X_2}(T(x))|DT(x)| - \pi_{X_1}(x)\right] \mathrm{d}x,$$

where $DT(x)$ denotes the Jacobian matrix of $T$ at $x$, $|DT(x)| = |\det DT(x)|$, and $\Psi : \mathbb{R}^{N_x} \to \mathbb{R}$ is a Lagrange multiplier enforcing the coupling of the two marginal PDFs under the desired transport map.

To simplify the calculation, we introduce the inverse transfer map $X_1 = S(X_2) = T^{-1}(X_2)$, and obtain the functional

$$\mathcal{L}[S, \Psi] = \frac{1}{2} \int_{\mathbb{R}^{N_x}} \|S(x) - x\|^2 \pi_{X_2}(x) \mathrm{d}x$$

$$+ \int_{\mathbb{R}^{N_x}} \left[\Psi(S(x))\pi_{X_2}(x) - \Psi(x)\pi_{X_1}(x)\right] \mathrm{d}x,$$

having made use of the change of variables formula.

To find the extrema of the functional, we compute the *variational derivatives* with respect to $S$ and $\Psi$. These are defined (in the weak sense) as

$$\int_{\mathbb{R}^{N_x}} \Phi(x)^{\mathrm{T}} \frac{\delta\mathcal{L}}{\delta S}(x)\mathrm{d}x = \lim_{\epsilon \to 0} \frac{1}{\epsilon} \left(\mathcal{L}[S + \epsilon\Phi, \Psi] - \mathcal{L}[S, \Psi]\right),$$

$$\int_{\mathbb{R}^{N_x}} \phi(x) \frac{\delta\mathcal{L}}{\delta \Psi}(x)\mathrm{d}x = \lim_{\epsilon \to 0} \frac{1}{\epsilon} \left(\mathcal{L}[S, \Psi + \epsilon\phi] - \mathcal{L}[S, \Psi]\right),$$

for all smooth test functions $\phi$ and maps $\Phi$ for which the limit is finite. At the extrema, the variational derivatives are zero, and after some calculation, we obtain the equations

$$\frac{\delta\mathcal{L}}{\delta S}(x) = \pi_{X_2}(x) \left[(S(x) - x) + \nabla_x\Psi(S(x))\right] = 0$$

and

$$\frac{\delta\mathcal{L}}{\delta \Psi}(x) = -\pi_{X_1}(x) + \pi_{X_2}(T(x))|DT(x)| = 0. \tag{2.21}$$

These equations characterise the critical points of the functional $\mathcal{L}$. The first equality implies

$$x_2 = T(x_1) = x_1 + \nabla_x\Psi(x_1) = \nabla_x \left(\frac{1}{2}x_1^{\mathrm{T}}x_1 + \Psi(x_1)\right) =: \nabla_x\psi(x_1)$$

and the second implies that $T$ transforms $\pi_{X_1}$ into $\pi_{X_2}$ as required.     □

---

[3] See Villani (2003) for a completely general proof and also for more general results in terms of subgradients of convex functions and weaker conditions on the two marginal measures.

**Example 2.31**  Consider two univariate PDFs $\pi_{X_1}$ and $\pi_{X_2}$ with cumulative distribution functions $F_{X_1}$ and $F_{X_2}$, respectively. Then, as already discussed, a coupling is achieved by

$$x_2 = T(x_1) = F_{X_2}^{-1}(F_{X_1}(x_1)),$$

which is also optimal under the $(\cdot)^2$ distance. Furthermore, the $L^2$-Wasserstein distance (2.16) between $\pi_{X_1}$ and $\pi_{X_2}$ is given by

$$
\begin{aligned}
W(\pi_{X_1}, \pi_{X_2})^2 &= \int_{\mathbb{R}} \int_{\mathbb{R}} (x_1 - x_2)^2 \delta\left(x_2 - F_{X_2}^{-1}(F_{X_1}(x_1))\right) \pi_{X_1}(x_1) \mathrm{d}x_1 \mathrm{d}x_2 \\
&= \int_0^1 \int_{\mathbb{R}} (F_{X_1}^{-1}(p) - x_2)^2 \delta\left(x_2 - F_{X_2}^{-1}(p)\right) \mathrm{d}x_2 \mathrm{d}p \\
&= \int_0^1 (F_{X_1}^{-1}(p) - F_{X_2}^{-1}(p))^2 \mathrm{d}p,
\end{aligned}
\tag{2.22}
$$

with $p = F_{X_1}(x_1)$ and $\mathrm{d}p = \pi_{X_1}(x_1)\mathrm{d}x_1$.

**Example 2.32**  Consider two Gaussian distributions $\mathrm{N}(\overline{x}_1, P_1)$ and $\mathrm{N}(\overline{x}_2, P_2)$ in $\mathbb{R}^{N_x}$, with means $\overline{x}_1$ and $\overline{x}_2$ and covariance matrices $P_1$ and $P_2$, respectively. We previously discussed the deterministic coupling (2.14). However, the induced affine transformation $x_2 = T(x_1)$ cannot be generated from a potential $\psi$ since the matrix $P_2^{1/2} P_1^{-1/2}$ is not symmetric. Indeed, the optimal coupling in the sense of Monge–Kantorovitch with cost function $c(x_1, x_2) = \|x_1 - x_2\|^2$ is provided by

$$x_2 = T(x_1) := \overline{x}_2 + P_2^{1/2} \left[ P_2^{1/2} P_1 P_2^{1/2} \right]^{-1/2} P_2^{1/2} (x_1 - \overline{x}_1).
\tag{2.23}$$

See Olkin & Pukelsheim (1982) for a derivation. The associated Wasserstein distance (2.16) between the two Gaussian distributions is

$$W(\mu_{X_1}, \mu_{X_2})^2 = \|\overline{x}_1 - \overline{x}_2\|^2 + \mathrm{trace}\left( P_1 + P_2 - 2 \left[ P_2^{1/2} P_1 P_2^{1/2} \right]^{1/2} \right).$$

We now make a generalisation that will be used later in the book. Assuming that a matrix $A \in \mathbb{R}^{N_x \times M}$ is given such that $P_2 = AA^{\mathrm{T}}$, clearly we can choose $A = P_2^{1/2}$ in which case $M = N_x$ and $A$ is symmetric. However, we allow for $A$ to be non-symmetric, and $M$ can be smaller than $N_x$ in the case where $P_2$ is not of full rank. An important observation is that we can replace $P_2^{1/2}$ in (2.23) by $A$ and $A^{\mathrm{T}}$, respectively, i.e.,

$$T(x_1) = \overline{x}_2 + A \left[ A^{\mathrm{T}} P_1 A \right]^{-1/2} A^{\mathrm{T}} (x_1 - \overline{x}_1).
\tag{2.24}$$

In order to describe the geometric structure of optimal couplings (whether deterministic or not) we need to introduce the two concepts of *cyclical monotonicity* and *subdifferentials* of *convex functions*. Cyclical monotonicity is a property of the support of a transference plan.

**Definition 2.33** (Support of a measure and cyclical monotonicity)   The *support* of a coupling $\mu_Z$ on $\mathcal{Z} = \mathcal{X} \times \mathcal{X}$ is the smallest closed set on which $\mu_Z$ is concentrated, i.e.

$$\operatorname{supp}(\mu_Z) := \bigcap \{ S \subset \mathcal{Z} : S \text{ closed and } \mu_Z(\mathcal{Z} \setminus S) = 0 \}.$$

The support of $\mu_Z$ is called *cyclically monotone* if for every set of points $(x_1^i, x_2^i) \in \operatorname{supp}(\mu_Z) \subset \mathcal{X} \times \mathcal{X}$, $i = 1, \ldots, I$, and any permutation $\sigma$ of $\{1, \ldots, I\}$, we have

$$\sum_{i=1}^I \| x_1^i - x_2^i \|^2 \leq \sum_{i=1}^I \| x_1^i - x_2^{\sigma(i)} \|^2. \tag{2.25}$$

Note that (2.25) is equivalent to

$$\sum_{i=1}^I (x_1^i)^{\mathrm{T}} (x_2^{\sigma(i)} - x_2^i) \leq 0.$$

We will find later that cyclical monotonicity implies that the support of a transference plan is contained in the subdifferential of an appropriate convex functional $\psi(x)$. If that convex function can be shown to be sufficiently regular then the transference plan is deterministic. This chain of arguments can be made rigorous, providing a proof of Theorem 2.30 (Villani 2009).

We next discuss an example for which the support of the coupling is finite.

---

**Example 2.34**   We return to the linear transport problem associated with the optimal coupling $\mu_{X_1 X_2}^*$ of the two discrete random variables $X_1$ and $X_2$ as discussed in Examples 2.28 and 2.29. From (2.19), we see that the support of the optimal coupling is defined by

$$(x_1 = a_j, x_2 = a_i) \in \operatorname{supp}(\mu_{X_1 X_2}^*) \qquad \text{if and only if } t_{ij}^* > 0. \tag{2.26}$$

Since the coefficients $a_i$ have been sorted, cyclical monotonicity is evident from the staircase-like structure of the non-zero entries in $T^*$.

Furthermore, let $T$ denote any coupling matrix, i.e., a matrix with non-negative entries and

$$\sum_{i=1}^M t_{ij} = 1/M, \qquad \sum_{j=1}^M t_{ij} = w_i,$$

and take any two pairs $(a_{j_1}, a_{i_1}) \in \mathbb{R}^2$ and $(a_{j_2}, a_{i_2}) \in \mathbb{R}^2$ such that $t_{i_1 j_1} > 0$ and $t_{i_2 j_2} > 0$. If this pair does not satisfy cyclical monotonicity, i.e.,

$$(a_{i_1} - a_{j_1})^2 + (a_{i_2} - a_{j_2})^2 > (a_{i_1} - a_{j_2})^2 + (a_{i_2} - a_{j_1})^2,$$

then there is a $T'$ with lower cost. Specifically, set

$$c = (a_{i_1} - a_{j_1})^2 + (a_{i_2} - a_{j_2})^2 - (a_{i_1} - a_{j_2})^2 - (a_{i_2} - a_{j_1})^2$$
$$= 2(a_{i_2} - a_{i_1})(a_{j_1} - a_{j_2}) > 0$$

and define the associated entries in $T'$ by

$$t'_{i_1 j_1} = t_{i_1 j_1} - \varepsilon, \ t'_{i_2 j_2} = t_{i_2 j_2} - \varepsilon, \ t'_{i_2 j_1} = t_{i_2 j_1} + \varepsilon, \ t'_{i_1 j_2} = t_{i_1 j_2} + \varepsilon$$

with $\varepsilon > 0$ chosen such that the new entries are all non-negative. Since the associated contribution to the cost for $T$ is given by

$$J = t_{i_1 j_1}(a_{i_1} - a_{j_1})^2 + t_{i_2 j_2}(a_{i_2} - a_{j_2})^2 + t_{i_2 j_1}(a_{i_2} - a_{j_1})^2 + t_{i_1 j_2}(a_{i_1} - a_{j_2})^2$$

we find that

$$J' = t'_{i_1 j_1}(a_{i_1} - a_{j_1})^2 + t'_{i_2 j_2}(a_{i_2} - a_{j_2})^2 + t'_{i_2 j_1}(a_{i_2} - a_{j_1})^2 + t'_{i_1 j_2}(a_{i_1} - a_{j_2})^2$$
$$= (t_{i_1 j_1} - \varepsilon)(a_{i_1} - a_{j_1})^2 + (t_{i_2 j_2} - \varepsilon)(a_{i_2} - a_{j_2})^2$$
$$\quad + (t_{i_2 j_1} + \varepsilon)(a_{i_2} - a_{j_1})^2 + (t_{i_1 j_2} + \varepsilon)(a_{i_1} - a_{j_2})^2$$
$$= J - \varepsilon c < J$$

for $T'$. The reduction in cost is maximised by choosing $\varepsilon$ such that either $t'_{i_1 j_1}$ or $t'_{i_2 j_2}$ becomes zero. More generally, unless a coupling matrix $T$ is cyclically monotone, we can find a better coupling.

---

We now generalise this last observation.

**Theorem 2.35** (Cyclical monotonicity)   If $\mu_Z^*$ is a solution to the Monge–Kantorovitch problem (2.15), then $\mu_Z^*$ has cyclically monotone support.

*Proof*   We prove the theorem by contradiction, i.e., we assume that there exists a set of points $(x_1^i, x_2^i) \in \mathrm{supp}\,(\mu_Z^*)$, $i = 1, \ldots, I$, and a permutation $\sigma$ of $\{1, \ldots, I\}$ such that

$$\sum_{i=1}^{I} \|x_1^i - x_2^i\|^2 > \sum_{i=1}^{I} \|x_1^i - x_2^{\sigma(i)}\|^2$$

for optimal $\mu_Z^*$. Let $c > 0$ be defined by

$$c = \sum_{i=1}^{I} \|x_1^i - x_2^i\|^2 - \sum_{i=1}^{I} \|x_1^i - x_2^{\sigma(i)}\|^2.$$

By continuity there exist neighbourhoods $\mathcal{U}(x_1^i)$ and $\mathcal{U}(x_2^i)$ for all $i$ such that

$$\|x_1^i - x_2^i\|^2 - \frac{c}{2I} < \|x_1 - x_2\|^2 \quad \text{for all} \quad (x_1, x_2) \in \mathcal{U}(x_1^i) \times \mathcal{U}(x_2^i)$$

and

$$\|x_1^i - x_2^{\sigma(i)}\|^2 + \frac{c}{2I} > \|x_1 - x_2\|^2 \quad \text{for all} \quad (x_1, x_2) \in \mathcal{U}(x_1^i) \times \mathcal{U}(x_2^{\sigma(i)}).$$

We also choose the neighbourhoods such that the sets $W_i = \mathcal{U}(x_1^i) \times \mathcal{U}(x_2^i)$ are subsets of the support of $\mu_Z^*$ for $i = 1, \ldots, I$. Next we introduce non-vanishing probability measures $\mu_Z^i$ on each of the sets $W_i$ with marginals denoted by $\mu_{X_1}^i$ and $\mu_{X_2}^i$, respectively, and measures $\tilde{\mu}_Z^i$ on $\tilde{W}_i = \mathcal{U}(x_1^i) \times \mathcal{U}(x_2^{\sigma(i)})$ by

$$\tilde{\mu}_Z^i(\mathrm{d}x_1, \mathrm{d}x_2) = \mu_{X_1}^i(\mathrm{d}x_1)\, \mu_{X_2}^{\sigma(i)}(\mathrm{d}x_2)$$

for $i = 1, \ldots, I$.

A new coupling $\tilde{\mu}_Z \in \Pi(\mu_{X_1}, \mu_{X_2})$ is now constructed via

$$\tilde{\mu}_Z = \mu_Z - \gamma \sum_{i=1}^{I} \mu_Z^i + \gamma \sum_{i=1}^{I} \tilde{\mu}_Z^i$$

with $\gamma > 0$ chosen small enough that $\tilde{\mu}_Z$ remains non-negative. It is obvious by construction that the marginals of $\tilde{\mu}_Z$ are indeed $\mu_{X_1}$ and $\mu_{X_2}$, respectively.
Finally, we demonstrate that

$$\Delta := \int_{\mathcal{Z}} \|x_1 - x_2\|^2 \mu_Z^*(\mathrm{d}x_1, \mathrm{d}x_2) - \int_{\mathcal{Z}} \|x_1 - x_2\|^2 \tilde{\mu}_Z(\mathrm{d}x_1, \mathrm{d}x_2) > 0,$$

which provides the desired contradiction. Indeed

$$\Delta = \gamma \sum_{i=1}^{I} \|x_1 - x_2\|^2 \mu_Z^i(\mathrm{d}x_1, \mathrm{d}x_2) - \gamma \sum_{i=1}^{I} \|x_1 - x_2\|^2 \tilde{\mu}_Z^i(\mathrm{d}x_1, \mathrm{d}x_2)$$

$$> \gamma \sum_{i=1}^{I} \left( \|x_1^i - x_2^i\|^2 - \frac{c}{2I} \right) - \gamma \sum_{i=1}^{I} \left( \|x_1^i - x_2^{\sigma(i)}\|^2 + \frac{c}{2I} \right)$$

$$= \gamma(c - c) = 0,$$

which completes the proof. $\qquad \square$

A fundamental theorem of convex analysis, *Rockafellar's theorem* (Villani 2003), states that cyclically monotone sets $S \subset \mathbb{R}^{N_x} \times \mathbb{R}^{N_x}$ are contained in the *subdifferential* of a convex function $\psi : \mathbb{R}^{N_x} \to \mathbb{R}$.

**Definition 2.36** (Subdifferential)   The subdifferential $\partial \psi$ of a convex function $\psi$ at a point $x \in \mathbb{R}^{N_x}$ is defined as the non-empty and convex set of all $m \in \mathbb{R}^{N_x}$ such that

$$\psi(x') \geq \psi(x) + m^{\mathrm{T}}(x' - x)$$

for all $x' \in \mathbb{R}^{N_x}$. We write $m \in \partial \psi(x)$.

---

**Example 2.37**   Consider the convex function $\psi(x) = |x|$, which is differentiable away from $x = 0$ with $\psi'(x) = 1$ for $x > 0$ and $\psi'(x) = -1$ for $x < 0$. At $x = 0$ we need to find the set of all $m$ such that

$$|x'| \geq mx'$$

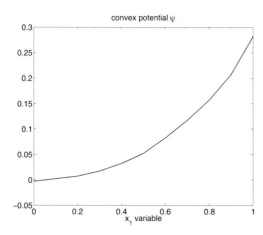

**Figure 2.5** Convex potential function $\psi$ for the coupling computed in Example 2.29. The function is piecewise linear and its subdifferential $\partial\psi(x_1)$ is defined as the derivative of $\psi$ whenever $x_1 \neq a_i$, $i = 1, \ldots, M$, and as the interval spanned by the left and right derivatives of $\psi$ whenever $x_1 = a_i$. These intervals include all possible cases $x_2 = a_i$ which are coupled to $x_1 = a_j$ by a non-zero entry in $t_{ij}^*$.

and we find that $m \in [-1, 1]$. This is the interval spanned by the left and right derivatives of $\psi$ at $x = 0$. In summary, we obtain the set-valued subdifferential

$$\partial\psi(x) = \begin{cases} -1 & \text{for } x < 0, \\ [-1, 1] & \text{for } x = 0, \\ 1 & \text{for } x > 0. \end{cases}$$

Given a cyclically monotone set $S \in \mathbb{R}^{N_x} \times \mathbb{R}^{N_x}$, a suitable potential $\psi$ can be defined as follows. Pick a particular pair $(x_1^0, x_2^0) \in S$. Then define

$$\psi(x) := \sup\{x_2^I(x - x_1^I) + x_2^{I-1}(x_1^I - x_1^{I-1}) + \cdots + x_2^0(x_1^1 - x_1^0)\}. \qquad (2.27)$$

Here the supremum is taken over all possible families of pairs $\{(x_1^i, x_2^i) \in S\}_{i=1}^I$ with integer $I \geq 1$. Cyclical monotonicity of $S$ implies that $\psi(x_1^0) \leq 0$ and the particular choice $I = 1$ with $x_1^1 = x_1^0$ and $x_2^1 = x_2^0$ leads to $\psi(x_1^0) = 0$.

**Example 2.38** If $S$ is finite, then (2.27) is constructive. Consider, for example, the coupling between $X_1$ and $X_2$ defined in Example 2.29 and set $S = \text{supp}\,(\mu_{X_1, X_2}^*)$. Because of (2.26), the set $S$ is defined by

$$(x_1 = a_j, x_2 = a_i) \in S \text{ if and only if } t_{ij}^* > 0.$$

Using $(x_1^0, x_2^0) = (a_1, a_1)$ in (2.27) leads to the convex potential $\psi(x_1)$ displayed in Figure 2.5.

A compact statement of Rockafellar's theorem is that $S \subset \partial\psi$ for a suitable convex potential $\psi$. An optimal transport map $T$ is obtained whenever $\psi$ is sufficiently regular in which case the subdifferential $\partial\psi(x)$ reduced to the classic gradient $\nabla_x\psi$ and $x_2 = T(x_1) = \nabla_x\psi(x_1)$. This happens, for example, when the involved (marginal) measures are absolutely continuous with bounded second-order moments. See Villani (2003) for more details.

While optimal couplings between continuous random variables are of broad theoretical and practical interest, their computational implementation is non-trivial. The case of discrete random variables with target space (2.17) can be dealt with by linear transport algorithms. We will come back to this issue in Chapter 5.

## Problems

**2.1**  Show the following.
(i)    If $X$ and $Y$ are independent, then $\mathrm{corr}(X, Y) = 0$.
(ii)   If $X = dY + b$, then $\mathrm{corr}(X, Y) = \mathrm{sgn}(d)$.
(iii)  $|\mathrm{corr}(X, Y)| \leq 1$ for any random variables $X$, $Y$ with bounded mean and variance. (Hint: Use the Cauchy–Schwarz inequality.)

**2.2**  Consider two independent univariate Gaussian random variables $X$ and $\Xi$ and define a third random variable $Y$ for given coefficient $h$ as follows:

$$Y = hX + \Xi.$$

Provided that $h \neq 0$, then $X = (Y - \Xi)/h$. Instead of this simple rearrangement, we now attempt to approximate $X$ in terms of $Y$ alone and make the linear *ansatz*

$$\hat{X} = aY + b.$$

Determine the unknown coefficients $a$ and $b$ through minimisation of the expected distance between $X$ and $\hat{X}$, i.e. $\mathbb{E}[(X - \hat{X})^2]$. Assume that $X \sim \mathrm{N}(\bar{x}, \sigma^2)$ and $\Xi \sim \mathrm{N}(0, r^2)$ are independent.[4] Hint: Find the derivatives of

$$\mathbb{E}\left[\left(X - \hat{X}\right)^2\right] = \mathbb{E}\left[(X - aY - b)^2\right]$$

with respect to $a$ and $b$.

**2.3**  Consider the joint PDF

$$\pi_{XY}(x, y) = \delta(y - h(x))\pi_X(x)$$

for given function $h : \mathbb{R}^{N_x} \to \mathbb{R}^{N_y}$, $N_x > N_y = 1$, and marginal PDF $\pi_X$ in $X$. We assume that the sets

$$A_y := \{x \in \mathbb{R}^{N_x} : h(x) = y\} \tag{2.28}$$

define smooth hypersurfaces in $\mathbb{R}^{N_x}$ for all $y \in \mathbb{R}$. Show that the marginal PDF $\pi_Y$ is given by

$$\pi_Y(y) = \int_{A_y} \pi_X(x)\mathrm{d}x.$$

Hint: Replace the Dirac delta function by

$$\delta_\varepsilon(s) = \begin{cases} 0 & \text{for } |s| \geq \varepsilon/2, \\ 1/\varepsilon & \text{otherwise,} \end{cases}$$

---

[4]  We will discuss such inverse problems in much more detail in Chapter 5. See also Appendix 2.4 at the end of this chapter.

and take the limit $\varepsilon \to 0$.

**2.4** Implement the iteration (1.28) for $k = 1, \ldots, K$ with $K = 10^9$. Plot a histogram for the resulting $I = 10^8$ iterates $\Xi_i$, defined by (1.10). Relative frequencies are obtained by normalising the histogram by the total sample size. In addition, compute the autocorrelation coefficients $C(\tau)$ for $\tau = 1, 2, 3$. The increase of the number of samples from $I = 10^7$ to $I = 10^8$ further improves the statistical significance of our results. However, it also increases the necessary computer time. Repeat the experiment with the coefficient 1.99999 in (1.28) replaced by 2.0 and 1.9, respectively. What do you observe in the histograms?

Next generate samples $\{\delta_j\}_{j=1}^J$ with $J = 5 \times 10^6$ of the accumulated measurement error (2.9) from the sequence $\{\Xi_i\}$ and plot their histogram or relative frequencies. Use the standard estimators

$$\bar{\delta}_J = \frac{1}{J} \sum_{j=1}^J \delta_j$$

for the mean and

$$\sigma_J^2 = \frac{1}{J-1} \sum_{j=1}^J (\delta_j - \bar{\delta}_J)^2$$

for the variance, respectively, in order to generate $J = 5 \times 10^6$ samples from the associated Gaussian $N(\bar{\delta}_J, \sigma_J^2)$. Use the Matlab function `randn` (or similar) to generate those samples, which we denote by $\Delta_j$. Compare the histogram for both samples sets $\{\delta_j\}$ and $\{\Delta_j\}$. See Example 2.21 for further details on how to verify whether a set of available samples (here the $\delta_j$ values), can be replaced by samples from an appropriate Gaussian random variable.

**2.5** Consider the two-dimensional Gaussian PDF $n(z; \bar{z}, P)$, $z = (x_1, x_2)$ from Example 2.18 with mean $\bar{z} = (\bar{x}_1, \bar{x}_2)$ and covariance matrix (2.6). Verify that

$$n(z; \bar{z}, P) = \frac{1}{2\pi |P|^{1/2}} \exp\left(-\frac{1}{2}(z - \bar{z})^{\mathrm{T}} P^{-1}(z - \bar{z})\right)$$

$$= \frac{1}{\sqrt{2\pi}\sigma_c} \exp\left(-\frac{1}{2\sigma_c^2}(x_1 - \bar{x}_c)^2\right) \frac{1}{\sqrt{2\pi}\sigma_{22}} \exp\left(-\frac{1}{2\sigma_{22}^2}(x_2 - \bar{x}_2)^2\right).$$

What are the corresponding formulas for the conditional PDF $\pi_{X_2}(x_2|x_1)$ and the marginal $\pi_{X_1}(x_1)$?

**2.6** Construct examples to show that a deterministic transport map to a measure $\mu_{X_2}$ cannot, in general, be defined in the case where the measure $\mu_{X_1}$ consists of finitely many point measures; for example,

$$\mu_{X_1}(\mathrm{d}x) = \frac{1}{M} \sum_{i=1}^M \mu_{x_i}(\mathrm{d}x) = \frac{1}{M} \sum_{i=1}^M \delta(x - x_i)\mathrm{d}x$$

for given $x_i \in \mathbb{R}$.

**2.7** Consider the two sets

$$\mathcal{X}_1 = \{a_1 = 1, a_2 = 2, a_3 = 3\} \quad \text{and} \quad \mathcal{X}_2 = \{b_1 = 1.5, b_2 = 2, b_3 = -1\}$$

with uniform probability vectors $\mathbb{P}(a_i) = \mathbb{P}(b_i) = 1/3$. A coupling is defined by a matrix $T \in \mathbb{R}^{3 \times 3}$ with $t_{ij} \geq 0$ and

$$\sum_{i=1}^{3} t_{ij} = \sum_{j=1}^{3} t_{ij} = 1/3.$$

Find the coupling that minimises

$$J(T) = \sum_{i,j=1}^{3} t_{ij} |b_i - a_j|^2.$$

What do you notice about the sparsity structure of the optimal coupling matrix $T^*$?

**2.8**   Prove that (2.24) is indeed equivalent to (2.23). You may assume that $M = N_x$ and $P_2$ has full rank.

**2.9**   The construction (2.27) can be applied to the coupling computed in Example 2.29. Find an explicit expression for the resulting potential $\psi$ and reproduce Figure 2.5 from Example 2.38. Hint: The potential $\psi$ is piecewise linear and all $a_i$ with $t_{ij}^* \neq 0$ for given $j$ satisfy

$$a_i \in \partial \psi(x = a_j).$$

## 2.3   Guide to literature

An elementary introduction to basic concepts from probability theory can be found in Chorin & Hald (2009) and Tijms (2012). A deeper mathematical treatment of random variables can, for example, be found in Jazwinski (1970) and Breźniak & Zastawniak (1999). The two monographs Villani (2003) and Villani (2009) provide an in-depth introduction to optimal transportation.

## 2.4   Appendix: Conditional expectation and best approximation

We have previously considered pairs of random variables $X$ and $Y$ which are related by smooth invertible maps $\psi : \mathbb{R}^{N_x} \to \mathbb{R}^{N_x}$. In this appendix, we consider the situation where

$$Y = h(X)$$

and $h : \mathbb{R}^{N_x} \to \mathbb{R}$ cannot be invertible if $N_x > 1$. We then assume that the sets

$$A_y := \{x \in \mathbb{R}^{N_x} : h(x) = y\}$$

define smooth hypersurfaces in $\mathbb{R}^{N_x}$ for all $y \in \mathbb{R}$, i.e., the sets $A_y$ foliate $\mathbb{R}^{N_x}$. Let us introduce the *conditional expectation* of $X$ given $y = Y(\omega)$:

$$\mathbb{E}[X|y] := \frac{\int_{A_y} x \pi_X(x) \mathrm{d}x}{\int_{A_y} \pi_X(x) \mathrm{d}x}.$$

This definition can be written more generally as

$$\mathbb{E}[X|y] = \int_{\mathbb{R}^{N_x}} x\pi_X(x|y)\mathrm{d}x$$

with the conditional PDF here formally given by

$$\pi_X(x|y) = \frac{\pi_{XY}(x,y)}{\pi_Y(y)} = \frac{\delta(y-h(x))\pi_X(x)}{\int_{A_y}\pi_X(x)\mathrm{d}x}.$$

Compare (2.28) from Problem 2.3.

The conditional expectation is a function of $y = Y(\omega)$, which we denote by $\phi^*(y)$, i.e., $\mathbb{E}[X|y] = \phi^*(y)$. The conditional expectation can be understood as a *best approximation* of $X$ in terms of functions $\phi : \mathbb{R} \to \mathbb{R}^{N_x}$ of $Y$. Indeed the functional

$$L[\phi] := \int_{\mathbb{R}} \int_{\mathbb{R}^{N_x}} \|x - \phi(y)\|^2 \pi_X(x|y)\pi_Y(y)\mathrm{d}x\mathrm{d}y$$

$$= \mathbb{E}[X^\mathrm{T}X] - 2\int_{\mathbb{R}}\int_{A_y} 2x^\mathrm{T}\phi(y)\pi_X(x)\mathrm{d}x\mathrm{d}y + \mathbb{E}[\phi(Y)^\mathrm{T}\phi(Y)]$$

$$= \int_{\mathbb{R}} \left(\phi(y)^\mathrm{T}\phi(y) - 2\phi^*(y)^\mathrm{T}\phi(y)\right)\pi_Y(y)\mathrm{d}y + \mathbb{E}[X^\mathrm{T}X]$$

is minimised for $\phi(y) = \phi^*(y)$.[5] In other words, in situations were we have access to realisations $y = Y(\omega)$ of $Y$ but not of $X$, $\hat{X}(\omega) := \phi^*(Y(\omega))$ provides an *estimate* for the unavailable $X(\omega)$ in the form of a best approximation. This is an example of *inference* which we will discuss in much more detail in Chapter 5. See also Chorin & Hald (2009) and Evans (2013) for a more detailed discussion of conditional expectation.

## 2.5     Appendix: Dual formulation of optimal linear transportation

In this appendix, we sketch the reformulation of a linear transport problem

$$\{t_{ij}^*\} = \arg\min_{\{t_{ij}\geq 0\}} \sum_{i,j=1}^M t_{ij}d_{ij}, \quad d_{ij} = \|a_i - a_j\|^2$$

subject to the constraint

$$\{t_{ij}\} \in \mathcal{S} := \left\{\{t_{ij}\geq 0\} : \sum_{i=1}^M t_{ij} = 1/M, \ \sum_{j=1}^M t_{ij} = w_i\right\}$$

---

[5] The concept of variational derivative is needed in order to demonstrate that $\phi^*$ is a critical point of $L$. Variational derivatives are discussed in Appendix 5.6.

as a min–max problem. First we introduce additional variables $u_i \in \mathbb{R}$ and $v_j \in \mathbb{R}$, $i, j = 1, \ldots, M$. Next we define an augmented Lagrangian

$$L = \sum_{i,j=1}^{M} t_{ij}d_{ij} + \sum_{i=1}^{M} u_i \left( w_i - \sum_{j=1}^{M} t_{ij} \right) + \sum_{j=1}^{M} v_j \left( 1/M - \sum_{i=1}^{M} t_{ij} \right)$$

and note that

$$\max_{\{u_i\},\{v_j\}} L = \begin{cases} \sum_{i,j=1}^{M} t_{ij}d_{ij} & \text{if } \{t_{ij}\} \in \mathcal{S}, \\ +\infty & \text{if } \{t_{ij}\} \notin \mathcal{S}. \end{cases}$$

Hence we can formulate the optimal transport problem as the following min–max problem:

$$\{t_{ij}^*\} = \arg \min_{\{t_{ij} \geq 0\}} \max_{\{u_i\},\{v_j\}} L.$$

Alternatively, consider first minimising and then maximising. In general

$$\min_{\{t_{ij} \geq 0\}} \max_{\{u_i\},\{v_j\}} L \geq \max_{\{u_i\},\{v_j\}} \min_{\{t_{ij} \geq 0\}} L$$

and equality holds if the dual problem

$$(\{u_i^*\}, \{v_j^*\}) = \arg \max \left\{ \sum_{i=1}^{M} u_i w_i + \frac{1}{M} \sum_{j=1}^{M} v_j \right\}$$

subject to the inequalities

$$d_{ij} \geq u_i + v_j, \tag{2.29}$$

$i, j = 1, \ldots, M$, also has a solution. The essential observation is that $L$ can be rewritten as

$$L = \sum_{i=1}^{M} w_i u_i + \frac{1}{M} \sum_{j=1}^{M} v_j + \sum_{i,j=1}^{M} t_{ij} \left( d_{ij} - v_j - u_i \right),$$

with $\min_{\{t_{ij} \geq 0\}} L = -\infty$ if (2.29) is not satisfied, and

$$\min_{\{t_{ij} \geq 0\}} L = \sum_{i=1}^{M} u_i w_i + \frac{1}{M} \sum_{j=1}^{M} v_j$$

if (2.29) holds.

# 3 Computational statistics

In Chapter 1 we introduced the idea of using models and data to estimate, or predict, the state of a system in the past, present or future. We highlighted that it is important to quantify uncertainty when making predictions. In Chapter 2 we introduced the concept of a random variable $X : \Omega \to \mathcal{X}$, whose outcome is characterised by a probability measure $\mu_X$ on $\mathcal{X}$. When we make a probabilistic prediction, instead of providing a single value $x_0 \in \mathcal{X}$, we provide a random variable $X$. The random variable describes the relative likelihood of different values and thus quantifies our uncertainty in the prediction. For real applications, the dimension of $\mathcal{X}$ is often very large, which means that $X$ itself is often very unwieldy. It is then convenient to communicate the uncertainty characterised by $X$ in terms of summary *statistics*, many of which take the form of *approximations* (also called *estimates* if such approximations involve realisations of random variables) to *expectation values* of scalar functions $f : \mathcal{X} \mapsto \mathbb{R}$,

$$\mathbb{E}[f(X)] = \int_{\mathcal{X}} f(x)\mu_X(\mathrm{d}x).$$

These are integrals which might be tackled by numerical quadrature, which we shall discuss first. However, when the dimension of $\mathcal{X}$ is even moderately large, numerical quadrature becomes very computationally intensive, which motivates the use of Monte Carlo methods for numerical integration. These methods then lead to ensemble prediction and filtering methods in later chapters.

In most cases discussed throughout this chapter $\mathcal{X} = \mathbb{R}^{N_x}$ and $\mu_X$ is absolute continuous with respect to the Lebesgue measure on $\mathbb{R}^{N_x}$. Then Definition 2.9 tells us that there exists a PDF $\pi_X$ such that

$$\mu_X(\mathrm{d}x) = \pi_X(x)\mathrm{d}x,$$

i.e.,

$$\mathbb{E}[f(X)] = \int_{\mathcal{X}} f(x)\pi_X(x)\mathrm{d}x,$$

provided the integral exists for the $f$ under consideration.

## 3.1      Deterministic quadrature

We first consider the simpler case of univariate random variables. We will often write $\overline{f}$ instead of $\mathbb{E}[f(X)]$ for simplicity. Under appropriate assumptions on $f$, expectation integrals can be approximated by *numerical quadrature rules*.

**Definition 3.1** (Numerical quadrature rules)   For a particular PDF $\pi_X$, a numerical quadrature rule for an integral

$$\overline{f} = \int_{\mathbb{R}} f(x)\pi_X(x)\mathrm{d}x,$$

with any choice of function $f$, is given by

$$\overline{f}_M := \sum_{i=1}^{M} b_i f(c_i). \tag{3.1}$$

Here $c_i \in \mathbb{R}$, $i = 1, \ldots, M$, denote the quadrature points and $b_i > 0$ denote their weights. Let $\Pi_k(\mathbb{R})$ denote the $(k+1)$-dimensional linear space of all polynomials of order $k$ or less, i.e. of the form

$$f(x) = a_0 + a_1 x + \cdots + a_k x^k.$$

A quadrature rule is of *order* $p$ if $\overline{f} = \overline{f}_M$ for all integrands $f(x) \in \Pi_{p-1}(\mathbb{R})$.

   Different quadrature rules are required for different PDFs $\pi_X$. We illustrate the application of quadrature rules to expectation integrals in the following example in which the PDF is the uniform distribution.

---

**Example 3.2**   Consider the case of a uniform distribution on the unit interval $[0, 1]$ and recall the notation $X \sim U[0, 1]$ for a random variable $X$ with PDF

$$\pi_X(x) = \begin{cases} 1 & \text{if } x \in [0, 1], \\ 0 & \text{otherwise.} \end{cases}$$

Expectation values are then simply given by

$$\overline{f} = \int_0^1 f(x)\mathrm{d}x. \tag{3.2}$$

The midpoint rule,

$$\overline{f} \approx \overline{f}_1 = f(1/2) \,,$$

is the lowest-order *Gauss–Legendre quadrature formula* with $M = 1$, $b_1 = 1$, $c_1 = 1/2$. It can be verified by explicit calculation that it integrates any linear function $f(x) = a_1 x + a_0$ exactly. The midpoint rule is therefore second-order accurate. With $M = 2$, Gauss–Legendre quadrature achieves fourth-order accuracy and the quadrature points and weights are given by

$$c_1 = \frac{1 - 1/\sqrt{3}}{2}, \quad c_2 = \frac{1 + 1/\sqrt{3}}{2}, \quad b_1 = b_2 = \frac{1}{2}.$$

More generally, Gauss–Legendre quadrature rules achieve order $p = 2M$ for $M$ quadrature points, for the uniform distribution.

In addition to (or as an alternative to) increasing the number of quadrature points $M$, the integral (3.2) may be split into a sum of integrals over finitely many non-overlapping subintervals of $[0, 1]$. Consider, for example, the formal decomposition

$$\overline{f} = \sum_{i=1}^{N_I} \int_{(i-1)\Delta x}^{i\Delta x} f(x)\mathrm{d}x, \tag{3.3}$$

where each subinterval is of length $\Delta x = 1/N_I$ with $N_I > 1$. A Gauss–Legendre quadrature rule can now be applied to each of the integrals in (3.3). Let us denote the numerical result by $\overline{f}_{M,N_I}$. If the function $f$ is $p$ times continuously differentiable, then

$$|\overline{f}_{M,N_I} - \overline{f}| = \mathcal{O}(\Delta x^{\min(p,q)}), \tag{3.4}$$

for a quadrature rule of order $q$. Hence high-order quadrature rules are only useful if $f$ is sufficiently smooth. We will come back to this issue in Example 3.4.

---

Another well-known family of quadrature rules are the Gauss–Hermite quadrature rules for univariate Gaussian random variables, discussed in the following example.

---

**Example 3.3** If $X'$ is a univariate Gaussian random variable with mean zero and variance one, then expectation values take the form

$$\mathbb{E}[f(X')] = \frac{1}{\sqrt{2\pi}} \int_{\mathbb{R}} f(x')e^{-(x')^2/2}\mathrm{d}x'.$$

With $M = 2$ in (3.1), the quadrature points and weights for the Gauss–Hermite quadrature rule of order four are given by

$$c_1 = -1, \quad c_2 = 1, \quad b_1 = b_2 = 1/2. \tag{3.5}$$

Assume that we want to use the same quadrature rule for approximating expectation values of another Gaussian random variable $X$ with mean $\overline{x} \neq 0$ and variance $\sigma^2 \neq 1$. We may rewrite $\mathbb{E}[f(X)]$ as an expectation over $X'$ as follows,

$$\mathbb{E}[f(X)] = \int_{\mathbb{R}} f(x)\pi_X(x)\mathrm{d}x$$

$$= \int_{\mathbb{R}} f(x)\frac{\pi_X(x)}{\pi_{X'}(x)}\pi_{X'}(x)\mathrm{d}x$$

$$= \mathbb{E}\left[f(X')\frac{\pi_X(X')}{\pi_{X'}(X')}\right].$$

This suggests the following quadrature formula for $\overline{f} = \mathbb{E}[f(X)]$ given by

$$\overline{f}_M = \sum_{i=1}^{M} b_i f(c_i) \frac{\pi_X(c_i)}{\pi_{X'}(c_i)} = \sum_{i=1}^{M} \hat{b}_i f(c_i),$$

with new weights

$$\hat{b}_i = b_i \frac{\pi_X(c_i)}{\pi_{X'}(c_i)}.$$

For constant $f = f_0$, we expect to obtain $\overline{f}_M = f_0$, but in general $\sum_i \hat{b}_i \neq 1$: the order of the quadrature rule has dropped from $p = 2M$ to $p = 0$! In order to recover $p = 1$, we could use the normalised weights

$$\tilde{b}_i = \frac{\hat{b}_i}{\sum_{j=1}^{M} \hat{b}_j} = \frac{b_i \frac{\pi_X(c_i)}{\pi_{X'}(c_i)}}{\sum_{j=1}^{M} b_j \frac{\pi_X(c_j)}{\pi_{X'}(c_j)}}. \tag{3.6}$$

A much better remedy is to realise that $X$ is also Gaussian distributed and that the quadrature rule could be adjusted by using a change-of-variables formula to change the quadrature points $c_i$ instead of the weights. Applying the transformation $x' = (x - \overline{x})/\sigma$ and $\mathrm{d}x = \sigma \mathrm{d}x'$, we get

$$\mathbb{E}[f(X)] = \frac{1}{\sqrt{2\pi}\sigma} \int_{-\infty}^{\infty} f(x) e^{-(x-\overline{x})^2/2\sigma^2} \mathrm{d}x$$

$$= \frac{1}{\sqrt{2\pi}} \int_{-\infty}^{\infty} f(\sigma x' + \overline{x}) e^{-(x')^2/2} \mathrm{d}x' = \mathbb{E}[f'(X')],$$

where $f'(x) = f(\sigma x + \overline{x})$. We conclude that Gauss–Hermite quadrature points for a Gaussian random variable with mean $\overline{x}$ and variance $\sigma^2$ are given by

$$\hat{c}_i = \sigma c_i + \overline{x}.$$

Note that a linear transformation does not change the order of a polynomial $f' \in \Pi_k(\mathbb{R})$ and, hence, the order of a quadrature rule is preserved.

---

In Example 3.3 we observed that when transforming between two Gaussian random variables with different means and variances, changing the quadrature points preserves the order of the quadrature rule, whereas changing the quadrature weights does not. The choice between changing the weights of a quadrature rule or changing the location of its quadrature points (or both) will be a recurring theme of this book.

The following example demonstrates the reduction in convergence rate that occurs for non-smooth functions.

---

**Example 3.4**   Let $\phi : [0, 1] \to [0, 1]$ denote the tent map defined by

$$\phi(x) = \begin{cases} 2x & \text{if } x \leq 1/2, \\ 2 - 2x & \text{otherwise.} \end{cases}$$

We compute expectation values with respect to $X \sim \mathrm{U}[0, 1/2]$ with PDF

$$\pi_X(x) = \begin{cases} 2 & \text{if } x \in [0, 1/2], \\ 0 & \text{otherwise,} \end{cases}$$

and $f$ given by application of $\phi$ $n$ times, i.e.,

$$f(x) = \underbrace{\phi(\phi(\cdots(\phi(x))\cdots))}_{n \text{ times}} = \phi^n(x), \qquad n \geq 1. \tag{3.7}$$

Since

$$
\begin{aligned}
\mathbb{E}[\phi^n(X)] &= 2 \int_0^{1/2} \phi^n(x)\mathrm{d}x = 2 \int_0^{1/2} \phi^{n-1}(\phi(x))\mathrm{d}x \\
&= 2 \int_0^{1/2} \phi^{n-1}(2x)\mathrm{d}x = \int_0^1 \phi^{n-1}(x)\mathrm{d}x \\
&= 2 \int_0^{1/2} \phi^{n-1}(x)\mathrm{d}x = \mathbb{E}[\phi^{n-1}(X)], \quad n > 1,
\end{aligned}
$$

and

$$\mathbb{E}[\phi(X)] = 2 \int_0^{1/2} \phi(x)\mathrm{d}x = 2 \int_0^{1/2} 2x\mathrm{d}x = 1/2,$$

the analytic value for $\bar{f} = \mathbb{E}[\phi^n(X)]$ is equal to $1/2$ for all $n \geq 1$. The midpoint rule for the interval $[0, 1/2]$ can be obtained by transforming the quadrature point $c_1 = 1/2$ to $\hat{c}_1 = 1/4$ while keeping the weight $b_1 = 1$ (compare the previous Example 3.3). The midpoint rule yields the exact result for $n = 1$. However, since

$$\phi^n(\hat{c}_1) = \begin{cases} 1/2 & \text{for } n = 1, \\ 1 & \text{for } n = 2, \\ 0 & \text{otherwise,} \end{cases}$$

the approximation errors for the implicit midpoint method increase to $0.5$ in absolute value for $n > 1$.

Even more revealing is the behaviour of the implicit midpoint rule applied to the formulation (3.3) with $f = \phi^n$. To examine this, we now fix $n = 50$ and increase the number of subintervals $N_I \gg 1$. Following the result (3.4), if $f$ were twice continuously differentiable, we could expect second-order convergence. This is not confirmed by the numerical results displayed in Figure 3.1. The reason is that $f = \phi^{50}$ is a highly irregular function. The numerical results indicate that the effective order of convergence drops to $p = 1$ in this case.

---

A quadrature rule with quadrature points $c_i$ and weights $b_i$ yields exact expectation value with respect to the *empirical measure* of the form

$$\mu_M(\mathrm{d}x) := \sum_{i=1}^M w_i \mu_{x_i}(\mathrm{d}x) = \sum_{i=1}^M w_i\, \delta(x - x_i)\mathrm{d}x, \tag{3.8}$$

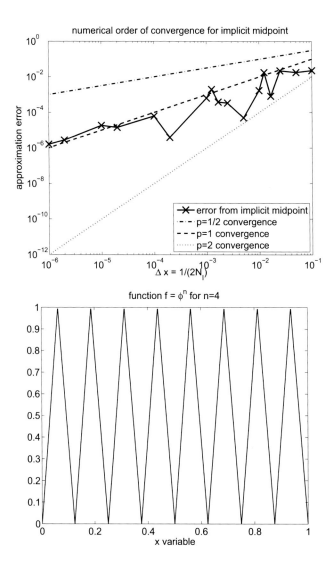

**Figure 3.1** Top: approximation errors from the midpoint rule applied to (3.3) with $f = \phi^n$, $n = 50$. The approximation error is displayed as a function of the interval length $\Delta x = 1/(2N_I)$ of subintervals. The classic order of the implicit midpoint order is $p = 2$ but only $p = 1$ is observed in this example, where $f$ is a highly irregular function. Bottom: plot of the function $\phi^n(x)$ for $n = 4$.

with weights $w_i = b_i$ and samples $x_i = c_i$. Recall that $\mu_{x_i}$ denotes the point measure centred at $x_i$ and that $\delta(\cdot)$ is the Dirac delta function. The empirical measure $\mu_M$ is a probability measure if $\sum_{i=1}^{M} w_i = 1$ since therefore

$$\int_{\mathbb{R}^{N_x}} \mu_M(\mathrm{d}x) = 1.$$

Proceeding, insertion of the empirical measure into the expectation formula gives

$$\overline{f} = \int_{\mathcal{X}} f(x)\mu_M(\mathrm{d}x) = \sum_{i=1}^{M} w_i f(x_i) = \sum_{i=1}^{M} b_i f(c_i), \tag{3.9}$$

as required. Hence, an interpretation of quadrature rules for expectation integrals is that we first approximate the measure $\mu_X$ by the empirical measure (3.8), and then evaluate all expectations exactly with respect to that measure. We shall see later in this chapter that if we take a sequence of quadrature rules with increasing number of quadrature points for which the expectations converge, then the corresponding sequence of empirical measures converges in a certain (weak) sense to $\mu_X$.

Gauss-type quadrature rules are extremely powerful whenever they are applicable. However, the data assimilation problems considered in this book lead to random variables in very high-dimensional spaces. Under those circumstances, standard quadrature rules, such as Gauss–Hermite or Gauss–Legendre, are no longer useful. For example, a straightforward approximation of an integral

$$\overline{f} = \int_0^1 \cdots \int_0^1 f(x_1, \ldots, x_{N_x}) \mathrm{d}x_1 \cdots \mathrm{d}x_{N_x} = \int_{[0,1]^{N_x}} f(x)\mathrm{d}x \tag{3.10}$$

in $\mathbb{R}^{N_x}$ by a product of $N_x$ one-dimensional quadrature rules, each with $M$ quadrature points, leads to a regular array of $M^{N_x}$ quadrature points in $\mathbb{R}^{N_x}$. This number quickly becomes very large as the dimension of the problem increases and the associated computational effort cannot be justified, especially in combination with a possible reduction of order as encountered in the previous example. This is often referred to as the "curse of dimensionality".

A popular method for reducing the computational effort of high-dimensional integrals of type (3.10) is the *analysis of variance* (ANOVA) representation of an integrand $f$. In order to demonstrate the basic idea, we set $N_x = 3$ and $x = (x_1, x_2, x_3)^{\mathrm{T}}$ in (3.10). We seek a decomposition of $f$ of the form

$$\begin{aligned} f(x_1, x_2, x_3) = {} & f_0 + f_1(x_1) + f_2(x_2) + f_3(x_3) + f_{12}(x_1, x_2) \\ & + f_{13}(x_1, x_3) + f_{23}(x_2, x_3) + f_{123}(x_1, x_2, x_3). \end{aligned} \tag{3.11}$$

Once such a decomposition is available, the first three non-trivial terms can be integrated by standard univariate quadrature rules. The next three terms require more work but still reduce to two-dimensional quadrature rules, while only the last term requires a full three-dimensional quadrature approach. The key idea of ANOVA is now to choose the decomposition such that the significant contributions to the integral come from the lower-order terms in (3.11). This can be achieved as follows. We define

$$f_0 = \mathbb{E}[f(X)] = \int_{[0,1]^3} f(x_1, x_2, x_3) \, \mathrm{d}x_1 \mathrm{d}x_2 \mathrm{d}x_3,$$

and set

$$f_l(x_l) = \int_{[0,1]^2} f(x) \prod_{j \neq l} \mathrm{d}x_j - f_0, \quad l = 1, 2, 3.$$

We then continue at the next level with

$$f_{lk}(x_l, x_k) = \int_{[0,1]} f(x)\mathrm{d}x_j - f_l(x_l) - f_k(x_k) - f_0, \quad j \neq k, \ j \neq l, \ k < l \leq 3.$$

We finally obtain

$$\begin{aligned} f_{123}(x) = f(x) &- f_{12}(x_1, x_2) - f_{13}(x_1, x_3) - f_{23}(x_2, x_3) \\ &- f_1(x_1) - f_2(x_2) - f_3(x_3) - f_0. \end{aligned} \tag{3.12}$$

The decomposition (3.12) has the desirable property that all terms in (3.11) are mutually orthogonal under the inner product

$$\langle g, f \rangle = \int_{[0,1]^3} g(x)f(x)\mathrm{d}x,$$

for two functions $f, g : [0, 1]^3 \to \mathbb{R}$. Hence the variance of the integrand, i.e.,

$$\sigma^2 = \int_{[0,1]^3} (f(x) - \mathbb{E}[f(X)])^2 \, \mathrm{d}x,$$

is equivalent to

$$\sigma^2 = \sigma_1^2 + \sigma_2^2 + \sigma_3^2 + \sigma_{12}^2 + \sigma_{23}^2 + \sigma_{13}^2 + \sigma_{123}^2, \tag{3.13}$$

with, for example,

$$\sigma_1^2 = \int_0^1 (f_1(x_1) - \mathbb{E}[f_1(X_1)])^2 \, \mathrm{d}x_1,$$

and the other variances defined accordingly.

ANOVA decompositions can easily be derived analytically for integrands which are sums or products of univariate functions. However, ANOVA decompositions cannot be used directly for designing high-dimensional quadrature rules since the constant $f_0$ term already requires the computation of a high-dimensional integral. This limitation of the classic ANOVA decomposition has led to the anchored ANOVA (Holtz 2011) decomposition. ANOVA approximations to an integral (3.10) are based on the observation that the individual variances in (3.13) decrease for sufficiently regular integrands $f(x)$ as the dimensionality of the involved functions in (3.11) increases. The number of quadrature points in each of the associated integrals may then be adjusted accordingly. Ultimately, ANOVA-type approximations lead to *sparse grid quadrature rules* (Holtz 2011). Sparse grid approximation can be very efficient provided the integrands in (3.10) are sufficiently regular.

Laplace's method is another efficient approximation method for expectation values in high dimensions. There are two key assumptions behind *Laplace's method*. First, there is a function $g$ such that

$$f(x)\pi_X(x) = e^{-g(x)},$$

and second, $g$ has a unique global minimum denoted by $x_0$. In that case we may expand $g$ about $x_0$ to obtain

$$g(x) = g(x_0) + \underbrace{g'(x_0)(x-x_0)}_{=0} + \frac{1}{2}g''(x_0)(x-x_0)^2 + \cdots$$

$$= g(x_0) + \frac{1}{2}g''(x_0)(x-x_0)^2 + \cdots,$$

where we have assumed $x \in \mathbb{R}$ for notational simplicity, and where primes denote differentiation with respect to $x$. Since $x_0$ is the unique minimum, we have $g''(x_0) > 0$. Substituting this expansion into $\overline{f}$ gives

$$\overline{f} \approx e^{-g(x_0)} \int_{\mathbb{R}} e^{-g''(x_0)(x-x_0)^2/2} dx.$$

Then, making use of the fact that

$$\int_{\mathbb{R}} e^{-g''(x_0)(x-x_0)^2/2} dx = \sqrt{\frac{2\pi}{g''(x_0)}},$$

we finally obtain the approximation

$$\overline{f} \approx e^{-g(x_0)} \sqrt{\frac{2\pi}{g''(x_0)}}.$$

This approximation becomes very useful in higher dimensions, since it always leads to a global integral of a multivariate Gaussian function which can be evaluated analytically. It is valid provided $g$ quickly increases away from $x_0$. In this case we may assume that significant contributions to the expectation value $\overline{f}$ are from regions near $x_0$, where the Taylor expansion of $g$ can be applied. On a more formal level the following asymptotic result holds.

**Lemma 3.5** (Laplace's method)  Assume that $\tilde{g} : [a,b] \to \mathbb{R}$ is twice differentiable and has a unique global minimum at $x_0 \in [a,b]$. Then

$$\lim_{\varepsilon \to 0} \frac{\int_a^b e^{-\tilde{g}(x)/\varepsilon} dx}{e^{-\tilde{g}(x_0)/\varepsilon} \sqrt{\frac{2\pi\varepsilon}{\tilde{g}''(x_0)}}} = 1.$$

We formally have $g(x) = \tilde{g}(x)/\varepsilon$ in our description of Laplace's method.

---

**Example 3.6**  We consider the approximation of

$$\mathbb{E}[\cos(X)] = \frac{1}{\sqrt{2\pi\varepsilon}} \int_{\mathbb{R}} \cos(x) e^{-x^2/(2\varepsilon)} dx$$

by Laplace's method, where $X$ is a Gaussian with mean zero and variance $\varepsilon > 0$. We first rewrite the integral as

$$\mathbb{E}[\cos(X)] = \frac{1}{\sqrt{2\pi\varepsilon}} \int_{\mathbb{R}} (\cos(x) + 1) e^{-x^2/(2\varepsilon)} \mathrm{d}x - \frac{1}{\sqrt{2\pi\varepsilon}} \int_{\mathbb{R}} e^{-x^2/(2\varepsilon)} \mathrm{d}x$$

$$= \frac{1}{\sqrt{2\pi\varepsilon}} \int_{\mathbb{R}} (\cos(x) + 1) e^{-x^2/(2\varepsilon)} \mathrm{d}x - 1,$$

and apply Laplace's method to the remaining integral,

$$I = \frac{1}{\sqrt{2\pi\varepsilon}} \int_{\mathbb{R}} (\cos(x) + 1) e^{-x^2/(2\varepsilon)} \mathrm{d}x$$

$$= \frac{1}{\sqrt{2\pi\varepsilon}} \int_{\mathbb{R}} e^{-x^2/(2\varepsilon) + \ln(\cos(x) + 1)} \mathrm{d}x.$$

Hence, using the notation of Lemma 3.5,

$$\tilde{g}(x) = \frac{x^2}{2} - \varepsilon \ln(\cos(x) + 1),$$

with a unique global minimum $x_0 = 0$ for all $\varepsilon > 0$ sufficiently small, since

$$\tilde{g}'(x) = x + \varepsilon \frac{\sin(x)}{1 + \cos(x)}.$$

Hence $\tilde{g}(x_0) = -\varepsilon \ln(2)$, and the second derivative satisfies

$$\tilde{g}''(x_0) = 1 + \frac{\varepsilon}{2}.$$

Finally we obtain the Laplace approximation

$$\mathbb{E}[\cos(X)] \approx \frac{e^{\ln(2)}}{\sqrt{1 + \varepsilon/2}} - 1 = \frac{2}{\sqrt{1 + \varepsilon/2}} - 1,$$

for $\varepsilon$ sufficiently small. We compare this approximation to the exact value of the integral, which is $e^{-\varepsilon/2}$, and to numerical approximations using the fourth-order Gauss–Hermite quadrature rule with quadrature points and weights given by (3.5). The results are displayed in Figure 3.2 for finite $\varepsilon$. These two approximation methods lead to virtually indistinguishable results.

## 3.2     Monte Carlo quadrature

We now introduce an extremely flexible and powerful family of methods for approximating integrals: *Monte Carlo methods*. Monte Carlo methods have been developed as random and mesh-free alternatives to grid-based quadrature rules. Monte Carlo methods can be used to approximate statistics, for example expectation values $\mathbb{E}[f(X)]$ of a random variable $X$. We begin by discussing the special case $f(x) = x$, i.e. the mean.

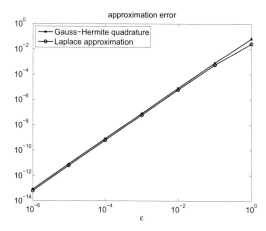

**Figure 3.2** Approximation errors for Laplace's method and the fourth-order Gauss–Hermite quadrature rule. Both methods display second-order accuracy in $\varepsilon$. However, while Laplace's method extends easily to higher dimensions, the same does not hold true for Gauss–Hermite quadrature rules.

**Definition 3.7** (Empirical mean)   Given a sequence $X_i$, $i = 1, \ldots, M$, of independent random variables[1] with identical PDF $\pi_X$ (so that they have a joint measure equal to the product PDF $\prod_{i=1}^{M} \pi_X(x_i)$), the *empirical mean* is

$$\overline{x}_M = \frac{1}{M} \sum_{i=1}^{M} x_i,$$

for independent samples $(x_1, x_2, \ldots, x_M) = (X_1(\omega), X_2(\omega), \ldots, X_M(\omega))$.

The empirical mean $\overline{x}_M$ constitutes a Monte Carlo approximation to the integral $\int_{\mathbb{R}} x \mu_X(\mathrm{d}x)$. Before we discuss the application of Monte Carlo approximations to more general integrals (in particular, expectation values), we need to understand the sense in which $\overline{x}_M$ provides an approximation to the mean $\overline{x}$ as $M \to \infty$. We note that $\overline{x}_M$ itself is the realisation of a random variable

$$\overline{X}_M = \frac{1}{M} \sum_{i=1}^{M} X_i. \tag{3.14}$$

We quantify the error in the empirical mean by using the *mean squared error* (MSE), given by

$$\begin{aligned}
\mathrm{MSE}(\overline{X}_M) &= \mathbb{E}[(\overline{X}_M - \overline{x})^2] \\
&= (\mathbb{E}[\overline{X}_M] - \overline{x})^2 + \mathbb{E}\left[(\overline{X}_M - \mathbb{E}[\overline{X}_M])^2\right],
\end{aligned} \tag{3.15}$$

as a measure for the approximation error. Here we have decomposed the MSE into two components: *squared bias* and *variance*. Such a decomposition is possible for any estimator and is known as the *bias-variance decomposition*. The bias measures the systematic deviation of the estimator from the true expectation value, whilst the variance measures the fluctuations in the estimator due to the use of random samples. The particular estimator $\overline{X}_M$ is called *unbiased* since

[1] Recall Definition 2.19.

$\mathbb{E}[\overline{X}_M] = \overline{x}$ for any $M \geq 1$. Furthermore, the variance of the estimator satisfies

$$\mathbb{E}\left[(\overline{X}_M - \mathbb{E}[\overline{X}_M])^2\right] = \frac{\sigma^2}{M}$$

provided that $\sigma^2 = \mathbb{E}[(X - \overline{x})^2] < \infty$. This result holds since the random variables $X_i$ in (3.14) are independent and identically distributed.

Estimators for other quantities may contain biases, as described in the following example.

---

**Example 3.8**    Consider the task of estimating the covariance matrix $P$ of a random variable $X$ with PDF $\pi_X$. We again assume that $X_i$, $i = 1, \ldots, M$, are independent and identically distributed random variables with PDF $\pi_X$. In analogy with the estimator (3.14) for the mean, we first consider the estimator

$$\hat{P}_M = \frac{1}{M} \sum_{i=1}^{M} (X_i - \overline{x}_M)(X_i - \overline{x}_M)^{\mathrm{T}}.$$

However, while the estimator for the mean is unbiased, the same does not hold for $\hat{P}_M$. We demonstrate this for $M = 2$ and $\mathbb{E}[X] = 0$, in which case we obtain

$$\mathbb{E}[\hat{P}_M] = \frac{1}{2}\mathbb{E}\left[\sum_{i=1}^{2}(X_i - \frac{1}{2}(X_1 + X_2))(X_i - \frac{1}{2}(X_1 + X_2))^{\mathrm{T}}\right]$$

$$= \frac{1}{2}\left(\frac{1}{2}\mathbb{E}[X_1 X_1^{\mathrm{T}}] + \frac{1}{2}\mathbb{E}[X_2 X_2^{\mathrm{T}}]\right)$$

$$= \frac{1}{2}P,$$

and the estimator is biased. An unbiased estimator is given by the modification

$$\hat{P}_M = \frac{1}{M-1} \sum_{i=1}^{M} (X_i - \overline{x}_M)(X_i - \overline{x}_M)^{\mathrm{T}}.$$

Since $(M-1)/M \to 1$ as $M \to \infty$, both estimators agree in the limit $M \to \infty$. Realisations $\hat{P}_M(\omega)$ of the estimator $\hat{P}_M$, i.e. actual estimates based on samples $x_i$, will be denoted by $P_M$ throughout this book.

---

We now discuss the convergence of a sequence of random variables such as (3.14) for $M \to \infty$ with independent and identically distributed samples $\{X_i\}$. We may first ask in what sense such a sequence of random variables may converge.

**Definition 3.9** (Convergence of sequences of random variables)    Let $X_M$, $M \geq 1$, denote a sequence of (univariate) random variables. Such a sequence converges with *probability one* to a random variable $X$ if

$$\mathbb{P}(\lim_{M \to \infty} X_M = X) = 1.$$

The sequence is said to *converge in probability* to $X$ if for every $\varepsilon > 0$ it holds that

$$\lim_{M \to \infty} \mathbb{P}(|X_M - X| > \varepsilon) = 0.$$

Finally, the sequence *converges weakly* (or in *distribution*) to $X$ if

$$\lim_{M \to \infty} \mathbb{E}[g(X_M)] = \mathbb{E}[g(X)],$$

for any bounded and continuous function $g$.

We also recall the *central limit theorem* and *Chebychev's inequality*, which are essential tools for studying the asymptotic behavior of estimators.

**Theorem 3.10** (Central limit theorem)  Given a sequence $X_i$, $i = 1, \ldots, M$, of independent univariate random variables with identical PDF $\pi_X$, mean $\bar{x}$, and finite variance $\sigma^2$, then the random variable $X_M$, defined as

$$X_M = \sqrt{\frac{M}{\sigma^2}} \left[ \frac{1}{M} \sum_{i=1}^{M} X_i - \bar{x} \right] = \sqrt{\frac{M}{\sigma^2}} (\overline{X}_M - \bar{x}), \qquad (3.16)$$

converges weakly to a Gaussian random variable with mean zero and variance one as $M \to \infty$.

For quadrature rules, we are able to quantify convergence of expectations as the number of quadrature points goes to infinity, if the function and PDF are sufficiently smooth. For the empirical mean, this is replaced by the concept of a confidence interval and its scaling as $M \to \infty$. Under repeated sampling of the empirical mean $\bar{x}_M$, a confidence interval is constructed such that the true mean value $\bar{x}$ is contained within the confidence interval with some chosen probability (typically 95% is used).

---

**Example 3.11**  Suppose $X_i$, $i = 1, \ldots, M$, are independent and identically distributed random variables with mean $\bar{x}$ and variance $\sigma^2$. Consider the estimator (3.14) with $M \gg 1$ such that the distribution of $\overline{X}_M$ can be well approximated by a Gaussian with mean $\bar{x}$ and variance

$$\sigma_M^2 = \frac{\sigma^2}{M},$$

according to the central limit theorem. The constant $c$ in the 95% *confidence interval* $I = [\bar{x}_M - c, \bar{x}_M + c]$ for a given estimate $\bar{x}_M = \overline{X}_M(\omega)$ is defined by the condition

$$\mathbb{P}\left(-c \leq \overline{X}_M - \bar{x} \leq c\right) \approx \int_{\bar{x}-c}^{\bar{x}+c} n(x; \bar{x}, \sigma_M^2) \, dx = 0.95.$$

It follows that

$$c \approx 1.96 \sigma_M = 1.96 \frac{\sigma}{M^{1/2}},$$

for a Gaussian distribution $N(\bar{x}, \sigma_M^2)$. Hence, averaged over many estimates $\bar{x}_M$, the true mean $\overline{x}$ will fall within the confidence interval $I \approx [\overline{x}_M - 1.96\sigma_M, \overline{x}_M + 1.96\sigma_M]$ in 95% of the cases.

Hence we may conclude that the empirical mean $\overline{x}_M$ converges with a rate of $M^{-1/2}$ to the mean $\overline{x}$. The same convergence rate can be derived without a Gaussian approximation using Chebychev's inequality, which we introduce next.

---

**Theorem 3.12** (Chebychev's inequality) Let the random variable $\overline{X}_M$ be defined by (3.14). Then *Chebychev's inequality* states that

$$\mathbb{P}\left(|\overline{X}_M - \overline{x}| \geq k\sigma_M\right) \leq \frac{1}{k^2}, \quad k > 0$$

with $\sigma_M^2 = \sigma^2/M$.

For example, set $k = 1/\sqrt{0.05} \approx 4.47$. Then the 95% *confidence interval I* of $X_M$ satisfies $I \subset [\overline{x}_M - k\sigma_M, \overline{x}_M + k\sigma_M]$ independently of whether $X_M$ is Gaussian or not, and goes to zero as $M \to \infty$ with rate $p = 1/2$.

*Proof* We introduce the indicator function of a set $I \subset \mathbb{R}$:

$$\chi_I(x) = \begin{cases} 1 & \text{if } x \in I, \\ 0 & \text{otherwise.} \end{cases}$$

Choose $I = \{x \in \mathbb{R} : |x| \geq k\sigma_M\}$, and introduce $Y_M = \overline{X}_M - \overline{x}$. Then

$$\mathbb{P}\left(|\overline{X}_M - \overline{x}| \geq k\sigma_M\right) = \mathbb{E}[\chi_I(Y_M)]$$

$$\leq \mathbb{E}\left[\left(\frac{Y_M}{k\sigma_M}\right)^2\right]$$

$$= \frac{1}{k^2\sigma_M^2}\mathbb{E}[(\overline{X}_M - \overline{x})^2] = \frac{1}{k^2}.$$

Here we have used the properties $y^2/(k\sigma_M)^2 \geq \chi_I(y)$ for all $y \in \mathbb{R}$, and $\mathbb{E}[(\overline{X}_M - \overline{x})^2] = \sigma_M^2$. $\qquad\square$

We also mention that the *strong law of large numbers* states that

$$\mathbb{P}(\lim_{M \to \infty} \overline{X}_M = \overline{x}) = 1,$$

provided $\mathbb{E}[\|X\|] < \infty$. In other words, the sequence $\overline{X}_M$ converges with probability one to the mean $\overline{x}$ of the underlying (univariate) random variables $X_i \sim \pi_X$. The *weak law of large numbers* is a statement of convergence in probability, i.e.,

$$\lim_{M \to \infty} \mathbb{P}(|\overline{X}_M - \overline{x}| > \varepsilon) = 0$$

for all $\varepsilon > 0$. Both laws imply that Monte Carlo approximations $\overline{x}_M$ converge to the mean $\overline{x}$ as $M \to \infty$. However, in contrast to the central limit theorem and Chebychev's inequality, they do not provide a rate of convergence.

Of course, Monte Carlo methods can be used to approximate the expectation value of functions more general than $f(x) = x$. In fact, in contrast with grid-based methods, for which certain smoothness assumptions have to be made on $f$ in order to achieve higher-order convergence, Monte Carlo methods can be applied to any $f$ as along as, for example, the second moment $\mathbb{E}[Y^2]$ of $Y = f(X)$ is bounded.

**Definition 3.13** (Monte Carlo approximation)  For a given PDF $\pi_X$ and a measurable function $f$, let $X_i$, $i = 1, \ldots, M$, be independent random variables with identical PDF $\pi_X$. Then the Monte Carlo approximation to $\mathbb{E}[f(X)]$ is given by

$$\overline{f}_M = \sum_{i=1}^{M} w_i f(x_i), \qquad (3.17)$$

where $(x_1, x_2, \ldots, x_M) = (X_1(\omega), X_2(\omega), \ldots, X_M(\omega))$ are the i.i.d. samples and $w_i = 1/M$ denote uniform weights.

---

**Example 3.14**  We return to Example 3.4 and approximate the integral

$$\overline{f} = \int_0^{1/2} 2f(x)\mathrm{d}x,$$

with $f$ defined by (3.7) and $n = 50$. In order to implement a Monte Carlo approximation, we need to simulate samples $x_i$ from $\mathrm{U}[0, 1/2]$. Most scientific computing software packages contain a pseudo random number generator which will simulate samples $\hat{x}_i$ from the $\mathrm{U}[0, 1]$ distribution. A simple change of variables can be used to define the Monte Carlo approximation

$$\overline{f}_M = \frac{1}{M} \sum_{i=1}^{M} f(\hat{x}_i/2).$$

The resulting errors for different $M$ for particular realisations of the random variables are displayed in Figure 3.3; a convergence rate of $1/\sqrt{M}$ on average can be observed. Note that the number of samples, $M$, of a Monte Carlo approximation corresponds to the number of subintervals $N_I$ in (3.3).

---

We shall see that Definition 3.13 is part of a more general framework in which an alternative joint distribution is used to generate the sample sequence $\{X_i\}$. This distribution can produce accurate estimates of statistics, provided that we also modify the weights.

**Definition 3.15** (Generalised Monte Carlo approximation)  A generalised Monte Carlo approximation to $\mathbb{E}[f(X)]$ uses Equation (3.17) but with a different (and possibly non-independent) joint distribution with PDF $\tilde{\pi}_M(x_1, \ldots, x_M)$ for the sequence of random variables $\{X_i\}$, and non-uniform weights $\{w_i\}$ subject to the conditions $w_i > 0$, $i = 1, \ldots, M$, and $\sum_{i=1}^{M} w_i = 1$.

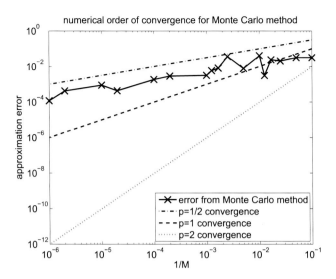

**Figure 3.3** Expectation value for $f$ defined by (3.7) with $n = 50$ resulting from a Monte Carlo approximation using $M$ independent samples from $X \sim \mathrm{U}[0, 1/2]$. We observe an order $1/\sqrt{M}$ convergence on average. Note that any specific error depends on the drawn samples and is therefore the outcome of a random experiment.

Appropriate choices for the weights $w_i$ of a generalised Monte Carlo method will be discussed shortly.

Approximation of expectations by standard quadrature rules can be incorporated into the (generalised) Monte Carlo framework by formally selecting the joint PDF $\tilde{\pi}_M$ as a product of Dirac delta functions, i.e.,

$$\tilde{\pi}_M(x_1, \ldots, x_M) = \prod_{i=1}^{M} \delta(x_i - c_i),$$

or, properly written as a measure,

$$\tilde{\mu}_M(\mathrm{d}x_1, \ldots, \mathrm{d}x_M) = \prod_{i=1}^{M} \mu_{c_i}(\mathrm{d}x_i),$$

and weights $w_i = b_i$. There is, however, a major difference: for a given quadrature rule, the realisations $(x_1, \ldots, x_M) = (c_1, \ldots, c_M)$ are always the same, but for a Monte Carlo scheme the samples – and hence the induced empirical measure (3.8) – will be different each time we draw realisations from the sequence of random variables $(X_1, X_2, \ldots, X_M)$ with joint PDF $\tilde{\pi}_M$. This renders the analysis of convergence of the induced empirical measure as $M \to \infty$ somewhat more complicated in the Monte Carlo case.

## 3.3        Sampling algorithms

We now discuss some practical aspects of how to implement Monte Carlo methods. Monte Carlo methods are easy to implement provided that it is possible to simulate the random variables $\{X_i\}$. Most scientific computing software packages provide (pseudo) random number generators for the uniform and the standard Gaussian distribution. The following techniques will allow us to move beyond those distributions.

The *transform method* is the first method we discuss for generating Monte Carlo samples from a PDF $\pi_X$ of a univariate random variable $X$. It is based on the idea of coupling which was introduced in Chapter 2.

**Lemma 3.16** (Transform method for sampling)    Let $X$ and $Y$ be random variables, and let $T$ be a transport map that defines a coupling between them. Let $\{x_i\}$ be a sequence of independent and identically distributed samples from $X$. Then $\{T(x_i)\}$ is a sequence of independent and identically distributed samples from $Y$.

*Proof*  First, it is clear that $\{T(X_i)\}$ are independent, identically distributed, since $\{X_i\}$ are. Further, $Y$ and $T(X)$ have the same law (weakly) if $\mathbb{E}[f(Y)] = \mathbb{E}[f(T(X))]$ for all suitable test functions $f$ (i.e., functions for which the expectations are finite). This is guaranteed by the definition of the transport map (2.12).        $\square$

In Example 2.25, we defined a transport map for univariate random variables, *via* the cumulative distribution function. This map can be used to transform the uniform distribution (which is easy to simulate on a computer) into other distributions, as described in the following example.

**Example 3.17**    Given a univariate random variable $X$ with PDF $\pi_X$ and cumulative distribution function

$$F_X(x) = \int_{-\infty}^{x} \pi_X(x')\mathrm{d}x',$$

we first draw $M$ samples $u_i$ from independent random variables $U_i$ with uniform distribution $\mathrm{U}[0,1]$ and then solve the implicit equation

$$F_X(x_i) = u_i, \qquad (3.18)$$

for $x_i \in \mathbb{R}$, $i = 1, \ldots, M$. The samples $x_i$ provide realisations from $M$ independent and identically distributed random variables with PDF $\pi_X$.

In order to generate univariate Gaussian random numbers using the transform method, we must evaluate the error function

$$\mathrm{erf}(t) = \frac{2}{\sqrt{\pi}} \int_0^t e^{-s^2}\mathrm{d}s,$$

and its inverse. Neither can be expressed in terms of elementary functions. This problem can be circumvented by generating a pair of independent Gaussian random variables from a pair of independent uniform random variables.

---

**Example 3.18**   We define a transport map between a pair of independent Gaussian random variables $X_1$, $X_2 \sim N(0,1)$ and a pair of independent uniform random variables $U_1$, $U_2 \sim U[0,1]$, as follows,

$$X_1 = \sqrt{-2 \ln U_1} \sin(2\pi U_2),$$
$$X_2 = \sqrt{-2 \ln U_1} \cos(2\pi U_2).$$

This is a transport map since

$$dx_1 dx_2 = \det \begin{pmatrix} -\frac{\sin(2\pi u_2)}{u_1 \sqrt{-2 \ln u_1}} & 2\pi\sqrt{-2 \ln u_1} \cos(2\pi u_2) \\ -\frac{\cos(2\pi u_2)}{u_1 \sqrt{-2 \ln u_1}} & -2\pi\sqrt{-2 \ln u_1} \sin(2\pi u_2) \end{pmatrix} du_1 du_2$$

$$= \left( 2\pi \frac{\cos(2\pi u_2)^2}{u_1} + 2\pi \frac{\sin(2\pi u_2)^2}{u_1} \right) du_1 du_2$$

$$= \frac{2\pi}{u_1} du_1 du_2.$$

We also find that

$$u_1 = e^{-(x_1^2 + x_2^2)/2},$$

and therefore

$$du_1 du_2 = \frac{1}{\sqrt{2\pi}} e^{-x_1^2/2} dx_1 \frac{1}{\sqrt{2\pi}} e^{-x_2^2/2} dx_2,$$

which implies

$$\mathbb{E}[f(X_1, X_2)] = \int_0^1 \int_0^1 f(x_1, x_2) du_1 du_2 = \mathbb{E}[\tilde{f}(U_1, U_2)],$$

with $\tilde{f}(u_1, u_2) = f(x_1(u_1, u_2), x_2(u_1, u_2))$. The resulting sampling method is called the *Box–Muller algorithm*.

---

**Example 3.19**   In this example, we discuss a multidimensional case of the transform approach. Mathematical software packages typically provide pseudo random number generators for multivariate Gaussian random variables with mean zero and covariance matrix $P = I$. As an example, consider two multivariate Gaussian distributions $N(\bar{x}_1, P_1)$ and $N(\bar{x}_2, P_2)$ in $\mathbb{R}^{N_x}$ with means $\bar{x}_1 = 0$ and $\bar{x}_2 \neq 0$, and covariance matrices $P_1 = I$ and $P_2 \neq I$, respectively. The coupling (2.14) leads to the well-known transformation

$$X_2 = \bar{x}_2 + P_2^{1/2} X_1,$$

which, in this particular case, coincides with the optimal coupling given by (2.23).

This transformation can be used to generate samples from a Gaussian distribution $N(\bar{x}, P)$ based on available random number generators.

As we have already discussed in Chapter 2 in the context of optimal transportation, there exist mappings $T$ which transform a random variable $X$ with PDF $\pi_X$ into another random variable $Y$ with PDF $\pi_Y$ under quite general assumptions. Furthermore, those maps can be generated by convex potentials $\psi$, i.e., $Y = T(X) = \nabla_x \psi(X)$. This result allows us to extend the transform method to more general multivariate random variables, at least theoretically. We will return to this issue in Chapter 5 when we discuss Bayesian inference; we will introduce an approximation scheme for transforming random variables based on linear transportation.

In many cases, obtaining an exact solution to (3.18) is intractable or expensive. In Example 3.3, whilst discussing Gauss–Hermite quadrature, we explored reformulating integrals with respect to a PDF $\pi_X$ as

$$\mathbb{E}[f(X)] = \int_{\mathbb{R}^{N_x}} f(x) \frac{\pi_X(x)}{\pi_{X'}(x)} \pi_{X'}(x) \mathrm{d}x.$$

This formula is also useful for generalised Monte Carlo approximation, in the case where $\pi_{X'}(x)$ denotes the PDF of a random variable $X'$ which we can easily draw samples from. We then use (3.17) with weights

$$w_i = \frac{\pi_X(x_i)/\pi_{X'}(x_i)}{\sum_{j=1}^{M} \pi_X(x_j)/\pi_{X'}(x_j)},$$

where $\{x_i\}$ are samples from $M$ independent and identically distributed random variables $X_i'$ with PDF $\pi_{X'}$. This is referred to as *importance sampling*, our second type of Monte Carlo method.

**Definition 3.20** (Importance sampling)  Let $X$ be a random variable with PDF $\pi_X$ and $X'$ be a second random variable with PDF $\pi_{X'}$ such that

$$\pi_X(x) = 0 \quad \text{if} \quad \pi_{X'}(x) = 0,$$

i.e., the measure $\mu_X(\mathrm{d}x) = \pi_X(x)\mathrm{d}x$ is *absolutely continuous* with respect to $\mu_{X'}(\mathrm{d}x) = \pi_{X'}(x)\mathrm{d}x$. Assume that we wish to obtain expectation formulas for $X$, but that it is much easier or efficient to sample from $X'$. Then, the importance sampling estimate of $\mathbb{E}[f(X)]$ is given by

$$\mathbb{E}[f(X)] \approx \sum_{i=1}^{M} w_i f(x_i'),$$

where $\{x_i'\}$ are $M$ independent samples from the random variable $X'$. The weights $\{w_i\}$ are given by

$$w_i \propto \frac{\pi_X(x_i')}{\pi_{X'}(x_i')},$$

where the constant of proportionality is chosen such that $\sum_i w_i = 1$.[2]

The choice of the random variable $X'$ might be determined by the availability of suitable random number generators and/or by accuracy considerations (minimising the variance of the resulting estimator).

In the following example, we illustrate importance sampling as a method for reducing the variance of a Monte Carlo estimator.

---

**Example 3.21**   We consider the approximation of the expectation value

$$\mathbb{E}[e^{-10X}\cos(X)] = \int_0^1 e^{-10x}\cos(x)\mathrm{d}x, \qquad (3.19)$$

with respect to $X \sim \mathrm{U}[0,1]$. Its analytic value is given by

$$\mathbb{E}[e^{-10X}\cos(X)] = \frac{10}{101} - \frac{10\cos(1) - \sin(1)}{101e^{10}}.$$

We can approximate this value by drawing $M$ independent samples $u_i$ from the uniform distribution $\mathrm{U}[0,1]$, i.e.,

$$\bar{x}_M = \frac{1}{M}\sum_{i=1}^M \cos(u_i)e^{-10u_i}.$$

Since $e^{-10x}$ decays very rapidly away from zero, it seems reasonable to replace the uniform samples $u_i$ by samples $x_i \in [0,1]$, which are concentrated around zero. For example, we may take $X'$ to have PDF

$$\pi_{X'}(x) = \begin{cases} \frac{10e^{-10x}}{1-e^{-10}} & \text{if } x \in [0,1], \\ 0 & \text{otherwise.} \end{cases}$$

Samples $x_i$ from this distribution can be generated using the transform method with cumulative distribution function

$$F_{X'}(x) = \begin{cases} 1 & \text{if } x \geq 1, \\ \frac{1-e^{-10x}}{1-e^{-10}} & \text{if } x \in [0,1), \\ 0 & \text{otherwise.} \end{cases}$$

We obtain the explicit formula

$$x_i = -0.1\ln(1 - u_i + u_i e^{-10})$$

for independent samples $u_i$ from the uniform distribution $\mathrm{U}[0,1]$. The expectation value (3.19) is now approximated by

$$\bar{x}_M = \frac{1}{M}\sum_{i=1}^M \cos(x_i)\frac{1-e^{-10}}{10}.$$

---

[2] Using unnormalised weights $w_i = \pi_X(x_i')/\pi_{X'}(x_i')$ leads to an unbiased estimator of $\mathbb{E}[f(X)]$. This is beneficial in certain situations but stops the associated measure (3.8) from being a probability measure. Unnormalised weights are implicitly applied in Example 3.21.

As illustrated in Figure 3.4, we observe in numerical experiments that the variance of this estimator,

$$\sigma_M^2 = \mathbb{E}[(\overline{X}_M - \mathbb{E}[\overline{X}_M])^2],$$

is reduced by a factor of about ten thousand in comparison to a standard Monte Carlo implementation meaning that the accuracy (width of the confidence intervals) is improved by a factor of one hundred.

It should be noted that the performance of importance sampling is rather sensitive to the integrand. For example, if we replace (3.19) by

$$\mathbb{E}[e^{-10X}\sin(X)] = \int_0^1 e^{-10x}\sin(x)\mathrm{d}x, \tag{3.20}$$

then the same importance sampling approach does not give any reduction in variance and there is no improvement in the associated estimator.

A third type of Monte Carlo methods is *rejection sampling*. Rejection sampling is based on two ingredients: a proposal PDF $\pi_P(x)$, and a constant $m > 1$ such that $\pi_X(x) < m\,\pi_P(x)$ for all $x \in \mathbb{R}^{N_x}$. Rejection sampling is summarised in the following algorithm.

**Algorithm 3.22** (Rejection sampling)   For $i = 1, \ldots, M$ do the following.

(i) Use a random number generator to generate a sample $x \in \mathbb{R}^{N_x}$ from a random variable $X'$ with PDF $\pi_P$ and draw a $u$ from the uniform distribution $\mathrm{U}[0, 1]$.

(ii) If

$$u < \frac{\pi_X(x)}{m\pi_P(x)},$$

then set $x_i = x$, increase $i$ by one, and go back to (i). Otherwise reject the proposal, $x$, and return to (i).

**Lemma 3.23** (Consistency of rejection sampling)   Rejection sampling generates samples $x_i$, $i = 1, \ldots, M$, from $M$ independent and identically distributed random variables $X_i$ with PDF $\pi_X$.

*Proof*   The independence of the accepted samples follows from their definition. The correct distribution follows from rearrangement of Equation (2.3) into the standard conditional probability identity[3]

$$\pi(x|\mathrm{accept}) = \frac{\mathbb{P}(\mathrm{accept}|x)\,\pi(x)}{\mathbb{P}(\mathrm{accept})},$$

where $\pi(x|\mathrm{accept})$ denotes the conditional PDF that a proposed $x$ is accepted,

---

[3] Much more shall be said about this formula in Chapter 5.

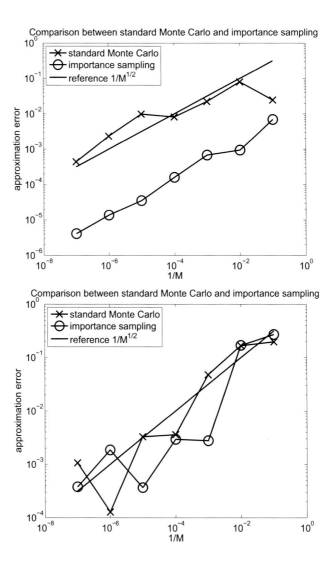

**Figure 3.4** Comparison between a standard Monte Carlo approximation to the expectation value (3.19) and an importance sampling Monte Carlo approximation. The top figure shows that an error reduction by a factor of about one hundred is achieved in this case. However, the same importance sampling approach applied to (3.20) does not lead to an improvement. See bottom figure. This result indicates that importance sampling for reducing the variance of estimators needs to be handled with great care.

and $\mathbb{P}(\text{accept}|x)$ is the conditional probability to reach acceptance for a given $x$. Note that $\mathbb{P}(\text{reject}|x) = 1 - \mathbb{P}(\text{accept}|x)$. Rejection sampling leads to

$$\mathbb{P}(\text{accept}|x) = \frac{\pi_X(x)}{m\pi_P(x)},$$

and

$$\pi(x) = \pi_P(x).$$

Hence

$$\mathbb{P}(\text{accept}) = \int_{\mathbb{R}^{N_x}} \mathbb{P}(\text{accept}|x)\pi(x)\mathrm{d}x = \int_{\mathbb{R}^{N_x}} \frac{\pi_X(x)}{m\pi_P(x)}\pi_P(x)\mathrm{d}x = \frac{1}{m},$$

and

$$\pi(x|\text{accept}) = \frac{\frac{\pi_X(x)}{m\pi_P(x)}\pi_P(x)}{1/m} = \pi_X(x),$$

as required.                                                                    □

There is a practical difficulty with rejection sampling: what is a good choice for the constant $m$? If $m$ is chosen too large, we will only rarely accept a proposed sample $x$ from the proposal density. We will learn about more efficient methods for sampling from a given PDF in Chapter 5.

---

**Example 3.24**   Rejection sampling can be given the following geometric interpretation. Step (i) of Algorithm 3.22 generates pairs $(x, u)$. We introduce the variable $y = um\pi_P(x)$ and plot the associated $(x, y)$ pairs in the plane. These pairs fill the area underneath $f(x) := m\pi_P(x)$ uniformly. In step (ii), we only retain those samples $x$ for which the associated $y$ is also underneath the graph of $g(x) := \pi_X(x)$. Hence the ratio of generated to accepted samples converges to the ratio of the two definite integrals associated with $f$ and $g$. Of course, since $g$ is obtained from a PDF $\pi_X$, we know that $g$ integrates to one. However, we may apply rejection sampling to any pair of functions $f(x) > g(x) \geq 0$. If the area enclosed by $f$ is known, then rejection sampling can be used to approximate the area defined by $g$. We consider the following specific example. Define $f$ by

$$f(x) = \begin{cases} 1 & \text{if } x \in [-1, 1], \\ 0 & \text{otherwise,} \end{cases}$$

and $g$ by

$$g(x) = \begin{cases} \sqrt{1 - x^2} & \text{if } x \in [-1, 1], \\ 0 & \text{otherwise.} \end{cases}$$

Then,

$$\int_{-1}^{1} f(x)\mathrm{d}x = 2 \quad \text{and} \quad \int_{-1}^{1} g(x)\mathrm{d}x = \frac{\pi}{2},$$

and rejection sampling can be used to approximate $\pi$. Numerical results are displayed in Figure 3.5.

---

We now return to the interpretation of Monte Carlo methods or quadrature rules as introducing empirical measures of type (3.8) with associated expectation values (3.9). Furthermore, we are interested in the cases for which the weights

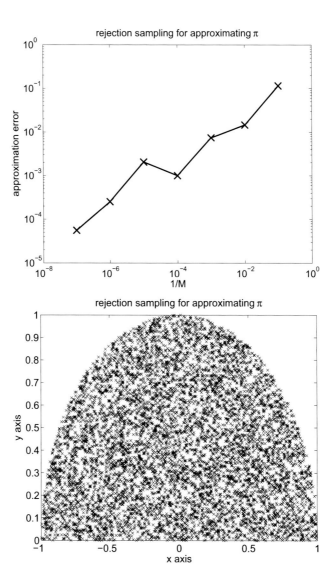

**Figure 3.5** Approximation of $\pi$ using rejection sampling. The bottom figure shows the accepted samples from a uniform distribution in $[-1, 1] \times [0, 1]$. The top figure shows the approximation error as a function of sample size $M$.

$w_i$ are non-uniform, i.e., $w_i \neq 1/M$. As we have already discussed, such cases arise for importance sampling or Gauss–Legendre quadrature rules. In the case of importance sampling in particular, it is often the case that very small weights can be obtained for some of the samples. For random variables that are expensive to simulate (such as those that are coupled to mechanistic models, which are encountered in data assimilation), these samples are not contributing much to the expectation value. This is inefficient. Hence, it is useful to replace the empirical measure $\mu_M$ with another measure $\tilde{\mu}_M$ with equal weights (but possibly duplicate samples). This is referred to as *resampling*. The aim is that $\mu_M$ and $\tilde{\mu}_M$ should both approximate the same distribution; this approximation is quantified in the weak sense by comparing expectation values for suitable test functions $f$. See Appendix 3.5 at the end of this chapter for more details.

A simple resampling method is called *independent resampling with replacement*, defined as follows.

**Definition 3.25** (Resampling)   Let $\mu_M$ be an empirical measure of the form (3.8). Resampling replaces $\mu_M$ by another empirical measure $\tilde{\mu}_M$ of the form

$$\tilde{\mu}_M(\mathrm{d}x) = \frac{1}{L}\sum_{i=1}^{M}\xi_i\delta(x-x_i)\mathrm{d}x, \qquad (3.21)$$

with corresponding expectation estimators

$$\overline{f}_\xi = \frac{1}{L}\sum_{i=1}^{M}\xi_i f(x_i), \qquad (3.22)$$

where $L > 0$ is a positive integer, and the weights $\{\xi_i\}$ are realisations of uni-variate discrete random variables $\Xi_i : \Omega \to S$ with integer-valued realisations in $S = \{0, 1, \ldots, L\}$ subject to

$$\sum_{i=1}^{M}\xi_i = L.$$

In this setting, $\overline{f}_\xi$ is a random estimator that depends on the outcome of $\{\xi_i\}$.

**Lemma 3.26** (Unbiased resampling)   Take the sequence $\Xi = \{\Xi_i\}$ of discrete random variables such that

$$\mathbb{E}[\Xi_i] = Lw_i.$$

Then,

$$\mathbb{E}[\overline{f}_\Xi] = \sum_{i=1}^{M}w_i f(x_i).$$

This means that, upon averaging over all possible realisations of $\{\xi_i\}$, the resampled empirical measure produces the same statistics as $\mu_M$. Any errors are due to the variance in the estimator.

*Proof*   For any suitable test function $f$ we obtain

$$\mathbb{E}[\overline{f}_\Xi] = \frac{1}{L}\sum_{i=1}^{M}(\mathbb{E}[\Xi_i])f(x_i) = \sum_{i=1}^{M}w_i f(x_i)$$

as required.                                                                 □

The interpretation of unbiased resampling is that we have replaced an empirical measure (3.8) with non-uniform weights $w_i$ by a new empirical measure (3.22) with uniform weights $\tilde{w}_j = 1/L$ and each sample $x_i$ being replaced by $\xi_i$ identical *offspring*. The total number of offspring is equal to $L$. In other words, the offspring $\{\xi_i\}_{i=1}^M$ follow a *multinomial distribution* defined by

$$\mathbb{P}(\xi_i = n_i, i = 1, \ldots, M) = \frac{M!}{\prod_{i=1}^M n_i!} \prod_{i=1}^M (w_i)^{n_i}, \tag{3.23}$$

with $n_i \geq 0$ such that $\sum_{i=1}^M n_i = L$.

We introduce the notation $\mathrm{Mult}(L; w_1, \ldots, w_M)$ to denote the multinomial distribution of $L$ independent trials, where the outcome of each trial is distributed among $M$ possible outcomes according to probabilities $\{w_i\}_{i=1}^M$. The following algorithm draws random samples from $\mathrm{Mult}(L; w_1, \ldots, w_M)$.

**Algorithm 3.27** (Multinomial samples)   The integer-valued variable $\bar{\xi}_i$, $i = 1, \ldots, M$, is set equal to zero initially.
    For $l = 1, \ldots, L$ do the following.

  (i)  Draw a number $u \in [0, 1]$ from the uniform distribution $\mathrm{U}[0, 1]$.
  (ii)  Determine the integer $i^* \in \{1, \ldots, M\}$ which satisfies

$$i^* = \arg\min_{i \geq 1} \sum_{j=1}^i w_j \geq u.$$

 (iii)  Increment $\bar{\xi}_{i^*}$ by one.

   The final integers $\{\bar{\xi}_i\}$ are distributed according to $\mathrm{Mult}(L; w_1, \ldots, w_M)$.

   Independent resampling with replacement will become important when we discuss *sequential Monte Carlo methods* in Chapter 6 (typically, $L = M$). Independent resampling leads to quite high variance errors, and is often replaced by *residual* or *systematic resampling*. We next summarise residual resampling, while we refer the reader to Arulampalam, Maskell, Gordon & Clapp (2002) for an algorithmic description of systematic resampling.

**Definition 3.28** (Residual resampling)   Given an empirical measure (3.8) *residual resampling* generates a total of $M$ offspring with

$$\xi_i = \lfloor M w_i \rfloor + \bar{\xi}_i,$$

offspring for each sample $x_i$, $i = 1, \ldots, M$. Here $\lfloor x \rfloor$ denotes the integer part of $x$ and the values $\{\bar{\xi}_i\}$ follow the multinomial distribution (3.23) with

$$L = M - \sum_{i=1}^M \lfloor M w_i \rfloor$$

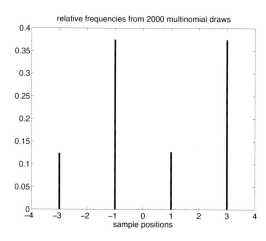

relative frequencies from 2000 multinomial draws

**Figure 3.6** Relative frequency of two thousand repeated draws from a multinomial distribution with probability vector $\overline{w} = (1/8, 3/8, 1/8, 3/8)$.

and new weights

$$\overline{w}_i = \frac{Mw_i - \lfloor Mw_i \rfloor}{\sum_{j=1}^{M}(Mw_j - \lfloor Mw_j \rfloor)}.$$

**Example 3.29** Consider four samples $x_1 = -3$, $x_2 = -1$, $x_3 = 1$, and $x_4 = 3$ with associated weights $w_1 = 1/16$, $w_2 = 3/16$, $w_3 = 5/16$, and $w_4 = 7/16$, respectively. Residual resampling leads to $\lfloor Mw_i \rfloor$ equal to zero for $i = 1, 2$ and $\lfloor Mw_i \rfloor = 1$ for $i = 3, 4$. The new weights $\overline{w}_i$ are then given by $\overline{w}_{1,3} = 1/8$, $\overline{w}_{2,4} = 3/8$, and $L = 2$. Drawing a total of two thousand samples from the associated multinomial distribution, we find that the relative frequency of the outcomes indeed reproduces the probabilities given by the probability vector $\overline{w} = (1/8, 3/8, 1/8, 3/8)$. See Figure 3.6.

We finally mention that linear transportation, as discussed in Chapter 2 in the context of coupling discrete random variables, can also be used for replacing an empirical measure with non-uniform weights by an empirical measure with equal weights. We will discuss this approach in more detail in Chapter 5.

## Problems

**3.1** The formal estimate in (3.4) can be made precise for the implicit midpoint rule applied to an integral (3.2). The order of the implicit midpoint method is $p = 2$ and

$$|\overline{f}_{1,N_I} - \overline{f}| \leq \frac{\max_{\xi \in [0,1]} |f''(\xi)|}{24} \Delta x^2$$

with $\Delta x = 1/N_I$ and $N_I$ the number of subintervals.

(i)   Generalise this estimate to integrals of the form

$$\overline{f} = \int_{-a}^{a} f(x)\mathrm{d}x, \qquad a > 0,$$

and corresponding approximations by the implicit midpoint rule over $N_I$ subintervals of length $\Delta x = 2a/N_I$.

(ii)  Apply this result to

$$\overline{f} = \int_{-3}^{3} e^{-x^2}\mathrm{d}x \tag{3.24}$$

and derive a lower bound $N_I^*$ that guarantees that $|\overline{f} - \overline{f}_{1,N_I}| \le 0.01$ for all $N_I \ge N_I^*$.

(iii)  Implement the implicit midpoint rule for (3.24) and compute the actual approximation error arising for $N_I = N_I^*$.

**3.2**  Repeat the experiments from Example 3.4 with the random variable $X \sim \mathrm{U}[0, 1/2]$ replaced by $X \sim \mathrm{U}[0, 1]$. Compare your results to those obtained in Example 3.4.

**3.3**  Determine the ANOVA decomposition for

$$f(x_1, x_2) = 12x_1 + 6x_2 - 6x_1x_2$$

and compute the associated variances $\sigma_1^2$, $\sigma_2^2$, and $\sigma_{12}^2$. Which terms in the ANOVA decomposition contribute most significantly to the total variance $\sigma^2$?

**3.4**  Consider a sequence $\{X_i\}_{i\ge 1}$ of independent and identically distributed univariate Gaussian random variables with mean zero and variance $\sigma^2 = 1$. Apply the central limit theorem to the induced sequence of random variables

$$Y_M = M^{-1/2}\sum_{i=1}^{M} X_i^2,$$

in order to determine the PDF $\pi_{Y_M}$ for $Y_M$ as $M \to \infty$.

**3.5**  Repeat the numerical experiment from Example 3.14 with $n = 1$, $10$, and $50$ in the definition (3.7) for the integrand $f$. Compare the resulting errors from the associated Monte Carlo approximations. Explain your findings in terms of the variance of $Y = \phi^n(X)$ with $X \sim \mathrm{U}[0, 1/2]$.

**3.6**  Consider a univariate random variable $X$ with smooth cumulative distribution function $F_X(x)$. A coupling between $X$ and a random variable $U \sim \mathrm{U}[0, 1]$ is provided by $X = F_X^{-1}(U)$. Such couplings form the basis of the transform method. Compute the associated Wasserstein distance

$$W(\pi_X, \pi_U) := \sqrt{\mathbb{E}[(F_X^{-1}(U) - U)^2]}$$

in the case where $X$ is Gaussian with mean zero and variance one.

**3.7**  Use rejection sampling in the setting of Example 3.24 to approximate $\pi$. Denote the number of generated $(x, u)$ pairs by $M$. Display the approximation error as a function of $1/M$ and compare your findings with those displayed in Figure 3.5.

**3.8** Implement Algorithm 3.27. The input parameters are the integers $M$, $L$, and a set of weights $w_i \geq 0$, $i = 1, \ldots, M$, with $\sum_{i=1}^{M} w_i = 1$. The output of the algorithm are $M$ integers $\overline{\xi}_i \geq 0$ which satisfy $\sum_{i=1}^{M} \overline{\xi}_i = L$. Verify your algorithm by checking that $\overline{\xi}_i / L \approx w_i$ for $L \gg M$.

## 3.4 Guide to literature

Basic concepts of numerical quadrature rules are covered in most textbooks on numerical analysis such as Süli & Mayers (2006). Sparse grid quadrature rules for high-dimensional integrals and their relation to ANOVA-type approximations are discussed in Holtz (2011); see also the survey paper by Bungartz & Griebel (2004). An introduction to Monte Carlo methods can be found, for example, in Liu (2001) and Robert & Casella (2004). Theoretical aspects of Monte Carlo and Quasi-Monte Carlo methods are covered by Caflisch (1998). Quasi-Monte Carlo methods increase the convergence rate of Monte Carlo methods by using low discrepancy (or quasi-random) samples $x_i$.

## 3.5 Appendix: Random probability measures

In this appendix, we give a brief introduction to random probability measures. We restrict the discussion to discrete measures and consider monomial resampling as a concrete example. Assume we are given $M$ fixed points $x_i \in \mathbb{R}^{N_x}$. Any set of weights $w_i \geq 0$, $i = 1, \ldots, M$, subject to $\sum_{i=1}^{M} w_i = 1$ leads to an empirical measure

$$\mu_M(\mathrm{d}x) = \sum_{i=1}^{M} w_i \delta(x_i - x)\mathrm{d}x. \tag{3.25}$$

We may now "randomise" this measure by considering the weights $\{w_i\}$ as the outcome of random variables $W_i : \Omega \to [0, 1]$, which satisfy $\sum_{i=1}^{M} W_i = 1$, i.e., $w_i = W_i(\omega)$. We introduce the notation $\mu_M^\Omega$ to emphasise that (3.25) is now viewed as the outcome of a random experiment. Next we introduce the distance of two such random measures $\mu_M^\Omega$ and $\nu_M^\Omega$ as follows:

$$d(\mu_M^\Omega, \nu_M^\Omega) = \sup_{|f| \leq 1} \sqrt{\mathbb{E}\left[\left(\sum_{i=1}^{M}(W_i - V_i)f(x_i)\right)^2\right]}. \tag{3.26}$$

Here the expectation is taken over all realisations of the two sets of random variables $\{W_i\}$ and $\{V_i\}$ associated with $\mu_M^\Omega$ and $\nu_M^\Omega$, respectively. We recall that

$$\sum_{i=1}^{M}(\overline{w}_i - \overline{v}_i)f(x_i) = \sum_{i=1}^{M}\overline{w}_i f(x_i) - \sum_{i=1}^{M}\overline{v}_i f(x_i) =: \mathbb{E}_{\mu_M^\Omega}[f] - \mathbb{E}_{\nu_M^\Omega}[f],$$

where $\overline{w}_i = \mathbb{E}[W_i]$ and $\overline{v}_i = \mathbb{E}[V_i]$.

In the case of monomial resampling, the measure $\mu_M^\Omega$ has fixed importance weights $\{w_i\}$, i.e., $w_i = W_i(\omega)$ for almost all $\omega \in \Omega$, and an expectation value $\mathbb{E}_{\mu_M^\Omega}[f]$, abbreviated by $\overline{f}_M$. The weights $v_i$ of the "random" resampling measure $\nu_M^\omega$ are given by $v_i(\omega) = \xi_i(\omega)/L$, where $\xi_i(\omega)$ counts how many times $x_i$ has been drawn under the resampling step and $\sum_{i=1}^M \xi_i(\omega) = L$. Furthermore, it holds that $\overline{v}_i = w_i$, or, equivalently,

$$\mathbb{E}[\Xi_i] = w_i L.$$

An alternative representation of realisations $\nu_M^\omega$ of the random measure $\nu_M^\Omega$ is

$$\nu_M^\omega(\mathrm{d}x) = \frac{1}{L} \sum_{l=1}^L \delta(x - X_l(\omega))\mathrm{d}x,$$

with $L$ independent and identically distributed discrete random variables

$$X_l : \Omega \to \{x_1, \ldots, x_M\},$$

such that $\mathbb{P}[X_l = x_i] = w_i$.

We now bound the distance $d(\mu_M^\Omega, \nu_M^\Omega)$ as a function of the resampling size $L$. First note that

$$\mathbb{E}_{\nu_M^\Omega}[f] - \mathbb{E}_{\mu_M^\Omega}[f] = \frac{1}{L} \sum_{l=1}^L (\mathbb{E}[f(X_l)] - \overline{f}_M) = 0,$$

and that

$$\mathbb{E}\left[(f(X_l) - \overline{f}_M)(f(X_k) - \overline{f}_M)\right] = 0$$

for $k \neq l$. These equalities hold since the the random variables $\{X_l\}$ are independent and identically distributed and satisfy $\mathbb{E}[f(X_l)] = \overline{f}_M$. Hence

$$d(\mu_M^\Omega, \nu_M^\Omega) = \sup_{|f| \leq 1} \sqrt{\mathbb{E}\left[\left(\frac{1}{L} \sum_{l=1}^L f(X_l) - \overline{f}_M\right)^2\right]}$$

$$= \frac{1}{L^{1/2}} \sup_{|f| \leq 1} \sqrt{\mathbb{E}\left[\frac{1}{L} \sum_{l=1}^L (f(X_l) - \overline{f}_M)^2\right]}$$

$$\leq \frac{4}{L^{1/2}},$$

since $|f(x_l) - \overline{f}_M| \leq 2$ under the assumption that $|f(x)| \leq 1$ for all $x \in \mathbb{R}^{N_x}$.

The discussion of this appendix can be extended to continuous random measures and can be used to prove the convergence of empirical measures generated from Monte Carlo importance sampling-resampling steps to the posterior PDF of Bayesian inference as the sample size $L = M \to \infty$. See Chapter 5.

## 3.6 Appendix: Polynomial chaos expansion

As an alternative to the numerical methods discussed in this chapter, here we consider approximating a random variable $X : \Omega \to \mathbb{R}^{N_x}$ by another random variable $\tilde{X} : \Omega \to \mathbb{R}^{N_x}$. Let us assume, for simplicity, that $N_x = 1$ and that there is a transformation $X = T(Y)$ with $Y$ a Gaussian random variable with mean zero and variance equal to one. Then $\tilde{X}$ can be defined by a finite truncation of the *polynomial chaos expansion* (PCE) of $X$,

$$X = T(Y) = \sum_{k \geq 0} \alpha_k H_k(Y),$$

where $\{\alpha_k\}$ are constant expansion coefficients, and $H_k(y)$ denotes the Hermite polynomial of order $k \geq 0$. Hermite polynomials satisfy the orthogonality relation $\mathbb{E}[H_k(Y)H_l(Y)] = 0$ for $k \neq l$ if $Y$ is $N(0,1)$.

Multiplying both sides of the expression by $H_k(Y)$, taking expectation and using the orthogonality relation, we obtain

$$\alpha_k = \frac{\mathbb{E}[T(Y)H_k(Y)]}{\mathbb{E}[H_k(Y)H_k(Y)]}.$$

The first four Hermite polynomials are given by $H_0(y) = 1$, $H_1(y) = y$, $H_2(y) = y^2 - 1$, and $H_3(y) = y^3 - 3y$.[4] Polynomial chaos expansions, also called *spectral expansions*, have become popular in the context of stochastic finite element methods for partial differential equations. See Smith (2014) for more details.

---

[4] The roots of these polynomials are also used to define the quadrature points $c_i$ of Gauss–Hermite quadrature rules. See Example 3.3. For example, the Gauss–Hermite quadrature rule of order four satisfies $H_2(c_i) = 0$, $i = 1, 2$.

# 4 Stochastic processes

In the previous two chapters, we discussed how probability measures can be used to express our uncertainty in estimating quantities. We also introduced some useful tools for calculating with probability measures. A key aspect of many physical systems of interest is that they evolve in time according to physical laws, such as (1.2). Having obtained a probability measure expressing our uncertainty in the system state at a particular snapshot in time, we would like to know how our uncertainty evolves in time. This motivates a probabilistic view of dynamical systems. It is also often the case that the models that we use are themselves random, often because they approximately represent some complex dynamical process by a simple random process. We can use the language of stochastic processes to describe such models and incorporate them into the probabilistic dynamical systems framework. In this book we do not discuss specific models, instead we are interested in qualitative properties that can be described in this framework.

In this chapter we will develop this framework in the context of forecasting. Dynamical systems and stochastic processes are among the most fundamental mathematical modelling tools; they find widespread use in science and engineering. This is a vast topic, and this chapter can only highlight those aspects which are of particular relevance to forecasting and data assimilation. We will primarily restrict the discussion to discrete-time systems and processes in order to keep mathematical details relatively elementary. For a more in-depth study we recommend the textbooks listed at the end of this chapter.

## 4.1 Dynamical systems and discrete-time Markov processes

We start with the concept of a *dynamical system*.

**Definition 4.1** (Dynamical system)  Given a *phase space* $\mathcal{B} \subset \mathbb{R}^{N_z}$ embedded into an $N_z$-dimensional Euclidian space, an *autonomous dynamical system* is a map $\psi : \mathcal{B} \to \mathcal{B}$. Given an *initial condition* $z^0 \in \mathcal{B}$, a dynamical system defines a solution sequence or *trajectory* $\{z^n\}_{n \geq 0}$ via the iteration

$$z^{n+1} = \psi(z^n). \tag{4.1}$$

If the map $\psi$ also depends on the iteration index $n$, then we call it a *non-autonomous dynamical system*.

Using this terminology, we find that (1.18) induces an autonomous dynamical system

$$\psi(z) = z + \delta t f(z), \tag{4.2}$$

while (1.2) defines a non-autonomous dynamical system

$$\psi_n(z) = z + \delta t \left(f(z) + g(t_n)\right), \qquad t_n = n\delta t,$$

for given $g(t_n)$.

From a forecasting perspective, if we do not know the precise value of the system state $z$, but instead only know that it lies in some subset $\mathcal{A}$ of phase space, we would like to know the minimum subset definitely containing the system state at later times. More generally, this is the setting for many questions of interest about the properties of dynamical systems. The theory of dynamical systems is less concerned about the behaviour of individual trajectories and instead focuses on the collective or typical behaviour of many trajectories. For example, we might ask whether trajectories remain bounded or whether they enter a compact subset of phase space after finitely many iterations. This perspective leads us to the consideration of sequences of sets

$$\mathcal{A}^{n+1} = \psi(\mathcal{A}^n), \qquad \mathcal{A}^0 = \mathcal{A},$$

where $z^{n+1} \in \mathcal{A}^{n+1}$ if and only if there exists a $z^n \in \mathcal{A}^n$ such that $z^{n+1} = \psi(z^n)$. A subset $\mathcal{A}$ of phase space is now called *forward invariant* if

$$\psi(\mathcal{A}) \subseteq \mathcal{A}.$$

In other words, if $z^{n_*} \in \mathcal{A}$ for some $n_*$, then $z^n \in \mathcal{A}$ for all $n \geq n_*$.

Let us explore this aspect further by means of Example 1.7.

---

**Example 4.2**  We recall the Lorenz-63 system (Lorenz 1963) and its discretisation in time by the forward Euler method, which gives rise to an autonomous dynamical system of type (4.2) with $\mathcal{B} = \mathbb{R}^3$, $z = (x, y, z)^{\mathrm{T}}$, and the vector field $f$ given by

$$f(z) = \begin{pmatrix} \sigma(y - x) \\ x(\rho - z) - y \\ xy - \beta z \end{pmatrix}, \tag{4.3}$$

with parameters $\sigma = 10$, $\rho = 28$, and $\beta = 8/3$.

A first observation is that $f(0) = 0$ and hence $z^n = 0$ for all $n > 0$ provided $z^0 = 0$. Therefore, $\mathcal{A} = \{0\}$ is forward invariant. However this is not an "interesting" forward invariant set since any initial condition $z^0 \neq 0$ with $\|z^0\|$ arbitrarily small will be repelled from the origin and will ultimately approach a much more interesting forward invariant set, which is called the *Lorenz attractor*. The set $\mathcal{A}$ defining the Lorenz attractor has a complicated geometric structure which is

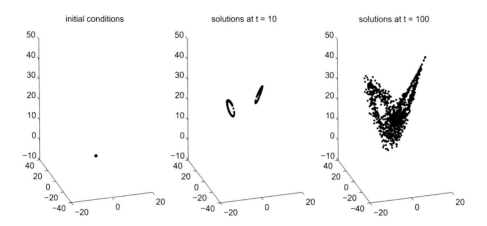

**Figure 4.1** Snapshots of $M = 1000$ solutions starting near the origin at time zero (left panel) at time $t = 10$ (middle panel) and at $t = 100$. The solutions start approaching a set closely resembling the set displayed in Figure 1.8.

beyond this introductory textbook, but it can be easily explored numerically. In fact, the qualitative structure of the Lorenz attractor is well represented by Figure 1.8.

A numerical demonstration of "attraction" is provided in Figure 4.1 where one thousand solutions with initial conditions close to zero are displayed at $t = 10$ and $t = 100$. The solutions approach the Lorenz attractor as time progresses.

Before giving a formal definition of an *attractor*, we first define the distance from a point to a set.

**Definition 4.3** (Distance from a point to a set)  For $z \in \mathcal{B}$, the distance from $z$ to a subset $\mathcal{A} \subset \mathcal{B}$ is

$$d(z, \mathcal{A}) := \inf_{z' \in \mathcal{A}} \|z - z'\|.$$

**Definition 4.4** (Attractor)  A compact set $\mathcal{A} \subset \mathcal{B}$ is called an *attractor* of a dynamical system $\psi$ if

(i) $\mathcal{A}$ is forward invariant;
(ii) $\mathcal{A}$ attracts a neighbourhood of itself, i.e., there exists $\delta > 0$ such that if $d(z^0, \mathcal{A}) < \delta$, then $d(z^n, \mathcal{A}) \to 0$, as $n \to \infty$; and
(iii) $\mathcal{A}$ is minimal, i.e., there is no $\mathcal{A}' \subset \mathcal{A}$ such that both $\mathcal{A}$ and $\mathcal{A}'$ are forward invariant and attracting.

**Example 4.5**  The identification of an attractor is often highly non-trivial. Let us consider, for example, the dynamical system defined by $\mathcal{B} = [0, 1] \subset \mathbb{R}$ and the tent map

$$\psi(z) := \begin{cases} 2z & \text{if } z \in [0, 1/2], \\ 2 - 2z & \text{otherwise.} \end{cases}$$

If we define $\mathcal{A}^0 = [0, 1/2]$, for example, then we find that $\mathcal{A}^1 = \mathcal{B} = [0, 1]$ after a single iteration. Clearly $\mathcal{B}$ is forward invariant. The choice $\mathcal{A}^0 = \{0, 1\}$ leads, on the other hand, after a single iteration to $\mathcal{A}^1 = \{0\}$ which itself is forward invariant. We find that $\mathcal{A} = \{0\}$ is attracting for certain initial conditions, since any $z^0 = 1/2^k$, $k = 0, 1, 2, \ldots$, will result in trajectories reaching $\{0\}$ after finitely many steps (in fact $k+1$ iterations). At the same time, there is no neighbourhood $\mathcal{U}$ of $\{0\}$ in $[0, 1]$ such that all $z^0 \in \mathcal{U}$ approach $\{0\}$ and, hence, $\{0\}$ is not an attractor as defined above. Furthermore, there are also periodic trajectories of period $n_* > 1$ by which we mean that

$$z^n = z^{n+n_*}$$

for all $n \geq 0$. For example, $z^0 = 2/5$ leads to $z^1 = 4/5$ and then back to $z^3 = 2/5 = z^0$. Hence $n_* = 2$ in this case and $\mathcal{A} = \{2/5, 4/5\}$ is forward invariant. Again these sets do not define attractors in the above sense. In fact, the tent map has only the whole set $\mathcal{B}$ as its attractor.

---

From the perspective of forecasting, rather than simply specifying a set that we think contains $z$, it is more useful to quantify our uncertainty[1] about where $z$ is by assigning probabilities to subsets $\mathcal{A} \subset \mathcal{B}$. We can then compare subsets based on where $z$ is most likely to be found. We will denote $\mathbb{P}^n(\mathcal{A})$ the probability of $z$ being in set $\mathcal{A}$ at time $n$. Once we have assigned probabilities $\mathbb{P}^0(\mathcal{A})$ to subsets at $n = 0$, their evolution is entirely determined by the dynamical system since

$$\mathbb{P}^{n+1}(\mathcal{A}) = \mathbb{P}^n(\mathcal{A}'), \quad n \geq 0,$$

with $\mathcal{A}' = \psi^{-1}(\mathcal{A})$ for all appropriate sets $\mathcal{A} \subset \mathcal{B}$. We have already encountered this transformation rule (or conservation law) for probabilities in Lemma 2.13 of Chapter 2.

Using the language of probability theory, as summarised in Chapter 2, we define a PDF $\pi_{Z^0}$ and a random variable $Z^0 : \Omega \to \mathcal{B}$ on phase space $\mathcal{B} \subset \mathbb{R}^{N_z}$ such that

$$\mathbb{P}^0(\mathcal{A}) = \int_{\mathcal{A}} \pi_{Z^0}(z^0) \mathrm{d}z^0.$$

After a single application of the dynamical system, we then obtain a random variable $Z^1 = \psi(Z^0)$, with marginal PDF $\pi_{Z^1}$ defined by

$$\mathbb{P}^1(\mathcal{A}) = \int_{\mathcal{A}} \pi_{Z^1}(z^1) \mathrm{d}z^1 = \int_{\psi^{-1}(\mathcal{A})} \pi_{Z^0}(z^0) \mathrm{d}z^0,$$

---

[1] Here we consider uncertainty to be a subjective quantity that will depend on prior knowledge and assumptions about $z$.

for all subsets $\mathcal{A} \subseteq \mathcal{B}$.

---

**Example 4.6**  We consider the scalar, linear iteration

$$z^{n+1} = dz^n + b,$$

with phase space $\mathcal{B} = \mathbb{R}$ and fixed parameters $d$ and $b$. Assume that $z^0$ is obtained from a Gaussian random variable $Z^0$ with mean $\bar{z}^0$ and variance $\sigma_0^2$. The PDF for $Z^0$ is

$$\pi_{Z^0}(z) = \mathrm{n}(z; \bar{z}^0, \sigma_0^2) = \frac{1}{\sqrt{2\pi\sigma_0^2}} e^{-\frac{1}{2}\left(\frac{z - \bar{z}^0}{\sigma_0}\right)^2}.$$

The random variable $Z^1$ is now defined by

$$Z^1 = dZ^0 + b,$$

which is again Gaussian with mean

$$\bar{z}^1 = \mathbb{E}[dZ^0 + b] = d\bar{z}^0 + b,$$

and variance

$$\sigma_1^2 = \mathbb{E}[(dZ^0 + b - \bar{z}^1)^2] = d^2\mathbb{E}[(Z^0 - \bar{z}^0)^2] = d^2\sigma_0^2.$$

By induction, $Z^n$ is Gaussian for $n \geq 0$, and the mean and variance are obtained from the recursions

$$\bar{z}^{n+1} = d\bar{z}^n + b, \quad \sigma_{n+1}^2 = d^2\sigma_n^2.$$

We denote the marginal distribution of $Z^n$ by $\pi_{Z^n}(z) = \mathrm{n}(z; \bar{z}^n, \sigma_n^2)$. Note that $Z^n$ and $Z^{n+1}$ are fully correlated since

$$\mathbb{E}[(Z^n - \bar{z}^n)(Z^{n+1} - \bar{z}^{n+1})] = \mathbb{E}[d(Z^n - \bar{z}^n)(Z^n - \bar{z}^n)] = d\sigma_n^2,$$

and the correlation becomes

$$\mathrm{corr}(Z^n, Z^{n+1}) = \frac{\mathbb{E}[(Z^n - \bar{z}^n)(Z^{n+1} - \bar{z}^{n+1})]}{\mathbb{E}[(Z^n - \bar{z}^n)^2]^{1/2}\,\mathbb{E}[(Z^{n+1} - \bar{z}^{n+1})^2]^{1/2}} = \begin{cases} 1 & \text{if } d > 0, \\ -1 & \text{if } d < 0. \end{cases}$$

This is, of course, not surprising since $Z^n$ and $Z^{n+1}$ are connected by a deterministic linear map.

If the parameter $d$ is chosen such that $|d| < 1$, then $\sigma_n \to 0$ as $n \to \infty$ and $\bar{z}^n$ tends to $\bar{z}^\infty = b/(1-d)$ as $n \to \infty$. Hence $\pi_n$ converges to the Dirac delta function $\delta(z - \bar{z}^\infty)$ as $n \to \infty$. On the other hand, if $|d| > 1$, the variances increase without bound and the mean tends to $\pm\infty$ unless $\bar{z}^0 = b = 0$. The particular case $d = 1$ and $b = 0$ leads to $\bar{z}^{n+1} = \bar{z}^n$ and $\sigma_{n+1} = \sigma_n$. In this case, the distribution $\pi_n$ is stationary, i.e., $\pi_n = \pi_0$ for all $n \geq 1$.

These considerations can be generalised to multivariate iterations

$$z^{n+1} = Dz^n + b, \tag{4.4}$$

$z^n \in \mathbb{R}^{N_z}$, in which case the mean of the associated random variables $Z^n$ is recursively given by

$$\bar{z}^{n+1} = D\bar{z}^n + b,$$

and the covariance matrices $P^n$ follow the recursion

$$
\begin{aligned}
P^{n+1} &= \mathbb{E}[(Z^{n+1} - \bar{z}^{n+1})(Z^{n+1} - \bar{z}^{n+1})^{\mathrm{T}}] \\
&= D\mathbb{E}[(Z^n - \bar{z}^n)(Z^n - \bar{z}^n)^{\mathrm{T}}]D^{\mathrm{T}} \\
&= DP^n D^{\mathrm{T}} .
\end{aligned}
$$

Furthermore, since (i) the degree of a polynomial $q(z)$ remains invariant under linear transformations of type (4.4) and (ii) any quadratic polynomial can be written as

$$q(z) = \frac{1}{2}(z - m)^{\mathrm{T}} P^{-1}(z - m) + c,$$

with $m, c \in \mathbb{R}^{N_z}$, $P \in \mathbb{R}^{N_z \times N_z}$ appropriately chosen, we may conclude that Gaussian PDFs remain Gaussian under any linear transformation and the marginal distribution of $Z^n$ is given by the PDF

$$\pi_{Z^n}(z) = \mathrm{n}(z; \bar{z}^n, P^n) = \frac{1}{(2\pi)^{N_z/2}|P^n|^{1/2}} \exp\left(-\frac{1}{2}(z - \bar{z}^n)^{\mathrm{T}}(P^n)^{-1}(z - \bar{z}^n)\right).$$

---

The probabilistic interpretation of dynamical systems is essential for quantifying forecast uncertainties arising from uncertainties in the initial conditions. At the same time we have seen in Chapter 1 that such uncertainties can be reduced by estimating initial conditions from available observations. Therefore we briefly discuss the relation between observations and initial conditions within an idealised dynamical systems perspective. We assume that we are given a dynamical system (4.1) with a unique attractor $\mathcal{A}$. We also assume that we have a scalar-valued forward or observation operator $h : \mathbb{R}^{N_z} \to \mathbb{R}$ and a sequence of observations $y^k \in \mathbb{R}$ for $k = 1, \ldots, N_{\mathrm{A}}$. These observations are related to an initial state $z^0$ of the dynamical system through

$$y^k = h(\psi^k(z^0)). \tag{4.5}$$

In other words these observations do not contain measurement errors and they are generated by our model. The goal is to reconstruct $z^0$ from the $N_{\mathrm{A}}$ observations. This is possible through the following fundamental result in dynamical systems theory.

**Theorem 4.7** (Takens' theorem)   Let $\psi$ be a smooth and invertible dynamical system with a unique attractor $\mathcal{A}$, let $h$ be a smooth forward operator, and let $\{y^k\}_{k=1}^{N_{\mathrm{A}}}$ be a sequence of noise-free observations given by (4.5) with $z^0 \in \mathcal{A}$. Then it is a generic property that $z^0 \in \mathcal{A}$ can be determined uniquely from the discrete set of observations $\{y^k\}_{k=1}^{N_{\mathrm{A}}}$, provided that $N_{\mathrm{A}} \geq 2N_z + 1$.

*Proof*   See Takens (1981) and Collet & Eckmann (2006).                    □

If we replace the sequence $\{y^k\}_{k=1}^{N_A}$ by noisy observations $\{y_{\text{obs}}^k\}_{k=1}^{N_A}$, such as those constructed in Chapter 1, the overdetermined system of equations

$$y_{\text{obs}}^k = h(\psi^k(z^0)), \qquad k = 1, \ldots, N_A \geq 2N_z + 1,$$

does not have a solution $z^0 \in \mathbb{R}^{N_z}$, in general. This situation can be compared to that of an overdetermined linear system of equations

$$Az = b \tag{4.6}$$

with $b \in \mathbb{R}^{N_A}$, $z \in \mathbb{R}^{N_z}$ and $N_z < N_A$. If (i) $A$ has rank $N_z$, and (ii) $b$ lies in the image of $A$, then there is a unique solution $z$ to this system of equations. However, if we perturb $b$ to become $\hat{b}$ such that $\hat{b}$ is no longer in the image of $A$, then there is no solution. It becomes necessary to replace (4.6) by the *least squares formulation*

$$z_* = \arg \min_{z \in \mathbb{R}^{N_z}} \|Az - \hat{b}\|^2,$$

which we have already encountered in Chapter 1. This discussion suggests that we should replace (4.5) by the minimisation of

$$L(z^0) = \frac{1}{2} \sum_{k=1}^{N_A} \left( y_{\text{obs}}^k - h(\psi^k(z^0)) \right)^2, \tag{4.7}$$

over initial conditions $z^0$, which is the same nonlinear least squares data assimilation formulation (1.20) from Chapter 1. Provided that (i) the differences between $y^k$ and $y_{\text{obs}}^k$ are sufficiently small and that (ii) we have enough observations, i.e., $N_A \geq 2N_z + 1$, we can generically expect that the minimisation problem (4.7) has a unique global minimiser.

We mention in passing that the bound $N_A \geq 2N_z + 1$ on the necessary number of observations can be improved to $N_A \geq 2N_A + 1$, where $N_A$ denotes the *box-counting dimension* of the attractor $\mathcal{A}$. We refer the reader to the dynamical systems literature for a mathematical definition of attractor dimension, but remark that the Lorenz-63 system possesses an attractor of box-counting dimension $N_A \approx 2.06$. Recall that we used $N_A = 5$ for the numerical experiments in Example 1.8, which is close to the theoretical bound of $N_A \geq 5.12$.

Our discussion has given a heuristic justification to the method of least squares as a tool for estimating model states from sufficiently long and accurate sequences of observations. In practice, state estimation problems typically have $N_z \gg N_A$ or $N_A \gg N_A$, respectively. Then the method of least squares is bound to fail; the *inverse problem* of estimating the state $z^0 \in \mathbb{R}^{N_z}$ from observations $\{y_{\text{obs}}^k\}_{k=1}^{N_A}$ becomes *ill posed*. This means that either estimates are not uniquely defined or they do not depend continuously on the observations. We will learn more about ill-posed inverse problems in Chapter 5, and about associated data assimilation techniques in the second part of this book.

Let us return to the discussion of dynamical systems without reference to random motion generated by modified tent map

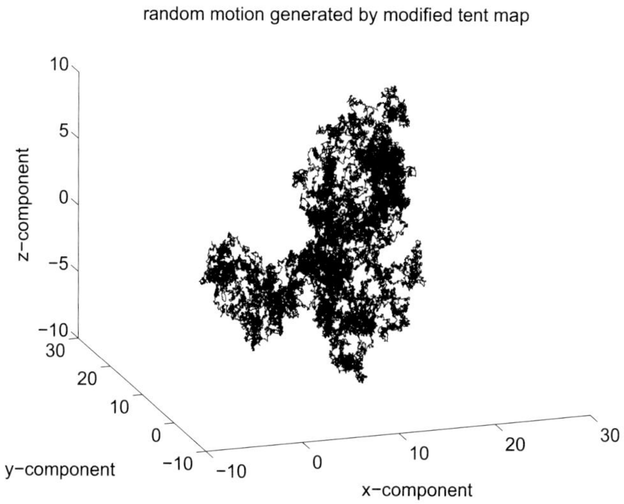

**Figure 4.2** Trajectory from a simulation with non-autonomous forcing in $\mathbb{R}^3$. Although the forcing is generated by a deterministic tent map, the trajectory resembles a "random walk".

observational data. So far we have exclusively discussed autonomous dynamical systems. We now turn our attention to non-autonomous systems. Recall that we introduced a non-autonomous forcing term in Example 1.1. We will investigate its impact in the following example with the drift term $f(z)$ set equal to zero for simplicity.

**Example 4.8** We consider the iteration

$$x^{n+1} = x^n + \delta t g_1^n, \tag{4.8}$$
$$y^{n+1} = y^n + \delta t g_2^n, \tag{4.9}$$
$$z^{n+1} = z^n + \delta t g_3^n, \tag{4.10}$$

in $\mathbb{R}^3$ with step-size $\delta t = 0.001$, initial condition

$$x^0 = y^0 = z^0 = 0,$$

and with the non-autonomous forcing $g(t_n) = g^n = (g_1^n, g_2^n, g_3^n)^{\mathrm{T}} \in \mathbb{R}^3$ generated as follows. Set $a = 1/\sqrt{\delta t}$ and, for $n \geq 0$, define recursively

$$g_i^{n+1} = \begin{cases} 1.99999 g_i^n + a/2 & \text{if } g_i^n \in [-a/2, 0), \\ -1.99999 g_i^n + a/2 & \text{otherwise,} \end{cases} \tag{4.11}$$

with initial values $g_1^0 = a(2^{-1/2} - 1/2)$, $g_2^0 = a(3^{-1/2} - 1/2)$, and $g_3^0 = a(5^{-1/2} - 1/2)$. Recall that $g_i^n \in [-a/2, a/2]$.

The resulting trajectory is stored over a time interval $t_0 = 0$ to $t_{\text{end}} = 200$ in intervals of $\Delta t_{\text{out}} = 0.05$. For later reference these trajectory values are denoted

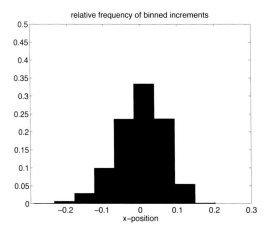

relative frequency of binned increments

**Figure 4.3** Relative frequency of binned solution increments $\Delta x^k := x(t_k) - x(t_{k-1})$ produced by the modified tent map iteration (4.8) with increments taken over time intervals $\Delta t_{\text{out}} = 0.05$.

by $x(t_k)$, $y(t_k)$, and $z(t_k)$, respectively, with $t_k = k\Delta t_{\text{out}}$ for $k \geq 0$. See Figure 4.2 for the numerical results.

The trajectory clearly displays "random walk" behaviour in $\mathbb{R}^3$. In order to analyse this phenomenon in more detail we define solution increments

$$\Delta x^k = x(t_k) - x(t_{k-1}),$$

for $k \geq 1$ with corresponding expressions for $\Delta y^k$ and $\Delta z^k$. Relative frequencies of the $\Delta x^k$ values are displayed in Figure 4.3. We approximate this distribution by a Gaussian with mean zero and variance $\sigma_x^2 \approx 0.0838\Delta t_{\text{out}}$.

We also compute the (normalised) autocorrelation coefficients (see Definition 4.19 later in this chapter)

$$C(\tau) = \frac{\sum_{k\geq 1} \Delta x^k \Delta x^{k+\tau}}{\sum_{k\geq 1} \Delta x^k \Delta x^k},$$

for $\tau = 0, 1, \ldots, 10$. By definition, $C(0) = 1$ and all other coefficients are found to be smaller than $10^{-2}$ in absolute value. In other words, increments can be treated as mutually uncorrelated. These findings suggest that we could approximate the iteration

$$x^{n+1} = x^n + \delta t g_1^n, \tag{4.12}$$

and the resulting output sequence $\{x(t_k)\}_{k\geq 0}$ with a stochastic difference equation

$$x(t_{k+1}) = x(t_k) + \xi^k, \tag{4.13}$$

where the increments $\{\xi^k\}$ are realisations of independent and Gaussian distributed random variables $\{\Xi^k\}$ with mean zero and variance $\sigma_x^2 \approx 0.0838\Delta t_{\text{out}}$. The same stochastic difference equations can be derived for the other two components of the state vector. We display a simulation result using these stochastic difference equations in Figure 4.4. The stochastic model (4.13) provides us with

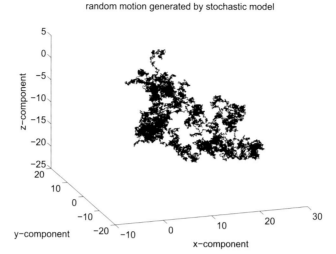

**Figure 4.4** Trajectory from the stochastic difference equation (4.13) in $x(k\Delta t_{\text{out}})$ and from related equations in $y(k\Delta t_{\text{out}})$ and $z(k\Delta t_{\text{out}})$. This trajectory should be compared qualitatively to the one displayed in Figure 4.2. Note, however, that we only see a particular realisation of our stochastic model. Hence the trajectories in both figures should not be compared on a point-wise level.

a simplified, imperfect model for the reference system (4.12). We will come back to this point later in this chapter.

We would like to incorporate random processes such as the stochastic recursion (4.13) into our probabilistic view of dynamical systems. We start the discussion with the following example.

**Example 4.9** We consider a sequence of univariate random variables $\{Z^n\}_{n\geq 0}$ defined by the recursion

$$Z^{n+1} = Z^n + \Xi^n, \quad n = 0, 1, 2, \dots \quad . \tag{4.14}$$

Here $\Xi^n \sim N(0, 1)$ are assumed to be independent with respect to each other and to $\{Z^k\}_{k=0}^n$ (but not $Z^k$ for $k > n$, of course). We will discuss this recursion probabilistically, which means that we want to understand how the probability measures for the sequence of random variables $\{Z^n\}$ are related. The recursion requires an initial condition, i.e. a specification of the probability distribution of $Z^0$. For simplicity we choose the Dirac measure centred at $z = 0$, i.e., the random variable $Z^0$ takes the value $Z^0(\omega) = 0$ with probability one. Hence we may simply conclude that $Z^1$ is distributed according to $N(0, 1)$ since we know that $\Xi^0 \sim N(0, 1)$ and $Z^0 = 0$ almost surely.

Computing the distribution of $Z^2$ is more involved. First we assume the value of $Z^1$ is known to be $z^1$. Then the conditional distribution of $Z^2$, given that $Z^1 = z^1$, is

$$Z^2|z^1 = z^1 + \Xi^1 \sim \mathrm{N}(z^1, 1).$$

Consequently, the joint probability density for $(Z^1, Z^2)$ is given by

$$\pi_{Z^1 Z^2}(z^1, z^2) = \frac{1}{2\pi} e^{-\frac{1}{2}(z^2 - z^1)^2} e^{-\frac{1}{2}(z^1)^2}.$$

The marginal distribution for $Z^2$, i.e. the distribution for $Z^2$ only, is obtained by integrating over $z = z^1$,

$$\begin{aligned}
\pi_{Z^2}(z') &= \frac{1}{2\pi} \int_{\mathbb{R}} e^{-\frac{1}{2}(z'-z)^2} e^{-\frac{1}{2}z^2} \mathrm{d}z \\
&= \frac{1}{2\pi} \int_{\mathbb{R}} e^{-\frac{1}{4}(z')^2} e^{-(z-z'/2)^2} \mathrm{d}z \\
&= \frac{1}{2\sqrt{\pi}} e^{-\frac{1}{4}(z')^2}.
\end{aligned}$$

Hence $Z^2 \sim \mathrm{N}(0, 2)$ and we find that

$$\pi_{Z^{n+1}}(z') = \int_{\mathbb{R}} \frac{1}{\sqrt{2\pi}} e^{-\frac{1}{2}(z'-z)^2} \pi_{Z^n}(z) \mathrm{d}z, \quad n \geq 0,$$

by induction. We see that the conditional PDF

$$\pi_{Z^{n+1}}(z'|z) = \frac{1}{\sqrt{2\pi}} e^{-\frac{1}{2}(z'-z)^2}$$

plays the role of a *transition probability density*. Since this PDF does not depend on time, we will drop the subscript and use the simpler notation $\pi(z'|z)$.

---

These Gaussian recursions are examples of (discrete-time) *stochastic processes*, which we now discuss in more generality.

**Definition 4.10** (Stochastic process)   Let $T$ be a set of indices. A *stochastic process* is a family $\{Z^t\}_{t \in T}$ of random variables $Z^t : \Omega \to \mathcal{Z}$ with joint probability space $(\Omega, \mathcal{F}, \mathbb{P})$.

The variable $t$ typically corresponds to time; we distinguish between continuous time $t \in [0, t_{\mathrm{end}}] \subset \mathbb{R}$ and discrete time $t_n = n\delta t$, $n \in \{0, 1, 2, \ldots\} = T$, with time increment $\delta t > 0$. In the discrete-time setting we generally prefer $Z^n$ to $Z^{t_n}$. We will also use the notation $Z(t)$ or $Z(t_n)$, respectively, whenever superscript indices would be more confusing.

A stochastic process can be seen as a function of two arguments: $t$ and $\omega$. For fixed $\omega \in \Omega$, $Z^t(\omega)$ becomes a function of $t \in T$, which we call a realisation or trajectory of the stochastic process. In the case of continuous processes, we will only consider processes for which $Z^t(\omega)$ is continuous in $t$. Alternatively, we can fix a time $t \in T$ and consider the random variable $Z^t(\cdot)$ and its distribution (as we did when we obtained the marginal distribution for $Z^2$ above). More generally, we can consider $l$-tuples $(t_1, t_2, \ldots, t_l)$ and associated $l$-tuples of random variables $(Z^{t_1}(\cdot), Z^{t_2}(\cdot), \ldots, Z^{t_l}(\cdot))$ with their joint distributions. This leads to concepts such as autocorrelation, which we shall discuss later in this chapter.

In Example 4.9, we introduced the idea of a transition probability density which allowed us to compute the distribution for $Z^{n+1}$ from that for $Z^n$. This generalises to the concept of Markov processes for discrete-time processes.

**Definition 4.11** (Discrete-time Markov processes)   The discrete-time stochastic process $\{Z^n\}_{n \in T}$ with $\mathcal{Z} = \mathbb{R}^{N_z}$ and $T = \{0, 1, 2, \ldots\}$ is called a (time-independent) *Markov process* if its joint PDFs can be written as

$$\pi_{Z^0 \ldots Z^n}(z^0, z^1, \ldots, z^n) = \pi(z^n | z^{n-1}) \pi(z^{n-1} | z^{n-2}) \cdots \pi(z^1 | z^0) \pi_{Z^0}(z^0) \quad (4.15)$$

for all $n \in \{1, 2, \ldots\} = T$. The associated marginal distributions

$$\pi_{Z^n}(z^n) = \int_{\mathcal{Z}} \cdots \int_{\mathcal{Z}} \pi_{Z^0 \ldots Z^n}(z^0, z^1, \ldots, z^n) dz^0 \cdots dz^{n-1},$$

i.e., the probability density functions for $Z^n$, $n = 1, 2, \ldots$, satisfy the *Chapman–Kolmogorov equation*

$$\pi_{Z^{n+1}}(z') = \int_{\mathcal{Z}} \pi(z' | z) \pi_{Z^n}(z) dz, \quad (4.16)$$

from which the marginal distributions can be computed recursively for given initial $\pi_{Z^0}$ in order to yield the family $\{\pi_{Z^n}\}_{n \in T}$. A Markov process is called *time dependent* if the conditional PDF $\pi(z' | z)$ depends on the time level $n$.

The Chapman–Kolmogorov equation (4.16) can be written in more abstract form as a linear iteration

$$\pi_{Z^{n+1}} = \mathcal{P} \pi_{Z^n}, \quad (4.17)$$

where the operator $\mathcal{P}$ is called the *transition operator*.[2]

Equation (4.15) for a Markov process should be compared with the disintegration formula in Equation (2.4) which is valid for arbitrary stochastic processes. Hence the above definition is equivalent to the more traditional definition which states that a process is Markov if the conditional distributions $\pi_{Z^n}(z^n | z^0, z^1, \ldots, z^{n-1})$, $n \geq 1$, satisfy

$$\pi_{Z^n}(z^n | z^0, z^1, \ldots, z^{n-1}) = \pi(z^n | z^{n-1}).$$

We also find that the Chapman–Kolmogorov equation (4.16) is obtained from the joint PDF

$$\pi_{Z^n Z^{n+1}}(z^n, z^{n+1}) = \pi(z^{n+1} | z^n) \pi_{Z^n}(z^n),$$

followed by marginalisation,

$$\pi_{Z^{n+1}}(z^{n+1}) = \int_{\mathcal{Z}} \pi_{Z^n Z^{n+1}}(z, z^{n+1}) dz,$$

---

[2] Transition operators will be discussed in more detail in Chapter 5.

to obtain $\pi_{Z^{n+1}}(z^{n+1})$.

In the context of forecasting, if the mechanistic model used for predictions is a discrete Markov process, and $\pi_0$ represents our uncertainty in the system state at time level $n = 0$, then repeated iteration of the Chapman–Kolmogorov equation provides our uncertainty in the system state, based on the model, at later times. This allows for a practical implementation since having calculated $z^{n+1}$ from $z^n$, $z^n$ can be discarded as it is not required to compute $z^{n+2}$. The Chapman–Kolmogorov equation is a crucial tool in propagating our uncertainty forwards in time using the mechanistic model.

---

**Example 4.12**   We consider a diffeomorphism $\psi : \mathcal{B} \to \mathcal{B}$ with $\mathcal{B} \subset \mathbb{R}^{N_z}$ and the associated dynamical system (4.1). If we view the initial condition as the realisation of a random variable $Z^0 \sim \pi_0$, then the dynamical system gives rise to a Markov process with (formal) transition probability density

$$\pi(z'|z) = \delta(z' - \psi(z)).$$

More precisely, it holds that $\mu(\mathrm{d}z'|z) = \mu_{\psi(z)}(\mathrm{d}z')$ in terms of probability measures. We have already encountered such transition probabilities in the context of transport maps in Chapter 2 and recall that

$$\pi_{Z^{n+1}}(z') = \pi_{Z^n}(\psi^{-1}(z'))|D\psi^{-1}(z')|$$

is the transformation formula for the associated marginal PDFs if $\psi$ is a diffeomorphism. Indeed,

$$\begin{aligned}
\pi_{Z^{n+1}}(z') &= \int_{\mathcal{B}} \pi(z'|z)\,\pi_{Z^n}(z)\mathrm{d}z \\
&= \int_{\mathcal{B}} \delta(z' - \psi(z))\,\pi_{Z^n}(z)\mathrm{d}z \\
&= \int_{\psi^{-1}(\mathcal{B})} \delta(z' - \hat{z})\pi_{Z^n}(\psi^{-1}(\hat{z}))|D\psi^{-1}(\hat{z})|\mathrm{d}\hat{z} \\
&= \pi_{Z^n}(\psi^{-1}(z'))|D\psi^{-1}(z')|.
\end{aligned}$$

---

We return to our mechanistic model (1.18) and combine it with our findings from Example 4.8 in order to find a better mechanistic model for our surrogate physical process, in terms of a stochastic Markov process.

---

**Example 4.13**   In our example data assimilation problem in Chapter 1, the surrogate physical process (1.2) and the mechanistic model (1.18) differ only by the missing non-autonomous driving term $g(t)$. In addition we have just found in Example 4.8 that the non-autonomous driving terms $(g_1^n, g_2^n, g_3^n)^{\mathrm{T}}$ give rise to a random walk like behaviour, which can be modelled by a stochastic difference equation. This suggests that we could replace the mechanistic model from

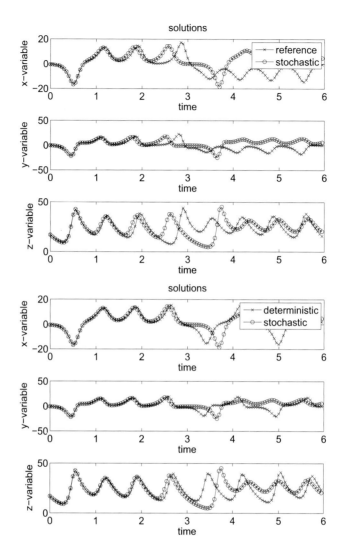

**Figure 4.5** Comparison between the behaviour of our modified stochastic model and the reference trajectory $z_{\text{ref}}(t)$, under the assumption that both start from the same initial condition at time $l = 0$. Note that the results (top panel) are similar to those displayed in Figure 1.9 for the deterministic model. We also compare the results from the deterministic and the stochastic models (bottom panel). The growth of uncertainty in the forecast is relatively well captured even though it appears slightly delayed when compared to the results in the top panel.

Example 1.7 by the following stochastic difference equations

$$x^{n+1} = x^n + \delta t \sigma (y^n - x^n) + \sqrt{\delta t} \xi_1^n, \tag{4.18}$$

$$y^{n+1} = y^n + \delta t \left( x^n (\rho - z^n) - y^n \right) + \sqrt{\delta t} \xi_2^n, \tag{4.19}$$

$$z^{n+1} = z^n + \delta t \left( x^n y^n - \beta z^n \right) + \sqrt{\delta t} \xi_3^n, \tag{4.20}$$

where $\{\xi_i^n\}$ are now realisations of independent Gaussian random variables with mean zero and variance 0.0838. We will discuss the mathematical properties of such stochastic difference equations in more detail in the next section.

In a general modelling context, the precise nature of the non-autonomous driving terms $g_i^n$ in (1.2) would be unknown to us and the additional random terms in (4.18)–(4.20) would be called a *parametrisation*[3] of those driving terms. Since our stochastic parametrisation can only provide an approximation, (4.18)–(4.20) is still an imperfect model! In fact, when we replace the deterministic model from Example 1.7 by our new stochastic model, we find that the quality of the predictions does not improve. The shape of the attractor also does not change significantly. Compare Figures 4.5 and 4.6. These findings warrant an explanation. Our parametrisation was based on an interpretation of the non-autonomous forcing terms $g_i^n$ in (1.2) as realisations of a stochastic process. We do not have direct access to these realisations and replace them therefore by some realisations $\xi_i^n$. However, the probability that

$$\sqrt{\delta t}\xi_i^n = \delta t g_i^n$$

is zero. Whilst we do not expect the stochastic parametrisation to help to reproduce particular trajectories, they may help to improve probabilistic forecasts. We will readdress this issue later in this book when we discuss probabilistic forecasting and data assimilation algorithms.

---

We complete this section by a discussion of the linear transition operator (4.17) in the context of finite state space models.

**Definition 4.14** (Discrete state space random processes)   A finite state space random process $\{Z^n\}_{n \in T}$ is one in which $Z^n$ can only take a finite set of values for each $n$, taken from the same finite state space $\mathcal{B} \subset \mathbb{R}^{N_z}$. We write $\mathcal{B} = \{a_1, a_2, \ldots, a_M\}$. The probability distribution for the random variable $Z^n : \Omega \to \mathcal{B}$ is then entirely characterised by an $M$-tuple of non-negative numbers $p^n(a_i) = \mathbb{P}(Z^n = a_i)$, $i = 1, \ldots, M$, which satisfy $\sum_i p^n(a_i) = 1$. A discrete-time Markov process is then defined through transition probabilities $p_{ij} = \mathbb{P}(Z^{n+1} = a_i | Z^n = a_j)$, which we collect in an $M \times M$ *transition matrix* P. This transition matrix replaces the transition operator in (4.17) for stochastic processes with finite state space. We obtain the linear recursion

$$p^{n+1}(a_i) = \sum_{j=1}^{M} p_{ij}\, p^n(a_j).$$

A matrix P with entries $p_{ij} = (\text{P})_{ij}$ such that (i) $p_{ij} \geq 0$ and (ii) $\sum_i p_{ij} = 1$ is called a *stochastic matrix*. By definition, a transition matrix is always a stochastic matrix.

---

[3] This is a standard term in weather prediction, ocean and climate modelling to indicate a model term that is an inprecise representation of physical processes that are otherwise unrealisable within the model.

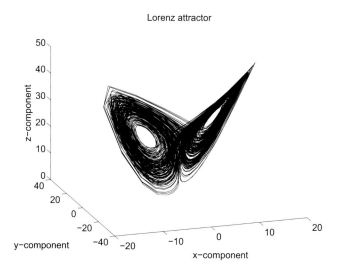

**Figure 4.6** Long trajectory from our improved mechanistic model which traces the model attractor. The shape of the attractor is nearly identical to the one displayed in Figure 1.8 for the model without stochastic driving terms.

Discrete state space random processes have many useful applications; in this book we shall discuss them as numerical discretisations of continuous state space processes. See Appendix 5.7.

## 4.2 Stochastic difference and differential equations

We will now examine the continuous time limit of stochastic difference models such as the one in Example 4.13. We start from the *stochastic difference equation*

$$Z^{n+1} = Z^n + \delta t f(Z^n) + \sqrt{2\delta t}\,\Xi^n, \quad t_{n+1} = t_n + \delta t, \tag{4.21}$$

where $\delta t > 0$ is a small parameter (the step-size), $f$ is a given (Lipschitz continuous) function, and $\Xi^n \sim \mathrm{N}(0, Q)$ are independent and identically distributed random variables with covariance matrix $Q$. Here we have written the stochastic difference equations directly in terms of the involved random variables $\{Z^n\}_{n\geq 0}$.

Equation (4.21) is a discrete-time Markov process, and so the time evolution of the associated marginal densities $\pi_{Z^n}$ is governed by the Chapman–Kolmogorov equation (4.16) with conditional PDF

$$\pi(z'|z) = \frac{1}{(4\pi\delta t)^{N_z/2}|Q|^{1/2}}$$

$$\times \exp\left(-\frac{1}{4\delta t}(z' - z - \delta t f(z))^{\mathrm{T}} Q^{-1}(z' - z - \delta t f(z))\right). \tag{4.22}$$

We wish to investigate the limit $\delta t \to 0$ for fixed final time $T > 0$. This can be achieved by defining $\delta t = T/N$ with $N \to \infty$ and iteration indices $n \in \{0, 1, \ldots, N\}$ in (4.21). Let us first consider the special case $N_z = 1$, $f(z) = 0$, and $Q = 1$ (univariate Gaussian random variable). We also drop the factor $\sqrt{2}$ in (4.21) and consider linear interpolation in between time-steps, i.e.,

$$Z(t) = Z^n + \sqrt{\delta t} \frac{t - t_n}{t_{n+1} - t_n} \Xi^n, \qquad t \in (t_n, t_{n+1}], \tag{4.23}$$

setting $Z^0(\omega) = 0$ with probability one. For each family of realisations $\{\xi^n = \Xi^n(\omega)\}_{n \geq 0}$ we obtain a piecewise linear and continuous function $Z(t, \omega)$. Furthermore, the limit $\delta t \to 0$ is well defined and the stochastic process $Z(t)$, $t \geq 0$, can be shown to converge weakly to a stochastic process called *Brownian motion*.[4]

**Definition 4.15** (Brownian motion)   Standard univariate *Brownian motion* is a stochastic process $W(t)$, $t \geq 0$, with the following properties:

(i) $W(0) = 0$,
(ii) realisations $W(t, \omega)$ are continuous in $t$,
(iii) $W(t_2) - W(t_1) \sim N(0, t_2 - t_1)$ for $t_2 > t_1 \geq 0$, and
(iv) increments $W(t_4) - W(t_3)$ and $W(t_2) - W(t_1)$ are mutually independent for $t_4 > t_3 \geq t_2 > t_1 \geq 0$.

It follows from our construction (4.23) that with probability one the Brownian motion is not differentiable, since

$$\frac{Z^{n+1} - Z^n}{\delta t} = \delta t^{-1/2} \Xi^n \sim N(0, \delta t^{-1})$$

and so the limit $\delta t \to 0$ is not well defined. Using the concept of Brownian motion, we can rewrite the stochastic difference equations (4.21) in the form

$$Z^{n+1} = Z^n + \delta t f(Z^n) + \sqrt{2} Q^{1/2} (W(t_{n+1}) - W(t_n)). \tag{4.24}$$

We now take the formal limit $\delta t \to 0$, which leads to a *stochastic differential equation* (SDE). While we will always use (4.24) and related approximations when doing computations, the underlying theory often manifests itself much more clearly in a SDE formulation. Below we summarise a few results particularly relevant in the context of this book. The reader is referred to Evans (2013) for more details. In particular, we must be careful with regard to the underlying stochastic calculus (Itô or Stratonovitch); this is not an issue for the simple SDEs considered in this chapter.

**Proposition 4.16** (Stochastic differential equation and Fokker–Planck equation) After taking the limit $\delta t \to 0$ in (4.24), we obtain the SDE

$$dZ = f(Z)dt + \sqrt{2} Q^{1/2} dW, \tag{4.25}$$

---

[4] A more rigorous discussion of Brownian motion can be found in Evans (2013).

where $W(t)$ denotes standard $N_z$-dimensional Brownian motion. The *Fokker–Planck equation*,

$$\frac{\partial \pi_Z}{\partial t} = -\nabla_z \cdot (\pi_Z f) + \nabla_z \cdot (Q \nabla_z \pi_Z), \qquad (4.26)$$

describes the time evolution of the marginal densities $\pi_Z(z, t)$. If $Q = 0$ (no noise), Equation (4.26) becomes

$$\frac{\partial \pi_Z}{\partial t} = \mathcal{L} \pi_Z, \qquad (4.27)$$

in which case it is called the Liouville, transport or continuity equation, with operator $\mathcal{L}$ defined by

$$\mathcal{L} \pi := -\nabla_z \cdot (\pi f). \qquad (4.28)$$

The Fokker–Planck equation for stochastic differential equations is the limit of the Chapman–Kolmogorov equation for stochastic difference equations. It has the same interpretation in the context of forecasting: if our mechanistic model is a stochastic differential equation of the form (4.25), then the Fokker–Planck equation (4.26) allows us to propagate our uncertainty in the system state forward in time.

We now proceed with an outline of a proof.

*Proof*  See Evans (2013) on the existence and uniqueness theory for SDEs. The difference equation (4.21) is called the Euler–Maruyama method for approximating the SDE (4.25). See Higham (2001) and Kloeden & Platen (1992) for a discussion on the convergence of (4.21) to (4.25) as $\delta t \to 0$. Here we shall provide a heuristic derivation of the Fokker–Planck equation (4.26). We formally use

$$Z^{n+1} - Z^n \to \mathrm{d}Z(t_n), \quad \delta t f(Z^n) \to f(Z(t_n))\mathrm{d}t, \quad W(t_{n+1}) - W(t_n) \to \mathrm{d}W(t_n).$$

The right hand side of (4.26) is the linear combination of a drift and a diffusion term. To simplify the discussion we derive both terms separately from (4.21) by first considering $f = 0$, $Q \neq 0$ and then $Q = 0$, $f \neq 0$. In order to simplify the derivation of the diffusion term even further, we also assume $z \in \mathbb{R}$ and $Q = 1$. In other words, we shall first show that if the discrete process $\{Z^n\}$ satisfies the stochastic difference equation

$$Z^{n+1} = Z^n + \sqrt{2}(W(t_{n+1}) - W(t_n)),$$

then the Chapman–Kolmogorov equation for the sequence of marginal PDFs $\{\pi_{Z^n}\}$ converges to the diffusion equation

$$\frac{\partial \pi_Z}{\partial t} = \frac{\partial^2 \pi_Z}{\partial z^2}.$$

In the case $f(z) = 0$, $Q = 1$, $N_z = 1$, the conditional PDF (4.22) reduces to

$$\pi(z'|z) = (4\pi \delta t)^{-1/2} \exp\left(-\frac{(z'-z)^2}{4\delta t}\right).$$

Under the variable substitution $\Delta z = z - z'$, the discrete-time Chapman–Kolmogorov equation (4.16) becomes

$$\pi^{n+1}(z') = \int_{\mathbb{R}} \frac{1}{\sqrt{4\pi\delta t}} e^{-\Delta z^2/(4\delta t)} \pi^n(z' + \Delta z) \mathrm{d}\Delta z, \tag{4.29}$$

where we have introduced the abbreviation $\pi^n(z)$ for the marginal distributions $\pi_{Z^n}(z)$. We now expand $\pi^n(z' + \Delta z)$ in $\Delta z$ about $\Delta z = 0$, i.e.,

$$\pi^n(z' + \Delta z) = \pi^n(z') + \Delta z \frac{\partial \pi^n}{\partial z}(z') + \frac{\Delta z^2}{2} \frac{\partial^2 \pi^n}{\partial z^2}(z') + \cdots,$$

and substitute the expansion into (4.29):

$$\begin{aligned}
\pi^{n+1}(z') &= \left( \int_{\mathbb{R}} \frac{1}{\sqrt{4\pi\delta t}} e^{-\Delta z^2/(4\delta t)} \mathrm{d}\Delta z \right) \pi^n(z') \\
&+ \left( \int_{\mathbb{R}} \frac{1}{\sqrt{4\pi\delta t}} e^{-\Delta z^2/(4\delta t)} \Delta z \mathrm{d}\Delta z \right) \frac{\partial \pi^n}{\partial z}(z') \\
&+ \frac{1}{2} \left( \int_{\mathbb{R}} \frac{1}{\sqrt{4\pi\delta t}} e^{-\Delta z^2/(4\delta t)} \Delta z^2 \mathrm{d}\Delta z \right) \frac{\partial^2 \pi^n}{\partial z^2}(z') + \cdots.
\end{aligned}$$

The three integrals correspond to the zeroth, first and second-order moments of the Gaussian distribution with mean zero and variance $2\delta t$. Hence their value is known, and we obtain

$$\pi^{n+1}(z') = \pi^n(z') + \delta t \frac{\partial^2 \pi^n}{\partial z^2}(z') + \cdots.$$

It can be shown that the neglected higher-order terms have magnitude $\mathcal{O}(\delta t^2)$. Therefore

$$\frac{\pi^{n+1}(z') - \pi^n(z')}{\delta t} = \frac{\partial^2 \pi^n}{\partial z^2}(z') + \mathcal{O}(\delta t),$$

and the diffusion equation is obtained upon taking the limit $\delta t \to 0$.

We now show that if the discrete process $\{Z^n\}$ satisfies the difference equation

$$Z^{n+1} = \psi(Z^n) := Z^n + \delta t f(Z^n),$$

then the Chapman–Kolmogorov equation for the sequence of marginal PDFs $\{\pi^n\}$ convergences to Liouville's equation (4.27). For $\delta t$ sufficiently small, $\psi$ is a diffeomorphism, and we may use the transformation rule for PDFs under a diffeomorphism $\psi$ (compare Example 4.12) in the form

$$\pi^{n+1}(\psi(z))|D\psi(z)| = \pi^n(z). \tag{4.30}$$

For $f$ and $\pi^{n+1}$ sufficiently smooth,[5] we may expand $|D\psi(z)|$ and $\pi^{n+1}(\psi(z))$ as power series in $\delta t$, to obtain

$$\pi^{n+1}(\psi(z)) = \pi^{n+1}(z) + \delta t \nabla_z \pi^{n+1}(z) \cdot f(z) + \mathcal{O}(\delta t^2), \tag{4.31}$$

$$|D\psi(z)| = 1 + \delta t \nabla_z \cdot f(z) + \mathcal{O}(\delta t^2), \tag{4.32}$$

---

[5]  A more rigorous proof requires careful examination of when, and in what sense, these formulas are valid.

and (4.30) then implies

$$\pi^n = \pi^{n+1} + \delta t \pi^{n+1} \nabla_z \cdot f + \delta t (\nabla_z \pi^{n+1}) \cdot f + \mathcal{O}(\delta t^2),$$

and

$$\frac{\pi^{n+1} - \pi^n}{\delta t} = -\nabla_x \cdot (\pi^{n+1} f) + \mathcal{O}(\delta t).$$

Taking the limit $\delta t \to 0$, we obtain (4.27). $\qquad \square$

In data assimilation, practical computations will rely on a chosen, fixed step-size $\delta t > 0$ for the dynamical model, which may be different from observation intervals $\Delta t_{\text{out}} = N_{\text{out}} \delta t$. In this context it is helpful to generalise the Chapman–Kolmogorov equation (4.16) to its $N_{\text{out}}$-fold recursive application which propagates a PDF $\pi_{Z^n}$ to $\pi_{Z^{n+N_{\text{out}}}}$ according to

$$\pi_{Z^{n+N_{\text{out}}}}(z) = \int_{\mathbb{R}^{N_z}} \cdots \int_{\mathbb{R}^{N_z}} \pi(z|z') \, \pi(z'|z'') \cdots$$
$$\pi(z^{(N_{\text{out}}-1)}|z^{(N_{\text{out}})}) \, \pi_{Z^n}(z^{(N_{\text{out}})}) \, \mathrm{d}z' \cdots \mathrm{d}z^{(N_{\text{out}})}$$
$$= \int_{\mathbb{R}^{N_z}} \pi_{N_{\text{out}}}(z|\tilde{z}) \, \pi_{Z^n}(\tilde{z}) \, \mathrm{d}\tilde{z}, \qquad (4.33)$$

where the one-step transition probability $\pi(z|z')$ is given by (4.22) and the implied $N_{\text{out}}$-step transition probability is denoted by $\pi_{N_{\text{out}}}(z|z')$. Let $\mathcal{P}_{\delta t}$ denote the transition operator (recall Definition 4.17) defined by (4.16) and (4.22). Similarly, let $\mathcal{P}_{\Delta t_{\text{out}}}$ be the transition operator associated with (4.33). Then

$$\mathcal{P}_{\Delta t_{\text{out}}} = \underbrace{\mathcal{P}_{\delta t} \cdots \mathcal{P}_{\delta t}}_{N_{\text{out}} \text{ times}} = (\mathcal{P}_{\delta t})^{N_{\text{out}}}.$$

The operator $\mathcal{P}_{\Delta t_{\text{out}}}$ transforms our uncertainty in the system state from one observation time to another.

We now discuss an important subclass of Markov processes,[6] known as *ergodic* processes, where it is possible make quantitative statements about averages over long time intervals. We start from the definition of the invariant measure.

**Definition 4.17** (Invariant measure)   Let $\pi_Z^*$ be a steady state solution to (4.17) (or (4.26) in the case of time-continuous processes). Then $\mu_Z^*(\mathrm{d}z) = \pi_Z^* \mathrm{d}z$ is called an *invariant measure* for the underlying Markov process.

If the random variable $Z^0$ has probability distribution with an invariant measure as its marginal PDF, i.e., $\pi_{Z^0} = \pi_Z^*$, then all subsequent random variables $Z^n$ with $n > 0$ will have the same marginal PDF. This means that expectation values $\mathbb{E}[f(Z^n)]$ are independent of $n$, with value

$$\mathbb{E}[f(Z^n)] = \int_{\mathcal{Z}} f(z) \pi_Z^*(z) \mathrm{d}z.$$

Such processes are called *stationary*.

---

[6] Discussed here in the context of discrete-time processes.

More generally, let us assume that the iteration (4.17) has a unique invariant measure $\pi_Z^*$ and that any initial PDF $\pi_{Z^0}$ converges to $\pi_Z^*$ in a weak sense, i.e.,

$$\mathbb{E}[g(Z^n)] \to \int_{\mathcal{Z}} g(z)\pi_Z^*(z)\mathrm{d}z$$

for all bounded and continuous functions $g$ as $n \to \infty$. This process of convergence is called *equilibration*, with $Z^n$ said to be "close to equilibrium" if $\pi_{Z^n} \approx \pi_Z^*(z)$. In other words, such a stochastic process becomes essentially stationary for $n$ sufficiently large, which motivates the following definition of ergodicity.

**Definition 4.18** (Ergodicity)   Let $\{Z^n\}$ be a discrete Markov process with unique invariant measure $\mu_Z^*$ and associated PDF $\pi_Z^*$. The process is said to be *ergodic* if time averages along specific process realisations $\{Z^n(\omega)\}$ converge almost surely to expectations with respect to $\pi_Z^*$, i.e.,

$$\lim_{N \to \infty} \frac{1}{N} \sum_{n=1}^{N} f(Z^n(\omega)) = \int_{\mathcal{Z}} f(z)\pi_Z^*(z)\mathrm{d}z,$$

for all functions $f$ with

$$\left| \int_{\mathcal{Z}} f(z)\pi_Z^*(z)\mathrm{d}z \right| < \infty.$$

Stochastic processes are often assumed to be ergodic, although it is only possible to prove ergodicity in special cases. Approximately speaking, a stochastic process is ergodic if the iterates of (4.17) converge to $\pi_Z^*$ sufficiently quickly for any initial PDF $\pi_{Z^0}$, and if the iterates decorrelate sufficiently rapidly. We will discuss a specific example in the context of Brownian dynamics in Chapter 5.

For ergodic processes, we can quantify the degree of independence between $Z^n$ and $Z^m$ for $n < m$, i.e. the amount of "memory" in the stochastic process, by using autocorrelation (the reader is reminded of Definition 2.17).

**Definition 4.19** (Autocorrelation)   Let $\{Z^n\}$ be a stochastic process in equilibrium, i.e., the process has invariant PDF $\pi_Z^*$, and $Z^0$ has PDF $\pi_Z^*$. Then the autocorrelation of the stochastic process is

$$C(\tau) = \frac{\mathbb{E}\left[(Z^{n+\tau} - \bar{z})(Z^n - \bar{z})\right]}{\mathbb{E}\left[(Z^n - \bar{z})^2\right]}, \quad \bar{z} = \int_{\mathcal{Z}} z\pi_Z^*(z)\mathrm{d}z,$$

for $\tau \geq 0$. If the stochastic process is ergodic, then this can be calculated from time averages along specific process realisations $\{Z^n(\omega)\}$,

$$C(\tau) = \frac{\lim_{N \to \infty} \frac{1}{N} \sum_{n=1}^{N} (Z^{n+\tau}(\omega) - \bar{z})(Z^n(\omega) - \bar{z})}{\lim_{N \to \infty} \frac{1}{N} \sum_{n=1}^{N} (Z^n(\omega) - \bar{z})^2}. \tag{4.34}$$

Equation (4.34) can be approximated by truncating after finite $N$, to provide an empirical estimate of independence of $Z^n$ and $Z^{n+\tau}$ for $\tau > 0$. This was used in Example 2.20 in Chapter 2, and Example 4.8 to test for near-independence of (deterministic) Markov processes.

## 4.3     Probabilistic forecasting and ensemble prediction

In probabilistic forecasting, our goal is to calculate marginal PDFs $\pi_Z(z,t)$ for a Markov process, given the initial PDF $\pi_Z(z,0)$. This is useful since we can use expectations to provide a forecast by computing the mean, together with variances and higher-order statistics that quantify the uncertainty. It may even be the case that the distribution becomes multimodal, suggesting very different outcomes are possible (for example, different possible tracks of a tropical storm). For high-dimensional models, the PDF $\pi_Z(z,t)$ is very unwieldy, and so we concentrate on computing expectations. This motivates a Monte Carlo approximation of the marginal PDFs $\pi_Z(z,t)$, $t \geq 0$, evolving under the SDE model (4.25).

**Definition 4.20** (Ensemble prediction)    A Monte Carlo approximation to the marginal PDFs $\pi_Z(z,t)$ which solve the Fokker–Planck equation (4.26) can be obtained from solving the SDEs

$$dz_i = f(z_i)dt + \sqrt{2}Q^{1/2}d\xi_i(t), \quad i = 1, \ldots, M, \tag{4.35}$$

where the processes $\{\xi_i(t)\}_{i=1}^M$ denote independent realisations of a standard $N_z$-dimensional Brownian motion $W(t) : \Omega \to \mathbb{R}^{N_z}$ and the initial conditions $z_i(0)$ are sampled independently from the initial PDF $\pi_Z(z,0)$. Approximations of expectations at later times $t > 0$ are obtained from

$$\bar{g}_M(t) = \frac{1}{M}\sum_{i=1}^{M} g(z_i(t)).$$

This approximation is an example of a *particle* or *ensemble prediction* method for the marginal PDFs; an analogous definition applies to stochastic difference equations (4.21).

We now discuss two examples.

---

**Example 4.21**    We return to the Lorenz-63 model with and without stochastic perturbations. We perform an ensemble prediction with the initial ensemble drawn from Gaussian distributions centred about the initial condition $z^0 = (x^0, y^0, z^0)$ given in Chapter 1 by (1.5) and variance 0.01 in each of the three components of the state vector. We then compute the empirical expectation value of the absolute value $|x(t)|$ of the x solution component, i.e.,

$$\overline{|x|}_M(t) = \frac{1}{M}\sum_{i=1}^{M} |x_i(t)|,$$

at initial time $t = 0$ and final time $t = 5$. We also estimate the variance

$$\mathrm{var}_M(t) = \frac{1}{M}\sum_{i=1}^{M}(|x_i(t)| - \overline{|x|}_M(t))^2.$$

Under the simplifying assumption of a Gaussian distribution, the 95% confidence

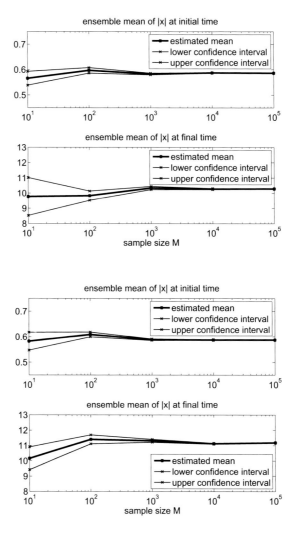

**Figure 4.7** Ensemble estimates for $\overline{|x|}$ and their confidence intervals for the deterministic Lorenz-63 model (see Example 4.2) in the top panel and the stochastically perturbed variant (see Example 4.13) for increasing ensemble size $M$ in the bottom panel. Both models display a similar behaviour. However the asymptotic values for $\overline{|x|}$ differ by about 10% at final time $t = 5$.

interval for the estimated expectation values is itself estimated by

$$\left[\overline{|x|}_M(t) - 1.96\sqrt{\frac{\mathrm{var}_M(t)}{M}}, \overline{|x|}_M(t) + 1.96\sqrt{\frac{\mathrm{var}_M(t)}{M}}\right].$$

The computed expectation values and the boundaries for their confidence intervals can be found in Figure 4.7 for the deterministic model (Example 4.2) as well as for the stochastically perturbed model (Example 4.13). The expectation values $\overline{|\mathbf{x}|}_M$ converge to approximately 11.16 for the stochastically perturbed model and 10.26 for the deterministic model, as the ensemble size $M$ is increased. There is also a systematic difference in the computed variance $\mathrm{var}_M(t)$. The deterministic model leads to a value of about 9.8 while the stochastically perturbed model leads to 12.5.

---

**Example 4.22** We consider the SDE

$$\mathrm{d}Z = \gamma(-Z^3 + Z)\mathrm{d}t + \sqrt{0.2}\mathrm{d}W(t), \tag{4.36}$$

on $\mathcal{Z} = \mathbb{R}$ for $\gamma > 0$. We note that

$$z^3 - z = \frac{\mathrm{d}}{\mathrm{d}z}\left(\frac{z^4}{4} - \frac{z^2}{2}\right),$$

i.e., the deterministic part of (4.36) is generated by the negative derivative of the potential

$$U(z) = \gamma\frac{z^4}{4} - \gamma\frac{z^2}{2}.$$

Stationary points of the deterministic part are characterised by $U'(z) = 0$, i.e., $0 = z(z^2 - 1)$ and we obtain three stationary points $z_0 = 0$, and $z_m = \pm 1$, respectively. Upon investigating the second derivative $U''(z) = 3z^2 - 1$, we find that $z_0 = 0$ is unstable (since $U$ is locally concave) while $z_m = \pm 1$ are stable (since $U$ is locally convex).

The shape of the potential $U$ is shown in Figure 4.8 for $1 \leq \gamma \leq 4$. We also show a typical trajectory for $\gamma = 1$ and $\gamma = 2$ which demonstrates that it becomes increasingly difficult for solutions to overcome the barrier between the two potential wells at $z_m = \pm 1$ in the limit of large $\gamma$. The occasions when $z(t)$ crosses this barrier becomes a *rare event*.[7]

We now use ensemble prediction to estimate the fraction of trajectories starting at $z_0 = 1$ that take a value $z(t) < 0$ at time $t = 1000$. The ensembles are generated numerically using the Euler–Maruyama method with step-size $\delta t = 0.01$. Table 4.1 shows the results as a function of the ensemble size and the parameter $\gamma$. A fraction of 0.5 implies that trajectories have statistically equilibrated while a small fraction implies that most trajectories have not been able to cross the barrier.

---

We mention that ensemble prediction leads to associated empirical measures

$$\mu_M(\mathrm{d}z, t) = \frac{1}{M}\sum_{i=1}^{M}\mu_{z_i(t)}(\mathrm{d}z) = \frac{1}{M}\sum_{i=1}^{M}\delta(z - z_i(t))\mathrm{d}z, \tag{4.37}$$

[7] The statistics of rare events is investigated under *extreme value theory* (EVT). In contrast with the laws of large numbers, as considered in Chapter 3, EVT deals with laws for small numbers. An introduction to EVT can be found in Coles (2001).

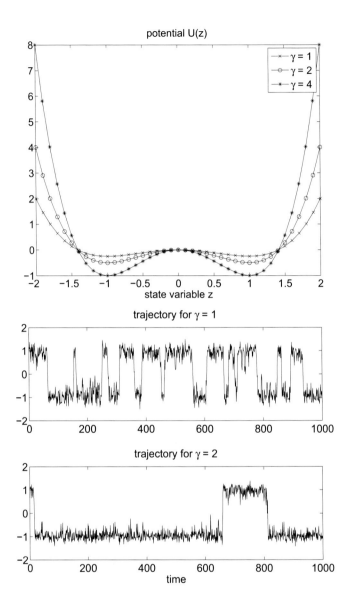

**Figure 4.8** We display the potential $U$ for different values of $\gamma$ in the top panel. The barrier between the two potential wells at $z_m = \pm 1$ increases as $\gamma$ increases. The effect on trajectories starting from $z_0 = 1$ can be seen in the bottom panel.

which provide a numerical approximation to uncertainties induced by uncertain initial conditions and stochastic forcing terms in an SDE model. These empirical measures were used in Example 4.22 to estimate the probability of a trajectory to be found in either the left or right potential well. These probabilities represent our uncertainty when forecasting whether a particular realisation $z(t)$ will satisfy

| $\gamma/M$ | 1 | 2 | 3 | 4 | 5 |
|---|---|---|---|---|---|
| 10 | 0.5 | 0.3 | 0.2 | 0 | 0 |
| 100 | 0.54 | 0.52 | 0.26 | 0.03 | 0.02 |
| 1000 | 0.512 | 0.515 | 0.26 | 0.043 | 0.002 |
| 10000 | 0.5009 | 0.4907 | 0.2539 | 0.0361 | 0.0044 |

Table 4.1 Fraction of trajectories starting from $z_0 = 1$ at $t = 0$ that take a value $z(t) < 0$ at $t = 1000$ in an ensemble of $M \in \{10, 100, 1000, 10000\}$ members and for parameter value $\gamma \in \{1, 2, 3, 4, 5\}$.

$z(t) > 0$ or $z(t) < 0$. However, it should be kept in mind that these uncertainties may not reflect forecast uncertainties with respect to the reference solution $z_{\text{ref}}(t)$, as introduced in Chapter 1 (or future partial observations of $z_{\text{ref}}(t)$), in the case of systematic model errors. We provide a brief discussion on this issue in the following section.

## 4.4 Scoring rules for probabilistic forecasting

We have seen that stochastic dynamical models, in the form of either a difference equation (4.21) or an SDE (4.25), allow us to forecast the PDFs $\pi_Z(z, t)$, $t \geq 0$, starting from some known initial PDF $\pi_Z(z, 0)$. Numerically, these PDFs can be approximated by ensemble prediction as discussed in the previous section; we obtain a good prediction of model statistics in the limit of large ensemble sizes. However, there will still be errors in the probabilistic forecast due to the use of an imperfect model (these could be numerical discretisation errors, or model errors such as incorrect values of parameters or simplifying assumptions in the model). In probabilistic forecasting, we need to assess the impact of these errors on statistics, which are the main "product" that we are interested in.

One difficulty in analysing the impact of model errors on statistics is that the model is of some physical system where we cannot measure the complete system state or construct exact solutions. One approach is to collect a time series of observations from the physical system, and to compare it with simulated observations from the model; this will determine how well *calibrated* the model is to the physical system.

We will assume that partial observations $y = h(z)$ of a physical process are available at equally spaced time instances $t_k = k\Delta t_{\text{out}}$, $k = 1, \ldots, N_{\text{obs}}$, with $\Delta t_{\text{out}} > 0$. We denote the observed values by $y_{\text{obs}}(t_k)$, and will ignore measurement errors throughout this section. For simplicity, we will also assume that the observed quantity is a scalar. Then, given a model predicted PDF $\pi_Z(z, t_k)$, we can deduce predicted probability measures $\mu_Y(dy, t_k)$ in the observable *via*

$$\mu_Y(A, t_k) = \int_{h^{-1}(A)} \pi_Z(z, t_k)\, dz$$

for all Borel sets $A \subset \mathbb{R}$. We will assume that there is a PDF $\pi_Y(y, t_k)$ such that

$\mu_Y(dy, t_k) = \pi_Y(y, t_k)dy$, i.e., the measures $\mu_Y(dy, t_k)$ are absolutely continuous with respect to the Lebesgue measure on $\mathbb{R}$.

We now introduce the probability integral transform as a tool for assessing the *calibration* of the predicted PDFs $\pi_Y(y, t_k)$ with respect to the data $y_{obs}(t_k) \in \mathbb{R}$.

**Definition 4.23** (Probability integral transform) Given a scalar random variable $Y$ with cumulative probability density function $F_Y$ (recalling Definition 2.6), the probability integral transform (PIT) defines a new random variable $P$ with

$$P = F_Y(Y). \tag{4.38}$$

**Lemma 4.24** (Uniform distribution for the PIT) Let $P$ be defined as the PIT of $Y$, as above, and assume that $F_Y$ is strictly monotonic increasing on the range of $Y$. Then $P \sim U[0, 1]$.

*Proof* Since $F_Y$ is strictly monotonic increasing on the range of $Y$, its inverse exists and is defined by

$$\mathbb{P}(Y < F_Y^{-1}(p)) = p.$$

Then, for $0 \le p \le 1$,

$$\mathbb{P}(P < p) = \mathbb{P}(F_Y(Y) < p) = \mathbb{P}(Y < F_Y^{-1}(p)) = p, \tag{4.39}$$

hence the result. □

This means that it is possible to check whether two random variables $Y_1$ and $Y_2$ have the same distribution by taking samples from $Y_2$, computing the PIT using $F_{Y_1}$, and comparing visually with the uniform distribution by plotting a histogram.

We can apply this to the calibration of dynamic models, if we assume that the observations $\{y_{obs}(t_k)\}$ are ergodic with respect to some stationary invariant measure. We also assume that the forecast PDFs $\pi_Y(y, t_k)$ become stationary as $t_k \to \infty$. Under these assumptions, we can combine the sequence of forecast PDFs $\pi_Y(y, t_k)$ together with observations $y_{obs}(t_k)$ for $t_k = k\Delta t_{out}$, $k = 1, \ldots, N_{obs}$ with $N_{obs}$ sufficiently large, to obtain PIT values

$$p_{t_k} = F_Y(y_{obs}(t_k), t_k).$$

Here $F_Y$ denotes the induced cumulative distribution function given by

$$F_Y(y, t_k) = \int_{-\infty}^{y} \pi_Y(y', t_k)\, dy'. \tag{4.40}$$

Since the forecast PDFs will not be available in general, in practice this has to be implemented using Monte Carlo ensemble forecasts $y_i(t_k) = h(z_i(t_k))$, $i = 1, \ldots, M$, instead of $\pi_Y(y, t_k)$. Let us denote by

$$F_{\bar{y}}(y) := \int_{-\infty}^{y} \mu_{\bar{y}}(dy') = \begin{cases} 0 & \text{for } y < \bar{y}, \\ 1 & \text{for } y \ge \bar{y}, \end{cases} \tag{4.41}$$

the cumulative distribution function of the point measure $\mu_{\bar{y}}(dy) = \delta(y - \bar{y})dy$.

Then the empirical measure (4.37), associated with a forecast ensemble $\{y_i(t_k)\}$, gives rise to an *empirical cumulative distribution function*

$$F_{\hat{Y}_M}(y, t_k) = \frac{1}{M} \sum_{i=1}^{M} F_{y_i(t_k)}(y), \qquad (4.42)$$

and associated PIT values $\hat{p}_{t_k} = F_{\hat{Y}_M}(y_{\text{obs}}(t_k), t_k)$, $k \geq 1$, which we then inspect to see whether they are uniformly distributed over their discrete range $\{0, 1/M, \ldots, (M-1)/M, 1\}$. The following algorithm provides a slightly simplified assessment of PIT values in terms of *rank histograms*.

**Algorithm 4.25** (Rank histogram)  Set $M+1$ counters $\xi_i$ equal to zero initially. For $k = 1, \ldots, N_{\text{obs}}$ do the following.

(i) Sort the (scalar) predicted observations $y_i = h(z_i(t_k))$, $i = 1, \ldots, M$, such that $y_1 \leq y_2 \leq \cdots \leq y_M$.
(ii) Define the $M+1$ intervals $I_1 = (-\infty, y_1]$, $I_{i+1} = (y_i, y_{i+1}]$ for $i = 1, \ldots, M-1$, and $I_{M+1} = (y_M, +\infty)$.
(iii) Find the interval $I_{i^*}$ containing the actual observation $y_{\text{obs}}(t_k)$, and increase the associated counter $\xi_{i^*}$ by one.

**Definition 4.26** (Calibrated ensemble forecast)  A Monte Carlo ensemble forecast $\{y_i(t_k)\}$, $k = 1, \ldots, N_{\text{obs}}$, is called *calibrated* if the histogram of ranks is flat, i.e.,

$$\xi_i \approx \frac{N_{\text{obs}}}{M+1}$$

for $N_{\text{obs}}$ sufficiently large.

If the ensemble consists of a single forecast $z(t_k)$, i.e., $M = 1$, then we simply need to count the cases for which $h(z(t_k)) > y_{\text{obs}}(t_k)$ and $h(z(t_k)) \leq y_{\text{obs}}(t_k)$, respectively. The forecast is calibrated if both events have equal probability.

In addition to calibration we might also want to compare different models by using forecast scores.

**Definition 4.27** (Forecast score)  Let $F_Y$ be the cumulative distribution function which is being forecast, and let $Y_{\text{obs}}$ be a random variable which is being forecast by $F_Y$. $Y_{\text{obs}}$ has PDF $\pi_{Y_{\text{obs}}}$. A *scoring rule* is a random variable $S(F_Y, Y_{\text{obs}})$ that assigns a scalar score to $F_Y$ based on the actually observed value of $y_{\text{obs}} = Y_{\text{obs}}(\omega)$. The expected value of the scoring rule is

$$\mathbb{E}\left[S(F_Y, Y_{\text{obs}})\right] = \int_{\mathcal{Y}} S(F_Y, y_{\text{obs}}) \pi_{Y_{\text{obs}}}(y_{\text{obs}}) dy_{\text{obs}}.$$

A scoring rule is:

(i) *proper* if

$$\mathbb{E}\left[S(F_Y, Y_{\text{obs}})\right] \geq \mathbb{E}\left[S(F_{Y_{\text{obs}}}, Y_{\text{obs}})\right],$$

for all cumulative distribution functions $F_Y$, where $F_{Y_{\text{obs}}}$ is the cumulative distribution function for $Y_{\text{obs}}$, and

(ii) *strictly proper* if

$$\mathbb{E}\left[S(F_Y, Y_{\text{obs}})\right] = \mathbb{E}\left[S(F_{Y_{\text{obs}}}, Y_{\text{obs}})\right] \implies F_Y = F_{Y_{\text{obs}}}.$$

If $S(F_Y, Y_{\text{obs}})$ is strictly proper then $d(F_Y, F_{Y_{\text{obs}}})$, defined by

$$d(F_Y, F_{Y_{\text{obs}}}) = \mathbb{E}\left[S(F_Y, Y_{\text{obs}})\right] - \mathbb{E}\left[S(F_{Y_{\text{obs}}}, Y_{\text{obs}})\right],$$

satisfies the properties of a *divergence*, i.e., $d(F_1, F_2) \geq 0$ for all $F_1$, $F_2$, and $d(F_1, F_2) = 0$ implies that $F_1 = F_2$.[8]

Given a proper scoring rule $S(F_Y, Y_{\text{obs}})$, we say that a prediction $F_1$ is more skilful than another prediction $F_2$ if

$$\mathbb{E}\left[S(F_1, Y_{\text{obs}})\right] < \mathbb{E}\left[S(F_2, Y_{\text{obs}})\right].$$

Of course, in our context, we do not have access to the probability distribution for the observations $\{y_{\text{obs}}(t_k)\}$. Instead we must again assume that the statistics of the observations are ergodic and stationary and that the distributions $F_Y(\cdot, t_k)$ become stationary as $k \to \infty$. We can then calculate the *empirical averaged scoring rule*

$$\overline{S}(\{F_Y(\cdot, t_k)\}, \{y_{\text{obs}}(t_k)\}) = \frac{1}{N_{\text{obs}}} \sum_{k=1}^{N_{\text{obs}}} S(F_Y(\cdot, t_k), y_{\text{obs}}(t_k)).$$

In addition, we do not have access to $F_Y(\cdot, t_k)$ either, and must use the empirical CDF given by (4.42) to approximate the scoring rule.

We now discuss a few examples of scoring rules.

**Definition 4.28** (Continuous ranked probability score)  Given a cumulative distribution function $F_Y(y)$ and an observed value $y_{\text{obs}}$ without observation errors, the *continuous ranked probability score* is defined by

$$S_{\text{crps}}(F_Y, y_{\text{obs}}) = \int_{-\infty}^{\infty} (F_Y(y) - F_{y_{\text{obs}}}(y))^2 \, dy, \tag{4.43}$$

where $F_{y_{\text{obs}}}$ is the empirical cumulative probability distribution function given by (4.41), with $\overline{y} = y_{\text{obs}}$.

**Lemma 4.29**  The continuous ranked probability score is strictly proper.

---

[8]  A divergence has all the properties of a distance as defined in topology except the triangle inequality property.

*Proof*  It can be shown that (see Problem 4.6)

$$\mathbb{E}\left[S_{\mathrm{crps}}(F_Y, Y_{\mathrm{obs}})\right] = \int_{-\infty}^{\infty} S_{\mathrm{crps}}(F_Y, y_{\mathrm{obs}})\, \pi_{Y_{\mathrm{obs}}}(y_{\mathrm{obs}})\mathrm{d}y_{\mathrm{obs}}$$

$$= \int_{-\infty}^{\infty} (F_Y(y) - F_{Y_{\mathrm{obs}}}(y))^2 \mathrm{d}y$$

$$+ \int_{-\infty}^{\infty} F_{Y_{\mathrm{obs}}}(y)(1 - F_{Y_{\mathrm{obs}}}(y))\mathrm{d}y, \qquad (4.44)$$

and hence

$$d_{\mathrm{crps}}(F_Y, F_{Y_{\mathrm{obs}}}) = \mathbb{E}\left[S_{\mathrm{crps}}(F_Y, Y_{\mathrm{obs}})\right] - \mathbb{E}\left[S_{\mathrm{crps}}(F_{Y_{\mathrm{obs}}}, Y_{\mathrm{obs}})\right]$$

$$= \int_{-\infty}^{\infty} (F_Y(y) - F_{Y_{\mathrm{obs}}}(y))^2 \mathrm{d}y \geq 0,$$

which is only equal to zero if $F_Y = F_{Y_{\mathrm{obs}}}$, hence the result.  □

The logarithmic scoring rule is another popular scoring rule.

**Definition 4.30** (Logarithmic scoring rule)  The *logarithmic scoring rule* is defined by

$$S_{\log}(F_Y, y_{\mathrm{obs}}) = -\ln \pi_Y(y_{\mathrm{obs}}),$$

where $\pi_Y(y) = F_Y'(y)$.

**Lemma 4.31**  The logarithmic scoring rule is strictly proper.

*Proof*  The implied expected score is

$$\mathbb{E}[S_{\log}(F_Y, Y_{\mathrm{obs}})] = \int_{-\infty}^{\infty} S_{\log}(F_Y, y_{\mathrm{obs}})\, \pi_{Y_{\mathrm{obs}}}(y_{\mathrm{obs}})\mathrm{d}y_{\mathrm{obs}}$$

$$= -\int_{-\infty}^{\infty} \ln \pi_Y(y_{\mathrm{obs}})\, \pi_{Y_{\mathrm{obs}}}(y_{\mathrm{obs}})\mathrm{d}y_{\mathrm{obs}},$$

which gives rise to the *Kullback–Leibler divergence*

$$d_{\mathrm{KL}}(F_Y, F_{Y_{\mathrm{obs}}}) = \mathbb{E}[S_{\log}(F_Y, Y_{\mathrm{obs}})] - \mathbb{E}[S_{\log}(F_{Y_{\mathrm{obs}}}, Y_{\mathrm{obs}})]$$

$$= \int_{-\infty}^{\infty} \ln \frac{\pi_{Y_{\mathrm{obs}}}(y_{\mathrm{obs}})}{\pi_Y(y_{\mathrm{obs}})} \pi_{Y_{\mathrm{obs}}}(y_{\mathrm{obs}})\mathrm{d}y_{\mathrm{obs}}. \qquad (4.45)$$

□

See Gneiting, Balabdaoui & Raftery (2007) for a more detailed discussion of scoring rules, and also Bröcker (2012) for computational aspects of the continuous ranked probability score.

Finally, we give an example of a proper but not strictly proper scoring rule.

**Definition 4.32** (Root mean square error)  The root mean square error scoring rule is

$$S(F_Y, y_{\mathrm{obs}}) = (\bar{y} - y_{\mathrm{obs}})^2,$$

where $\bar{y} = \mathbb{E}[Y]$ denotes the mean with respect to the cumulative distribution function $F_Y$.

Application of the scoring rule in our framework gives rise to the *root mean square error* (RMSE)

$$\text{RMSE}(F_Y) = \sqrt{\frac{1}{N_{\text{obs}}} \sum_{k=1}^{N_{\text{obs}}} (\bar{y}_M(t_k) - y_{\text{obs}}(t_k))^2}, \quad \bar{y}_M(t_k) = \frac{1}{M} \sum_{i=1}^{M} y_i(t_k),$$

which is widely used as a simple metric to assess the quality of a family of ensemble forecasts $\{y_i(t_k)\}$, $k = 1, \ldots, N_{\text{obs}}$.

**Lemma 4.33** The root mean square error scoring rule is proper but not strictly proper.

*Proof* The expected score is

$$\int_{-\infty}^{\infty} S(F_Y, y_{\text{obs}}) \, \pi_{Y_{\text{obs}}}(y_{\text{obs}}) \mathrm{d}y_{\text{obs}} = (\bar{y} - \bar{y}_{\text{obs}})^2 + \mathbb{E}[(Y_{\text{obs}} - \bar{y}_{\text{obs}})^2]$$

and we find that

$$d(F_Y, F_{Y_{\text{obs}}}) = (\bar{y} - \bar{y}_{\text{obs}})^2 \geq 0.$$

This expression does not define a divergence since there exist many distribution functions $F_Y$ and $F_{Y_{\text{obs}}}$ with $F_Y \neq F_{Y_{\text{obs}}}$ and $\bar{y} = \bar{y}_{\text{obs}}$. □

While it is straightforward to compute the RMSE for an ensemble $y_i(t_k) = h(z_i(t_k))$ of $M$ model forecasts with respect to an observed $y_{\text{obs}}(t_k)$, computing the continuous ranked probability score is slightly more technical. Using the empirical cumulative distribution function (4.42) instead of $F_Y$ in the definition of the continuous ranked probability score, $S_{\text{crps}}(F_{\hat{Y}_M}, y_{\text{obs}})$ can be explicitly evaluated and we obtain

$$S_{\text{crps}}(F_{\hat{Y}_M}, y_{\text{obs}}) = \frac{2}{M} \sum_{i=1}^{M} \frac{i - 1/2}{M} (y_{\text{obs}} - y_i)_+$$

$$+ \frac{2}{M} \sum_{i=1}^{M} \left(1 - \frac{i - 1/2}{M}\right) (y_i - y_{\text{obs}})_+. \tag{4.46}$$

Here $(y)_+ = 0$ if $y \leq 0$ and $(y)_+ = y$ for $y > 0$. For a single member forecast $y(t_k) = h(z(t_k))$, i.e., $M = 1$, this formula reduces to

$$S_{\text{crps}}(F_{\hat{Y}_M}(\cdot, t_k), y_{\text{obs}}(t_k)) = |y(t_k) - y_{\text{obs}}(t_k)|.$$

**Example 4.34** We apply the rank histogram and the empirical averaged continuous ranked probability score (ACRPS),

$$\bar{S}_{\text{crps}}(\{F_{\hat{Y}_M}(\cdot, t_k)\}, \{y_{\text{obs}}(t_k)\}) = \frac{1}{N_{\text{obs}}} \sum_{k=1}^{N_{\text{obs}}} S_{\text{crps}}(F_{\hat{Y}_M}(\cdot, t_k), y_{\text{obs}}(t_k)),$$

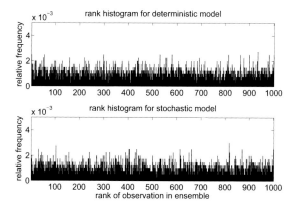

**Figure 4.9** Rank histograms for the deterministic and the stochastically perturbed Lorenz-63 models. Both models are found to be calibrated with respect to the observations according to their essentially flat rank histograms.

to our deterministic and stochastically perturbed Lorenz-63 models. The unperturbed observations are provided by the reference model described in Example 1.1 from Chapter 1. We use a total of 4000 data points collected in intervals of $\Delta t_{\text{out}} = 0.05$. The x-component of the state vector is observed and formula (4.46) is used for evaluating the ACRPS. The computations are based on $M = 1000$ ensemble forecasts from each model. Initial conditions are generated by perturbing the values of the reference solution at time zero by random numbers with mean zero and variance $\sigma^2 = 0.01$. The resulting score for the deterministic model is 9.0049 while the stochastically perturbed model leads to 8.9786. We also run the reference model from Example 1.1 with the same random initial conditions and obtain a score of 8.9572. Hence we may conclude that the stochastically perturbed model performs nearly as well as the reference model for the given initial conditions closely followed by the deterministic model. Furthermore, the rank histograms for the deterministic and the stochastically perturbed model are displayed in Figure 4.9 and reveal that both imperfect models can be considered as calibrated.

We now investigate the impact of numerical time-stepping errors. We have already mentioned this additional source of forecast errors in Chapter 1. In order to investigate the impact of numerical errors on calibration and scoring we replace the deterministic model, which we write abstractly as

$$z^{n+1} = z^n + \delta t f(z^n), \quad t_{n+1} = t_n + \delta t,$$

by either the explicit Euler approximation

$$z^{n+1} = z^n + \Delta t f(z^n), \quad t_{n+1} = t_n + \Delta t,$$

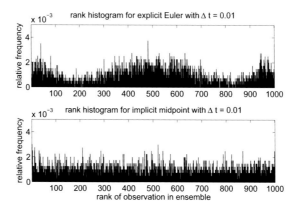

**Figure 4.10** Effect of different time-stepping methods on calibration. While the Euler method with step-size $\Delta t = 0.01 = 10\delta t$ leads to non-calibrated forecasts, the implicit midpoint is still calibrated even though the step-size has increased by a factor of ten.

with $\Delta t = 10\delta t = 0.01$, or the implicit midpoint rule

$$z^{n+1} = z^n + \Delta t f\left((z^{n+1} + z^n)/2\right).$$

In both cases we only investigate the deterministic model and still retain $\Delta t_{\mathrm{out}} = 0.05$. The computed ACRPS for the explicit Euler approximation is 9.2786 while the implicit midpoint leads to 8.9823. We note an increase in the score for the explicit Euler approximation. This increase is also confirmed by the rank histogram for the Euler method, which is no longer flat. See Figure 4.10. This is in contrast to the implicit midpoint method, which despite the much longer time-step, still leads to a flat rank histogram and, therefore, to calibrated forecasts.

## Problems

**4.1**   Generate an ensemble of initial conditions $z_i^0 \sim \mathrm{N}(0, \delta I)$ for $i = 1, \dots, M$, with $M = 1000$, $\delta = 0.1$, $I$ the $3 \times 3$ identity matrix. Propagate these initial conditions under the dynamical system defined by (4.2) with step-size $\delta t = 0.001$ and the right hand side given by the Lorenz-63 model. Plot the resulting solution ensembles at $t_n = 10$, 100, and 1000. Increase the ensemble size to $M = 10000$ and, if computationally feasible, to $M = 100000$. The resulting ensemble at $t = 1000$ should rather closely resemble the Lorenz attractor from Chapter 1. Repeat the experiments, starting the initial ensemble from a different point $\bar{z}$ in phase space, i.e., $z_i^0 \sim \mathrm{N}(\bar{z}, \delta I)$. What is the impact on the resulting ensemble at later times?

**4.2**   Implement the iteration (4.9) with $g_2^n$ generated by the modified tent map iteration (4.11), $\delta t = 0.001$, and initial conditions $y^0 = 0$, $g_2^0 = a(3^{-1/2} - 1/2)$. Output the resulting trajectory $y^n$, $n \geq 0$ every 50 iterations and generate a total of 1000000 outputs. By computing the sample mean, variance, skewness, and kurtosis (see Chapter 2), discuss whether or not the increments

$$\Delta y^k = y^{50k} - y^{50(k-1)}, \qquad k \geq 1,$$

can be approximately viewed as samples from a Gaussian random variable.

**4.3** Consider a transition matrix $P \in \mathbb{R}^{M \times M}$ which we assume to be also symmetric, i.e., $P^T = P$. Eigenvectors $v \in \mathbb{R}^M$ with eigenvalue $\lambda = 1$ are called *stationary* under the transition matrix P.

(i) Show that all eigenvalues $\lambda$ of P are real and satisfy $\lambda \in [-1, 1]$.

(ii) A transition matrix P is called *geometrically ergodic* if it possesses a unique stationary eigenvector and all other eigenvalues $\lambda$ satisfy $|\lambda| <$ $1$.[9] Show that the entries $v_i^*$ of a stationary eigenvector $v^*$ of a geometrically ergodic transition matrix satisfy $v_i^* \geq 0$ and can be normalised to $\sum_{i=1}^M v_i^* = 1$. (Of course, if $v^*$ is an eigenvector so is $-v^*$.) Show that other eigenvectors $v$ satisfy $\sum_{i=1}^M v_i = 0$.

**4.4** The time evolution of the marginal PDFs $\pi_Z(z, t)$ under an SDE (4.25) is given by the Fokker–Planck equation (4.26). For scalar-valued SDEs the invariance condition for a PDF reduces to

$$\frac{\partial}{\partial z} \left( f(z) \pi_Z^*(z) - \frac{\partial \pi_Z^*(z)}{\partial z} \right) = 0.$$

Determine all functions $\pi_Z^*$ which satisfy this differential equation. Under which conditions on $f$ are those functions normalisable, i.e.,

$$\int_{\mathbb{R}} \pi_Z^*(z) dz < \infty?$$

Hint: Consider first the special case $f(z) = az$ for $a < 0$ and $a > 0$.

**4.5** Consider the linear SDE

$$dZ = -Z dt + \sqrt{2} dW(t),$$

with initial PDF $\pi_Z(z, 0) = n(z; -1, 0.01)$. Since the SDE is linear, the time-evolved PDFs $\pi_Z(z, t)$ will remain Gaussian. Find analytic expressions for the mean $\bar{z}(t)$ and the variance $\sigma^2(t)$. Next apply the Euler–Maruyama method to the SDE with step-size $\delta t = 0.01$ over a time interval $[0, 100]$. Generate an ensemble of M solutions $\{z_i^n\}_{n \geq 0}$ with initial conditions drawn from $\pi_Z(z, 0)$. Verify that the estimated means $\bar{z}_M$ and $\sigma_M^2$ converge to their analytic counterparts as $M \to \infty$. Study the impact of the step-size on the estimates by increasing its value to $\delta t = 0.1$ and $\delta t = 1.0$.

**4.6** Show that the two parts of (4.44) are indeed equivalent using the definition of the continuous ranked probability score (4.43). Hint: Show first that

$$\int_{-\infty}^{\infty} F_Y(y) F_{y_{\text{obs}}}(y) \pi_{Y_{\text{obs}}}(y_{\text{obs}}) dy_{\text{obs}} = F_Y(y) F_{Y_{\text{obs}}}(y).$$

[9] We will reencounter transition matrices in Chapter 5 when we discuss Brownian dynamics and spatio-temporal discretisation of its associated Fokker–Planck equation.

**4.7**   Verify that the Kullback–Leibler divergence (4.45) of two univariate Gaussians $X_i \sim \mathrm{N}(\overline{x}_i, \sigma_i^2)$, $i = 1, 2$, is given by

$$
d_{\mathrm{KL}}(F_{X_1}, F_{X_2}) = \int_{\mathbb{R}} \ln \frac{\pi_{X_1}(x)}{\pi_{X_2}(x)} \pi_{X_1}(x)\mathrm{d}x
$$

$$
= \frac{1}{2}\left(\sigma_2^{-2}\sigma_1^2 + \sigma_2^{-2}(\overline{x}_2 - \overline{x}_1)^2 - 1 - 2\ln\frac{\sigma_1}{\sigma_2}\right).
$$

According to Example 2.32 the Wasserstein distance between $\pi_{X_1}$ and $\pi_{X_2}$ is given by

$$
W(\pi_{X_1}, \pi_{X_2})^2 = (\overline{x}_1 - \overline{x}_2)^2 + (\sigma_1 - \sigma_2)^2.
$$

**4.8**   Replace the implicit midpoint method in Example 4.34 by the implicit Euler method

$$
z^{n+1} = z^n + \Delta t f(z^{n+1}) \tag{4.47}
$$

and compute the resulting rank histograms for $M = 100$ ensemble members and for step-sizes $\Delta t = 0.001$ and $\Delta t = 0.01$. Either fixed point iteration or Newton's method (Süli & Mayers 2006) can be used to solve the resulting nonlinear equation (4.47) for $z^{n+1}$. All other computational details can be found in Example 4.34.

## 4.5       Guide to literature

Gardiner (2004), Jazwinski (1970), Chorin & Hald (2009), and Pavliotis (2014) provide an introduction to various aspects of stochastic processes. A more foundational axiomatic treatment is provided in Breźniak & Zastawniak (1999), Øksendal (2000), Lasota & Mackey (1994), and Meyn & Tweedie (1993). An elementary introduction to stochastic differential equations can be found in Evans (2013) and numerical issues are discussed in Higham (2001) and Kloeden & Platen (1992). Verhulst (2000) and Collet & Eckmann (2006) provide an introduction to differential equations and dynamical systems while an in depth treatment of dynamical systems can be found in Katok & Hasselblatt (1995). The reader is referred to Gneiting et al. (2007) and Bröcker (2012) for a discussion of scoring rules and calibration.

# 5 Bayesian inference

In this chapter, we define Bayesian inference, explain what it is used for and introduce some mathematical tools for applying it.

We are required to make inferences whenever we need to make a decision in light of incomplete information. Sometimes the information is incomplete because of partial measurements. For example, it can be difficult determine from a photograph whether the ball crossed the goal line in a football match because the information is incomplete: three-dimensional reality has been projected into a two-dimensional image, and in addition, the picture is only a snapshot in time and we cannot determine the speed and direction in which the ball is moving. The information is partial because we only see the situation from one angle, and at one moment in time. Also, sometimes the information is incomplete because of inaccurate measurements. In our example, this would occur if the photographic image was fuzzy, so we could not even determine exactly where the ball and the goal line are in the photograph. Incomplete information results in uncertainties which make decision-making difficult. However, often we have to make a decision anyway, despite the presence of uncertainty. In this situation, we have to combine the incomplete information with preconceived assumptions. We do this all the time in our daily lives, without even thinking about it; it is called "intuition". Intuition can be surprisingly successful in some situations, for example we are somehow able to control cars at high speeds on motorways with relatively few accidents. However, in some other situations, intuition can fail miserably. To increase skill in decision making, in predicting the spread of tuberculosis in cattle for example, it is necessary to adopt a more rigorous approach.

When making an inference we have to decide how much to trust the incomplete information and how much to trust prior assumptions (assumptions based on previous experience before taking the measurement). If we take an uncertain measurement that does not match our previous experience, do we assume that the situation is changing and take notice of the measurement, or do we neglect the measurement, assuming that an error was made? If a mathematical approach is to be useful, it needs to be able to guide us in these situations. In *Bayesian inference*, this question is resolved by quantifying our uncertainty in the measurements as probabilities. In addition, the uncertainty in our prior assumptions (prior uncertainty), and our uncertainty about the situation after taking the measurements (posterior uncertainty), are also quantified as probabilities. The step of treating uncertainties in our prior knowledge (or belief) as probabilities constitutes a bold mathematical abstraction. However, this abstraction leads to the relationship between measurement uncertainty, prior uncertainty, and posterior uncertainty being completely described by *Bayes' theorem*, the central tool of Bayesian inference. Later in this book we will explain that prior knowledge can be acquired from mathematical models and, depending on the modeller and the model, ensemble forecasts will be given a probabilistic interpretation. The main task of Bayesian inference is then to evaluate the posterior uncertainty accurately and in a computationally efficient way.

## 5.1     Inverse problems from a probabilistic perspective

In this chapter we introduce the framework of Bayesian inference, illustrated with some simple examples. Mathematical theories of inference are concerned with determining the value of some variable $x$ of interest, which could be a single number (for example the price of cotton), an array of numbers organised into a vector (for example the position of a space probe travelling towards Jupiter), or a function (for example the distribution of temperature in the world's oceans). From a more mathematical perspective, the variable of interest could, for example, be the state $z$ of a dynamical system or, more generally, of a stochastic process as considered in Chapter 4. We refer to $x \in \mathcal{X}$ as the *parameters* with *parameter space* $\mathcal{X}$. In Bayesian statistics, we use probability to quantify our uncertainty about $x$; this requires us to regard $x$ as a realisation of a random variable $X : \Omega \to \mathcal{X}$. A typical inference model is then the following.

**Definition 5.1** (Inference model[1])   Consider a *random parameter vector* $X : \Omega \to \mathcal{X} = \mathbb{R}^{N_x}$, and an *observation noise variable* $\Xi : \Omega \to \mathcal{Y} = \mathbb{R}^{N_y}$, both over a probability space $(\Omega, \mathcal{F}, \mathbb{P})$. Assume that $X$ and $\Xi$ are independent random variables. Then the *observed variable* $Y : \Omega \to \mathcal{Y} \in \mathbb{R}^{N_y}$ is a random variable defined by

$$Y = h(X) + \Xi, \tag{5.1}$$

where $h : \mathcal{X} \to \mathcal{Y}$ is a continuous map, called the *forward map*.

The goal of Bayesian inference is to estimate our uncertainty in the state variable $X$ after we have observed one or more realisations of the random variable $Y$.

We now describe a simple inference problem that leads to a low-dimensional linear inference model, closely related to the discussions from Chapter 1.

---

**Example 5.2**   Assume that a scalar variable $z \in \mathbb{R}$ varies in time according to the following linear model

$$z(t) = b_1 t + b_0, \tag{5.2}$$

where $b_0$ and $b_1$ are unknown parameters. In contrast with the modelling scenario described in Chapter 1, here we assume that (5.2) is also used for generating the reference trajectory $z_{\mathrm{ref}}(t)$, but now with unknown parameter values $b_0$ and $b_1$.

---

[1]  This model can of course be generalised in many ways, $Y$ may be a nonlinear function of $\Xi$, and $X$ and $\Xi$ may not be independent variables. Also, here $X$ and $Y$ are taken from vector spaces but they could be taken from any chosen mathematical sets.

This modelling scenario is often referred to as a *perfect model scenario*. Our goal is to estimate the parameters $b_0$ and $b_1$ from observations of $y_{obs}(t_k)$ taken at a set of discrete times $t_k$, $k = 1, \ldots, N_{obs}$. We assume that the observations are made with a measurement device that introduces an error which is normally distributed with mean zero and variance $\sigma^2 > 0$, and that the observation errors at different times are statistically independent. Then the measurement process can be described mathematically as follows:

$$y_{obs}(t_k) = b_1 t_k + b_0 + \xi^k, \quad k = 1, \ldots, N_{obs}.$$

The measurement errors $\xi^k$ are viewed as independent realisations of $N(0, \sigma^2)$. This can be rewritten in the form of (5.1) with

$$Y = (Y(t_1), Y(t_2), \ldots, Y(t_{N_{obs}}))^T \in \mathbb{R}^{N_{obs}},$$

$x = (b_0, b_1)^T \in \mathbb{R}^2$,

$$h(x) = \begin{pmatrix} b_0 + b_1 t_1 \\ b_0 + b_1 t_2 \\ \vdots \\ b_0 + b_1 t_{N_{obs}} \end{pmatrix},$$

and $\xi = (\xi^1, \ldots, \xi^{N_{obs}})^T$ is a realisation of $\Xi \sim N(0, \sigma^2 I)$.

In order to infer information about the state variable $X$ from realisations of $Y$, we need to know how the probability distribution for $Y$ relates to the probability distribution for $X$. Lemma 2.13 from Chapter 2 can be used to prove the following formula for $\pi_Y$.

**Theorem 5.3** (Distribution of observation variable $Y$)  Assume that $X$ and $\Xi$ are absolutely continuous with PDFs $\pi_X$ and $\pi_\Xi$ respectively, and $Y$ is related to $X$ and $\Xi$ via (5.1). Then $Y$ is also absolutely continuous with PDF

$$\pi_Y(y) = \int_{\mathbb{R}^{N_x}} \pi_\Xi(y - h(x))\pi_X(x)dx. \tag{5.3}$$

If $X$ is a deterministic variable, i.e., $X(\omega) = x_0$ almost surely for an appropriate $x_0 \in \mathcal{X}$, then the PDF simplifies to

$$\pi_Y(y) = \pi_\Xi(y - h(x_0)).$$

*Proof*   First we compute the conditional PDF $\pi_Y$ in the case of a fixed parameter value $X = x_0$. If $X$ is deterministic then the only source of uncertainty is $\Xi$. We use Lemma 2.13 with transformation $\Phi(\xi) = h(x_0) + \xi$, its inverse $\Phi^{-1}(y) = y - h(x_0)$, and Jacobian $D\Phi^{-1}(y) = I$ to obtain

$$\pi_Y(y) = \pi_\Xi(y - h(x_0)).$$

In the case of a deterministic parameter $X = x_0$, the proof is complete. If $X$ is a random variable, then the same reasoning gives the conditional PDF for $X = x_0$

$$\pi_Y(y|x_0) = \pi_\Xi(y - h(x_0)),$$

and the joint distribution $\pi_{XY}$ of $(X, Y)$ satisfies

$$\pi_{XY}(x, y) = \pi_Y(y|x)\pi_X(x).$$

Finally we marginalise, i.e.,

$$\pi_Y(y) = \int_{\mathbb{R}^{N_x}} \pi_{XY}(x, y)\mathrm{d}x = \int_{\mathbb{R}^{N_x}} \pi_Y(y|x)\pi_X(x)\mathrm{d}x,$$

and obtain Equation (5.3).                                                 □

---

**Example 5.4**   In this example we will calculate $\pi_Y$ for the case in which $X$ and $\Xi$ are multivariate normal random variables with means $\bar{x}$ and zero, and covariance matrices $P$ and $R$, respectively. The forward operator $h : \mathbb{R}^{N_x} \to \mathbb{R}^{N_y}$ is a linear map defined by

$$h(x) = Hx,$$

where $H$ is an $(N_x \times N_y)$-dimensional matrix. Equation (5.3) then becomes

$$\pi_Y(y) \propto \int_{\mathbb{R}^{N_x}} \exp\left(-\frac{1}{2}(y - Hx)^{\mathrm{T}}R^{-1}(y - Hx)\right)$$

$$\times \exp\left(-\frac{1}{2}(x - \bar{x})^{\mathrm{T}}P^{-1}(x - \bar{x})\right)\mathrm{d}x,$$

where we have left out the constant of proportionality since we can always normalise the PDF at the end of the calculation. Next we use the completing-the-square formula

$$x^{\mathrm{T}}Cx - 2d^{\mathrm{T}}x = (x - C^{-1}d)^{\mathrm{T}}C(x - C^{-1}d) - d^{\mathrm{T}}C^{-1}d,$$

to reformulate the exponent in the integrand

$$I = -\frac{1}{2}\left\{(Hx - y)^{\mathrm{T}}R^{-1}(Hx - y) + (x - \bar{x})^{\mathrm{T}}P^{-1}(x - \bar{x})\right\},$$

as

$$I = -\frac{1}{2}\left\{(x - C^{-1}d)^{\mathrm{T}}C(x - C^{-1}d) - d^{\mathrm{T}}C^{-1}d + y^{\mathrm{T}}R^{-1}y + \bar{x}^{\mathrm{T}}P^{-1}\bar{x}\right\},$$

where

$$C = P^{-1} + H^{\mathrm{T}}R^{-1}H, \quad d = H^{\mathrm{T}}R^{-1}y + P^{-1}\bar{x}.$$

Since the $x$ dependence in $I$ reduces to a normalisation constant under marginalisation, we obtain

$$\pi_Y(y) \propto \exp\left(-\frac{1}{2}(y^{\mathrm{T}}R^{-1}y - d^{\mathrm{T}}C^{-1}d)\right).$$

---

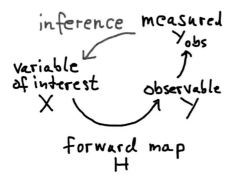

**Figure 5.1** Schematic representation of the loop created by the forward map $H$, which links the desired variable $x$ to an observable quantity $y$, an actual observation $y_{obs}$, and its inference back onto the variable of interest $x$. Bayesian inference treats $x$ and $y$ as random variables and we use the notations $X$ and $Y$ instead.

If we quantify the uncertainty in the measurement device using the random variable $\Xi$, and quantify our uncertainty in the parameters using the random variable $X$, then Theorem 5.3 shows us how to quantify our uncertainty in the measured values using the random variable $Y$. This is often referred to as the *forward problem* which, as we have seen, can be solved using a simple transformation of variables. However, this simple transformation can already be very challenging to compute for large $N_x$, since it involves integration over a large number of dimensions. Hence we either have to restrict ourselves to (or approximate by) cases for which the integrals are simple to evaluate (such as the case of linear transformations of Gaussian variables given in Example 5.4), or adopt Monte Carlo methods as discussed in Chapter 3.

Having said that, we are actually more interested in the *inverse inference problem* in which we have obtained an observation which is modelled as a random observation variable $y \in \mathcal{Y}$, and we wish to *infer* the uncertainty in the parameters $x \in \mathcal{X}$. See Figure 5.1 for a schematic representation of the connection between the forward problem, an observation, and the inference problem. An example of such an inference problem is in oil recovery. Oil engineers try to learn about the structure of oil reservoirs deep under the ground by various techniques such as taking seismic readings at the surface, and by drilling holes so that pressure and electrostatic measurements can be taken at depth. In that case, the parameters $x \in \mathcal{X}$ would contain all the variables required to describe the state of the oil reservoir and the surrounding geology, for example, the oil concentration field and the rock porosity field. The observation variable $y \in \mathcal{Y}$ would contain all of the observational data obtained. The forward operator $h$ would be a numerical model that simulates the oil reservoir (perhaps containing fluid and solid mechanics and solving the electrostatic equations) and the resulting observations. The oil engineers wish to quantify their uncertainty about the structure of the oil reservoir, having observed a value $y_{obs}$ of the observation variable. This uncertainty can then be used to assess the chance of drilling for oil being profitable, which ultimately informs a decision by oil companies about whether to invest.

Bayesian inference provides a mathematical framework to solve such inference problems. The main tool is Bayes' theorem which yields a conditional PDF for the parameters $x$ given an observation $y_{\mathrm{obs}}$.

**Theorem 5.5** (Bayes' theorem)  Given a particular observation value $y_{\mathrm{obs}} \in \mathbb{R}^{N_y}$, the conditional PDF $\pi_X(x|y_{\mathrm{obs}})$ is given by *Bayes' formula*,

$$\pi_X(x|y_{\mathrm{obs}}) = \frac{\pi_Y(y_{\mathrm{obs}}|x)\pi_X(x)}{\pi_Y(y_{\mathrm{obs}})}. \tag{5.4}$$

*Proof*  The proof is obtained by exchanging the variables $X$ and $Y$ in the definition of marginalisation and conditional PDFs to obtain

$$\pi_{XY}(x, y) = \pi_Y(y|x)\pi_X(x) = \pi_X(x|y)\pi_Y(y),$$

and, hence,

$$\pi_X(x|y) = \frac{\pi_Y(y|x)\pi_X(x)}{\pi_Y(y)}. \qquad \square$$

Here $\pi_X$ quantifies our uncertainty about the parameters $X$ *before* observing $y_{\mathrm{obs}}$ (and hence we call it the *prior PDF*), whilst $\pi_X(x|y_{\mathrm{obs}})$ quantifies our uncertainty *after* observing $y_{\mathrm{obs}}$ (and hence we call it the *posterior PDF*). The conditional PDF $\pi_Y(y|x)$ quantifies the likelihood of observing $y$ given a particular value of $x$, and hence it is often called the *likelihood function*. The real power of this formula comes from the fact that $\pi_Y(y_{\mathrm{obs}})$ is simply a normalisation factor; we know that $\pi_X(x|y_{\mathrm{obs}})$ must integrate to 1, so we can compute any normalisation factor as a post-processing step. This means that Equation (5.4) can be written as

$$\pi_X(x|y_{\mathrm{obs}}) \propto \pi_Y(y_{\mathrm{obs}}|x)\pi_X(x) = \pi_\Xi(y_{\mathrm{obs}} - h(x))\pi_X(x).$$

We note, however, that the normalisation factor $\pi_Y(y_{\mathrm{obs}})$ can become important when comparing different models. Under such circumstances the factor $\pi_Y(y_{\mathrm{obs}})$ is also referred to as the *evidence*. We will return to this topic in Chapter 9.

We use the formulas developed in Example 5.4 to evaluate the posterior distribution for Gaussian distributions with linear observation operator in the following example.

---

**Example 5.6**  Return to the notation of Example 5.4, and assume that we have observed a particular value $y_{\mathrm{obs}}$ of the observation variable $Y$. From the calculations in that example we obtain

$$\pi_X(x|y) \propto \exp\left(-\frac{1}{2}\left((y - Hx)^{\mathrm{T}}R^{-1}(y - Hx) + (x - \bar{x})^{\mathrm{T}}P^{-1}(x - \bar{x})\right)\right)$$

$$\propto \exp\left(-\frac{1}{2}(x - C^{-1}d)^{\mathrm{T}}C(x - C^{-1}d)\right),$$

with $C$ and $d$ defined as before. This means that $\pi_X(x|y_{\text{obs}}) = n(x; \bar{x}^{\text{a}}, P^{\text{a}})$ with covariance matrix $P^{\text{a}} = C^{-1} = (P^{-1} + H^{\text{T}}R^{-1}H)^{-1}$ and mean

$$\bar{x}^{\text{a}} = C^{-1}d$$
$$= \bar{x} - P^{\text{a}}H^{\text{T}}R^{-1}(H\bar{x} - y_{\text{obs}}).$$

We now make a connection to Examples 1.2 and 1.8 from Chapter 1 and Example 2.20 from Chapter 2. The state variable $z$ takes the role of the parameter $x$ in all of these examples.

---

**Example 5.7** We introduced the (scalar) measurement model (1.8) in Chapter 1. In addition we considered a particular case in Example 1.2, analysing it further in Example 2.20. The key conclusion was that (1.8) can be replaced by the stochastic measurement model

$$Y = h(z_{\text{ref}}(t)) + \Xi(t),$$

where $\Xi(t)$ is a Gaussian random variable with mean zero and variance $R$. Following our previous discussion, with the state variable $z$ now replacing the parameter variable $x$, this model gives rise to the conditional PDF (likelihood)

$$\pi_Y(y|z) = \frac{1}{\sqrt{2\pi R}}e^{-\frac{(y-h(z))^2}{2R}}.$$

A more complex case was considered in Example 1.8, where $N_{\text{obs}}$ observations $y_{\text{obs}}(t_k)$ in observation intervals $\Delta t_{\text{out}}$ were considered simultaneously. Using the notation of Chapter 1, we obtain

$$y_{\text{obs}}(t_1) = H\psi(z^0) + \xi^1,$$
$$y_{\text{obs}}(t_2) = H\psi^2(z^0) + \xi^2,$$
$$\vdots$$
$$y_{\text{obs}}(t_{N_A}) = H\psi^{N_A}(z^0) + \xi^{N_A},$$

where the variables $\{\xi^k\}$ are realisations of independent and identically distributed Gaussian random variables with mean zero and variance $R$. Note that we have replaced $z_{\text{ref}}(t_k)$ by $\psi^k(z^0)$; this is justified if the model errors $e^n$, as defined by (1.19), are sufficiently small and their accumulative effect can be ignored over the interval $[0, t_{N_A}]$. Under this assumption, we obtain the likelihood function

$$\pi_{Y_{t_{1:N_A}}}(y_{t_{1:N_A}}^{\text{obs}}|z) = \frac{1}{(2\pi R)^{N_A/2}}\Pi_{k=1}^{N_A}\exp\left(-\frac{(y_{\text{obs}}(t_k) - H\psi^k(z))^2}{2R}\right), \quad (5.5)$$

where $y_{t_{1:N_A}}^{\text{obs}} \in \mathbb{R}^{N_A}$ represents the values of all measurements $y_{\text{obs}}(t_k) \in \mathbb{R}$ from $t_1$ to $t_{N_A}$. The nonlinear method of least squares, as introduced in Example 1.8, can now be viewed as *maximising the likelihood*, i.e., finding the minimiser of

(1.20) is equivalent to finding the maximiser $z_*^0$ of (5.5) for given $y_{t_{1:N_A}}^{\text{obs}}$. Indeed, we find that

$$\ln \pi_{Y_{t_{1:N_A}}} \left( y_{t_{1:N_A}}^{\text{obs}} | z \right) = -R^{-1}L(z) - \frac{N_A}{2} \ln(2\pi R),$$

with $L$ defined by (1.20) and, consequently,

$$\nabla_z \pi_{Y_{t_{1:N_A}}} \left( y_{t_{1:N_A}}^{\text{obs}} | z \right) = 0 \quad \text{if and only if} \quad \nabla_z L(z) = 0,$$

which justifies the statement. In other words, we have used *maximum likelihood estimates* (MLEs) in order to perform data assimilation in Example 1.8. We will now introduce Bayesian estimates which will replace MLEs as a tool for performing data assimilation in Chapter 6.

---

Having obtained a posterior PDF $\pi_X(x|y_{\text{obs}})$, it is often necessary to provide an appropriate point estimate of $x$. Bayesian estimates for $x$ are defined as follows.

**Definition 5.8** (Bayesian estimate)   Given a posterior PDF $\pi_X(x|y_{\text{obs}})$ we define a *Bayesian estimate* $\hat{x} \in \mathcal{X}$ by

$$\hat{x} = \arg \min_{x' \in \mathcal{X}} \int_{\mathcal{X}} \ell(x', x)\pi_X(x|y_{\text{obs}})\mathrm{d}x,$$

where $\ell(x', x)$ is an appropriate *loss function*. Popular choices include the *maximum a posteriori (MAP) estimate* with $\hat{x}$ corresponding to the modal value (global maximum) of $\pi_X(x|y_{\text{obs}})$. The MAP estimate formally corresponds to the loss function

$$\ell_\varepsilon(x', x) = \begin{cases} 1 & \text{if } \|x' - x\| > \varepsilon, \\ 0 & \text{otherwise}, \end{cases}$$

in the limit $\varepsilon \to 0$. The *posterior median estimate* corresponds to $\ell(x', x) = \|x' - x\|$ while the *posterior mean estimate*,

$$\hat{x} = \int_{\mathcal{X}} x\pi_X(x|y_{\text{obs}})\mathrm{d}x,$$

results from $\ell(x', x) = \|x' - x\|^2$.[2]

The MLE is formally obtained as a special case of the MAP estimate with the prior PDF (formally) set equal to a constant. This step is justified provided that

$$\int_{\mathbb{R}^{N_x}} \pi_Y(y|x)\mathrm{d}x < \infty. \tag{5.6}$$

This situation is referred to as a *non-informative prior*. Condition (5.6) does not hold for most practical data assimilation problems since the dimension of

---

[2]   These estimates $\hat{x}$ are themselves realisations of random variables $\hat{X}$, called *estimators*, which depend on $y_{\text{obs}} = Y(\omega)$. Compare Appendix 2.4 for the special case of the posterior mean estimator under vanishing measurement errors $\Xi \equiv 0$ and Appendix 5.5 for the best linear unbiased (BLUE) estimator.

parameter space $\mathbb{R}^{N_x}$ is larger than the dimension of observation space $\mathbb{R}^{N_y}$ and a proper/informative prior is essential for obtaining Bayesian estimates.

Note that the MAP estimate, the posterior mean and the posterior median coincide for Gaussian random variables. This does not hold generally, as we demonstrate in the following example.

---

**Example 5.9** We consider a nonlinear forward map given by

$$y = h(x) = \frac{7}{12}x^3 - \frac{7}{2}x^2 + 8x.$$

The observed value is $y_{\text{obs}} = 2$ and the measurement error is normal with mean zero and variance equal to one. The likelihood function is therefore

$$\pi_Y(y_{\text{obs}}|x) = \frac{1}{\sqrt{2\pi}}e^{-\frac{(h(x)-2)^2}{2}}.$$

The prior is assumed to be normal with mean $\bar{x} = -2$ and variance $\sigma^2 = 1/2$. Hence the posterior is

$$\pi_X(x|2) \propto \frac{1}{\sqrt{2\pi}}e^{-(x+2)^2 - \frac{1}{2}(h(x)-2)^2}. \tag{5.7}$$

In order to compute the posterior PDF we introduce a computational grid $x_j = j\Delta x$ with grid spacing $\Delta x = 0.0001$ sufficiently small in order to compute the posterior mean, median and MAP value from the grid values $\pi_X(x_j|2)$ to an accuracy of four leading digits. We obtain $\bar{x} \approx 0.2095$, a median of approximately 0.2006 and a MAP value of approximately 0.1837. A coarser grid is used to display the prior, likelihood, and posterior in Figure 5.2. Note that the uncertainty in the prior is significantly larger than the measurement error in the forward model and that the observed $y_{\text{obs}} = 2$ is in the tail of the prior Gaussian distribution.

---

We now discuss an important example where the posterior can be computed analytically.

---

**Example 5.10** Consider the case of a scalar observation with $\Xi \sim N(0, R)$. Then

$$\pi_Y(y|x) = \pi_\Xi(y - h(x)) = \frac{1}{\sqrt{2\pi R}}e^{-\frac{1}{2R}(h(x)-y)^2}.$$

We also assume that $X \sim N(\bar{x}, P)$ and that $h(x) = Hx$. Then, the posterior distribution of $X$ given an observed $y = y_{\text{obs}}$ is also Gaussian with mean

$$\bar{x}^{\text{a}} = \bar{x} - P^{\text{a}}H^{\text{T}}R^{-1}(H\bar{x} - y_{\text{obs}})$$
$$= \bar{x} - PH^{\text{T}}(HPH^{\text{T}} + R)^{-1}(H\bar{x} - y_{\text{obs}}), \tag{5.8}$$

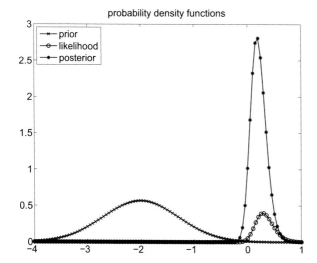

probability density functions

**Figure 5.2** Prior, likelihood and posterior distributions for a univariate example with nonlinear forward operator. The prior is chosen to be rather uninformative and also has a mean quite far away from the observed value. As a result, we find that the posterior is relatively close to the likelihood.

and covariance matrix

$$P^{\mathrm{a}} = (P^{-1} + H^{\mathrm{T}} R^{-1} H)^{-1}$$
$$= P - PH^{\mathrm{T}}(HPH^{\mathrm{T}} + R)^{-1}HP. \tag{5.9}$$

These are the famous *Kalman update formulas*. Both formulas can be verified by direct calculations using the results from Example 5.6.

We note that $\bar{x}^{\mathrm{a}}$ solves the minimisation problem

$$\bar{x}^{\mathrm{a}} = \arg\min_{x \in \mathbb{R}^{N_x}} \left\{ \frac{1}{2}(x - \bar{x})^{\mathrm{T}} P^{-1}(x - \bar{x}) + \frac{1}{2R}(Hx - y_{\mathrm{obs}})^2 \right\}, \tag{5.10}$$

which can be viewed as a Tikhonov regularisation of the *ill-posed inverse problem*

$$y_{\mathrm{obs}} = Hx, \quad x \in \mathbb{R}^{N_x},$$

for $N_x > 1$. A standard Tikhonov regularisation would use $\bar{x} = 0$ and $P^{-1} = \delta I$ with the regularisation parameter $\delta > 0$ appropriately chosen. In the Bayesian approach to inverse problems, the regularisation term is instead determined by the prior PDF $\pi_X$.

**Example 5.11**  We extend the previous example to a Gaussian mixture prior on $X$:

$$\pi_X(x) = \sum_{j=1}^{J} \frac{\alpha_j}{(2\pi)^{N_x/2}|P_j|^{1/2}} \exp\left( -\frac{1}{2}(x - \bar{x}_j)^{\mathrm{T}} P_j^{-1}(x - \bar{x}_j) \right)$$
$$= \sum_{j=1}^{J} \alpha_j \, \mathrm{n}(x; \bar{x}_j, P_j), \tag{5.11}$$

where $\alpha_j > 0$, $j = 1, \ldots, J$, denote the mixture weights which sum to one. The posterior distribution is again a Gaussian mixture

$$\pi_X(x|y_{\text{obs}}) = \sum_{j=1}^{J} \alpha_j^{\text{a}} \, \mathrm{n}(x; \overline{x}_j^{\text{a}}, P_j^{\text{a}}),$$

with new means

$$\overline{x}_j^{\text{a}} = \overline{x}_j - P_j H^{\mathrm{T}} (H P_j H^{\mathrm{T}} + R)^{-1} (H \overline{x}_j - y_{\text{obs}}),$$

new covariance matrices

$$P_j^{\text{a}} = P_j - P_j H^{\mathrm{T}} (H P_j H^{\mathrm{T}} + R)^{-1} H P_j,$$

and new weights

$$\alpha_j^{\text{a}} \propto \frac{\alpha_j}{\sqrt{2\pi(H P_j H^{\mathrm{T}} + R)}} \exp\left( -\frac{(H \overline{x}_j - y_{\text{obs}})^2}{2(H P_j H^{\mathrm{T}} + R)} \right),$$

where the constant of proportionality is chosen such that the weights $\alpha_j^{\text{a}}$ sum to one.

---

We mention that Bayes' formula must be replaced by the Radon–Nikodym derivative in cases where the prior distribution is not absolutely continuous with respect to the Lebesgue measure (or in the case that the space $\mathcal{X}$ does not admit a Lebesgue measure). Consider as an example the case of an empirical measure $\mu_X$ centred about the $M$ samples $x_i \in \mathcal{X}$, $i = 1, \ldots, M$, i.e.,

$$\mu_X(\mathrm{d}x) = \frac{1}{M} \sum_{i=1}^{M} \mu_{x_i}(\mathrm{d}x) = \frac{1}{M} \sum_{i=1}^{M} \delta(x - x_i) \mathrm{d}x.$$

Then the resulting posterior measure $\mu_X(\cdot|y_{\text{obs}})$ is absolutely continuous with respect to $\mu_X$ and the associated *Radon–Nikodym derivative* is given by

$$\frac{\mathrm{d}\mu_X(x|y_{\text{obs}})}{\mathrm{d}\mu_X(x)} \propto \pi_{\Xi}(y_{\text{obs}} - h(x)).$$

Furthermore, since

$$\int_{\mathcal{X}} g(x) \mu_X(\mathrm{d}x|y_{\text{obs}}) = \int_{\mathcal{X}} g(x) \frac{\mathrm{d}\mu_X(x|y_{\text{obs}})}{\mathrm{d}\mu_X(x)} \mu_X(\mathrm{d}x)$$

for any sufficiently regular function $g$, the posterior measure is given by

$$\mu_X(\mathrm{d}x|y_{\text{obs}}) = \sum_{i=1}^{M} w_i \, \mu_{x_i}(\mathrm{d}x) = \sum_{i=1}^{M} w_i \delta(x - x_i) \mathrm{d}x,$$

with weights $w_i \geq 0$ defined by

$$w_i \propto \pi_{\Xi}(y_{\text{obs}} - h(x_i)),$$

and the constant of proportionality is determined by the condition $\sum_{i=1}^{M} w_i = 1$.

## 5.2    Sampling the posterior

We usually want to summarise our uncertainty, formally represented by the posterior PDF $\pi_X(x|y_{\mathrm{obs}})$, in terms of expectation values

$$\bar{g} = \int_{\mathcal{X}} g(x)\pi_X(x|y_{\mathrm{obs}})\mathrm{d}x,$$

where $g$ could, for example, stand for the variance or correlation. Apart from a few special examples, these integrals are intractable, and it becomes necessary to use Monte Carlo methods to approximate them. Recall that a standard Monte Carlo method would be based on samples $x_i$, $i = 1, \ldots, M$, from the posterior distribution. In some cases such samples are easy to generate by the methods discussed in Chapter 3; in other cases these methods can become computationally demanding. In this section, we therefore introduce an alternative method for generating samples from a desired distribution $\pi_X$. This method is based on *Brownian dynamics* and *invariant measures*.

A Brownian dynamics model is an SDE of type (4.25) with the vector field $f$ being generated by a potential $U : \mathbb{R}^{N_x} \to \mathbb{R}$. We also set $Q = I$ in (4.25). Note that we are shifting focus from an SDE as a model of a physical process towards its use as a tool for generating samples $x_i$ from a PDF $\pi_X(x)$. In order to emphasise this shift in focus we will denote the independent variable by $\tau$ instead of $t$ as used previously.

**Definition 5.12** (Brownian dynamics and canonical distribution)    We consider *Brownian dynamics*

$$\mathrm{d}X = -\nabla_x U(X)\mathrm{d}\tau + \sqrt{2}\mathrm{d}W, \tag{5.12}$$

where $U : \mathbb{R}^{N_x} \to \mathbb{R}$ is an appropriate potential, the independent variable is denoted by $\tau$, and $W(\tau)$ denotes standard Brownian motion. We introduce the *canonical PDF*

$$\pi_X^*(x) = C^{-1}\exp(-U(x)), \qquad C = \int_{\mathbb{R}^{N_x}} \exp(-U(x))\mathrm{d}x, \tag{5.13}$$

provided $C < \infty$. Following (4.28), we also define the linear operator

$$\mathcal{L}\pi := \nabla_x \cdot (\pi \nabla_x U) + \nabla_x \cdot \nabla_x \pi, \tag{5.14}$$

and write the Fokker–Planck equation for Brownian dynamics in the abstract operator form

$$\frac{\partial \pi_X}{\partial \tau} = \mathcal{L}\pi_X. \tag{5.15}$$

**Proposition 5.13** (Stationary distribution)    The canonical distribution (5.13) satisfies $\mathcal{L}\pi_X^* = 0$ which implies that the canonical PDF is stationary under the associated Fokker–Planck equation.

*Proof*  The proposition follows from $\nabla_x \pi_X^* = -\pi_X^* \nabla_x U$ and

$$\nabla_x \cdot (\pi_X^* \nabla_x U) + \nabla_x \cdot \nabla_x \pi_X^* = \nabla_x \cdot (\pi_X^* \nabla_x U + \nabla_x \pi_X^*) = 0. \qquad \square$$

Note that the Fokker–Planck equation can also be reformulated as a gradient flow towards the stationary solution $\pi_X^*$:

$$\frac{\partial \pi_X}{\partial \tau} = \nabla_x \cdot (\pi_X \nabla_x U(x) + \nabla_x \pi_X)$$

$$= \nabla_x \cdot \left( \pi_X^* \nabla_x \left( \frac{\pi_X}{\pi_X^*} \right) \right). \tag{5.16}$$

Equation (5.16) has the structure of a weighted diffusion equation with standard diffusion formally obtained for $\pi_X^* \equiv 1$. See Appendix 5.6 for more details.

We now illustrate how Brownian dynamics in conjunction with Proposition 5.13 can be used to sample from a posterior PDF $\pi_X(x|y_{\text{obs}})$. A key observation is that the posterior PDF becomes the stationary distribution of Brownian dynamics, provided that the potential $U$ is chosen according to

$$U(x) = -\ln \pi_X(x|y_{\text{obs}})$$
$$= -\ln \pi_X(x) - \ln \pi_Y(y_{\text{obs}}|x) + \ln \pi_Y(y_{\text{obs}}).$$

Since the dynamics does not depend on a constant added or subtracted from $U(x)$, we may actually use

$$U(x) = -\ln \pi_X(x) - \ln \pi_Y(y_{\text{obs}}|x), \tag{5.17}$$

which provides a huge simplification in practice since it avoids the computation of the evidence $\pi_Y(y_{\text{obs}})$.

If the Brownian dynamics is ergodic, then expectations from the posterior can be computed by using time integrals according to

$$\mathbb{E}[g(X)] = \int_{\mathbb{R}^{N_x}} g(x) \pi_X^*(x) \mathrm{d}x$$

$$= \lim_{T \to \infty} \frac{1}{T} \int_0^T g(x(\tau)) \mathrm{d}\tau \approx \lim_{N \to \infty} \frac{1}{N} \sum_{n=1}^N g(x(\tau_n)).$$

Here $x(\tau)$ denotes a particular realisation of Brownian dynamics and $\tau_n = n \Delta \tau$ with step-size $\Delta \tau > 0$. This is an example of a generalised Monte Carlo method, as defined in Definition 3.15, with equal weights $w_i = 1/N$. It is generalised since the sample points $x(\tau_n)$ are not independent.

---

**Example 5.14**  We continue with Example 5.9 and recall the posterior (5.7) which, according to (5.17), corresponds to the potential

$$U(x) = (x+2)^2 + \frac{1}{2}(h(x) - 2)^2,$$

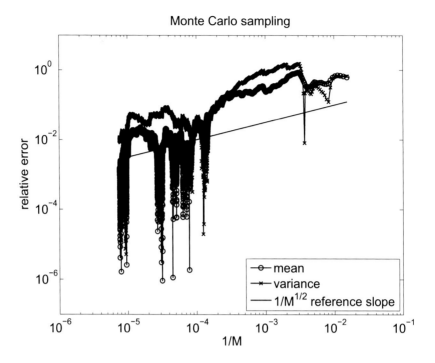

**Figure 5.3** Relative errors in the posterior mean and the variance along trajectories of (5.18) of length $M$. The typical Monte Carlo $M^{-1/2}$ convergence rate can be observed even though the samples $x_i$ are correlated.

with gradient

$$\nabla_x U(x) = U'(x) = 2(x+2) + \left( \frac{7}{12}x^3 - \frac{7}{2}x^2 + 8x - 2 \right) \left( \frac{7}{4}x^2 - 7x + 8 \right).$$

We now conduct a long simulation with the Euler–Maruyama method (compare (4.21) from Chapter 4):

$$x^{n+1} = x^n - \Delta\tau U'(x^n) + \sqrt{2\Delta\tau}\,\xi^n, \tag{5.18}$$

where the variables $\{\xi^n\}$ are realisations of independent Gaussian random variables with mean zero and variance one. The step-size is set equal to $\Delta\tau = 0.001$ (it is small for stability reasons) and we start from $x^0 = -2$ (the centre of the prior PDF). Time has no physical meaning here: we are not modelling a physical process but merely exploiting the sampling property of the Brownian dynamics. We disregard the first one thousand time-steps and then store every iterate from (5.18) until we have a total of $M_{\max} = 130000$ samples, which we denote by $\{x_i\}_{i=1}^{M_{\max}}$. To illustrate the behaviour of (5.18) as a sampling device we consider probability densities computed from binned prior and posterior samples

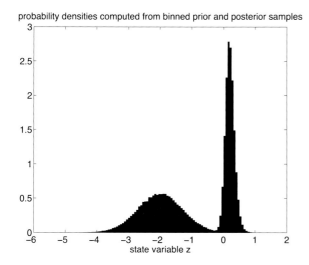

**Figure 5.4** Approximative probability densities from binned samples drawn from the posterior using Brownian dynamics with a Gaussian prior using a standard random number generator. The result agrees well with the distributions displayed in Figure 5.2.

the convergence of the empirical mean,

$$\overline{x}_M = \frac{1}{M} \sum_{i=1}^{M} x_i,$$

to the posterior mean $\overline{x} \approx 0.2095$ (as computed in Example 5.9) as a function of sample size (length of the trajectory) $M \leq M_{\text{max}}$. We also consider the approximation to the posterior variance,

$$\sigma_M^2 = \frac{1}{M} \sum_{i=1}^{M} (x_i - \overline{x}_M)^2,$$

and monitor convergence to its asymptotic value $\sigma^2 \approx 0.0211$. We display the relative errors $|\overline{x}_M - \overline{x}|/|\overline{x}|$ and $|\sigma_M^2 - \sigma^2|/\sigma^2$, respectively, in Figure 5.3. The typical Monte Carlo $M^{-1/2}$ convergence rate is observed numerically.

Finally $M = 130000$ samples $\hat{x}_i$ are generated from the prior PDF using a standard normal random number generator. The probability densities resulting from the binned samples $\{x_i\}$ and $\{\hat{x}_i\}$ are displayed in Figure 5.4; note the similarity with the PDFs displayed in Figure 5.2. These approximative densities are obtained from the relative frequencies of the binned samples scaled by the inverses of the bin widths.

---

While Brownian dynamics samples asymptotically from its stationary distribution $\pi_X^*$, subsequent samples are not independent. This is different from the Monte Carlo methods we considered in Chapter 3. It is the case, however, that the two random variables $X(\tau_n)$ and $X(\tau_m)$ become almost independent for $\tau_n - \tau_m \gg 1$. This is called decorrelation. Our tool for understanding decorrelation is the linear Fokker–Planck equation (5.15).[3] If all solutions of the Fokker–Planck equation converge to the stationary PDF $\pi_X^*$ in the limit $\tau \to \infty$, then for any random variable $X(\tau_n)$, we have $\pi_X(x, \tau_n) \approx \pi_X^*(x)$ for large $\tau_n$, independently of the distribution of $X(\tau_m)$. This means that $X(\tau_n)$ and $X(\tau_m)$ are becoming independent in the limit $\tau_n - \tau_m \to \infty$. To determine whether solutions of the Fokker–Planck equation do indeed converge to the stationary PDF, we need to study the spectral properties of $\mathcal{L}$.

To analyse the eigenvalues of $\mathcal{L}$, we introduce the weighted inner product

$$\langle \pi_1, \pi_2 \rangle_* = \int_{\mathbb{R}^{N_x}} \pi_X^*(x)^{-1} \pi_1(x) \pi_2(x) \, dx$$

in the space of all integrable functions such that $\|\pi\|_* = \langle \pi, \pi \rangle_*^{1/2} < \infty$. Since

$$
\begin{aligned}
\langle \mathcal{L}\pi_1, \pi_2 \rangle_* &= \int_{\mathbb{R}^{N_x}} (\pi_X^*)^{-1} \pi_2 \nabla_x \cdot (\pi_1 \nabla_x U + \nabla_x \pi_1) dx \\
&= -\int_{\mathbb{R}^{N_x}} \nabla_x ((\pi_X^*)^{-1} \pi_2) \cdot (\pi_1 \nabla_x U + \nabla_x \pi_1) dx \\
&= -\int_{\mathbb{R}^{N_x}} (\pi_X^*)^{-1} (\nabla_x \pi_2 + \pi_2 \nabla_x U) \cdot (\pi_1 \nabla_x U + \nabla_x \pi_1) dx \\
&= -\int_{\mathbb{R}^{N_x}} \nabla_x ((\pi_X^*)^{-1} \pi_1) \cdot (\pi_2 \nabla_x U + \nabla_x \pi_2) dx \\
&= \int_{\mathbb{R}^{N_x}} (\pi_X^*)^{-1} \pi_1 \nabla_x \cdot (\pi_2 \nabla_x U + \nabla_x \pi_2) dx = \langle \pi_1, \mathcal{L}\pi_2 \rangle_*,
\end{aligned}
$$

we may conclude that $\mathcal{L}$ is self-adjoint with respect to the inner product $\langle \cdot, \cdot \rangle_*$. Hence the spectrum $\sigma(\mathcal{L})$ of $\mathcal{L}$ is on the real axis. Furthermore, since

$$
\begin{aligned}
\langle \mathcal{L}\pi, \pi \rangle_* &= \int_{\mathbb{R}^{N_x}} (\pi_X^*)^{-1} \pi \nabla_x \cdot (\pi \nabla_x U + \nabla_x \pi) dx \\
&= -\int_{\mathbb{R}^{N_x}} (\pi_X^*)^{-1} (\nabla_x \pi + \pi \nabla_x U) \cdot (\pi \nabla_x U + \nabla_x \pi) \, dx \\
&= -\|\pi \nabla_x U + \nabla_x \pi\|_*^2 \\
&\leq 0,
\end{aligned}
$$

all eigenvalues of $\mathcal{L}$ have to be non-positive. We express this by writing $\sigma(\mathcal{L}) \subset \{\lambda \in \mathbb{R} : \lambda \leq 0\}$.

To determine whether solutions converge to the stationary PDF, first we must ask whether (5.13) is the only eigenfunction (up to scaling by a constant) with eigenvalue zero. Second, in the case that (5.13) is indeed the only stationary PDF for (5.15), we must ask whether the remaining spectrum of $\mathcal{L}$ is bounded away from zero. If it is, then the non-zero eigenvalue with smallest magnitude determines the rate at which solutions converge to the stationary PDF, since all the non-stationary eigenfunctions will decay by at least that rate.

---

[3] Although we are discussing a discrete time process, we know that it converges to a continuous time process where the decorrelation process is somewhat easier to explain. Similar arguments can be made for the discrete time process.

Indeed, if (i) $U$ is smooth, (ii) $\int_{\mathcal{X}} \exp(-U(x))\mathrm{d}x < \infty$, and (iii) there is a constant $c > 0$ such that the Hessian matrix, $D^2 U(x)$, of second-order derivatives satisfies

$$v^{\mathrm{T}} D^2 U(x) v \geq c\|v\|^2,$$

for all $v \in \mathbb{R}^{N_x}$ and all $x \in \mathbb{R}^{N_x}$, then the canonical PDF (5.13) is the unique invariant density and

$$\sup[\sigma(\mathcal{L}) \setminus \{0\}] \leq -c. \tag{5.19}$$

See Pavliotis (2014) for a derivation of this result. Furthermore, solutions to the Fokker–Planck equation (5.15) can be written in semi-group form

$$\pi_X(\cdot, \tau) = e^{\tau \mathcal{L}} \pi_X(\cdot, 0). \tag{5.20}$$

This means that the non-stationary contributions in $\pi_X(x, 0)$ decay at least as quickly as $e^{-c\tau}$ as $\tau \to \infty$. A numerical approximation to the operator $e^{\tau \mathcal{L}}$ is discussed in Appendix 5.7. There we also perform numerical experiments to verify the bound (5.19) for Brownian dynamics with a particular choice of potential $U(x)$.

If Brownian dynamics fulfills a spectral gap condition of type (5.19), then

$$\overline{X}_M = \frac{1}{M} \sum_{n=1}^{M} X^n \tag{5.21}$$

satisfies a central limit theorem and a strong law of large numbers (compare Chapter 3) even though the random variables $X^n = X(\tau_n)$ are correlated. Here $X(\tau)$, $\tau \geq 0$, denotes the stochastic process induced by Brownian dynamics.

If Brownian dynamics is discretised by the Euler–Maruyama method (4.21), time-stepping errors lead to sampling errors which imply that the associated estimator (5.21) is inconsistent as $M \to \infty$, where $X^n$ now refers to the numerical approximation at $\tau_n = n\Delta\tau$. However, the inconsistency vanishes as $\Delta\tau \to 0$. The inconsistency can also be eliminated for finite step-sizes by combining (4.21) with a *Metropolis accept-reject criterion*. (See Definition 5.15 below.) The resulting Metropolis adjusted time-stepping method gives rise to a particular instance of a *Markov chain Monte Carlo (MCMC) method*, called the *Metropolis adjusted Langevin algorithm (MALA)* or *hybrid Monte Carlo (HMC) method* (Liu 2001). We remark that the Euler–Maruyama method (4.21) without a Metropolis criterion often leads to satisfactory results provided $\Delta\tau$ is chosen appropriately.

MCMC methods provide a flexible tool for generating samples from a desired PDF $\pi_X^*$. The basic idea is to combine a Markov process with symmetric transition PDF $\pi(z'|z) = \pi(z|z')$ in combination with a Metropolis accept/reject criterion in order to generate a modified Markov process with $\pi_X^*$ as an invariant PDF. This is a very broad topic; here we summarise the key ideas in the case of a finite state space $\mathcal{X} = \{a_1, a_2, \ldots, a_M\}$. We assume that we have a symmetric Markov chain on $\mathcal{X}$ with stochastic transition matrix $P \in \mathbb{R}^{M \times M}$, i.e., $p_{ij} = p_{ji}$.

**Definition 5.15** (Discrete state space Markov chain Monte Carlo (MCMC) method)
Given a desired probability distribution $p^* \in \mathbb{R}^M$ and a symmetric stochastic transition matrix $P \in \mathbb{R}^{M \times M}$ over a discrete state-space $\mathcal{X} = \{a_1, a_2, \ldots, a_M\}$, the modified Markov chain with stochastic transition matrix $\tilde{P}$ with entries

$$\tilde{p}_{ij} = (1 - \alpha_{ij})\delta_{ij} + \alpha_{ij}p_{ij}, \qquad \alpha_{ij} = 1 \wedge (p_i^*/p_j^*), \qquad (5.22)$$

gives rise to a *MCMC* method. The coefficients $\alpha_{ij} \in [0, 1]$ define the *Metropolis accept/rejection criterion*. Here $\delta_{ij}$ denotes the Kronecker symbol with values $\delta_{ii} = 1$ and $\delta_{ij} = 0$ for $i \neq j$ and

$$a \wedge b = \min\{a, b\}.$$

The invariance of $p^*$ under (5.22) follows from the *detailed balance* condition

$$\tilde{p}_{ij}p_j^* = \tilde{p}_{ji}p_i^* \qquad (5.23)$$

for all pairs $i, j = 1, \ldots, M$ since (5.23) implies

$$\sum_j \tilde{p}_{ij}p_j^* = \sum_j \tilde{p}_{ji}p_i^* = p_i^*.$$

Detailed balance is satisfied by (5.22) since $p_{ij} = p_{ji}$. In terms of practical implementation of (5.22) we proceed as follows. If the chain is in state $a_j$, draw a proposal state $a_i$ from $\mathcal{X}$ with probability $p_{ij}$. Next draw a uniform random number $\xi$ and accept the proposal if $\alpha_{ij} > \xi$ otherwise remain in the current state $a_j$. If $p^*$ is the only invariant probability vector and all other eigenvalues $\lambda_l$ of the induced Markov chain

$$p^{n+1} = \tilde{P}p^n$$

satisfy $|\lambda_l| < 1 - c$ for a $c > 0$, then again a central limit theorem and a strong law of large numbers hold for samples generated by the MCMC method.

## 5.3 Optimal coupling approach to Bayesian inference

In this section, we summarise the application of optimal transportation, as outlined in Chapter 2, to Bayesian inference. In the Bayesian context, it is often the case that we have samples from the prior distribution, but we wish to compute statistics from the posterior distribution. Recall that we introduced importance sampling in Chapter 3 as a form of Monte Carlo method which is used when we have samples from one distribution but we wish to compute statistics from another distribution. In this section, we will combine importance sampling with a transformation step which is based on the idea of optimal coupling and optimal transportation. This transformation step allows us to transform prior samples into posterior ones in a completely deterministic manner. Such transformations will become important when we discuss recursive applications of Bayes' theorem in Part II of this book.

To prepare for the transition to a recursive application of Bayes' theorem in the context of data assimilation, we introduce the terms *forecast* and *analysis* random variables (these are names which are used in the geosciences context and have different names in other fields). The forecast random variable gives rise to the prior distribution and a Bayesian assimilation of data then leads to the analysis random variable with its marginal distribution equal to the posterior PDF.

More specifically, given a prior or *forecast* random variable $X^f : \Omega \rightarrow \mathbb{R}^{N_x}$, we denote its PDF by $\pi_{X^f}(x)$, $x \in \mathbb{R}^{N_x}$, and consider the *assimilation* of an observed $y_{obs} \in \mathbb{R}^{N_y}$ with likelihood function $\pi_Y(y|x)$. The posterior or *analysis* PDF is given by

$$\pi_{X^a}(x|y_{obs}) = \frac{\pi_Y(y_{obs}|x)\pi_{X^f}(x)}{\int_{\mathbb{R}^{N_x}} \pi_Y(y_{obs}|x)\pi_{X^f}(x)\mathrm{d}x}, \tag{5.24}$$

according to Bayes' theorem.[4] It is important to emphasise that Bayes' theorem does not determine the random variable $X^a$ as a transformation from $X^f$. Instead Bayes' theorem only determines the marginal PDF $\pi_{X^a}(x|y_{obs})$; for given marginal PDF there are many possible couplings in general. Computing optimal couplings between $X^f$ and $X^a$ is the subject of this section.

Typically, the forecast random variable $X^f$ and its PDF are not available explicitly. Instead we assume that an ensemble of forecasts $x_i^f \in \mathbb{R}^{N_x}$, $i = 1,\ldots,M$, is given, which are considered as realisations $X_i^f(\omega)$, $\omega \in \Omega$, of $M$ independent (or dependent) random variables $X_i^f : \Omega \rightarrow \mathbb{R}^{N_x}$ with law $\pi_{X^f}$. Applying the importance sampling technique (see Chapter 3), we obtain the following estimator for $\mathbb{E}[g(X^a)]$ with respect to the posterior PDF $\pi_{X^a}(x|y_{obs})$ using the forecast ensemble:

$$\bar{g}_M^a = \sum_{i=1}^{M} w_i g(x_i^f),$$

with weights

$$w_i = \frac{\pi_Y(y_{obs}|x_i^f)}{\sum_{j=1}^{M} \pi_Y(y_{obs}|x_j^f)}. \tag{5.25}$$

This estimator is consistent (recall from Chapter 3 that an estimator is called consistent if the root mean square error between the estimator $\bar{g}_M^a$ and the exact expectation value $\bar{g}^a = \mathbb{E}[g(X^a)]$ vanishes as $M \rightarrow \infty$).

---

**Example 5.16**   We return to the Bayesian inference problem of Example 5.9. Instead of the Brownian dynamics sampling approach considered in Example 5.14 we now consider importance sampling by drawing $M$ samples $x_i$ from the

---

[4] Note that we will switch to the notation $Z^f$ and $Z^a$, respectively, in Part II of this book when the random variables under consideration come from a dynamical system or a more general Markov process.

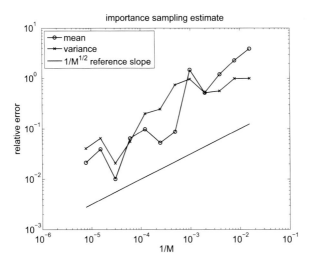

**Figure 5.5** Relative errors in the posterior mean and variance obtained from importance sampling with the samples drawn from the Gaussian prior. The relative errors are defined as in Example 5.14. The error behaviour is qualitatively similar to that displayed in Figure 5.3.

Gaussian prior $N(-2, 1/2)$ with posterior weights

$$w_i \propto e^{-\frac{1}{2}(h(x_i)-2)^2}.$$

The relative errors (as defined in Example 5.14) in the posterior mean and variance,

$$\bar{x}_M = \sum_{i=1}^{M} w_i x_i, \qquad \sigma_M^2 = \sum_{i=1}^{M} w_i (x_i - \bar{x}_M)^2,$$

are displayed in Figure 5.5 for a range of values of the ensemble size $M$. We observe an $M^{-1/2}$ convergence behaviour on average; the overall errors are comparable to those obtained from (5.18) in Example 5.14. We remark that examples could be easily constructed where importance sampling is more efficient than Monte Carlo sampling using Brownian dynamics and *vice versa*. Importance sampling is efficient if the posterior does not differ much from the prior and the prior is easy to sample from.

---

Instead of using weighted forecast samples, an alternative is to attempt to transform the samples $x_i^f = X_i^f(\omega)$ with $X_i^f \sim \pi_{X^f}$ into samples $x_i^a$ from the posterior distribution $\pi_{X^a}(x|y_{\text{obs}})$. Then we can use the estimator

$$\bar{g}_M^a = \frac{1}{M} \sum_{i=1}^{M} g(x_i^a),$$

with equal weights. In other words, we are looking for a coupling between the prior and posterior PDFs as discussed in Chapter 2.

Recall from Chapter 2 that for univariate random variables $X_1 = X^f$ and $X_2 = X^a$ with PDFs $\pi_{X^f}$ and $\pi_{X^a}$ respectively, the transformation is characterised by

$$F_{X^a}(x_i^a) = F_{X^f}(x_i^f), \tag{5.26}$$

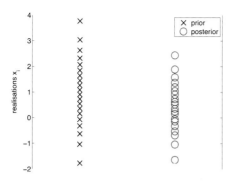

**Figure 5.6** Prior $x_i^{\mathrm{f}}$ and posterior $x_i^{\mathrm{a}}$ realisations from the transform method for $M = 20$.

where $F_{X^{\mathrm{f}}}$ and $F_{X^{\mathrm{a}}}$ denote the cumulative distribution functions of $X^{\mathrm{f}}$ and $X^{\mathrm{a}}$, respectively. Equation (5.26) requires knowledge of the associated PDFs; the extension to multivariate random variables is non-trivial. Instead, we propose an alternative approach that does not require explicit knowledge of the underlying PDFs and that easily generalises to multivariate random variables. This approach combines importance sampling with the idea of optimal transportation.

We have already discussed monomial resampling in Chapter 3, which can be used to generate posterior samples $\{x_i^{\mathrm{a}}\}$ from weighted prior samples $\{x_i^{\mathrm{f}}, w_i\}$. Monomial resampling effectively defines a *coupling* between the two discrete random variables $X_M^{\mathrm{f}} : \Omega \to \mathcal{X}_M$ and $X_M^{\mathrm{a}} : \Omega \to \mathcal{X}_M$ with realisations in $\mathcal{X}_M = \{x_1^{\mathrm{f}}, \ldots, x_M^{\mathrm{f}}\}$ and probability vector $p^{\mathrm{f}} = (1/M, \ldots, 1/M)^{\mathrm{T}}$ for $X_M^{\mathrm{f}}$ and $p^{\mathrm{a}} = (w_1, \ldots, w_M)^{\mathrm{T}}$ for $X_M^{\mathrm{a}}$, respectively. Here a coupling between $p^{\mathrm{f}}$ and $p^{\mathrm{a}}$ is an $M \times M$ matrix $T$ with non-negative entries $t_{ij} = (T)_{ij} \geq 0$ such that

$$\sum_{i=1}^{M} t_{ij} = \frac{1}{M}, \qquad \sum_{j=1}^{M} t_{ij} = w_i; \qquad (5.27)$$

compare Chapter 2.

Instead of defining a coupling $T$ through monomial resampling,[5] we seek the coupling $T^*$ that minimises the expected Euclidean distance

$$\mathbb{E}[\|X_M^{\mathrm{f}} - X_M^{\mathrm{a}}\|^2] = \sum_{i,j=1}^{M} t_{ij} \|x_i^{\mathrm{f}} - x_j^{\mathrm{f}}\|^2. \qquad (5.28)$$

As already discussed in Examples 2.28 and 2.34, the desired coupling $T^*$ is obtained by solving a linear transport problem. Since (5.27) leads to $2M - 1$ independent constraints, the matrix $T^*$ contains at most $2M - 1$ non-zero entries. Having computed $T^*$, the stochastic transition matrix $\mathrm{P} = M\,T^* \in \mathbb{R}^{M \times M}$ on $\mathcal{X}_M$ then has the property that the probability vectors $p^{\mathrm{f}}$ and $p^{\mathrm{a}}$ satisfy $p^{\mathrm{a}} = \mathrm{P}p^{\mathrm{f}}$.

---

[5] More precisely, monomial resampling can be interpreted as leading to a matrix $T$ with entries $t_{ij} = w_i/M$, which treats $X_M^{\mathrm{f}}$ and $X_M^{\mathrm{a}}$ as independent random variables.

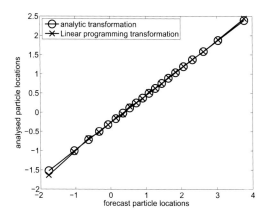

**Figure 5.7** Exact and numerical ensemble transform map for $M = 20$. The Gaussian case leads to the exact transformation being linear. The numerical approximation deviates from linearity mostly in the tails.

Given a set of $M$ realisations $x_j^f$, $j = 1, \ldots, M$, from the prior PDF and importance weights $w_i \propto \pi_Y(y_{\text{obs}} | x_i^f)$, a Monte Carlo resampling step proceeds now as follows.

(i) Compute the coupling matrix $T^*$ which is optimal under the cost function (5.28) and define discrete random variables $\hat{X}_j^a$, $j = 1, \ldots, M$, with law

$$\hat{X}_j^a \sim \begin{pmatrix} p_{1j} \\ \vdots \\ p_{Mj} \end{pmatrix}. \tag{5.29}$$

Here $p_{ij}$ denotes the $(i, j)$th entry of $\mathbf{P} = MT^*$ and each column vector in $\mathbf{P}$ defines a probability vector, i.e., $\sum_{i=1}^M p_{ij} = 1$.

(ii) An analysis ensemble $\{x_j^a\}$ of size $M$ is obtained by collecting a single realisation from each random variable $\hat{X}_j^a$, i.e., $x_j^a := \hat{X}_j^a(\omega)$ for $j = 1, \ldots, M$. This ensemble of equally weighted samples allows for the approximation of expectation values with respect to the posterior distribution $\pi_{X^a}(x | y_{\text{obs}})$.

The outlined procedure leads to a particular instance of resampling with replacement. The main difference with the resampling techniques discussed in Chapter 3 is that the resampling is chosen such that the expected distance (5.28) between the prior and posterior samples is minimised (which is equivalent to maximising the correlation between the prior and posterior samples).

We now introduce a further modification which replaces the random resampling step by a linear transformation. The modification is based on the observation that the expectation values of the random variables (5.29) are given by

$$\bar{x}_j^a = \mathbb{E}[\hat{X}_j^a] = \sum_{i=1}^M x_i^f p_{ij}. \tag{5.30}$$

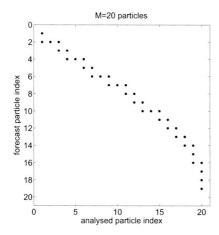

**Figure 5.8** Non-zero entries in the matrix P for $M = 20$, which indicate the support of the coupling. There are a total of $2M - 1 = 39$ non-zero entries. The banded structure reveals the spatial locality and the cyclical monotonicity of the resampling step.

We use this result to propose the deterministic transformation

$$x_j^a := \overline{x}_j^a = \sum_{i=1}^{M} x_i^f p_{ij}, \tag{5.31}$$

$j = 1, \ldots, M$, hoping that

$$\overline{g}_M^a = \frac{1}{M} \sum_{j=1}^{M} g(\overline{x}_j^a)$$

still provides a consistent estimator for $\mathbb{E}[g(X^a)]$ as $M \to \infty$. Indeed, consistency for the posterior mean, i.e., $g(x) = x$, follows from

$$\overline{x}_M^a = \frac{1}{M} \sum_{j=1}^{M} x_j^a = \frac{1}{M} \sum_{j=1}^{M} \sum_{i=1}^{M} p_{ij} x_i^f = \sum_{i,j} t_{ij}^* x_i^f = \sum_{i=1}^{M} w_i x_i^f.$$

Consistency for a general $g$ is less obvious. Before investigating the theoretical properties of the proposed transformation (5.31) we discuss an example, which indicates that (5.31) leads to a consistent approximation to (5.26) in the limit $M \to \infty$.

---

**Example 5.17**   We take the univariate Gaussian with mean $\overline{x} = 1$ and variance $\sigma^2 = 2$ as the PDF for the prior random variable $X^f$. Realisations of $X^f$ are generated using

$$x_i^f = 1 + 2\,\mathrm{erf}^{-1}(2u_i - 1), \quad u_i = \frac{1}{2M} + \frac{i-1}{M}$$

for $i = 1, \ldots, M$. The likelihood function is

$$\pi_Y(y_{\mathrm{obs}}|x) = \frac{1}{\sqrt{4\pi}} \exp\left(\frac{-(y_{\mathrm{obs}} - x)^2}{4}\right)$$

with assumed observed value $y_{\mathrm{obs}} = 0.1$. Bayes' formula yields a posterior distribution which is Gaussian with mean $\overline{x} = 0.55$ and variance $\sigma^2 = 1$. Since

**Table 5.1** Estimated posterior first- to fourth-order moments from the ensemble transform method applied to a Gaussian scalar Bayesian inference problem.

|  | $\overline{x}$ | $\sigma^2$ | $\mathbb{E}[(X - \overline{x})^3]$ | $\mathbb{E}[(X - \overline{x})^4]$ |
|---|---|---|---|---|
| $M = 10$ | 0.5361 | 1.0898 | −0.0137 | 2.3205 |
| $M = 40$ | 0.5473 | 1.0241 | 0.0058 | 2.7954 |
| $M = 100$ | 0.5493 | 1.0098 | −0.0037 | 2.9167 |

we are dealing with univariate random variables in this example, the matrix $T^*$ of the associated optimal transport problem can be computed efficiently by the algorithm described in Appendix 5.8 at the end of this chapter. The prior and posterior realisations from the transform method are shown for $M = 20$ in Figure 5.6. We also display the analytic transform, which is a straight line in the case of Gaussian distributions,[6] and the approximative transform using optimal transport in Figure 5.7. The locations of the non-zero entries of the stochastic transition matrix P are displayed in Figure 5.8, which shows a banded structure of local interactions. The staircase-like arrangement is due to cyclical monotonicity of the support of $T^*$. More generally, we obtain the posterior estimates for the first four moments displayed in Table 5.1, which indicate convergences as $M \to \infty$. In fact, since non-random samples $\{x_i^{\mathrm{f}}\}$ are being used, the convergence rate is first-order in $1/M$.

We now proceed with a theoretical investigation of the transformation (5.31). Our convergence result is based on the following lemma and general results from McCann (1995).

**Lemma 5.18**   The set $\mathcal{T}$ consisting of all pairs $(x_j^{\mathrm{f}}, \overline{x}_j^{\mathrm{a}})$, $j = 1, \ldots, M$, with $\overline{x}_j^{\mathrm{a}}$ defined by (5.30), is cyclically monotone.

*Proof*   Let $\mathcal{I}_j$ denote the set of indices $i$ where $p_{ij} = Mt_{ij}^* > 0$. From Theorem 2.35, the optimal coupling $T^*$ satisfies cyclical monotonicity. Hence let $\mathcal{S}$ denote the support of $\mu^*_{X_M^{\mathrm{f}} X_M^{\mathrm{a}}}$, i.e., the set of all $(x_j^{\mathrm{f}}, x_i^{\mathrm{f}}) \in \mathcal{X}_M \times \mathcal{X}_M$ such that $t_{ij}^* > 0$. (Compare Example 2.34.) Then

$$\langle \xi_1^{\mathrm{a}}, \xi_2^{\mathrm{f}} - \xi_1^{\mathrm{f}} \rangle + \langle \xi_2^{\mathrm{a}}, \xi_3^{\mathrm{f}} - \xi_2^{\mathrm{f}} \rangle + \cdots + \langle \xi_l^{\mathrm{a}}, \xi_{l+1}^{\mathrm{f}} - \xi_l^{\mathrm{f}} \rangle + \cdots + \langle \xi_L^{\mathrm{a}}, \xi_1^{\mathrm{f}} - \xi_L^{\mathrm{f}} \rangle \leq 0 \quad (5.32)$$

for any set of pairs $(\xi_l^{\mathrm{f}}, \xi_l^{\mathrm{a}}) \in \mathcal{S}$, $l = 1, \ldots, L$. In particular, (5.32) holds for sequences containing a term of type

$$\langle \xi_l^{\mathrm{a}}, \xi_{l+1}^{\mathrm{f}} - \xi_l^{\mathrm{f}} \rangle = \langle x_i^{\mathrm{f}}, \xi_{l+1}^{\mathrm{f}} - x_j^{\mathrm{f}} \rangle$$

with $\xi_l^{\mathrm{f}} = x_j^{\mathrm{f}}$ and $\xi_l^{\mathrm{a}} = x_i^{\mathrm{f}}$ for an appropriate index $j$ and $i \in \mathcal{I}_j$. By linearity

---

[6] Gaussian random variables are transformed into each other by shifting their centres and scaling the anomalies. As already discussed in Chapter 2, this is equivalent to a linear transformation.

of $\langle x_i^{\mathrm{f}}, \xi_{l+1}^{\mathrm{f}} - x_j^{\mathrm{f}} \rangle$ in each of its two arguments, (5.32) then also applies to linear combinations giving rise to

$$\sum_{i=1}^{M} p_{ij} \left\{ \langle \xi_1^{\mathrm{a}}, \xi_2^{\mathrm{f}} - \xi_1^{\mathrm{f}} \rangle + \langle \xi_2^{\mathrm{a}}, \xi_3^{\mathrm{f}} - \xi_2^{\mathrm{f}} \rangle + \cdots + \langle x_i^{\mathrm{f}}, \xi_{l+1}^{\mathrm{f}} - x_j^{\mathrm{f}} \rangle + \cdots + \langle \xi_L^{\mathrm{a}}, \xi_1^{\mathrm{f}} - \xi_L^{\mathrm{f}} \rangle \right\}$$

$$= \langle \xi_1^{\mathrm{a}}, \xi_2^{\mathrm{f}} - \xi_1^{\mathrm{f}} \rangle + \langle \xi_2^{\mathrm{a}}, \xi_3^{\mathrm{f}} - \xi_2^{\mathrm{f}} \rangle + \cdots + \langle \overline{x}_j^{\mathrm{a}}, \xi_{l+1}^{\mathrm{f}} - x_j^{\mathrm{f}} \rangle + \cdots + \langle \xi_L^{\mathrm{a}}, \xi_1^{\mathrm{f}} - \xi_L^{\mathrm{f}} \rangle \le 0$$

since $\sum_{i=1}^{M} p_{ij} = 1$ and $p_{ij} > 0$ if and only if $i \in \mathcal{I}_j$. We finally use $\xi_l^{\mathrm{f}} = x_j^{\mathrm{f}}$ and $\overline{\xi}_l^{\mathrm{a}} = \overline{x}_j^{\mathrm{a}}$ and apply the same procedure to all indices $l' \in \{1, \ldots, L\} \setminus \{l\}$ resulting in

$$\langle \overline{\xi}_1^{\mathrm{a}}, \xi_2^{\mathrm{f}} - \xi_1^{\mathrm{f}} \rangle + \langle \overline{\xi}_2^{\mathrm{a}}, \xi_3^{\mathrm{f}} - \xi_2^{\mathrm{f}} \rangle + \cdots + \langle \overline{\xi}_l^{\mathrm{a}}, \xi_{l+1}^{\mathrm{f}} - \xi_l^{\mathrm{f}} \rangle + \cdots + \langle \overline{\xi}_L^{\mathrm{a}}, \xi_1^{\mathrm{f}} - \xi_L^{\mathrm{f}} \rangle \le 0.$$

Hence the set $\mathcal{T}$ is cyclically monotone. □

**Theorem 5.19**   Assume that the ensemble $\mathcal{X}_M^{\mathrm{f}} = \{x_i^{\mathrm{f}}\}_{i=1}^{M}$ consists of realisations from $M$ independent and identically distributed random variables $X_i^{\mathrm{f}} : \Omega \to \mathbb{R}^{N_x}$ with PDF $\pi_{X^{\mathrm{f}}}$. Define the set $\mathcal{X}_M^{\mathrm{a}} = \{\overline{x}_j^{\mathrm{a}}\}_{j=1}^{M}$ with the means $\{\overline{x}_j^{\mathrm{a}}\}$ given by (5.30). Then the associated maps $\Psi_M : \mathcal{X}_M^{\mathrm{f}} \to \mathcal{X}_M^{\mathrm{a}}$ defined for fixed $M$ by

$$\overline{x}_j^{\mathrm{a}} = \Psi_M(x_j^{\mathrm{f}}), \qquad j = 1, \ldots, M,$$

converge weakly to a map $\Psi : \mathbb{R}^{N_x} \to \mathbb{R}^{N_x}$ for $M \to \infty$. Furthermore, the random variable defined by $X^{\mathrm{a}} = \Psi(X^{\mathrm{f}})$ has distribution (5.24) and the expected distance between $X^{\mathrm{a}}$ and $X^{\mathrm{f}}$ is minimised among all such mappings.

The essence of this theorem can be found in McCann (1995). The only significant difference here is that McCann (1995) considers optimal couplings between $M$ independent samples $\{x_i^{\mathrm{f}}\}$ from the prior $\pi_{X^{\mathrm{f}}}$ and $M$ independent samples $\{x_i^{\mathrm{a}}\}$ from the posterior $\pi_{X^{\mathrm{a}}}$. The optimal coupling $\hat{\Psi}_M : \hat{\mathcal{X}}_M^{\mathrm{f}} \to \hat{\mathcal{X}}_M^{\mathrm{a}}$ between the uniform distribution on $\hat{\mathcal{X}}_M^{\mathrm{f}} = \{x_i^{\mathrm{f}}\}$ and the uniform distribution on $\hat{\mathcal{X}}_M^{\mathrm{a}} = \{x_i^{\mathrm{a}}\}$ is obtained by solving the associated assignment problem. Hence we only need to demonstrate that we may replace $\hat{\mathcal{X}}_M^{\mathrm{a}}$ and $\hat{\Psi}_M$ in the proof of McCann (1995) by the associated quantities defined in Theorem 5.19.

*Proof*   The maps $\Psi_M$, $M \ge 1$, define a sequence of couplings between discrete random variables on $\mathcal{X}_M^{\mathrm{f}}$ and $\mathcal{X}_M^{\mathrm{a}}$, which satisfy cyclical monotonicity according to Lemma 5.18. We may now follow the proof of Theorem 6 in McCann (1995) and conclude that these couplings converge weakly to a continuous coupling, i.e., a probability measure $\mu_{\tilde{X}^{\mathrm{f}}\tilde{X}^{\mathrm{a}}}$ on $\mathbb{R}^{N_x} \times \mathbb{R}^{N_x}$ with marginals $\pi_{\tilde{X}^{\mathrm{f}}}$ and $\pi_{\tilde{X}^{\mathrm{a}}}$, respectively. By construction it is clear that $\pi_{\tilde{X}^{\mathrm{f}}} = \pi_{X^{\mathrm{f}}}$. We still need to show that $\pi_{\tilde{X}^{\mathrm{a}}}(x) = \pi_{X^{\mathrm{a}}}(x|y_{\mathrm{obs}})$ and that the support of $\mu_{\tilde{X}^{\mathrm{f}}\tilde{X}^{\mathrm{a}}}$ is the graph of a map $\Psi$. The latter property follows from the fact that $\mu_{\tilde{X}^{\mathrm{f}}\tilde{X}^{\mathrm{a}}}$ is cyclically monotone and that the probability measure for $X^{\mathrm{f}}$ is absolutely continuous with respect to the Lebesgue measure on $\mathbb{R}^{N_x}$. Hence the Main Theorem of McCann (1995) can be applied to guarantee the existence and uniqueness of the map $\Psi$, which itself is the gradient of a convex potential $\psi$. The potential $\psi$ can be taken as the limit of a family of convex potentials $\psi_M$ on $\mathbb{R}^{N_x}$ such that

$$\mathcal{S}_M \subset \partial \psi_M,$$

i.e., the support $\mathcal{S}_M$ of the coupling $\mu^*_{X^f_M, X^a_M}$ induced by $T^*$ for fixed $M$ is included in the subdifferential of $\psi_M$ (see Theorem 2.27 in Villani (2003)), as well as

$$\mathcal{T}_M := \{(x^f_1, \bar{x}^a_1), \ldots, (x^f_M, \bar{x}^a_M)\} \subset \partial \psi_M.$$

This proves that $\mathcal{S}_M$ approaches $\mathcal{T}_M$ as $M \to \infty$ and $\pi_{\tilde{X}^a}(x) = \pi_{X^a}(x|y_{\text{obs}})$ since the weights $\{w_i\}$ are defined by importance sampling, which provides a consistent approximation to the posterior PDF. The coupling $\mu_{\tilde{X}^f \tilde{X}^a}$ solves the Monge–Kantorovitch problem with cost $c(x, y) = \|x - y\|^2$ (Villani 2003, Villani 2009). $\qquad \square$

In particular, this theorem implies that the variance of the random vectors $\hat{X}^a_j$, as defined by (5.29), vanishes as $M \to \infty$, and so the error replacing $\hat{X}^a_j$ by its mean vanishes in that limit.

---

**Example 5.20**   We return to the problem set out in Example 5.9 and implement importance sampling from the Gaussian prior as described in Example 5.16. Instead of estimating posterior expectation values from the samples $x^f_i$ with weights $w_i$, we now apply the linear transform method in order to generate posterior samples $x^a_i$ with uniform weights $w_i = 1/M$. The resulting estimates for the posterior mean and variance are displayed in Figure 5.9. We note that the results are almost identical to those displayed in Figure 5.5. This observation should be expected since the transform method starts by defining importance weights. Hence, the results from the transform method should not be more accurate than those obtained from importance sampling alone. At the same time we note that the transform method is not degrading the results either. In Chapters 7 and 8, we will find that samples with uniform weights are preferable when considering the recursive application of Bayes' theorem in the context of data assimilation.

---

## Problems

**5.1**   Consider a two-dimensional state variable $z \in \mathbb{R}^2$, a linear map $\psi(z) = Az$, and a linear forward operator $H = (1, 0)^T$. Formulate the associated MLE estimator for given $N_A \geq 1$ and given observations $y_{\text{obs}}(t_k) = H\psi^k(z) + \xi^k$, $\xi^k \sim N(0, R)$, $k = 1, \ldots, N_A$. Discuss necessary and sufficient conditions on $N_A$ and $A$ for the existence of a unique minimiser.

**5.2**   Show that the posterior median estimate $\hat{x}$, given by

$$\int_{-\infty}^{\hat{x}} \pi_X(x|y_{\text{obs}}) = 1/2,$$

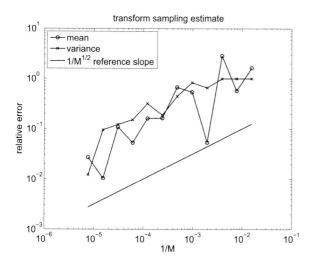

transform sampling estimate

**Figure 5.9** Relative errors for the posterior mean and variance for importance sampling combined with the transform method. We note that the results are essentially identical to those displayed in Figure 5.5. The results indicate that the transform method does not degrade the estimates (at the same time it cannot improve them since the transform method is entirely based on the prior samples $x_i^f$ and their importance weights $w_i$). The transform method will turn out to be advantageous when considering recursive applications of Bayesian inference. See Part II.

is indeed the minimiser with respect to the loss function $\ell(x, x') = \|x - x'\|$.

**5.3**  Compute the MAP estimate for the problem described in Example 5.9 by minimising the cost functional

$$L(x) = \frac{1}{2}\left(2 - \frac{7}{12}x^3 + \frac{7}{2}x^2 - 8x\right)^2 + (x+2)^2.$$

Compare the steepest decent method

$$x^{(l+1)} = x^{(l)} - L'(x^{(l)})$$

to Newton's method

$$x^{(l+1)} = x^{(l)} - \frac{L'(x^{(l)})}{L''(x^{(l)})}.$$

In both cases the iteration is started with $x^{(0)} = -2$.

**5.4**  Verify that (5.8)–(5.9) are mathematically equivalent to the formulas already derived for $\bar{x}^a$ and $P^a$ in Example 5.6.

**5.5**  Consider the linear Brownian dynamics model,

$$x^{n+1} = x^n - \Delta\tau x^n + \sqrt{2\Delta\tau}\xi^n, \tag{5.33}$$

with $\Delta\tau = 0.01$ and initial value $x^0 = 0$. This model has the Gaussian distribution $N(0, 1)$ as the invariant distribution in the limit $\Delta\tau \to 0$. Use the model in order to generate a total of $M_{\max} = 13000$ samples $x_i$ from the Gaussian distribution by storing every tenth iterate of (5.33). Compute empirical means and variances and compare those with the estimates obtained from $M$ independent samples using a standard random number generator. Plot the resulting approximation errors as a function of $1/M$.

**5.6**  Implement the transform method for univariate random variables as a subroutine using the algorithm from Appendix 5.8. Use $M$, $\{x_i^f\}$, and $w_i$ as inputs and provide the transformed ensemble $\{x_i^a\}$ as output. Apply your algorithm to Example 5.20. Prove that the algorithm does indeed solve the associated linear transport problem.

**5.7**   Consider a discrete Markov chain with three possible states $\mathcal{X} = \{1, 2, 3\}$ and transition matrix

$$P = \begin{pmatrix} 1/3 & 1/3 & 1/3 \\ 1/3 & 1/3 & 1/3 \\ 1/3 & 1/3 & 1/3 \end{pmatrix}.$$

What is the invariant discrete probability distribution for this Markov chain? Following Definition 5.15, use this discrete Markov chain to construct an MCMC sampler $\tilde{P}$ for the discrete probability distribution $p^* = (4/12, 3/12, 5/12)$. Implement the MCMC sampler and verify its correctness by computing relative frequencies of occurrence of each state $a_i = i$, $i = 1, 2, 3$.

**5.8**   The time evolution of the marginal PDF $\pi_X(x, t)$ under Brownian dynamics is characterised by the Fokker–Planck equation (5.16). A numerical discretisation of this partial differential equation is discussed in Appendix 5.7 and leads to an approximation of the operator $e^{\tau \mathcal{L}}$ in (5.20) by a Markov chain.

(i)   Using Equation (5.44), show that $\pi_j^n = \pi_j^*$ for all $j \in \mathbb{Z}$ is an invariant probability vector for the Markov chain.

(ii)   Implement the discretisation (5.44) for the problem described in Example 5.25 from Appendix 5.7 but with a coarser mesh-size of $\Delta x = 0.2$ and a total of $N_{\text{grid}} = 41$ grid points. The time-step is $\Delta \tau = \Delta x^2 / 4 = 0.1$. Compute all eigenvalues $\mu_l \in [-1, 1]$ and eigenvectors $v_l \in \mathbb{R}^{N_{\text{grid}}}$ of the associated Markov chain $P_{N_{\text{grid}}}$. Determine the coefficients $\beta_l = (\pi^0)^{\mathrm{T}} v_l$, where $\pi^0 \in \mathbb{R}^{N_{\text{grid}}}$ denotes the vector representation of the prior PDF with entries $\pi_k^0 = \mathrm{n}(x_k; -1, 1/2)$, $k = 1, \ldots, N_{\text{grid}}$ and grid points

$$x_k = \left( -\frac{N_{\text{grid}} - 1}{2} + k - 1 \right) \Delta x \in [-4, 4].$$

The time evolution of the initial vector $\pi^0$ is then explicitly given by

$$\pi^n = \sum_{l=1}^{N_{\text{grid}}} \beta_l v_l (\mu_l)^n.$$

What can you conclude about the convergence to the stationary distribution?

## 5.4        Guide to literature

Bayesian inference and a Bayesian perspective on inverse problems are discussed, in Kaipio & Somersalo (2005), Neal (1996), Lewis, Lakshmivarahan & Dhall (2006), and Robert (2001), for example. A discussion of infinite-dimensional Bayesian inference problems can be found in Stuart (2010) and Tarantola (2005), for example. We point to Hastie, Tibshirani & Friedman (2009) for a discussion of estimation and regression methods from a bias-variance perspective. Markov chain Monte Carlo methods are covered in Liu (2001) and Robert & Casella (2004). The two monographs Villani (2003) and Villani (2009) provide an in-depth introduction to optimal transportation and coupling of random variables. The link between Bayesian inference and optimal transportation is discussed by Moselhy & Marzouk (2012), Reich (2011), and Reich & Cotter (2013). The linear transformation method was introduced by Reich (2013*b*). Linear programming/transport and algorithmic implementations are covered in Nocedal & Wright (2006). A discussion of Brownian dynamics and its ergodic properties can, for example, be found in Pavliotis (2014).

## 5.5    Appendix: BLUE estimator

We have encountered several Bayesian estimators such as the posterior mean, and the maximum a posteriori estimator (MAP), in Definition 5.8. In this appendix, we briefly discuss another estimator which replaces the generally nonlinear conditional expectation (posterior mean) $\hat{X} = \phi^*(Y)$ with $\phi^* : \mathbb{R}^{N_x} \to \mathbb{R}^{N_y}$ defined by

$$\phi^*(y) = \int_{\mathbb{R}^{N_x}} x \pi_X(x|y) \mathrm{d}x.$$

We start from our familiar forward model

$$Y = h(X) + \Xi.$$

Here $\Xi$ is assumed to be centred, i.e., $\mathbb{E}[\Xi] = 0$ and independent of $X$.[7] No further assumptions about $X$ and $\Xi$ are being made. Instead we postulate a linear estimator of the form

$$\hat{X} = AY + b,$$

where $A \in \mathbb{R}^{N_x \times N_y}$ and $b \in \mathbb{R}^{N_x}$ are determined by minimising the expected distance $\mathbb{E}[\|X - \hat{X}\|^2]$. More specifically,

$$\mathbb{E}[\|X - \hat{X}\|^2] = \mathbb{E}[X^{\mathrm{T}}X] - 2\mathbb{E}[X^{\mathrm{T}}(AY+b)] + \mathbb{E}[(AY+b)^{\mathrm{T}}(AY+b)],$$

and minimisation leads to

$$\nabla_A \mathbb{E}[\|X - \hat{X}\|^2] = 2A\mathbb{E}[YY^{\mathrm{T}}] - 2\mathbb{E}[XY^{\mathrm{T}}] + 2b\mathbb{E}[Y^{\mathrm{T}}] = 0,$$

as well as

$$\nabla_b \mathbb{E}[\|X - \hat{X}\|^2] = -2\mathbb{E}[X] + 2b + 2A\mathbb{E}[Y] = 0.$$

The last equality implies

$$b = \overline{x} - A\overline{y}$$

---

[7] Conditional expectation for the special case $\Xi \equiv 0$ was discussed in Appendix 2.4.

with $\bar{y} = \mathbb{E}[h(X)]$. Upon substitution into the first equation, we obtain

$$0 = A(\mathbb{E}[YY^{\mathrm{T}}] - \bar{y}\,\bar{y}^{\mathrm{T}}) - (\mathbb{E}[XY^{\mathrm{T}}] - \bar{x}\,\bar{y}^{\mathrm{T}})$$
$$= AP_{yy} - P_{xy},$$

which finally yields the estimator

$$\hat{X} = \bar{x} + P_{xy}P_{yy}^{-1}(Y - \bar{y}). \tag{5.34}$$

This estimator is called the *best linear unbiased estimator* (BLUE).

Furthermore, let $P_{hh}$ denote the covariance matrix of $h(X)$ and $R$ the covariance matrix of $\Xi$, respectively. Since $X$ and $\Xi$ are assumed to be uncorrelated it holds that

$$P_{yy} = P_{hh} + R.$$

If, in addition, the forward operator is linear and $h(X) = HX$, then $P_{xy} = P_{xx}H^{\mathrm{T}}$, $P_{hh} = HP_{xx}H^{\mathrm{T}}$, and the BLUE estimator reduces to the Kalman estimate (5.8) for the mean, i.e.,

$$\hat{X} = \bar{x} + P_{xx}H^{\mathrm{T}}(HP_{xx}H^{\mathrm{T}} + R)^{-1}(Y - H\bar{x}),$$

once $Y$ is replaced by the observed value $y_{\text{obs}} = Y(\omega)$.

Since

$$X - \hat{X} = X - \bar{x} - P_{xy}P_{yy}^{-1}(Y - H\bar{x}),$$

the covariance matrix $\mathbb{E}[(X - \hat{X})(X - \hat{X})^{\mathrm{T}}]$ satisfies

$$\mathbb{E}[(X - \hat{X})(X - \hat{X})^{\mathrm{T}}] = P_{xx} - 2P_{xy}P_{yy}^{-1}P_{xy}^{\mathrm{T}} + P_{xy}P_{yy}^{-1}P_{yy}P_{yy}^{-1}P_{xy}^{\mathrm{T}}$$
$$= P_{xx} - P_{xx}H^{\mathrm{T}}(HP_{xx}H^{\mathrm{T}} + R)^{-1}HP_{xx},$$

which is the Kalman update formula (5.9) for the covariance matrix in $x$ under a linear forward operator $H$.

## 5.6      Appendix: A geometric view on Brownian dynamics

Following Otto (2001) and Villani (2003), in this appendix we demonstrate that certain evolution equations for PDFs, such as the diffusion equation and the Fokker–Planck equation for Brownian dynamics, possess a gradient flow structure. This helps to characterise their evolution towards an equilibrium state.

We first introduce some notation.

**Definition 5.21** (Differential geometric structure on manifold of probability densities)   We formally introduce the *manifold of all PDFs on* $\mathcal{Z} = \mathbb{R}^{N_z}$

$$\mathcal{M} = \left\{ \pi : \mathbb{R}^{N_z} \to \mathbb{R} : \pi(z) \geq 0, \int_{\mathbb{R}^{N_z}} \pi(z)\mathrm{d}z = 1 \right\},$$

with *tangent space*

$$T_\pi \mathcal{M} = \left\{ \phi : \mathbb{R}^{N_z} \to \mathbb{R} : \int_{\mathbb{R}^{N_z}} \phi(z) dz = 0 \right\}.$$

It is a manifold rather than a vector space due to the constraint that the PDF must be positive, and integrate to 1; neither of these properties is invariant under linear transformations.

The *variational derivative* of a functional $F : \mathcal{M} \to \mathbb{R}$ is defined as

$$\int_{\mathbb{R}^{N_z}} \frac{\delta F}{\delta \pi} \phi \, dz = \lim_{\epsilon \to 0} \frac{F(\pi + \epsilon \phi) - F(\pi)}{\epsilon},$$

where $\phi$ is a function such that $\int_{\mathbb{R}^{N_z}} \phi dz = 0$, i.e., $\phi \in T_\pi \mathcal{M}$.

Consider the potential $V : \mathcal{M} \to \mathbb{R}$ given by

$$V(\pi_Z) = \int_{\mathbb{R}^{N_z}} \pi_Z \ln \pi_Z dz, \tag{5.35}$$

which has variational derivative

$$\frac{\delta V}{\delta \pi_Z} = \ln \pi_Z,$$

since

$$V(\pi_Z + \epsilon \phi) = V(\pi_Z) + \epsilon \int_{\mathbb{R}^{N_z}} (\phi \ln \pi_Z + \phi) dz + \mathcal{O}(\epsilon^2)$$

$$= V(\pi_Z) + \epsilon \int_{\mathbb{R}^{N_z}} \ln \pi_Z \phi \, dz + \mathcal{O}(\epsilon^2),$$

having made use of the fact that $\phi$ integrates to zero. Hence we find that the diffusion part of the Fokker–Planck equation is equivalent to

$$\frac{\partial \pi_Z}{\partial t} = \nabla_z \cdot (Q \nabla_z \pi_Z) = \nabla_z \cdot \left\{ \pi_Z Q \nabla_z \frac{\delta V}{\delta \pi_Z} \right\}. \tag{5.36}$$

**Proposition 5.22** (Gradient on the manifold of probability densities)  Let $g_\pi$ be a metric tensor defined on $T_\pi \mathcal{M}$ as

$$g_\pi(\phi_1, \phi_2) = \int_{\mathbb{R}^{N_z}} (\nabla_z \psi_1) \cdot (M \nabla_z \psi_2) \, \pi \, dz$$

with potentials $\psi_i$, $i = 1, 2$, determined by the elliptic partial differential equation (PDE)

$$-\nabla_z \cdot (\pi M \nabla_z \psi_i) = \phi_i,$$

where $M \in \mathbb{R}^{N_z \times N_z}$ is a symmetric, positive-definite matrix.

Then, the gradient of potential $F(\pi)$ under $g_\pi$ satisfies

$$\operatorname{grad}_\pi F(\pi) = -\nabla_x \cdot \left( \pi M \nabla_z \frac{\delta F}{\delta \pi} \right). \tag{5.37}$$

*Proof*  Given the metric tensor $g_\pi$, the gradient of a functional $F(\pi)$ is defined by

$$g_\pi(\text{grad}_\pi F(\pi), \phi) = \int_{\mathbb{R}^{N_z}} \frac{\delta F}{\delta \pi} \phi \, dz, \tag{5.38}$$

which has to hold for all $\phi \in T_\pi \mathcal{M}$. Since

$$\phi = -\nabla_z \cdot (\pi M \nabla_z \psi_1),$$

and

$$\text{grad}_\pi F(\pi) = -\nabla_z \cdot (\pi M \nabla_z \psi_2),$$

for suitable potentials $\psi_1$ and $\psi_2$, respectively, we need to demonstrate that $\psi_2 = \frac{\delta F}{\delta \pi}$ is consistent with (5.38). Indeed, we find that

$$\int_{\mathbb{R}^{N_z}} \frac{\delta F}{\delta \pi} \phi \, dz = -\int_{\mathbb{R}^{N_z}} \frac{\delta F}{\delta \pi} \nabla_z \cdot (\pi M \nabla_z \psi_1) \, dz$$

$$= \int_{\mathbb{R}^{N_z}} \pi \nabla_z \frac{\delta F}{\delta \pi} \cdot (M \nabla_x \psi_1) \, dz$$

$$= \int_{\mathbb{R}^{N_z}} (\nabla_z \psi_2) \cdot (M \nabla_z \psi_1) \pi \, dz$$

$$= g_\pi(\phi_2, \phi_1) ,$$

with $\phi_1 = \phi$ and $\phi_2 = \text{grad}_\pi F(\pi)$.  $\square$

It follows that the diffusion part of the Fokker–Planck equation can be viewed as a gradient flow on the manifold $\mathcal{M}$. More precisely, set $F(\pi) = V(\pi_Z)$ and $M = Q$ to reformulate (5.36) as a gradient flow

$$\frac{\partial \pi_Z}{\partial t} = -\text{grad}_{\pi_Z} V(\pi_Z),$$

with potential (5.35). We note that

$$\frac{dV}{dt} = \int_{\mathbb{R}^{N_z}} \frac{\delta V}{\delta \pi_Z} \frac{\partial \pi_Z}{\partial t} \, dz$$

$$= -\int_{\mathbb{R}^{N_z}} \left(\nabla_z \frac{\delta V}{\delta \pi_Z}\right) \cdot \left(Q \nabla_z \frac{\delta V}{\delta \pi_Z}\right) \pi_Z \, dz \leq 0.$$

While we have considered the diffusion equation so far, it turns out that the entire Fokker–Planck equation (4.26) can be viewed as a gradient system on the manifold $\mathcal{M}$ of all PDFs $\pi_Z$ in the case of Brownian dynamics.

**Proposition 5.23** (Geometric structure of Brownian dynamics)   The Fokker–Planck equation (4.26) with $f(z) = -\nabla_z U(z)$ and $Q = I$ (Brownian dynamics) can be formulated as a gradient system

$$\frac{\partial \pi_Z}{\partial t} = -\text{grad}_{\pi_Z} V_{\text{BD}}(\pi_Z), \tag{5.39}$$

with potential

$$V_{\mathrm{BD}}(\pi_Z) = \int_{\mathbb{R}^{N_z}} \pi_Z \ln \pi_Z \, \mathrm{d}z - \int_{\mathbb{R}^{N_z}} \pi_Z \ln \pi_Z^* \, \mathrm{d}z.$$

The canonical PDF (5.13) satisfies $V_{\mathrm{BD}}(\pi_Z^*) = 0$. Note that $V_{\mathrm{BD}}(\pi_Z)$ is equal to the *Kullback–Leibler divergence*,

$$d_{\mathrm{KL}}(\pi_Z | \pi_Z^*) = \int_{\mathbb{R}^{N_z}} \pi_Z \ln \frac{\pi_Z}{\pi_Z^*} \, \mathrm{d}z \ ,$$

between $\pi_Z$ and $\pi_Z^*$.

*Proof*  This follows from the definition of the gradient on the manifold $\mathcal{M}$ of PDFs. $\qquad\qquad\qquad\qquad\qquad\qquad\qquad\qquad\qquad\qquad\qquad\qquad\square$

There is an interesting generalisation of the *implicit Euler method* to gradient flows on $\mathcal{M}$ which we now state.

**Proposition 5.24** (Implicit Euler method for geometric formulation of Brownian dynamics)  The following abstract formulation of an implicit Euler method applied to (5.39) can be given on the manifold $\mathcal{M}$ of PDFs:

$$\pi_Z(t_{n+1}) = \arg\inf_{\pi_Z} \left( W(\pi_Z(t_n), \pi_Z)^2 + \delta t V_{\mathrm{BD}}(\pi_Z) \right),$$

where $W(\pi_Z(t_n), \pi_Z)$ denotes the $L^2$-Wasserstein distance between the two PDFs $\pi_Z(z)$ and $\pi_Z(z, t_n)$ and $\delta t > 0$ is the step-size.

*Proof*  We assume for simplicity that the solution $\pi_Z(t_{n+1})$ is obtained from $\pi_Z(t_n)$ through an appropriate transport map $z_2 = T(z_1)$. Furthermore the transport map shall be of the form $z_2 = z_1 + \delta t \nabla_z \psi(z_1)$, where $\psi$ is an appropriate potential. Hence the cost functional induced by the implicit Euler approximation can be replaced by

$$\begin{aligned}
\mathcal{L}[\nabla_z \psi] &= W(\pi_Z(t_n), \pi_Z)^2 + \delta t V_{\mathrm{BD}}(\pi_Z) \\
&= \frac{\delta t^2}{2} \int_{\mathcal{Z}} \|\nabla_z \psi\|^2 \pi_Z(t_n) \mathrm{d}z + \delta t V_{\mathrm{BD}}(\pi_Z),
\end{aligned}$$

with $\pi_Z$ given by

$$\pi_Z = \pi_Z(t_n) - \delta t \nabla_z \cdot (\pi_Z(t_n) \nabla_z \psi) + \mathcal{O}(\delta t^2),$$

in terms of the potential $\psi$. Next we take variations with respect to $\nabla_z \psi$. After some algebra using variational derivatives, we obtain

$$\frac{\delta \mathcal{L}}{\delta \nabla_z \psi} = \delta t^2 \pi_Z(t_n) \nabla_z \psi + \delta t^2 \pi_Z(t_n) \nabla_z \frac{\delta V_{\mathrm{BD}}}{\delta \pi_Z} + \mathcal{O}(\delta t^3).$$

Setting the variational derivative to zero yields

$$\nabla_z \psi = -\nabla_z \frac{\delta V_{\mathrm{BD}}}{\delta \pi_Z} + \mathcal{O}(\delta t),$$

and, therefore,

$$\frac{z_2 - z_1}{\delta t} = -\nabla_z \frac{\delta V_{\mathrm{BD}}}{\delta \pi_Z}(z_1) + \mathcal{O}(\delta t), \tag{5.40}$$

and the desired result follows from taking the limit $\delta t \to 0$. □

At this point, we mention another interesting link between the geometric structure on the manifold $\mathcal{M}$ of PDFs on $\mathcal{Z} = \mathbb{R}^{N_z}$ and optimal transportation as discussed in Chapter 2. In particular, it has been shown by Benamou & Brenier (2000) that the $L^2$-Wasserstein distance between two PDFs $\pi_{Z_1} \in \mathcal{M}$ and $\pi_{Z_2} \in \mathcal{M}$ can be equivalently defined as follows.

(i) We minimise

$$\mathcal{L}[v] = \frac{1}{2}\int_0^1 \int_{\mathbb{R}^{N_z}} \pi(z,s)\|v(z,s)\|^2 dz ds, \tag{5.41}$$

over all velocity fields $v(z,s) \in \mathbb{R}^{N_z}$ such that the associated time-evolved PDFs $\pi(z,s)$ satisfy the continuity equation

$$\frac{\partial \pi}{\partial s} = -\nabla_z \cdot (\pi v),$$

subject to the boundary conditions $\pi(z,0) = \pi_{Z_1}(z)$ and $\pi(z,1) = \pi_{Z_2}(z)$.

(ii) We then set $W_2(\pi_{Z_1}, \pi_{Z_2})^2 = \mathcal{L}[v^*]$, where $v^*$ denotes the minimiser.

(iii) Furthermore, the optimal transport map is given as the time-one flow map of

$$\frac{\mathrm{d}z}{\mathrm{d}s} = v^*(z,s),$$

and $v^*$ is defined as the gradient of a potential.

We finally discuss an application of the formulation (5.40) in the context of ensemble prediction methods for the underlying SDE (4.25) with $f(z) = -\nabla_z U(z)$. More specifically, we introduce the alternative ensemble equations

$$\frac{\mathrm{d}z_i}{\mathrm{d}t} = -\nabla_z \frac{\delta V_{\mathrm{BD}}}{\delta \pi_Z}(z_i)$$

$$= -\nabla_z U(z_i) - \frac{1}{\pi_Z(z_i,t)}\nabla_z \pi_Z(z_i,t), \tag{5.42}$$

$i = 1, \ldots, M$. In contrast with the SDEs (4.35), this formulation requires the PDF $\pi_Z(z,t)$, which is not explicitly available in general. However, a Gaussian approximation can be obtained from the available ensemble $z_i(t)$, $i = 1, \ldots, M$, using

$$\pi_Z(z,t) \approx \frac{1}{(2\pi)^{N_z/2}|P_M|^{1/2}}\exp\left(-\frac{1}{2}(z - \bar{z}_M(t))^{\mathrm{T}}P_M(t)^{-1}(z - \bar{z}_M(t))\right),$$

with empirical mean $\bar{z}_M$ and empirical covariance matrix $P_M$. Substituting this Gaussian approximation into (5.42) as well as replacing the gradient of $U$ by a general vector field $f$ and the noise covariance matrix $I$ by $Q$ yields the ensemble evolution equations

$$\frac{dz_i}{dt} = f(z_i) + QP_M^{-1}(z_i - \bar{z}_M),$$

$(5.43)$

which converges to the analytic solution for $M \to \infty$ in the case when the vector field $f$ is linear, i.e., $f(z) = Az + u$, and the initial PDF is Gaussian.

Note the plus sign in front of the second term in (5.43), which leads to increased spread in the ensemble members in agreement with what diffusion is meant to achieve. Switching the sign to a minus would instead drive the ensemble members closer together.

## 5.7     Appendix: Discrete Fokker–Planck equation

In this appendix, we explore the convergence to equilibrium of Brownian dynamics, through numerical experiments and in the one-dimensional case. We will do this by studying the convergence to equilibrium of the corresponding Fokker–Planck equation, directly approximating the densities using finite differences in phase space. In the language of Chapter 3, this is equivalent to using a deterministic quadrature rule in phase space, rather than using Monte Carlo approximation.

We formulate an appropriate finite-dimensional approximation to the operator $e^{\tau \mathcal{L}}$ in (5.20) for given step-size $\tau = \Delta\tau$ (which will also allow us to estimate the constant $c$ in the spectral estimate (5.19)). In particular, we start from the Fokker–Planck formulation (5.16) and introduce a space-time grid $(x_j, \tau_n) = (j\Delta x, n\Delta\tau)$ for $n \geq 0$ and $j \in \mathbb{Z}$. The associated grid values $\pi_X^*(x_j)$ are denoted by $\pi_j^*$ and the numerical approximations to $\pi_X(x_j, \tau_n)$ by $\pi_j^n$. A straightforward generalisation of the standard central difference approximation for the diffusion equation results in

$$\frac{\pi_j^{n+1} - \pi_j^n}{\Delta\tau} = \frac{\pi_{j+1/2}^* \left( \frac{\pi_{j+1}^n}{\pi_{j+1}^*} - \frac{\pi_j^n}{\pi_j^*} \right) - \pi_{j-1/2}^* \left( \frac{\pi_j^n}{\pi_j^*} - \frac{\pi_{j-1}^n}{\pi_{j-1}^*} \right)}{\Delta x^2},$$

$(5.44)$

with $\pi_{j\pm1/2}^* = \pi_X^*(x_{j\pm1/2})$. We next write this scheme in discrete Markov chain form (recall Definition 4.14 from Chapter 4 and formally set $\pi_i^n = p_n(i)$), and use the recurrence

$$\pi_j^{n+1} = p_{j,j+1}\pi_{j+1}^n + p_{j,j}\pi_j^n + p_{j,j-1}\pi_{j-1}^n,$$

with transition probabilities

$$p_{j,j} = 1 - \frac{\Delta\tau}{\Delta x^2} \frac{\pi_{j+1/2}^* + \pi_{j-1/2}^*}{\pi_j^*}, \quad p_{j,j\pm1} = \frac{\Delta\tau}{\Delta x^2} \frac{\pi_{j\pm1/2}^*}{\pi_{j\pm1}^*}.$$

These probabilities sum to one, i.e. $\sum_{i\in\mathbb{Z}} p_{i,j} = 1$, as required, and are all non-negative provided

$$\Delta \tau \leq \frac{\Delta x^2 \pi_j^*}{\pi_{j+1/2}^* + \pi_{j-1/2}^*}.$$

Upon formally defining infinite-dimensional probability vectors $\pi^n = \{\pi_j^n\}_{j \in \mathbb{Z}}$, $n \geq 0$, we rewrite this approximation in the discrete Markov chain formulation

$$\pi^{n+1} = P\pi^n,$$

where P denotes the *transition operator* with entries $p_{i,j}$ and $i, j \in \mathbb{Z}$.

So far we have considered a discrete grid with an infinite number of grid points. To compute the eigenvectors and eigenvalues on a computer, we need to further approximate the problem by restricting the grid to a finite domain $|j| \leq (N_{\text{grid}} - 1)/2$ for odd $N_{\text{grid}} > 0$. Furthermore, to guarantee accurate results, $N_{\text{grid}}$ must be chosen sufficiently large that the solution to the infinite domain problem has almost no probability outside the finite domain. In order to obtain a finite-dimensional transition matrix $\mathfrak{P}_{N_{\text{grid}}} \in \mathbb{R}^{N_{\text{grid}} \times N_{\text{grid}}}$ we introduce indices $l, k \in \{1, \dots, N_{\text{grid}}\}$ via

$$l = j + \frac{1}{2}(N_{\text{grid}} + 1), \qquad |j| \leq \frac{1}{2}(N_{\text{grid}} - 1),$$

and

$$k = i + \frac{1}{2}(N_{\text{grid}} + 1), \qquad |i| \leq \frac{1}{2}(N_{\text{grid}} - 1),$$

respectively. The entries of $\mathfrak{P}_{N_{\text{grid}}}$ are denoted by $\mathfrak{p}_{k,l}$ and are related to the entries of P by $\mathfrak{p}_{k,l} = p_{i,j}$. Since we also wish the resulting finite-dimensional matrix $\mathfrak{P}_{N_{\text{grid}}}$ to define a Markov chain we need to enforce that

$$\sum_{l=1}^{N_{\text{grid}}} \mathfrak{p}_{l,k} = 1,$$

for all $k = 1, \dots, N_{\text{grid}}$. This is achieved by redefining the first and last diagonal entries in $P_{N_{\text{grid}}}$ by

$$\mathfrak{p}_{1,1} = 1 - \mathfrak{p}_{2,1}, \qquad \mathfrak{p}_{N_{\text{grid}}, N_{\text{grid}}} = 1 - \mathfrak{p}_{N_{\text{grid}} - 1, N_{\text{grid}}}.$$

The matrix $\mathfrak{P}_{N_{\text{grid}}}$ provides an approximation to the propagator $e^{\Delta \tau \mathcal{L}}$. All eigenvalues of $\mathfrak{P}_{N_{\text{grid}}}$ are contained in the unit disc $\{\lambda \in \mathbb{C} : |\lambda| \leq 1\}$ of the complex plane and invariant distributions have eigenvalue one.

These ideas are made more concrete in the following example.

---

**Example 5.25**   Consider the Gaussian prior $\pi_X(x) = n(x; -1, 1/2)$, the likelihood

$$\pi_Y(y|x) = n(y; x, 1),$$

and an observed $y_{\text{obs}} = 1$. The resulting posterior PDF is then $\pi_X(x|y_{\text{obs}}) =$

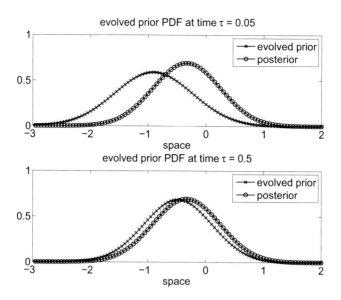

**Figure 5.10** Time evolution of the PDF under a Fokker–Planck equation with initial condition equal to the prior PDF and the posterior PDF as the stationary PDF. The time-evolved PDF is close to the stationary PDF at $\tau = 0.5$.

$n(x; -1/3, 1/3)$. The associated Brownian dynamics model is therefore

$$dX = -\frac{1}{3}\left(x + \frac{1}{3}\right)dt + \sqrt{2}dW$$

and $c = 3$ in (5.19). Instead of simulating Brownian dynamics, we implement the finite difference approximation (5.44) with $\pi_X^*$ given by the posterior distribution $\pi_X(x|y_{\mathrm{obs}})$. The mesh-size is $\Delta x = 0.05$, the number of grid points is $N_{\mathrm{grid}} = 161$, and the step-size is $\Delta\tau = 6.25 \times 10^{-4}$. The eigenvalues of the associated Fokker–Planck operator $\mathcal{L}$ can be approximated by computing the eigenvalues of $\mathfrak{P}_{N_{\mathrm{grid}}}$, taking their logarithm and finally dividing by $\Delta\tau$. We find that $\mathfrak{P}_{N_{\mathrm{grid}}}$ has a single eigenvalue equal to one, and that applying this procedure to the next largest eigenvalue $\mu$ gives $\lambda := \Delta\tau^{-1}\ln\mu \approx -3.00$. This eigenvalue determines the time-scale on which an initial PDF will approach the stationary posterior PDF; it agrees with the theoretical bound provided by (5.19). We demonstrate the approach to the stationary posterior distribution by starting from the prior distribution at $\tau = 0$ and display the evolved PDFs at time $\tau = 0.05$ and $\tau = 0.5$ in Figure 5.10. Note that $e^{0.05\lambda} \approx 0.8607$ and $e^{0.5\lambda} \approx 0.2231$. The time-scale of $1/\lambda$ determines the decorrelation time of a Monte Carlo sampling method based on the associated Brownian dynamics formulation (5.18).

## 5.8        Appendix: Linear transport algorithm in one dimension

The linear transport problem of finding the optimal transport matrix $T^*$ in the case of samples $\{x_i^{\mathrm{f}}\}$ from a univariate random variable can be solved efficiently by the following algorithm. The key observation is that scalar samples $x_i^{\mathrm{f}}$ can be sorted such that $x_1^{\mathrm{f}} \leq x_2^{\mathrm{f}} \leq \cdots \leq x_M^{\mathrm{f}}$.

The algorithm is described in the following pseudocode.

```
SORT SCALAR SAMPLES xf IN ASCENDING ORDER
COMPUTE ARRAY OF IMPORTANCE WEIGHTS w

FOR i = 1 : M
  w0(i) = 1 / M
END
i = M
j = M
WHILE i * j >= 1
  IF w(i) < w0(j)
      t(i,j) = w(i)
      w0(j) = w0(j) - w(i)
      i = i - 1
  ELSE
      t(i,j) = w0(j)
      w(i) = w(i) - w0(j)
      j = j - 1
  END
END
```

# Part II

## Bayesian Data Assimilation

# 6    Basic data assimilation algorithms

In this chapter, we return to the state estimation problem for dynamical systems as initially raised in Chapter 1. However, in contrast to Chapter 1, data assimilation algorithms will be based on a probabilistic interpretation of model-based forecasts in addition to measurement processes. Hence state estimation from partial and noisy observations can be put into the framework of Bayesian inference with model-based forecast uncertainties taking the role of prior distributions. Most of the mathematical ingredients have already been provided in the previous chapters. The goal of this chapter is to provide a concise mathematical formulation of the state estimation problem and to derive the *Kalman filter* for linear dynamical systems and Gaussian random variables on the one hand, and *particle filters* (also called sequential Monte Carlo methods) for general nonlinear dynamical systems and non-Gaussian distributions on the other. We will also touch upon *variational data assimilation* techniques as a natural link between the method of least squares, as considered in Chapter 1, and the assimilation techniques to be discussed in the remainder of this book. Applications of state estimation include, for example, weather forecasting, robotics, tracking using the global positioning system (GPS), and econometrics. In each of these cases partial and noisy observations are used in conjunction with a dynamical model in order to forecast future events. It is also often necessary to quantify forecast uncertainties; this is essential for taking decisions and/or for controlling the system under consideration.

In order to provide the necessary mathematical framework, we assume a model in the form of a stochastic difference equation

$$Z^{n+1} = Z^n + \delta t f(Z^n) + \sqrt{2\delta t}\,\Xi^n, \qquad t_{n+1} = t_n + \delta t, \qquad (6.1)$$

where $\Xi^n : \Omega \to \mathbb{R}^{N_z}$ are independent and identically distributed Gaussian random variables with mean zero and covariance matrix $Q$, $\delta t > 0$ is a given step-size, and $f : \mathbb{R}^{N_z} \to \mathbb{R}^{N_z}$ is a given vector field. We also assume that the marginal distribution $\pi_Z(z, 0)$ for $Z^0$ is given. This marginal distribution characterises our uncertainty about the initial state of our model at time $t = 0$. Recall that the time evolution of the marginal PDFs $\pi_Z(z, t_n)$ $(n \geq 1)$ under (6.1) is given recursively by the Chapman–Kolmogorov equation,

$$\pi_Z(z', t_{n+1}) = \int_{\mathbb{R}^{N_z}} \pi(z'|z)\pi_Z(z, t_n)\mathrm{d}z,$$

with transition kernel (conditional PDF)

$$\pi(z'|z) = \frac{1}{(4\pi\delta t)^{N_z/2}|Q|^{1/2}}$$

$$\times \exp\left(-\frac{1}{4\delta t}(z' - z - \delta t f(z))^{\mathrm{T}} Q^{-1}(z' - z - \delta t f(z))\right).$$

In addition to the stochastic dynamical model (6.1) and its initial PDF, we assume that noisy partial observations

$$y_{\mathrm{obs}}(t_k) \in \mathbb{R}^{N_y}, \quad t_k = k\Delta t_{\mathrm{out}}, \quad k = 1, 2, \ldots,$$

become available in regular time intervals of width $\Delta t_{\mathrm{out}} > 0$. We also assume that these observations are related to the unknown reference trajectory $z_{\mathrm{ref}}(t)$ of the dynamical model (6.1) by

$$Y^k = h(z_{\mathrm{ref}}(t_k), t_k) + \Sigma^k, \tag{6.2}$$

i.e., $y_{\mathrm{obs}}(t_k) = h(z_{\mathrm{ref}}(t_k), t_k) + \Sigma^k(\omega)$, where $\Sigma^k$ denotes a Gaussian random variable with mean zero and covariance matrix $R$ and $h(\cdot, t_k) : \mathbb{R}^{N_z} \to \mathbb{R}^{N_y}$ is the forward operator at observation time $t_k$. The conditional PDF for $Y_k$ given a state $z$ is therefore given by

$$\pi_Y(y|z, t_k) = \frac{1}{(2\pi)^{N_y/2}|R|^{1/2}} \exp\left(-\frac{1}{2}(y - h(z, t_k))^{\mathrm{T}} R^{-1}(y - h(z, t_k))\right). \tag{6.3}$$

We finally assume that the measurement errors, as represented by $\Sigma^k$, are mutually independent. The desired $z_{\mathrm{ref}}(t_n)$ is obtained from (6.1) with generally unknown initial condition $z_{\mathrm{ref}}(0)$ at $t = 0$ and unknown realisations $\xi^n = \Xi^n(\omega_{\mathrm{ref}})$. In other words, we view the unknown $z_{\mathrm{ref}}(t_n)$ as a particular realisation $Z^n(\omega_{\mathrm{ref}})$, $n \geq 0$, of the stochastic dynamical model (6.1). We call this scenario the *perfect model scenario* since the surrogate physical process and our mathematical forecasts use the same mathematical model. Data assimilation is used to infer information about $z_{\mathrm{ref}}(t_n)$ from the infinitely many possible realisations of a stochastic dynamical system (6.1), constrained only by the initial PDF $\pi_Z(z, t_0)$ and partial observations $y_{\mathrm{obs}}(t_k)$, to produce an estimate $\hat{z}(t_n)$ such that $\hat{z}(t_n)$ is close to $z_{\mathrm{ref}}(t_n)$ under an appropriate norm. It is also often necessary to quantify the uncertainty in the estimated states explicitly.

We distinguish three possible scenarios for obtaining such an estimate and its uncertainty in terms of probability densities.

**Definition 6.1** (Prediction, filtering and smoothing)   In the case where there are no observations available, our knowledge about a process $z_{\mathrm{ref}}(t)$ is encoded in the marginal PDFs $\pi_Z(z, t_n)$ for $Z^n$. When we are given observations $y_{\mathrm{obs}}(t_k)$, $k = 1, \ldots, N_{\mathrm{obs}}$, collected in an $N_y \times N_{\mathrm{obs}}$ matrix

$$y_{t_{1:N_{\mathrm{obs}}}}^{\mathrm{obs}} = (y_{\mathrm{obs}}(t_1), y_{\mathrm{obs}}(t_2), \ldots, y_{\mathrm{obs}}(t_{N_{\mathrm{obs}}})) \in \mathbb{R}^{N_y \times N_{\mathrm{obs}}},$$

our knowledge is encoded in the conditional, marginal PDFs $\pi_Z(z, t_n | y_{t_{1:N_{\mathrm{obs}}}}^{\mathrm{obs}})$ for

$Z^n | y_{t_{1:N_{obs}}}^{obs}$ . The task of calculating these PDFs takes one of the following three names:

(i) *prediction* if $t_n > t_{N_{obs}}$,
(ii) *filtering* if $t_n = t_{N_{obs}}$, and
(iii) *smoothing* if $t_n < t_{N_{obs}}$.

In each of the three cases, an estimate $\hat{z}(t_n)$ can be obtained by using an appropriate Bayesian estimate as introduced in (5.8).[1]

The Kalman and particle filters are, as their names indicate, primarily related to the filtering problem, while variational data assimilation is equivalent to solving a smoothing problem with $t_n = 0$.

We continue with a closer inspection of the filtering problem and derive recursive representations of the conditional, marginal PDFs $\pi_Z(z, t_k | y_{t_{1:k}}^{obs})$ for $k = 1, \ldots, N_{obs}$. Let us assume, for simplicity, that

$$\Delta t_{out} = N_{out} \delta t,$$

in which case the $N_{out}$-fold application of the Chapman–Kolmogorov equation leads from the initial PDF $\pi_Z(z, 0)$ at $t = 0$ to

$$\pi_Z(z', t_1) = \int_{\mathbb{R}^{N_z}} \pi_{N_{out}}(z'|z)\pi_Z(z, 0)dz,$$

with the transition kernel $\pi_{N_{out}}(z'|z)$ appropriately defined (see Equation (4.33)). Suppose an observation $y_{obs}(t_1)$ is available at $t_1$; then the filtering problem with $N_{obs} = 1$ is solved via Bayes' theorem by

$$\pi_Z(z, t_1 | y_{t_{1:1}}^{obs}) = \frac{\pi_Y(y_{obs}(t_1)|z, t_1)\, \pi_Z(z, t_1)}{\int_{\mathbb{R}^{N_z}} \pi_Y(y_{obs}(t_1)|z, t_1)\, \pi_Z(z, t_1)\, dz},$$

with

$$\pi_Y(y|z, t_1) = \frac{1}{(2\pi)^{N_y/2}|R|^{1/2}} \exp\left(-\frac{1}{2}(y - h(z, t_1))^T R^{-1}(y - h(z, t_1))\right).$$

Furthermore, the prediction problem with $t_n > t_1$, conditioned on having observed $y_{obs}(t_1)$, can again be solved by applying the Chapman–Kolmogorov equation. We obtain, in particular,

$$\pi_Z(z', t_2 | y_{t_{1:1}}^{obs}) = \int_{\mathbb{R}^{N_z}} \pi_{N_{out}}(z'|z)\pi_Z(z, t_1 | y_{t_{1:1}}^{obs})dz,$$

for $n = 2N_{out}$, i.e., $t_n = t_2$. If we now set $N_{obs} = 2$ in Definition 6.1, then the associated filtering problem is solved by yet another application of Bayes' formula:

$$\pi_Z(z, t_2 | y_{t_{1:2}}^{obs}) = \frac{\pi_Y(y_{obs}(t_2)|z, t_2)\, \pi_Z(z, t_2 | y_{t_{1:1}}^{obs})}{\int_{\mathbb{R}^{N_z}} \pi_Y(y_{obs}(t_2)|z, t_2)\, \pi_Z(z, t_2 | y_{t_{1:1}}^{obs})\, dz}.$$

---

[1] These estimates are themselves realisations of random variables $\hat{Z}(t_n)$ which are conditioned on the sequence of random observations $y_{t_{1:N_{obs}}}^{obs} = Y_{t_{1:N_{obs}}}(\omega)$ with $Y_{t_{1:N_{obs}}} := (Y(t_1), \ldots, Y(t_{N_{obs}}))$. See Chapter 9 for more details.

These steps can be repeated recursively to solve the filtering problem from Definition 6.1 for any $N_{\mathrm{obs}} \geq 1$. More precisely, given the conditional PDF $\pi_Z(z, t_{k-1} | y_{t_{1:k-1}}^{\mathrm{obs}})$ for the filtering problem at $t = t_{k-1}$, the Chapman–Kolmogorov equation

$$\pi_Z(z, t_k | y_{t_{1:k-1}}^{\mathrm{obs}}) = \int_{\mathbb{R}^{N_z}} \pi_{N_{\mathrm{out}}}(z|z')\pi_Z(z', t_{k-1} | y_{t_{1:k-1}}^{\mathrm{obs}})dz', \qquad (6.4)$$

yields the marginal PDF for the prediction problem at $t = t_k$ conditioned on having observed $y_{t_{1:k-1}}^{\mathrm{obs}}$. This marginal PDF is then used as a prior for assimilating an observation $y_{\mathrm{obs}}(t_k)$ via Bayes' theorem

$$\pi_Z(z, t_k | y_{t_{1:k}}^{\mathrm{obs}}) = \frac{\pi_Y(y_{\mathrm{obs}}(t_k)|z, t_k)\,\pi_Z(z, t_k | y_{t_{1:k-1}}^{\mathrm{obs}})}{\int_{\mathbb{R}^{N_z}} \pi_Y(y_{\mathrm{obs}}(t_k)|z, t_k)\,\pi_Z(z, t_k | y_{t_{1:k-1}}^{\mathrm{obs}})\,dz}, \qquad (6.5)$$

which solves the filtering problem for $t = t_k$.

We summarise the recursive approach to *sequential data assimilation* in the following definition.

**Definition 6.2** (Sequential data assimilation)    Given a stochastic dynamical system (6.1) with initial PDF $\pi(z, 0)$ and observations $y_{\mathrm{obs}}(t)$ for $t = t_1, \ldots, t_{N_{\mathrm{obs}}}$ in observation intervals of $\Delta t_{\mathrm{out}} = N_{\mathrm{out}}\delta t$, $N_{\mathrm{out}} \geq 1$, and forward model (6.2), the marginal filtering distributions $\pi_Z(z, t_k | y_{t_{1:k}}^{\mathrm{obs}})$, $k = 1, \ldots, N_{\mathrm{obs}}$, are recursively defined by first solving the prediction problem (6.4) followed by the Bayesian assimilation step (6.5).

An important remark has to be made at this point. Sequential data assimilation, as stated above, provides us with a sequence of marginal filtering distributions $\pi_Z(z, t_k | y_{t_{1:k}}^{\mathrm{obs}})$ for conditioned random variables $\tilde{Z}(t_k) := Z(t_k)|y_{t_{1:k}}^{\mathrm{obs}}$, $k = 1, \ldots, N_{\mathrm{obs}}$. However, it does *not* specify joint distributions $\pi_{\tilde{Z}_{t_{0:k}}}(\tilde{z}_{t_{0:k}}|y_{t_{1:k}}^{\mathrm{obs}})$ for the family of conditioned random variables

$$\tilde{Z}_{t_{0:k}} = (\tilde{Z}(t_0), \tilde{Z}(t_1), \ldots, \tilde{Z}(t_k)).$$

In particular, nothing is being said about mutual dependencies amongst $\tilde{Z}(t_{k_1})$ and $\tilde{Z}(t_{k_2})$ for $k_1 \neq k_2$. In order to define such families of random variables and their joint distributions we need to employ the concept of coupling as introduced in Chapter 2. This will be the subject of Chapter 7, allowing us to give the families $\tilde{Z}_{t_{0:k}}$ an interpretation in terms of Markov processes, which is at the heart of the McKean approach to data assimilation. In this chapter, we continue with a traditional discussion of the filtering problem purely at the level of marginal PDFs.

In order to simplify the subsequent discussions, we assume from now on that the forward operator $h$ in (6.2) does not explicitly depend on time and the associated conditional PDF (6.3) simplifies to

$$\pi_Y(y|z) = \frac{1}{(2\pi)^{N_y/2}|R|^{1/2}} \exp\left(-\frac{1}{2}(y - h(z))^\mathrm{T} R^{-1}(y - h(z))\right).$$

## 6.1    Kalman filter for linear model systems

There is a particular case for which the sequential filtering formulation from the previous section can be implemented algorithmically in closed form; namely when the initial PDF is Gaussian, the evolution model is linear,

$$Z^{n+1} = Z^n + \delta t(DZ^n + b) + \sqrt{2\delta t}\Xi^n, \tag{6.6}$$

and the forward model is also linear,

$$Y^k = Hz_{\text{ref}}(t_k) + \Sigma^k.$$

Here $H \in \mathbb{R}^{N_y \times N_z}$, $D \in \mathbb{R}^{N_z \times N_z}$ and $b \in \mathbb{R}^{N_z}$ denote constant matrices and a constant vector, respectively. The random variables $\Xi^n$ and $\Sigma^k$ are independent and Gaussian with mean zero and covariance matrices $Q$ and $R$, respectively. As we have already discussed in Example 4.6, a Gaussian random variable remains Gaussian under linear transformations, and a linear transformation can be found to link any two Gaussian random variables provided that their variances have the same rank. We also know that if both the prior and the likelihood are Gaussian, then so is the posterior, as discussed in Chapter 5. Hence we only need to keep track of the mean $\overline{z}$ and the covariance matrix $P$ of the associated Gaussian distributions $N(\overline{z}, P)$. Following standard notation from meteorology, we denote variables arising from a prediction step by superscript "f" (forecast) and those arising from the assimilation of data via Bayes' theorem by superscript "a" (analysis). In order to simplify notation we also introduce the shorthand

$$z_k^{\text{f}} = z^{\text{f}}(t_k), \quad z_k^{\text{a}} = z^{\text{a}}(t_k), \quad P_k^{\text{f}} = P^{\text{f}}(t_k), \quad P_k^{\text{a}} = P^{\text{a}}(t_k).$$

Hence we are dealing with sequences of Gaussian distributions

$$\pi(z, t_k | y_{t_{1:k-1}}^{\text{obs}}) = n(z; \overline{z}_k^{\text{f}}, P_k^{\text{f}}), \qquad \pi(z, t_k | y_{t_{1:k}}^{\text{obs}}) = n(z; \overline{z}_k^{\text{a}}, P_k^{\text{a}}),$$

in terms of given mean vectors and covariance matrices.

We now derive explicit recursive formulas for these mean vectors and covariance matrices. Upon recalling Example 4.6, we find that a single propagation step under the linear model leads to the update

$$\overline{z}^{n+1} = [I + \delta t D]\overline{z}^n + \delta t b, \tag{6.7}$$

for the mean, and the update

$$P^{n+1} = [I + \delta t D]P^n[I + \delta t D]^{\text{T}} + 2\delta t Q, \tag{6.8}$$

for the covariance matrix, where $Q$ is the covariance matrix of the stochastic forcing terms $\Xi^n$. Here we have also made use of the facts that $\mathbb{E}[\Xi^n] = 0$, and $\Xi^n$ and $Z^n$ are uncorrelated.

The update step is repeated $N_{\text{out}}$ times to propagate the mean and the covariance matrix over a time interval $\Delta t_{\text{out}} = \delta t N_{\text{out}}$. This results in an explicit transformation of the analysis pair $(\bar{z}^{\mathrm{a}}(\mathbf{t}_{k-1}), P^{\mathrm{a}}(\mathbf{t}_{k-1}))$ into the forecast pair $(\bar{z}^{\mathrm{f}}(\mathbf{t}_k), P^{\mathrm{f}}(\mathbf{t}_k))$, given by

$$\bar{z}^{\mathrm{f}}(\mathbf{t}_k) = [I + \delta t D]^{N_{\mathrm{out}}} \bar{z}^{\mathrm{a}}(\mathbf{t}_{k-1}) + \delta t \sum_{i=1}^{N_{\mathrm{out}}} [I + \delta t D]^{i-1} b,$$

and

$$P^{\mathrm{f}}(\mathbf{t}_k) = [I + \delta t D]^{N_{\mathrm{out}}} P^{\mathrm{a}}(\mathbf{t}_{k-1}) ([I + \delta t D]^{N_{\mathrm{out}}})^{\mathrm{T}}$$
$$+ 2\delta t \sum_{i=1}^{N_{\mathrm{out}}} [I + \delta t D]^{i-1} Q ([I + \delta t D]^{i-1})^{\mathrm{T}}.$$

We now analyse the Bayesian assimilation step in more detail. Recall the general formulas from Example 5.6 in Chapter 5. Applied to our situation with an appropriate identification of symbols (i.e., $b := 0$, $A := H$, $P := P_k^{\mathrm{f}}$, $\bar{x} := \bar{z}_k^{\mathrm{f}}$, $P^{\mathrm{a}} := P_k^{\mathrm{a}}$, $\bar{x}^{\mathrm{a}} := \bar{z}_k^{\mathrm{a}}$, and $y_{\mathrm{obs}} := y_{\mathrm{obs}}(\mathbf{t}_k)$), we obtain

$$(P_k^{\mathrm{a}})^{-1} = (P_k^{\mathrm{f}})^{-1} + H^{\mathrm{T}} R^{-1} H,$$

and

$$\bar{z}_k^{\mathrm{a}} = \bar{z}_k^{\mathrm{f}} - P_k^{\mathrm{a}} H^{\mathrm{T}} R^{-1} (H \bar{z}_k^{\mathrm{f}} - y_{\mathrm{obs}}(\mathbf{t}_k)).$$

We now employ the *Sherman–Morrison–Woodbury matrix inversion formula* (see Golub & Loan (1996)),

$$(M + U^{\mathrm{T}} N U)^{-1} = M^{-1} - M^{-1} U^{\mathrm{T}} (N^{-1} + U M^{-1} U^{\mathrm{T}})^{-1} U M^{-1}, \qquad (6.9)$$

with $M = (P_k^{\mathrm{f}})^{-1}$, $U = H$ and $N = R^{-1}$ to reformulate the covariance matrix update as

$$P_k^{\mathrm{a}} = P_k^{\mathrm{f}} - P_k^{\mathrm{f}} H^{\mathrm{T}} (R + H P_k^{\mathrm{f}} H^{\mathrm{T}})^{-1} H P_k^{\mathrm{f}}$$
$$= P_k^{\mathrm{f}} - K H P_k^{\mathrm{f}},$$

with *Kalman gain matrix*

$$K = P_k^{\mathrm{f}} H^{\mathrm{T}} (R + H P_k^{\mathrm{f}} H^{\mathrm{T}})^{-1}.$$

Using the Kalman gain matrix, the update for the mean can also be reformulated as

$$\bar{z}_k^{\mathrm{a}} = \bar{z}_k^{\mathrm{f}} - K (H \bar{z}_k^{\mathrm{f}} - y_{\mathrm{obs}}(\mathbf{t}_k)),$$

since

$$(P_k^{\mathrm{f}} - K H P_k^{\mathrm{f}}) H^{\mathrm{T}} R^{-1} = P_k^{\mathrm{f}} H^{\mathrm{T}} [I - (H P_k^{\mathrm{f}} H^{\mathrm{T}} + R)^{-1} H P_k^{\mathrm{f}} H^{\mathrm{T}}] R^{-1}$$
$$= P_k^{\mathrm{f}} H^{\mathrm{T}} (R + H P_k^{\mathrm{f}} H^{\mathrm{T}})^{-1}.$$

See also formulas (5.8) and (5.9) from Example 5.10 in Chapter 5.

After collecting all of these formulas, we have derived the celebrated Kalman filter.

**Algorithm 6.3** (Kalman Filter)   Given a mean $\bar{z}_0^a$ and a covariance matrix $P_0^a$ at time $t = 0$ and a sequence of observations $y_{\text{obs}}(t_k)$ with error covariance matrix $R$, $t_k = k\Delta t_{\text{out}}$ and observation interval $\Delta t_{\text{out}} = \delta t N_{\text{out}}$, the following sequence of steps is performed for $k \geq 1$.

(i) Set $\bar{z}^0 := \bar{z}_{k-1}^a$, $P^0 := P_{k-1}^a$ and iteratively determine $\bar{z}^{n+1}$ and $P^{n+1}$ for $n = 0, \ldots, N_{\text{out}} - 1$ via

$$\bar{z}^{n+1} = [I + \delta t D]\bar{z}^n + \delta t b, \tag{6.10}$$

$$P^{n+1} = [I + \delta t D]P^n[I + \delta t D]^{\text{T}} + 2\delta t Q. \tag{6.11}$$

Set $\bar{z}_k^f := \bar{z}^{N_{\text{out}}}$ and $P_k^f := P^{N_{\text{out}}}$.

(ii) Compute the Kalman gain matrix

$$K = P_k^f H^{\text{T}}(R + H P_k^f H^{\text{T}})^{-1},$$

and update the mean and covariance matrix according to

$$\bar{z}_k^a := \bar{z}_k^f - K(H\bar{z}_k^f - y_{\text{obs}}(t_k)), \tag{6.12}$$

$$P_k^a := P_k^f - KHP_k^f. \tag{6.13}$$

The performance of the Kalman filter is now demonstrated for a one-dimensional example.

---

**Example 6.4**   Consider the scalar stochastic difference equation

$$Z^{n+1} = Z^n + \delta t d Z^n + \delta t b + \sqrt{2\delta t}\, \Xi^n \tag{6.14}$$

with $d = -0.1$, $b = 1$, $\Xi^n \sim \text{N}(0,1)$, and $\delta t = 0.01$. The initial condition has probability distribution $Z^0 \sim \text{N}(10, 2)$. Observations are given in intervals of $\Delta t_{\text{out}} = 0.05$ (i.e., $N_{\text{out}} = 5$), the forward operator is $H = 1$, and the measurement error has distribution $\text{N}(0, 1)$. The reference trajectory $z_{\text{ref}}(t)$ is generated from the same model (6.14) with initial condition $z_{\text{ref}}(0) = 10$. This setting corresponds to the *perfect model* scenario. A simple inspection of the Kalman filter equations for the variances reveals that they are independent of the actual observations and, indeed, we find that the analysis and forecast variances quickly converge to stationary values $P_*^a \approx 0.2666$ and $P_*^f \approx 0.3636$, respectively (see the right panel in Figure 6.1, where we also display the analysis means $\bar{z}_k^a$ and the observed values $y_{\text{obs}}(t_k)$). As an immediate consequence the Kalman gain matrix also becomes stationary with $K \approx 0.2666$.

We now investigate an imperfect model scenario, which is more relevant for practical applications. Here we make the model "imperfect" by choosing that the trajectory $z_{\text{ref}}(t)$ is still obtained from (6.14) with $d = -0.1$ while the Kalman filter implementation is based on $d = -0.5$. All other parameters are as specified before (but could have been modified as well). The imperfect model scenario can be recognised from the fact that about 73% of the observed values $y_{\text{obs}}(t_k)$ are larger than the analysis $\bar{z}_k^a$, confirming that the model (6.14) is no longer calibrated. The difference between the perfect and the imperfect model scenario can

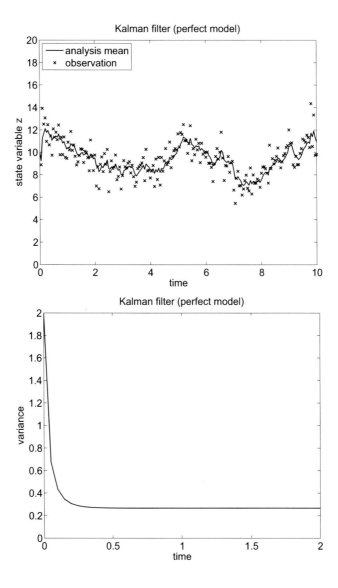

**Figure 6.1** Top panel: analysis $\bar{z}_k^a$ and observed values $y_{\mathrm{obs}}(t_k)$ for the Kalman filter under the perfect model scenario. Here "perfect" refers to the fact that the reference solution is generated from the same model that is used for filtering. Bottom panel: time evolution of the analysis variances. A rapid convergence to a stationary value can be observed.

be assessed in terms of time averaged root mean square error (RMSE), and the averaged continuously ranked probability score (ACRPS), as defined in Chapter 4. A long simulation over $N_{\mathrm{obs}} = 10^8$ observations reveals that the perfect model scenario leads to slightly better scores (imperfect model, time averaged RMSE $=$ 0.7692; perfect model, time averaged RMSE $= 0.5162$; imperfect model, ACRPS

$= 0.6345$; perfect model, ACRPS $= 0.4118$). The asymptotic value for the analysis variances is slightly reduced for the imperfect model scenario (imperfect model, $P_*^a = 0.2530$; perfect model $P_*^a = 0.2666$). See Figure 6.2. It should be noted that the perfect/imperfect model experiments are based on one and the same set of observations $y_{obs}(t_k)$. In summary, we find that the performance of the Kalman filter is quite robust with respect to the change in $d$ in (6.14).

## 6.2 Variational data assimilation

In Chapter 1, a nonlinear method of least squares was used to estimate model states from observations. This was a particular instance of a *variational data assimilation* technique; such techniques are based on minimising appropriate cost functionals subject to model constraints. In this section, a connection will be established between the Kalman filter and a variational data assimilation technique called four-dimensional variational data assimilation (*4DVar*). The name 4DVar arose in meteorology since the models are partial differential equations in three spatial dimensions and one temporal dimension: this is mostly not the case in this book since we concentrate on finite-dimensional examples. Nonetheless, we will use the term 4DVar to emphasise the time dimension.

It is assumed throughout this section that the stochastic model perturbations $\Xi^n$ vanish, i.e., the model error covariance matrix is $Q = 0$. We also set $b = 0$ for notational convenience. The $N_{out}$-fold application of the model dynamics (6.1) can therefore be reduced to

$$z(t_k) = \Psi z(t_{k-1}), \qquad \Psi := (I + \delta t D)^{N_{out}} \in \mathbb{R}^{N_z \times N_z},$$

and the Kalman filter equations are reformulated as follows. For $k = 1, \ldots, N_{obs}$ define

$$\bar{z}_k^f = \Psi \bar{z}_{k-1}^a, \tag{6.15}$$

$$P_k^f = \Psi P_{k-1}^a \Psi^T, \tag{6.16}$$

$$(P_k^a)^{-1} = (P_k^f)^{-1} + H^T R^{-1} H, \tag{6.17}$$

$$\bar{z}_k^a = \bar{z}_k^f - P_k^a H^T R^{-1} (H\bar{z}_k^f - y_{obs}(t_k)), \tag{6.18}$$

recursively from given initial mean $\bar{z}_0^a$, initial covariance matrix $P_0^a$, and a sequence of observations $y_{obs}(t_k)$, $k = 1, \ldots, N_{obs}$.

In this section, we demonstrate that variational data assimilation is closely related to the *smoothing problem*: determine the marginal distribution at $t_0 = 0$ from observations at $t_k$, $k = 1, \ldots, N_{obs}$. These marginal distributions are again Gaussian under the assumptions stated (linear model and initial Gaussian) and we introduce the notation

$$\pi_Z(z, t_0 | y_{t_{1:k}}^{obs}) = n(z; \bar{z}_{0:k}^s, P_{0:k}^s) \tag{6.19}$$

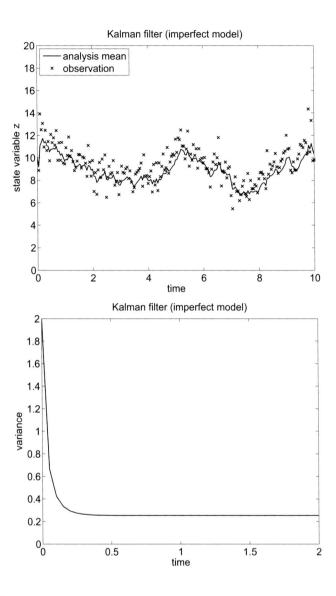

**Figure 6.2** We repeat the experiment from Figure 6.1 but with the Kalman filter being implemented for a modified model with $d = -0.5$ instead of $d = -0.1$. The Kalman filter is still able to track the reference solution and only a careful analysis of the time series reveals a difference between the imperfect and the perfect model scenarios. For example, we notice that more observations are located above the analysis in the plot on the top, showing that the model is no longer calibrated.

in terms of the involved mean vectors $\overline{z}^{\mathrm{s}}_{0:k}$ and covariance matrices $P^{\mathrm{s}}_{0:k}$.

In order to introduce 4DVar, we first demonstrate that $\overline{z}^{\mathrm{a}}_1$, as determined by

(6.18) with $k = 1$, is also the minimiser of the functional

$$\tilde{L}(z') = \frac{1}{2}(z' - \bar{z}_1^f)^T (P_1^f)^{-1}(z' - \bar{z}_1^f)$$
$$+ \frac{1}{2}(Hz' - y_{\text{obs}}(t_1))^T R^{-1}(Hz' - y_{\text{obs}}(t_1)). \qquad (6.20)$$

Indeed, we find that

$$\nabla_z \tilde{L}(z') = (P_1^f)^{-1}(z' - \bar{z}_1^f) + H^T R^{-1}(Hz' - y_{\text{obs}}(t_1)),$$

and the condition $\nabla_z \tilde{L}(\bar{z}_1^a) = 0$ leads to

$$\left\{ (P_1^f)^{-1} + H^T R^{-1} H \right\} \bar{z}_1^a = (P_1^f)^{-1}\bar{z}_1^f + H^T R^{-1}y_{\text{obs}}(t_1).$$

Since

$$P_k^a(P_k^f)^{-1} = \left\{ (P_k^f)^{-1} + H^T R^{-1} H \right\}^{-1}(P_k^f)^{-1}$$
$$= I - \left\{ (P_k^f)^{-1} + H^T R^{-1} H \right\}^{-1} H^T R^{-1} H$$
$$= I - P_k^a H^T R^{-1} H,$$

the desired (6.18) follows for $k = 1$. It also follows that the marginal filtering distribution at $t_1$ is given by

$$\pi(z', t_1 | y_{t_1:1}^{\text{obs}}) \propto e^{-\tilde{L}(z')}.$$

Upon introducing $z = \Psi^{-1}z'$, we can rewrite (6.20) as

$$L(z) := \frac{1}{2}(\Psi z - \bar{z}_1^f)^T (P_1^f)^{-1}(\Psi z - \bar{z}_1^f)$$
$$+ \frac{1}{2}(H\Psi z - y_{\text{obs}}(t_1))^T R^{-1}(H\Psi z - y_{\text{obs}}(t_1))$$
$$= \frac{1}{2}(z - \bar{z}_0^a)^T (P_0^a)^{-1}(z - \bar{z}_0^a) + \frac{1}{2}(H\Psi z - y_{\text{obs}}(t_1))^T R^{-1}(H\Psi z - y_{\text{obs}}(t_1)).$$

The associated PDF

$$\pi(z, t_0 | y_{t_1:1}^{\text{obs}}) \propto e^{-L(z)}, \qquad (6.21)$$

solves the smoothing problem at time $t_0 = 0$ with data given up to $t_1$. If we denote the minimiser of $L$ by $\bar{z}_{0:1}^s$, then we have $\bar{z}_{0:1}^s = \Psi^{-1}\bar{z}_1^a$, by definition. Hence it follows from our discussion that we can first solve the filtering problem up to $t_1$, and then apply the inverse operator $\Psi^{-1}$ to obtain the mean $\bar{z}_{0:1}^s$ of the smoothing problem. Furthermore, the Hessian matrix $\mathcal{H}$ of second derivatives of $L(z)$ with respect to $z$ is

$$\mathcal{H} = (P_0^a)^{-1} + \Psi^T H^T R^{-1} H \Psi = \Psi^T((P_1^f)^{-1} + H^T R^{-1} H)\Psi = \Psi^T (P_1^a)^{-1}\Psi.$$

The Hessian is equivalent to the inverse of the smoother covariance matrix at $t_0$, i.e.,

$$P_{0:1}^s := \mathcal{H}^{-1} = \Psi^{-1} P_1^a \Psi^{-T}.$$

Hence $L(z)$ can equivalently be written as

$$L(z) = \frac{1}{2}(z - z_{0:1}^{\mathrm{s}})^{\mathrm{T}}(P_{0:1}^{\mathrm{s}})^{-1}(z - z_{0:1}^{\mathrm{s}}),$$

in agreement with (6.21) and (6.19).

This statement can actually be generalised to $k > 1$ and leads to the cost functional

$$L(z) = \frac{1}{2}(z - \overline{z}_0^{\mathrm{a}})^{\mathrm{T}}(P_0^{\mathrm{a}})^{-1}(z - \overline{z}_0^{\mathrm{a}})$$

$$+ \frac{1}{2}\sum_{k=1}^{N_{\mathrm{obs}}}(H\Psi^k z - y_{\mathrm{obs}}(t_k))^{\mathrm{T}}R^{-1}(H\Psi^k z - y_{\mathrm{obs}}(t_k)), \qquad (6.22)$$

for the smoothing problem at $t_0 = 0$ with data up to $t_{N_{\mathrm{obs}}}$. The corresponding mean, $\overline{x}_{0:N_{\mathrm{obs}}}^{\mathrm{s}}$, is determined by

$$\nabla_z L(\overline{z}_{0:N_{\mathrm{obs}}}^{\mathrm{s}}) = 0.$$

This is, in fact, the linear variant of 4DVar. In this linear setting without stochastic model contributions, our discussion suggests that 4DVar is equivalent to first running a Kalman filter up to $t_{N_{\mathrm{obs}}}$ resulting in $\overline{z}_{N_{\mathrm{obs}}}^{\mathrm{a}}$, then applying the inverse dynamic operator $\Psi^{-1}$ $N_{\mathrm{obs}}$-times to obtain

$$\overline{z}_{0:N_{\mathrm{obs}}}^{\mathrm{s}} = \Psi^{-N_{\mathrm{obs}}}\overline{z}_{N_{\mathrm{obs}}}^{\mathrm{a}}.$$

Similarly, we obtain the smoothing covariance matrix

$$P_{0:N_{\mathrm{obs}}}^{\mathrm{s}} = \Psi^{-N_{\mathrm{obs}}}P_{N_{\mathrm{obs}}}^{\mathrm{a}}(\Psi^{-N_{\mathrm{obs}}})^{\mathrm{T}}.$$

**Proposition 6.5** (Variational formulation of the optimal state estimation) Let the analysis random variable $Z_0^{\mathrm{a}}$ have mean $\overline{z}_0^{\mathrm{a}}$ and covariance matrix $P_0^{\mathrm{a}}$ at time $t_0 = 0$. Assume that a sequence of observations $y_{\mathrm{obs}}(t_k)$, with $k = 1, \ldots, N_{\mathrm{obs}}$ is given. We also assume deterministic model dynamics and define $\Psi := (I + \delta t D)^{N_{\mathrm{out}}} \in \mathbb{R}^{N_z \times N_z}$. Finding the analysis mean $\overline{z}_{N_{\mathrm{obs}}}^{\mathrm{a}}$ from the associated Kalman filtering problem is then equivalent to minimising (6.22) with respect to $z$, denoting the minimiser by $\overline{z}_{0:N_{\mathrm{obs}}}^{\mathrm{s}}$, and setting

$$\overline{z}_{N_{\mathrm{obs}}}^{\mathrm{a}} = \Psi^{N_{\mathrm{obs}}}\overline{z}_{0:N_{\mathrm{obs}}}^{\mathrm{s}}.$$

The associated analysis covariance matrix is determined by

$$P_{N_{\mathrm{obs}}}^{\mathrm{a}} = \Psi^{N_{\mathrm{obs}}}\mathcal{H}^{-1}(\Psi^{N_{\mathrm{obs}}})^{\mathrm{T}},$$

where $\mathcal{H} \in \mathbb{R}^{N_z \times N_z}$ is the Hessian matrix of second partial derivatives of $L$ with respect to $z$ given by

$$\mathcal{H} = (P_0^{\mathrm{a}})^{-1} + \sum_{k=1}^{N_{\mathrm{obs}}}(\Psi^k)^{\mathrm{T}}H^{\mathrm{T}}R^{-1}H\Psi^k.$$

*Proof* We have already shown the validity of the result for $N_{obs} = 1$. The case $N_{obs} = 2$ follows from

$$L(z) = \frac{1}{2}(z - \bar{z}_0^a)^T(P_0^a)^{-1}(z - \bar{z}_0^a)$$

$$+ \frac{1}{2}\sum_{k=1}^{2}(H\Psi^k z - y_{obs}(t_k))^T R^{-1}(H\Psi^k z - y_{obs}(t_k))$$

$$= \frac{1}{2}(z - \bar{z}_{0:1}^s)^T(P_{0:1}^s)^{-1}(z - \bar{z}_{0:1}^s)$$

$$+ \frac{1}{2}(H\Psi^2 z - y_{obs}(t_2))^T R^{-1}(H\Psi^2 z - y_{obs}(t_2)),$$

with $\bar{z}_{0:1}^s = \Psi^{-1}\bar{z}_1^a$ and $P_{0:1}^s = \Psi^{-1}P_1^a\Psi^{-T}$. We next introduce $z' = \Psi^2 z$ and note that $L(z)$ becomes equivalent to

$$\tilde{L}(z') = \frac{1}{2}(\Psi^{-2}z' - \bar{z}_{0:1}^s)^T(P_{0:1}^s)^{-1}(\Psi^{-2}z' - \bar{z}_{0:1}^s)$$

$$+ \frac{1}{2}(Hz' - y_{obs}(t_2))^T R^{-1}(Hz' - y_{obs}(t_2))$$

$$= \frac{1}{2}(z' - \bar{z}_2^f)^T(P_2^f)^{-1}(z' - \bar{z}_2^f) + \frac{1}{2}(Hz' - y_{obs}(t_2))^T R^{-1}(Hz' - y_{obs}(t_2))$$

$$= \frac{1}{2}(z' - \bar{z}_2^a)^T(P_2^a)^{-1}(z' - \bar{z}_2^a)$$

following arguments previously made for the case $N_{obs} = 1$. The desired result for $N_{obs} = 2$ follows from

$$L(z) = \frac{1}{2}(z - \Psi^{-2}\bar{z}_2^a)^T(\Psi^2)^T(P_2^a)^{-1}\Psi^2(z - \Psi^{-2}\bar{z}_2^a)$$

$$= \frac{1}{2}(z - \bar{z}_{0:2}^s)^T(P_{0:2}^s)^{-1}(z - \bar{z}_{0:2}^s).$$

This argument can recursively be generalised to any $N_{obs} > 2$. □

Hence we may view the marginal smoothing PDF,

$$\pi_Z(z, t_0|y_{t_1:N_{obs}}^{obs}) \propto e^{-L(z)},$$

as the posterior distribution at $t_0 = 0$ corresponding to the Gaussian prior $N(\bar{z}_0^a, P_0^a)$ and the compound likelihood function

$$\pi_{Y_{t_1:N_{obs}}}(y_{t_1:N_{obs}}|z) \propto \prod_{k=1}^{N_{obs}} e^{-\frac{1}{2}(H\Psi^k z - y(t_k))^T R^{-1}(H\Psi^k z - y(t_k))}.$$

Therefore $\bar{z}_{0:N_{obs}}^s$ is the mean of the posterior PDF $\pi_Z(z, t_0|y_{t_1:N_{obs}}^{obs})$, or equivalently, the associated MAP estimator (see Definition 5.8)

This reformulation of the smoothing problem allows for a generalisation to nonlinear dynamical systems of type

$$z^{n+1} = z^n + \delta t f(z^n), \tag{6.23}$$

as considered in Chapters 1 and 4. If $\Delta t_{out} = \delta t N_{out}$ (as assumed before), then we define the map $\psi$ as the result of an $N_{\text{out}}$-fold application of (6.23) and formally introduce the iteration

$$z_{k+1} = \psi(z_k), \tag{6.24}$$

in order to describe the model dynamics in between observations. Again, we have assumed that stochastic contributions to the model dynamics can be ignored, e.g., $\psi$ could correspond to any deterministic dynamical system considered in Chapter 4.

**Definition 6.6** (Four-dimensional variational data assimilation (4DVar))   Let a mean $\bar{z}_0^{\text{a}}$ and a covariance matrix $P_0^{\text{a}}$ at time $t = 0$ be given as well as a sequence of observations $y_{\text{obs}}(t_k)$ with $k = 1, \ldots, N_{\text{obs}}$. The model dynamics in between observations is described by (6.24). Then the smoothing distribution at $t_0 = 0$ is given by

$$\pi_Z(z, t_0 | y_{t_{1:N_{\text{obs}}}}^{\text{obs}}) \propto e^{-\frac{1}{2}(z - \bar{z}_0^{\text{a}})^{\text{T}}(P_0^{\text{a}})^{-1}(z - \bar{z}_0^{\text{a}})} \pi_{Y_{t_{1:N_{\text{obs}}}}}(y_{t_{1:N_{\text{obs}}}}^{\text{obs}} | z),$$

up to a normalisation constant independent of $z$. The associated MAP estimator, denoted by $\hat{z}_{0:N_{\text{obs}}}^{\text{s}}$, is the minimiser of the functional $L(z)$ defined by

$$L(z) = \frac{1}{2}(z - \bar{z}_0^{\text{a}})^{\text{T}}(P_0^{\text{a}})^{-1}(z - \bar{z}_0^{\text{a}})$$

$$+ \frac{1}{2} \sum_{k=1}^{N_{\text{obs}}} (H\psi^k(z) - y_{\text{obs}}(t_k))^{\text{T}} R^{-1}(H\psi^k(z) - y_{\text{obs}}(t_k)). \tag{6.25}$$

The associated $\hat{z}_{N_{\text{obs}}}^{\text{a}} = \psi^{N_{\text{obs}}}(\hat{z}_{0:N_{\text{obs}}}^{\text{s}})$ provides the MAP estimator at the end of the observation interval $t_{N_{\text{obs}}}$. The process of obtaining the MAP estimator is called *4DVar*. Recall that the MAP estimator is equivalent to the posterior mean $\bar{z}_{0:N_{\text{obs}}}^{\text{s}}$ if the smoothing distribution is Gaussian. However, the MAP estimator and the posterior mean take different values in general.

Instead of applying 4DVar to a complete set of observations, we can also apply 4DVar recursively to patches of observations from intervals

$$[0, t_{N_A}], \quad [t_{N_A}, t_{2N_A}], \quad \ldots$$

with the integer $N_A$ chosen appropriately (compare with Example 1.8). In this recursive setting, we often assume a fixed background covariance matrix $B$ instead of an observation adjusted $(P_0^{\text{a}})$, $(P_{N_A}^{\text{a}})$, etc. Furthermore, the MAP estimator at the end of the last patch is used as the background mean in the cost functional for the next patch. Consider, for example, the second patch over the interval $[t_{N_A}, t_{2N_A}]$. The associated 4DVar functional becomes

$$L(z) = \frac{1}{2}(z - \hat{z}_{N_A}^{\text{a}})^{\text{T}} B^{-1}(z - \hat{z}_{N_A}^{\text{a}})$$

$$+ \frac{1}{2} \sum_{k=1}^{N_A} (H\psi^k(z) - y_{\text{obs}}(t_{k+N_A}))^{\text{T}} R^{-1}(H\psi^k(z) - y_{\text{obs}}(t_{k+N_A})), \tag{6.26}$$

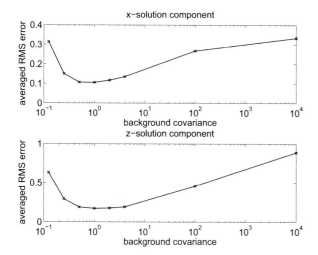

**Figure 6.3** Time averaged RMSEs over 40 data assimilation cycles each consisting of $N_A = 5$ observations. Results are displayed for various strengths $\delta > 0$ of the background covariance matrix $B = \delta I_3$. Observations are ignored in the limit $\delta \to 0$, while $\delta \to \infty$ recovers the assimilation experiment conducted in Experiment 1.8 of Chapter 1. The results demonstrate that an optimal choice of the background covariance can lead to a substantial reduction of the RMSE.

with the analysis $\hat{z}^a_{N_A}$ obtained from the assimilation of the first patch of observations. The minimiser of this functional, denoted by $\hat{z}^s_{N_A:2N_A}$, provides the background state via $\hat{z}^a_{2N_A} := \psi^{N_A}(\hat{z}^s_{N_A:2N_A})$ for the next assimilation cycle.

We return now to Example 1.8 from Chapter 1 and find that there we used a data assimilation technique rather close in spirit to 4DVar. The only difference being that, instead of (6.26), in Example 1.8 we minimised

$$L(z) = \frac{1}{2}\sum_{k=1}^{N_A}(H\psi^k(z) - y_{\mathrm{obs}}(t_k))^{\mathrm{T}}R^{-1}(H\psi^k(z) - y_{\mathrm{obs}}(t_k)), \qquad (6.27)$$

i.e., the prior distribution was ignored. In the following example, we repeat the numerical experiment from Example 1.8 with a proper 4DVar implementation and the background covariance matrix $B$ appropriately chosen.

---

**Example 6.7** We repeat the data assimilation experiment from Example 1.8. Recall that we assimilated data over assimilation windows consisting of patches of 5 observations, i.e., $N_A = 5$, with each observation separated by $\Delta t_{\mathrm{out}} = 0.05 = 50\delta t$ time units. A total of 40 assimilation cycles were performed. Following the discussion from Example 2.20, we model the measurement error as a Gaussian random variable with mean zero and variance $R = 1/15$. This parameter is used in the cost functional (6.25). We also use a constant prior (also called background) covariance matrix $B = \delta I$ for all assimilation windows. The parameter $\delta > 0$ was varied over a range of values to determine an optimal value. The resulting time averaged RMSEs in the observed x and the unobserved z variable can be found in Figure 6.3. Note that $\delta \to \infty$ leads back to the assimilation experiment conducted in Experiment 1.8 while $\delta \to 0$ implies that observations are ignored and the smoothed values are identified with their forecasted values.

---

In addition to improved behaviour of (6.25) compared with (6.27) for an optimised choice of $P_0^a = B$, it should also be kept in mind that minimising (6.27) becomes ill posed whenever the available set of observations is not sufficient to guarantee a well-defined minimiser. The same situation can, in principle, also arise for (6.25). However, the background term in (6.25) can always be chosen such that the associated $L$ possesses a unique minimiser. In contrast, in Appendix 6.5 we discuss the relation between (6.25) and (6.27) as $N_{obs} \to \infty$ by means of a simple example. This example demonstrates that both (6.25) and (6.27) lead asymptotically to the same estimator/minimiser.

We conclude this discussion by emphasising that 4DVar provides a mathematically elegant approach to state estimation in the context of smoothing. In combination with Monte Carlo sampling, variational data assimilation can also be used to compute expectation values with respect to $\pi_Z(z, t_0 | y_{t_1:N_{obs}}^{obs})$. The impact of stochastic model contributions on state estimation within a variational framework is discussed in Appendix 6.6.

We now provide some implementation details of the 4DVar method for the interested reader, which could be skipped during a first reading. The gradient descent method

$$z^{(l+1)} = z^{(l)} - \alpha \nabla_z L(z^{(l)}), \qquad l = 0, 1, \ldots,$$

is often used for finding local minima of the 4DVar cost functional (6.26). The parameter $\alpha > 0$ is chosen such that $L(z^{(l+1)}) \leq L(z^{(l)})$. We used $\alpha = 0.01$ in Example 6.7. More sophisticated methods for adaptively determining an appropriate step-length $\alpha$ are available (Nocedal & Wright 2006). In any case, an efficient method for computing the gradient $\nabla_z L(z)$ is crucial for the implementation of the gradient method. In order to avoid the construction of large dense matrices, the *adjoint method* should be used for calculating the gradient at a $z = z^{(l)}$. For simplicity we describe the procedure for $N_A = 2$ in (6.26). The first step of the adjoint method is a forward trajectory calculation resulting in $z_1 = \psi(z_0)$ and $z_2 = \psi(z_1)$ with $z_0 = z^{(l)}$ in our particular case. Simultaneously, we compute the two residuals

$$r_1 := Hz_1 - y_{obs}(t_{N_A+1}), \qquad r_2 := Hz_2 - y_{obs}(t_{N_A+2}).$$

The second step is a backward sweep starting at the last observation index $N_A + 2$. Hence, we start in our case with

$$a_2 = H^T R^{-1} r_2$$

and then set

$$a_1 = H^T R^{-1} r_1 + (D\psi(z_1))^T a_2.$$

Here $D\psi(z)$ denotes the Jacobian matrix of partial derivatives of $\psi$ at $z$. Finally

$$\nabla_z L(z^{(l)}) = B^{-1}(z^{(l)} - \hat{z}_{N_A}^a) + (D\psi(z^{(l)}))^T a_1.$$

Note that the entire calculation involves only matrix–vector multiplications. We find that the convergence rate of the gradient method with $B = \delta I$ increases as $\delta > 0$ becomes smaller. This can be explained by the fact that the scaled functional $\delta L(z)$ converges to an isotropic quadratic functional as $\delta \to 0$. To completely specify a single step of the gradient method, we still need to provide an efficient method for computing $D\psi(z_0)^{\mathrm{T}} a_1$ and $D\psi(z_1)^{\mathrm{T}} a_2$. Here we make use of the fact that $\psi$ is defined as the $N_{\mathrm{out}}$-fold application of the model (6.23). We explain the basic idea for $N_{\mathrm{out}} = 2$ and for $D\psi(z_1)^{\mathrm{T}} a_2$. Again we start with a forward sweep resulting in

$$z_{1,1} := z_1 + \delta t f(z_1), \qquad z_{1,2} := z_{1,1} + \delta t f(z_{1,1}).$$

Note that $z_{1,2} = z_2$ by definition. These calculations are followed by a backward sweep defining two vectors $a_{2,1}$ and $a_{2,0}$ by

$$a_{2,1} = (I + \delta t D f(z_{1,1}))^{\mathrm{T}} a_2,$$

and

$$a_{2,0} = (I + \delta t D f(z_1))^{\mathrm{T}} a_{2,1},$$

respectively. Then

$$D\psi(z_1)^{\mathrm{T}} a_2 = a_{2,0}$$

as can be verified by applying the chain rule of differentiation. Note that the calculation of, for example, $a_{2,1}$ can be interpreted as a single explicit Euler step applied to the *adjoint differential equation*

$$\frac{\mathrm{d}a}{\mathrm{d}t} = -Df(z(t))^{\mathrm{T}} a,$$

backward in time along $z(t) = z_{1,1}$, i.e., with step-size $-\delta t < 0$, and for given end value $a_2$.

Beyond simple gradient descent minimisation, we could consider more advanced minimisation techniques such as Gauss–Newton and the nonlinear conjugate gradient method. We refer the reader to textbooks such as Nocedal & Wright (2006).

# 6.3 Particle filters

While 4DVar is a powerful data assimilation method, it is not consistent with a Bayesian perspective unless the prior distribution at $t_0$ is indeed Gaussian. This assumption is typically violated when 4DVar is applied recursively over patches of observations. Computing the mode of a posterior distribution can also be misleading in cases where the smoothing distribution is multimodal. We therefore discuss a proper Bayesian generalisation of the Kalman filter to nonlinear dynamical models and non-Gaussian distributions in the remainder of this chapter. This generalisation, a *sequential Monte Carlo method* called the *particle filter*, relies on ensemble prediction for nonlinear dynamical systems as introduced in Chapter 4, combined with an importance sampling approach, introduced in Chapter 3 and further elaborated on in the context of Bayesian inference in Chapter 5.

We first recall the ensemble prediction approach to the approximation of marginal PDFs $\pi_Z(z,t)$ of an SDE model,

$$\mathrm{d}Z = f(Z)\mathrm{d}t + \sqrt{2}Q^{1/2}\mathrm{d}W(t) \,,$$

as outlined in Definition 4.20 from Chapter 4. In fact, as before, we replace the continuous ensemble formulation (4.35) by an ensemble of time-discrete approximations

$$z_i^{n+1} = z_i^n + \delta t f(z_i^n) + \sqrt{2\delta t}Q^{1/2}\xi_i^n, \qquad i = 1,\dots,M, \qquad (6.28)$$

$n \geq 0$, with the values $\{\xi_i^n\}$ denoting realisations of independent and identically distributed Gaussian random variables with mean zero and covariance matrix equal to the identity matrix. The initial conditions $z_i^0$ at $t = 0$ are realisations of a random variable with PDF $\pi_Z(z,0)$. Recall that the ensemble prediction method is just a Monte Carlo implementation of the prediction step (6.4).

The idea of particle filters is to combine ensemble prediction with importance sampling. Each ensemble member is assigned a weight $w_i^0 = 1/M$ at $t = 0$. These weights are kept constant during each ensemble prediction step (6.28) provided that there is no observation to be assimilated. We now assume that after $N_{\mathrm{out}}$ steps under (6.28), an observation $y_{\mathrm{obs}}(t_1)$ becomes available at $t_1 = \Delta t_{\mathrm{out}} := \delta t N_{\mathrm{out}}$ with likelihood function $\pi_Y(y_{\mathrm{obs}}(t_1)|z)$. Then, an application of Bayes' formula to the forecast ensemble $z_i^{\mathrm{f}}(t_1) = z_i^{N_{\mathrm{out}}}$ leads to rescaling the weights according to

$$w_i^1 = \frac{w_i^0 \pi_Y(y_{\mathrm{obs}}(t_1)|z_i^{\mathrm{f}}(t_1))}{\sum_{j=1}^M w_j^0 \pi_Y(y_{\mathrm{obs}}(t_1)|z_j^{\mathrm{f}}(t_1))} = \frac{\pi_Y(y_{\mathrm{obs}}(t_1)|z_i^{\mathrm{f}}(t_1))}{\sum_{j=1}^M \pi_Y(y_{\mathrm{obs}}(t_1)|z_j^{\mathrm{f}}(t_1))},$$

$i = 1,\dots,M$, since $w_i^0 = 1/M$. Compare Equation (5.25) from Chapter 5.

The new weights $w_i^1$ are again kept constant whilst the states are incremented according to (6.28), until a second set of observations $y_{\mathrm{obs}}(t_2)$ becomes available at $t_2 = 2\Delta t_{\mathrm{out}}$ and a new forecast ensemble is defined by

$$z_i^{\mathrm{f}}(t_2) = z_i^{2N_{\mathrm{out}}}.$$

At that point the weights are changed to

$$w_i^2 = \frac{w_i^1 \pi_Y(y_{\mathrm{obs}}(t_2)|z_i^{\mathrm{f}}(t_2))}{\sum_{j=1}^M w_j^1 \pi_Y(y_{\mathrm{obs}}(t_2)|z_j^{\mathrm{f}}(t_2))}, \qquad i = 1,\dots,M.$$

More generally, we obtain the update formula

$$w_i^k = \frac{w_i^{k-1} \pi_Y(y_{\mathrm{obs}}(t_k)|z_i^{\mathrm{f}}(t_k))}{\sum_{j=1}^M w_j^{k-1} \pi_Y(y_{\mathrm{obs}}(t_k)|z_j^{\mathrm{f}}(t_k))}, \qquad z_i^{\mathrm{f}}(t_k) = z_i^{kN_{\mathrm{out}}}, \qquad (6.29)$$

with the variables $\{z_i^n\}$, $n \geq 0$, obtained by simple propagation of the initial ensemble $\{z_i^0\}$ under the discrete model dynamics (6.28) throughout the whole assimilation process. This update means that more weight is given to ensemble members which produce simulated observations that are more "likely" in terms of the actual observations and the observation noise model, i.e. the likelihood.

Posterior expectation values of functions $g : \mathbb{R}^{N_z} \to \mathbb{R}$ at $\mathsf{t}_k$ are approximated by

$$\bar{g}_M^{\mathrm{a}}(\mathsf{t}_k) = \sum_{i=1}^{M} w_i^k g(z_i^{\mathrm{f}}(\mathsf{t}_k)),$$

while approximations to prior expectation values are based on

$$\bar{g}_M^{\mathrm{f}}(\mathsf{t}_k) = \sum_{i=1}^{M} w_i^{k-1} g(z_i^{\mathrm{f}}(\mathsf{t}_k)).$$

We now demonstrate that the posterior estimator is consistent with the assumption of a prior empirical distribution, formally given by

$$\mu_Z^{\mathrm{f}}(\mathrm{d}z, \mathsf{t}_k | y_{\mathsf{t}_{1:k-1}}^{\mathrm{obs}}) = \sum_{i=1}^{M} w_i^{k-1} \delta(z - z_i^{\mathrm{f}}(\mathsf{t}_k)) \mathrm{d}z,$$

and an application of Bayes' formula. Indeed, upon defining the posterior measure according to Bayes' formula,

$$
\begin{aligned}
\mu_Z(\mathrm{d}z, \mathsf{t}_k | y_{\mathsf{t}_{1:k}}^{\mathrm{obs}}) &= \frac{\pi_Y(y_{\mathrm{obs}}(\mathsf{t}_k)|z) \sum_{i=1}^{M} w_i^{k-1} \delta(z - z_i^{\mathrm{f}}(\mathsf{t}_k)) \mathrm{d}z}{\int_{\mathbb{R}^{N_z}} \pi_Y(y_{\mathrm{obs}}(\mathsf{t}_k)|z) \sum_{j=1}^{M} w_j^{k-1} \delta(z - z_j^{\mathrm{f}}(\mathsf{t}_k)) \mathrm{d}z} \\
&= \frac{\sum_{i=1}^{M} w_i^{k-1} \pi_Y(y_{\mathrm{obs}}(\mathsf{t}_k)|z) \, \delta(z - z_i^{\mathrm{f}}(\mathsf{t}_k)) \mathrm{d}z}{\sum_{j=1}^{M} w_j^{k-1} \pi_Y(y_{\mathrm{obs}}(\mathsf{t}_k)|z_j^{\mathrm{f}}(\mathsf{t}_k))} \\
&= \sum_{i=1}^{M} w_i^k \delta(z - z_i^{\mathrm{f}}(\mathsf{t}_k)) \mathrm{d}z,
\end{aligned}
$$

we obtain

$$
\begin{aligned}
\bar{g}_M^{\mathrm{a}}(\mathsf{t}_k) &= \int_{\mathbb{R}^{N_z}} g(z) \mu_Z(\mathrm{d}z, \mathsf{t}_k | y_{\mathsf{t}_{1:k}}^{\mathrm{obs}}) \\
&= \sum_{i=1}^{M} w_i^k g(z_i^{\mathrm{f}}(\mathsf{t}_k)),
\end{aligned}
$$

as desired. The resulting particle filter is often referred to as *sequential importance sampling* (SIS) filter.

It is to be expected that the weights will become non-uniform after a few assimilation steps. In order to quantify the non-uniformity in the weights we introduce the *effective sample size*.

**Definition 6.8** (Effective sample size)  Given a set of weights $w_i \geq 0$, $i = 1, \ldots, M$, the *effective sample size* is defined by

$$M_{\mathrm{effective}} = \frac{1}{\sum_{i=1}^{M} w_i^2}. \qquad (6.30)$$

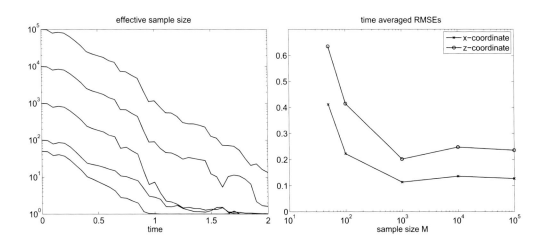

**Figure 6.4** Assimilation results from the Lorenz-63 model over a time period $[0, 2]$ and for various ensemble sizes $M$. Filtering is performed with a sequential importance sampling (SIS) filter. The left panel displays the evolution of the effective sample sizes while the right panel shows the time averaged RMSEs as a function of the ensemble size $M$. In these experiments we found that the filter fails to converge over an extended time window $[0, 3]$ due to a collapse of the effective sample size, even with ensembles of size $M \leq 10^5$.

The effective sample size is equal to $M$ in the case of uniform weights $w_i = 1/M$. In the extreme non-uniform case $w_i = 1$ for one single ensemble member $i$ and $w_j = 0$ for all $j \neq i$, we obtain $M_{\text{effective}} = 1$.

The effective sample size is used to quantify the weight non-uniformity for the following example.

**Example 6.9**   We return to the modified Lorenz-63 model introduced in Chapter 1. Recall that the process of generating the underlying physical process $z_{\text{ref}}(t)$ was described in Example 1.1. The generation of partial observations in the x-variable was laid out in Example 1.2. We now use these observations together with the stochastic Lorenz-63 model (4.18)–(4.20) from Example 4.13 to implement an SIS filter. The required likelihood function is given by

$$\pi_Y\left(x_{\text{obs}}(t_k)|z_i^{\text{f}}(t_k)\right) = \frac{1}{\sqrt{2\pi R}} e^{-\frac{1}{2R}\left(x_{\text{obs}}(t_k) - x_i^{\text{f}}(t_k)\right)^2},$$

with error variance $R = 1/15$. See Example 2.20 from Chapter 2. As for Examples 1.8 and 6.7, observations are collected every $\Delta t_{\text{out}} = 0.05$ time units. The initial PDF is Gaussian with mean $\bar{z} = (-0.587, -0.563, 16.87)$ and diagonal covariance matrix $P = \sigma^2 I$ with $\sigma = 0.1$.

Numerical results for the resulting effective sample sizes as a function of time and the time averaged RMSEs as a function of the ensemble size $M$ can be found in Figure 6.4. Notice that the effective sample size decays rather quickly, and that the RMSEs converge as $M$ is increased for fixed assimilation intervals (here $[0, 2]$). However, the SIS filter is found to fail to converge on the extended assimilation interval $[0, 3]$ for ensembles of size $M \leq 10^5$. Here the RMSEs are defined as in Example 6.7 with the analysis mean now defined by

$$\bar{z}_k^{\mathrm{a}} = \sum_{i=1}^{M} w_i^k z_i^{\mathrm{f}}(\mathsf{t}_k).$$

We may conclude that an SIS particle filter is not competitive with an optimally implemented 4DVar algorithm for this particular example. Indeed the RMSEs from Example 6.7 are comparable to those displayed in Figure 6.4 but the achievable 4DVar assimilation windows are much longer.

---

The previous example clearly illuminates the need to modify the particle filter to avoid the collapse of the effective sample size. The resampling strategies discussed towards the end of Chapter 3 are natural candidates for this. Such modified particle filters are collectively called *sequential importance resampling* (SIR) filters. Other names often found in the literature are *bootstrap filter* and *condensation algorithm* (del Moral 2004).

**Algorithm 6.10** (Sequential Importance resampling (SIR) filter)   Given an initial distribution $\pi_Z(z, 0)$, we draw $M$ independent realisations $z_i(\mathsf{t}_0)$ from this distribution with equal weights $w_i^0 = 1/M$.
 The following steps are performed recursively for $k = 1, \ldots, N_{\mathrm{obs}}$.

(i) In between observations, the ensemble is propagated under an evolution model, such as (6.28), with constant weights $w_i^{k-1}$ producing a forecast ensemble $\{z_i^{\mathrm{f}}(\mathsf{t}_k)\}_{i=1}^{M}$.

(ii) An observation $y_{\mathrm{obs}}(\mathsf{t}_k)$ at $\mathsf{t}_k = k\Delta t_{\mathrm{out}} = \delta t k N_{\mathrm{out}}$ results in a change of weights from $w_i^{k-1}$ to $w_i^k$, $i = 1, \ldots, M$, according to (6.29).

(iii) After each change of weights, the effective sample size is evaluated according to (6.30).

    (a) If $M_{\mathrm{effective}}$ drops below $M/2$, a new set of $M$ equally weighted ensemble members $z_i^{\mathrm{a}}(\mathsf{t}_k)$ is generated from the forecast ensemble $z_i^{\mathrm{f}}(\mathsf{t}_k)$ by the method of residual resampling. See Algorithm 3.27 from Chapter 3. Finally we return to (i) with the resampled ensemble, i.e., with ensemble members given by

$$z_i(\mathsf{t}_k) := z_i^{\mathrm{a}}(\mathsf{t}_k),$$

    weights given by $w_i^k := 1/M$, and $k$ incremented by one.

    (b) Otherwise we continue in (i) with $z_i(\mathsf{t}_k) = z_i^{\mathrm{f}}(\mathsf{t}_k)$, weights $w_i^k$ as computed under (ii), and increment $k$ by one.

The threshold for resampling can, of course, be chosen to be different from $M/2$. In fact, we could simply resample after each assimilation step. We now apply the SIR filter to the data assimilation experiment from Example 6.9.

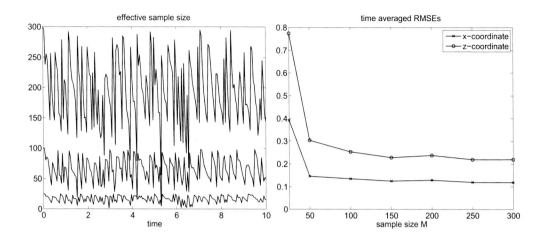

**Figure 6.5** Assimilation results from the Lorenz-63 model over a time period $[0, 10]$ and varying ensemble sizes $M \in [30, 300]$. Filtering is performed with an SIR filter. The left panel displays the evolution of the effective sample sizes for $M = 30, 100$ and $300$ while the right panel shows the time averaged RMSEs as a function of the ensemble size $M$. We notice that resampling helps to keep the effective sample size stabilised and the filter is able to follow the surrogate physical process as represented by $z_{\mathrm{ref}}(t)$. When averaged over $[0, 10]$, the RMSEs quickly converge as $M$ increases and the size of the errors are comparable to those obtained from an optimised 4DVar implementation for $M \geq 100$. See Figure 6.3.

---

**Example 6.11**   We repeat the experiment from Example 6.9 with the SIS filter being replaced by the SIR filter described in the previous algorithm. The SIR filter is able to successfully track the reference solution as given by $z_{\mathrm{ref}}(t)$. The RMSEs averaged over a time period $[0, 10]$ are similar to those from an optimised 4DVar technique. See Figures 6.5 and 6.3. However the SIR filter is easier to implement since no iterative minimisation of a cost functional is required.

---

It can be shown (see Bain & Crisan (2009) and del Moral (2004), for example) that the SIR filter provides a consistent Monte Carlo implementation of the abstract Bayesian filtering problem, as outlined at the beginning of this chapter, within a perfect model setting. However, in Example 6.11 an imperfect model setting was used, i.e., the reference trajectory and the forecasts were generated by different models. There are very few rigorous results about the convergence of particle filters under imperfect model scenarios, but the previous example demonstrates that skilful forecasts are nevertheless possible.

We finally demonstrate, using numerical experiments, that an SIR filter is able to reproduce the results from a Kalman filter in the case of a linear dynamical model and a Gaussian distribution on the initial conditions.

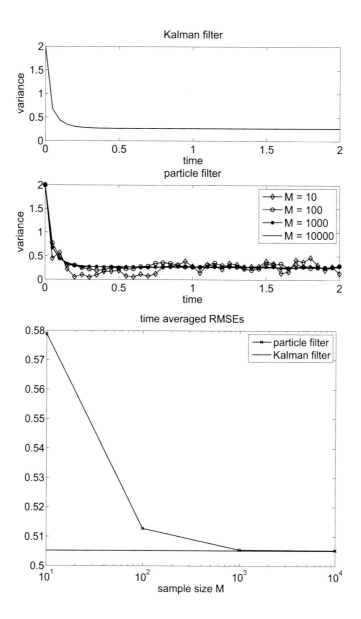

**Figure 6.6** Comparison of the SIR filter to the Kalman filter for a scalar linear model and a Gaussian initial distribution. While the top panel displays the behaviour in terms of posterior variances, the bottom one gives the resulting time averaged RMSEs for both filters. The convergence of the SIR filter to the (optimal) Kalman solution as $M$ increases is clearly visible.

**Example 6.12**     We repeat the perfect model experiment from Example 6.4 and replace the Kalman filter by the SIR filter with increasing sample sizes $M$.

Again we find that the SIR filter converges as $M$ is increased and, furthermore, a comparison with the Kalman filter reveals that the SIR filter converges to the same asymptotic value of the posterior variance. See Figure 6.6. We also compare the time averaged RMSEs from the Kalman and the SIR filter and again find asymptotic convergence as $M \to \infty$.

An SIR resampling step generally produces an equally weighted analysis ensemble with some of its members being identical. If the model dynamic is deterministic, then these ensemble members will remain identical for all times; eventually the effective ensemble size may collapse as for an SIS particle filter. *Particle rejuvenation* is often used to generated mutually distinct analysis ensemble members.

**Definition 6.13** (Particle rejuvenation)   Let $\{z_i^{\mathrm{a}}\}$ denote an equally weighted analysis ensemble with some ensemble members being identical, i.e., there exist indices $i_1$ and $i_2$ such that $z_{i_1}^{\mathrm{a}} - z_{i_2}^{\mathrm{a}}$. Let $B \subset \mathbb{R}^{N_z \times N_z}$ denote a given covariance matrix and $\tau > 0$ a given *bandwidth parameter*. Then *particle rejuvenation* replaces each analysis ensemble member $z_i^{\mathrm{a}}$, $i = 1, \ldots, M$, by a single draw from the Gaussian distribution $\mathrm{N}(z_i^{\mathrm{a}}, \tau B)$. Note that the analysis ensemble remains unaltered for $\tau = 0$ and that $B$ can be chosen to be the empirical covariance matrix of the forecast ensemble.

Particle rejuvenation was not applied in the previous examples since the underlying dynamical models are stochastic. However, in Chapters 7 and 8, we will find that the introduction of particle rejuvenation is essential for good performance of particle filters in many contexts.

## Problems

**6.1**   Derive the update formulas (6.7) and (6.8) from the dynamical model equations (6.6).

**6.2**   Repeat the imperfect model experiment from Example 6.4 with the parameter $d$ in (6.14) set to $d = 0.5$. The reference trajectory is still generated with $d = -0.1$. Compute the asymptotic value $P_*^{\mathrm{a}}$, the analysis means $\{\bar{z}_k^{\mathrm{a}}\}$, and the time averaged RMSE. Compare your results to those from the perfect and imperfect model settings from Example 6.4.

**6.3**   The derivation of linear 4DVar was based on the simplified assumption that the dynamical system satisfies $z^{n+1} = (I + \delta t D)z^n$. How do the results change if we were to consider the more general linear system with affine term

$$z^{n+1} = (I + \delta D)z^n + \delta t b?$$

**6.4**   Consider the trivial dynamical model $z^{n+1} = z^n$ for $z^n \in \mathbb{R}^{N_z}$ and $n \geq 0$. The initial conditions $z^0$ are Gaussian distributed with mean zero and covariance matrix $P^0 = I$. For simplicity, the reference trajectory is given by $z_{\mathrm{ref}}^n = 0$ for all $n \geq 0$. We will consider a time-dependent observation operator where a different component of the state vector $z$ is observed at each time-step. At time index $n$, we observe the $n$th entry of the state vector $z$, which we denote by $z(n)$. In other words, the forward operator $H \in \mathbb{R}^{1 \times N_z}$ is time dependent and given by $H(t_n) = e_n^T$ and $N_{out} = 1$. The measurement errors are independent and Gaussian distributed with mean zero and variance $R = 0.16$. Hence, we obtain the time-dependent conditional PDF

$$\pi_Y(y_{obs}^n | z, t_n) \propto e^{-\frac{(y_{obs}^n - e_n^T z^n)^2}{2R}},$$

with $y_{obs}^n = \xi^n$ and $\xi^n \sim N(0, R)$. Apply the Kalman formulas to this problem to derive the sequence of analyis means $\bar{z}_n^a$ and covariance matrices $P_n^a$ for $n = 1, \ldots, N_z$. Be careful to note that the forward operator $H$ is time dependent. Finally discuss the dependence of the final $\bar{z}_{N_z}^a$ and $P_{N_z}^a$ on the dimension of state space $N_z$.

**6.5** Implement the SIS particle filter for the data assimilation scenario in Problem 6.4. How does the particle filter behave for fixed ensemble size $M = 10$ and increasing values of the dimension of state space $N_z \in \{1, 10, 20, \ldots, 100, 200\}$? Repeat each experiment one thousand times and average over the resulting normalised RMSEs at the final iteration $n = N_z$, i.e.,

$$\text{RMSE} = \frac{1}{N_z^{1/2}} \left\| \sum_{i=1}^M w_i^{N_z} z_i^{N_z} \right\|,$$

noting that for this model, $z_i^{N_z} = z_i^0$. Also monitor the effective sample size (6.30) as a function of the iteration index $n = 0, \ldots, N_z$.

**6.6** The behaviour of the SIS particle filter observed in Problem 6.5 is an example of the *curse of dimensionality* for dynamical systems with high-dimensional state spaces. We will discuss filter algorithms for high-dimensional systems in Chapter 8. Here we illustrate one of their basic ideas for the data assimilation problem from Problem 6.4. Note that the Kalman filter updates each entry of the state vector individually while the particle filter of Problem 6.5 couples all entries through a change in the particle weights $w_i^n \geq 0$. A more appropriate approach would be to *localise* the impact of an observation $y_{obs}^n$ onto the corresponding entry of the ensemble vectors $z_i^n \in \mathbb{R}^{N_z}$, $i = 1, \ldots, M$. This leads to vectors of weights $w_i^n \in \mathbb{R}^{N_z}$ with their $k$th entry denoted by $w_i^n(k)$. Those entries individually satisfy

$$\sum_k w_i^n(k) = 1;$$

surprisingly only the $n$th entry is updated at the $n$th assimilation step using

$$w_i^n(n) \propto w_i^{n-1}(n) e^{-\frac{(y_{obs}^n - e_n^T z_i^n)^2}{2R}}, \qquad i = 1, \ldots, M,$$

with $w_i^{n-1}(n) = 1/M$. Implement the associated localised SIS filter and compare your results with those from Problem 6.5 in terms of the RMSE defined by

$$\text{RMSE} = \frac{1}{N_z^{1/2}} \sqrt{\sum_{i=1}^{M} \sum_{n=1}^{N_z} \left( w_i^{N_z}(n) z_i^{N_z}(n) \right)^2}.$$

**6.7**  Implement the SIR filter for the stochastically perturbed Lorenz-63 model (4.18)–(4.20) from Example 4.13. Use the same model to generate a reference trajectory $\{z_{\text{ref}}^n\}_{n \geq 0}$ from the initial condition

$$z_{\text{ref}}^0 = (-0.587, -0.563, 16.87).$$

Use this reference trajectory to generate a total of $N_{\text{obs}} = 100000$ observations of the x-components in time intervals of $\Delta t_{\text{out}} = 0.01$ and with measurement error variance $R$. Compute time averaged RMSEs for ensemble sizes varying between $M = 50$ and $M = 1000$ and for measurement error variances $R = 0.1$ and $R = 1.0$. The initial PDF is Gaussian with mean $\bar{z} = z_{\text{ref}}^0$ and diagonal covariance matrix $P = \sigma^2 I$ with $\sigma = 0.1$. In addition to varying values of the measurement error variance $R$, it is also interesting to explore different observation intervals $\Delta t_{\text{out}}$ and/or different variances $\sigma$ in the initial PDF $N(z_{\text{ref}}^0, \sigma^2 I)$.

## 6.4        Guide to literature

Tarantola (2005) is a very readable introduction to data assimilation, whilst Jazwinski (1970) is still an excellent monograph on the classic theory of filtering and Bayesian data assimilation. The linear filter theory (Kalman filter) can, for example, be found in Simon (2006). A broad range of assimilation techniques, including variational ones, is discussed in Lewis et al. (2006). Also, see Särkkä (2013) for a stronger emphasis on the Bayesian approach to smoothing and filtering. Practical aspects of particle filters/sequential Monte Carlo methods can be found in Doucet et al. (2001), Robert (2001), and Arulampalam et al. (2002), while del Moral (2004), Bain & Crisan (2009) and Künsch (2005) provide a more theoretical perspective. Bengtsson, Bickel & Li (2008) discuss the applicability of particle filters to high-dimensional systems.

A discussion of data assimilation in a meteorological and geophysical context is provided by Daley (1993) and Kalnay (2002).

An introduction to minimisation algorithms can be found in Nocedal & Wright (2006).

## 6.5        Appendix: Posterior consistency

Bayes' formula tells us how to adjust our probability distribution having received noisy observations. If a series of measurements is taken, then we expect to reduce our uncertainty in the system state as each measurement is made, even if the measurements are noisy. It seems reasonable to expect that the probability measure converges to the Dirac measure centred on the true value, in the limit of many observations with observation noise of fixed variance. This is called *posterior consistency*. Posterior consistency is often used as a way of verifying Bayesian data assimilation algorithms, or even debugging algorithm code.

The conditions under which posterior consistency is expected under a given data assimilation scheme are very technical, and a subject of current research. Here, we consider a very simple case, namely the trivial iteration

$$z^{n+1} = z^n, \quad t_{n+1} = t_n + 1,$$

where we wish to estimate the initial state $z^0$ from observations $y_{\rm obs}(t_n)$ at $t_n = n$, $n = 1, 2, \ldots, N_{\rm obs}$. The reference solution is simply given by $z_{\rm ref}^n = z^0$ under a perfect model assumption. We further assume for simplicity the forward model

$$y_{\rm obs}(t_n) = z^0 + \xi_n,$$

where the variables $\{\xi_n\}$ are independent realisations of a Gaussian random variable with mean zero and covariance matrix $R$.

This very much simplified data assimilation problem allows us to compare maximum likelihood based estimators, such as (6.27), with Bayesian ones, such as (6.25). Without further restriction of generality we also assume that $z$ and $y$ are univariate.

Since the measurement errors are assumed to be mutually independent, the likelihood function of $N_{\rm obs}$ observations is simply given by

$$l(z, y_{t_{1:N_{\rm obs}}}^{\rm obs}) := \prod_{n=1}^{N_{\rm obs}} \pi_Y(y_{\rm obs}(t_n)|z),$$

with

$$\pi_Y(y|z) = \frac{1}{\sqrt{2\pi R}} e^{-\frac{1}{2R}(y-z)^2}.$$

The maximum likelihood estimate of $z^0$, denoted by $\hat{z}^0$, is now defined as the minimiser of the negative log likelihood function

$$L_{\rm MLE}(z) = -\ln l(z, y_{t_{1:N_{\rm obs}}}^{\rm obs}) = \sum_{n=1}^{N_{\rm obs}} \frac{1}{2R}(y_{\rm obs}(t_n) - z)^2 + \frac{N_{\rm obs}}{2} \ln(2\pi R),$$

and we recognise the method of least squares applied to the residuals

$$r_n := z - y_{\rm obs}(t_n),$$

up to an insignificant additive constant. Since $\hat{z}^0$ has to satisfy

$$L_{\rm MLE}'(\hat{z}^0) = \frac{1}{R} \sum_{n=1}^{N_{\rm obs}} (\hat{z}^0 - y_{\rm obs}(t_n)) = 0,$$

the maximum likelihood estimate is given by

$$\hat{z}^0 = \frac{1}{N_{\text{obs}}} \sum_{n=1}^{N_{\text{obs}}} y_{\text{obs}}(t_n),$$

which determines $\hat{z}^0$ as the mean over the available observations.

Since the observations $y_{\text{obs}}(t_n)$ are realisations of random variables $Y(t_n)$, the estimator $\hat{z}^0$ is also the realisation of an appropriately defined random variable $\hat{Z}^0$. Within our simple model setting, the distribution of $\hat{Z}^0$ is Gaussian for any $N_{\text{obs}} \geq 1$ with mean $\hat{z}^0$ and variance $\sigma^2 = R/N_{\text{obs}}$.

How does this picture change for the associated Bayesian MAP estimate $\bar{z}^0$, which is based on minimising

$$L_{\text{MAP}}(z) = \frac{1}{2B}(\bar{z}^0 - z)^2 + L_{\text{MLE}}(z),$$

in the case of a Gaussian prior $\text{N}(\bar{z}^0, B)$? Straightforward calculations lead to the equation

$$L'_{\text{MAP}}(\bar{z}^0) = \frac{1}{B}(\bar{z}^0 - \bar{z}^0) + \frac{1}{R} \sum_{n=1}^{N_{\text{obs}}} (\bar{z}^0 - y_{\text{obs}}(t_n)) = 0.$$

Hence

$$\bar{z}^0 + \frac{R}{B N_{\text{obs}}}(\bar{z}^0 - \bar{z}^0) = \frac{1}{N_{\text{obs}}} \sum_{n=1}^{N_{\text{obs}}} y_{\text{obs}}(t_n)$$

and $\bar{z}^0 \to \hat{z}^0$ as $N_{\text{obs}} \to \infty$. In other words, the maximum likelihood estimator $\hat{z}^0$ is recovered asymptotically as the number of observations is increased.

## 6.6      Appendix: Weak constraint 4DVar

Our discussion of variational data assimilation techniques has been based on deterministic models leading to a relation

$$z^{\text{f}}_{k+1} = \psi(z^{\text{a}}_k) \tag{6.31}$$

between the analysis at time $t_k$ and the forecast at $t_{k+1}$. In this appendix, we briefly describe an extension of the 4DVar functional (6.25) to models containing stochastic contributions. This extension, known as *weak constraint 4DVar*, formally replaces the perfect model (6.31) by

$$z^{\text{f}}_{k+1} = \psi(z^{\text{a}}_k) + w_{k+1},$$

with the new variables $w_k$, $k = 1, \ldots, N_{\text{obs}}$, representing stochastic model contributions. These contributions are assumed to be Gaussian with mean zero and covariance matrix $\hat{Q} \in \mathbb{R}^{N_z \times N_z}$. Furthermore, the functional (6.25) is replaced by

$$L = \frac{1}{2}(z_0 - \overline{z}_0^{\mathrm{a}})^{\mathrm{T}}(P_0^{\mathrm{a}})^{-1}(z_0 - \overline{z}_0^{\mathrm{a}}) + \frac{1}{2}\sum_{k=1}^{N_{\mathrm{obs}}} w_k^{\mathrm{T}}\hat{Q}^{-1}w_k$$

$$+ \frac{1}{2}\sum_{k=1}^{N_{\mathrm{obs}}}(Hz_k - y_{\mathrm{obs}}(t_k))^{\mathrm{T}}R^{-1}(Hz_k - y_{\mathrm{obs}}(t_k)), \qquad (6.32)$$

subject to

$$w_k := z_k - \psi(z_{k-1}). \qquad (6.33)$$

These modifications to 4DVar have the important consequence that the functional (6.32) now depends on a whole sequence $z_0, z_1, \ldots, z_{N_{\mathrm{obs}}}$ of states. Critical points are given by the $N_z \times (N_{\mathrm{obs}} + 1)$ nonlinear equations

$$\nabla_{z_0} L = (P_0^{\mathrm{a}})^{-1}(z_0 - \overline{z}_0^{\mathrm{a}}) - D\psi(z_0)^{\mathrm{T}}\hat{Q}^{-1}w_1 = 0,$$

$$\nabla_{z_k} L = -D\psi(z_k)^{\mathrm{T}}\hat{Q}^{-1}w_{k+1} + \hat{Q}^{-1}w_k + H^{\mathrm{T}}R^{-1}r_k = 0,$$

for $k = 1, \ldots, N_{\mathrm{obs}} - 1$, and

$$\nabla_{z_{N_{\mathrm{obs}}}} L = \hat{Q}^{-1}w_{N_{\mathrm{obs}}} + H^{\mathrm{T}}R^{-1}r_{N_{\mathrm{obs}}} = 0$$

with model contributions (6.33) and residuals

$$r_k := Hz_k - y_{\mathrm{obs}}(t_k).$$

Weak constraint 4DVar can be shown to reduce to the associated Kalman smoother equations in the case of linear models and Gaussian uncertainties in the initial conditions and model errors (Jazwinski 1970).

Standard 4DVar is recovered in the formal limit $\hat{Q} \to 0$.

# 7  McKean approach to data assimilation

The previous chapter introduced some well-established data assimilation algorithms. On the one hand, the Kalman filter provides a way to convert from a forecast PDF to an analysis PDF, under the assumption of a linear model, a Gaussian forecast PDF and Gaussian observation error. On the other hand, the particle filter transforms an empirical PDF from forecast to analysis by altering the weights, and can be used in completely general situations. In this chapter we will develop a framework that unifies these two approaches, by taking a coupling and optimal transportation perspective. We will use this framework in this (and the following) chapter to explore a number of data assimilation algorithms which attempt to deal with the major drawback of the particle filter, namely the requirement of relative large ensemble sizes for good state estimates.

We start by recalling that a Markov process gives rise to families of random variables

$$Z_{t_{0:N}} := (Z^0, Z^1, \ldots, Z^N) : \Omega \to \mathbb{R}^{N_z \times N+1},$$

with joint PDFs given by

$$\pi_{Z_{t_{0:N}}}(z_{t_{0:N}}) = \pi_Z(z^0, t_0)\pi(z^1|z^0)\cdots\pi(z^N|z^{N-1}),$$

where $\pi(z'|z)$ denotes the transition kernel of the Markov process and $\pi_Z(z, t_0)$ is the initial PDF. The marginal PDFs $\pi_Z(z, t_n)$ for the random variables $Z^n$, $n = 1, \ldots, N$, are recursively determined by the Chapman–Kolmogorov equation

$$\pi_Z(z', t_n) = \int_{\mathbb{R}^{N_z}} \pi(z'|z)\pi_Z(z, t_{n-1})\mathrm{d}z.$$

Ensemble prediction methods produce realisations (or samples) of $Z_{t_{0:N}}$, based on the recursive structure of the underlying Markov process. More precisely, given a set of $M$ ensemble members $z_i^{n-1}$ at $t_{n-1}$, this ensemble is subsequently transformed into an ensemble at $t_n$ according to a (stochastic) model which we write as

$$z_i^n = Z_i^n(\omega_i), \qquad Z_i^n \sim \pi(\cdot|z_i^{n-1}),$$

for $i = 1, \ldots, M$, i.e., $z_i^n$ is taken as the realisation of a random variable with PDF $\pi(\cdot|z_i^{n-1})$. We have discussed several methods for generating realisations from a PDF $\pi_Z(z) := \pi(z|z_i^{n-1})$ in Chapter 3. After having completed this process for

$n = 1, \ldots, N$ we may formally write

$$Z_{t_{0:N}}(\omega_i) := (z_i^0, z_i^1, \ldots, z_i^N),$$

for $i = 1, \ldots, M$.

Furthermore, since the ensemble values $\{z_i^n\}$ at time $t_n$ are samples from $\pi(z, t_n)$, the ensemble induced PDF

$$\pi_M(z', t_{n+1}) = \frac{1}{M} \sum_{i=1}^{M} \pi(z'|z_i^n),$$

converges weakly to $\pi_Z(z', t_{n+1})$ and the new ensemble $\{z_i^{n+1}\}$ at $t_{n+1}$ can be used to approximate the expectation value

$$\mathbb{E}[g(Z^{n+1})] \approx \frac{1}{M} \sum_{i=1}^{M} g(z_i^{n+1}),$$

of any continuous and bounded function $g$.

Bayesian data assimilation algorithms combine ensemble prediction for Markov processes with a recursive application of Bayes' formula

$$\pi_{Z^a}(z|y_{\text{obs}}) = \frac{\pi_Y(y_{\text{obs}}|z)\pi_{Z^f}(z)}{\pi_Y(y_{\text{obs}})}, \tag{7.1}$$

which transforms a forecast PDF $\pi_{Z^f}(z)$ into an analysis PDF $\pi_{Z^a}(z|y_{\text{obs}})$ under the likelihood $\pi_Y(y_{\text{obs}}|z)$ of an observation $y_{\text{obs}}$. One of the challenges of merging ensemble prediction methods and Bayesian data assimilation algorithms lies in the fact that Bayes' formula does not come in the form of a Chapman–Kolmogorov equation. The SIR particle filter works around that problem by implementing Bayes' formula as an importance resampling step in order to obtain an analysis ensemble with uniform weights.

The *McKean approach*[1] to data assimilation pushes importance resampling a step further by putting Bayes' formula directly into the framework of Markov chains. The Markov chain defines the transition from a forecast ensemble into an analysis ensemble at an observation time $t_k$, with all ensemble members keeping equal weights. The desired Markov chain will only be applied once and has to produce an analysis which is consistent with Bayes' formula (7.1). We summarise this in a formal definition. A broader perspective on the McKean approach and, more generally, interacting particle systems can be found in del Moral (2004).

[1] McKean (1966) pioneered the study of stochastic processes that are generated by stochastic differential equations for which the diffusion term depends on the time-evolving marginal distributions $\pi_Z(z, t)$. Such stochastic differential equations are fundamentally different from the ones considered in Chapter 4, and lead to interacting particle/ensemble approximations. More precisely, Monte Carlo sampling paths $\{z_i(t)\}_{t \in [0,T]}$, $i = 1, \ldots, M$, are no longer independent if samples $\{z_i(t)\}$ at time $t$ are used to approximate the marginal PDF $\pi_Z(z, t)$ by, e.g., the ensemble induced empirical measure. Here we utilise a generalisation of this idea which allows for Markov transition kernels $\pi(z', t_n|z)$ that depend on the marginal distribution $\pi_Z(z, t_n)$.

**Definition 7.1** (McKean approach)    Let $b(z'|z)$ be a transition kernel such that Bayes' formula (7.1) becomes equivalent to a Chapman–Kolmogorov equation,

$$\pi_{Z^{\mathrm{a}}}(z^{\mathrm{a}}|y_{\mathrm{obs}}) = \int_{\mathbb{R}^{N_z}} b(z^{\mathrm{a}}|z^{\mathrm{f}})\pi_{Z^{\mathrm{f}}}(z^{\mathrm{f}})\mathrm{d}z^{\mathrm{f}}.$$

Given an ensemble $z_i^{\mathrm{f}}$ which follows the forecast PDF, an analysis ensemble can be obtained from

$$z_i^{\mathrm{a}} = Z_i^{\mathrm{a}}(\omega), \qquad Z_i^{\mathrm{a}} \sim b(\cdot|z_i^{\mathrm{f}}),$$

$i = 1,\ldots,M$, i.e., the analysis samples $z_i^{\mathrm{a}}$ are realisations of random variables $Z_i^{\mathrm{a}}$ with PDFs $b(z|z_i^{\mathrm{f}})$. This Monte Carlo approach to Bayesian inference is called the *McKean approach*.

The transition kernel $b(z'|z)$ will, in general, depend on both the observed value $y_{\mathrm{obs}}$ as well as the forecast PDF $\pi_{Z^{\mathrm{f}}}$. In this sense, the induced Markov process will be non-autonomous; this is contrary to most of the Markov processes considered in Chapter 4.

---

**Example 7.2**    The following transition kernel can be found in del Moral (2004):

$$b(z^{\mathrm{a}}|z^{\mathrm{f}}) = \varepsilon\pi_Y(y_{\mathrm{obs}}|z^{\mathrm{f}})\delta(z^{\mathrm{a}} - z^{\mathrm{f}}) + (1 - \varepsilon\pi_Y(y_{\mathrm{obs}}|z^{\mathrm{f}}))\pi_{Z^{\mathrm{a}}}(z^{\mathrm{a}}|y_{\mathrm{obs}}).$$

Here $\varepsilon \geq 0$ is chosen such that

$$1 - \varepsilon\pi_Y(y_{\mathrm{obs}}|z) \geq 0,$$

for all $z \in \mathbb{R}^{N_z}$. Indeed we find that

$$\int_{\mathbb{R}^{N_z}} b(z^{\mathrm{a}}|z^{\mathrm{f}})\pi_{Z^{\mathrm{f}}}(z^{\mathrm{f}})\mathrm{d}z^{\mathrm{f}} = \varepsilon\pi_Y(y_{\mathrm{obs}}|z^{\mathrm{a}})\pi_{Z^{\mathrm{f}}}(z^{\mathrm{a}}) + \pi_{Z^{\mathrm{a}}}(z^{\mathrm{a}}|y_{\mathrm{obs}})$$

$$- \varepsilon\pi_{Z^{\mathrm{a}}}(z^{\mathrm{a}}|y_{\mathrm{obs}}) \int_{\mathbb{R}^{N_z}} \pi_Y(y_{\mathrm{obs}}|z^{\mathrm{f}})\pi_{Z^{\mathrm{f}}}(z^{\mathrm{f}})\mathrm{d}z^{\mathrm{f}}$$

$$= \pi_{Z^{\mathrm{a}}}(z^{\mathrm{a}}|y_{\mathrm{obs}})$$

$$+ \varepsilon\left\{\pi_Y(y_{\mathrm{obs}}|z^{\mathrm{a}})\pi_{Z^{\mathrm{f}}}(z^{\mathrm{a}}) - \pi_{Z^{\mathrm{a}}}(z^{\mathrm{a}}|y_{\mathrm{obs}})\pi_Y(y_{\mathrm{obs}})\right\}$$

$$= \pi_{Z^{\mathrm{a}}}(z^{\mathrm{a}}|y_{\mathrm{obs}}).$$

This choice of a transition kernel implies that the state remains at $z^{\mathrm{f}}$ with probability $p = \varepsilon\pi_y(y_{\mathrm{obs}}|z^{\mathrm{f}})$, otherwise we draw a new sample from the analysis PDF $\pi_{Z^{\mathrm{a}}}(z^{\mathrm{a}}|y_{\mathrm{obs}})$. The particular choice $\varepsilon = 0$ implies zero correlation between the forecast and analysis ensembles.

---

In order to apply the McKean approach to data assimilation, we need to find an appropriate transition kernel $b(z^{\mathrm{a}}|z^{\mathrm{f}})$. There are many possibilities for doing so. The kernels considered in this chapter are based on the concept of coupling two probability measures. Recalling the definition in Chapter 2, a Bayes' formula coupling between the forecast and the analysis PDFs is a joint measure $\mu_{Z^fZ^a}$ such that the marginals satisfy

$$\pi_{Z^f}(z^f)dz^f = \int_{z^a \in \mathbb{R}^{N_z}} \mu_{Z^fZ^a}(dz^f, dz^a),$$

and

$$\pi_{Z^a}(z^a|y_{\mathrm{obs}})dz^a = \int_{z^f \in \mathbb{R}^{N_z}} \mu_{Z^fZ^a}(dz^f, dz^a),$$

respectively. Once such a coupling is available we obtain the desired transition PDF $b(z^a|z^f)$ from the disintegration formula

$$b(z^a|z^f)\,\pi_{Z^f}(z^f)\,dz^f dz^a = \mu_{Z^fZ^a}(dz^f, dz^a).$$

We recall from Chapter 2 that couplings can often be made deterministic and are then given in the form of a transport map, i.e., there exists a transformation $z^a = T(z^f)$ such that

$$\mu_{Z^fZ^a}(dz^f, dz^a) = \delta(z^a - T(z^f))\,\pi_{Z^f}(z^f)\,dz^f dz^a,$$

in which case we have

$$b(z^a|z^f) = \delta(z^a - T(z^f)),$$

formally. In this case, a Monte Carlo implementation of the McKean approach to Bayesian inference reduces to the simple mathematical formula

$$z_i^a = T(z_i^f), \qquad i = 1, \ldots, M. \tag{7.2}$$

In addition to finding appropriate couplings there is another major challenge for implementing the McKean approach in practice. This challenge is related to the fact that the forecast PDF is often not available explicitly. Indeed, an ensemble prediction method will only provide us with a forecast ensemble $z_i^f$, $i = 1, \ldots, M$, from which we will have to estimate a statistical model in the form of a forecast PDF (or measure) $\pi_{Z^f}$. See Figure 7.1 for a graphical presentation of the complete ensemble-based implementation of a McKean approach for Bayesian inference.

A statistical model for the forecast PDF $\pi_{Z^f}$ can be either parametric or non-parametric. A simple parametric model is the Gaussian $N(\bar{z}_M^f, P_M^f)$ with its mean $\bar{z}_M^f$ and covariance matrix $P_M^f$ estimated from the prior or forecast ensemble $z_i^f$, $i = 1, \ldots, M$, i.e.,

$$\bar{z}_M^f = \frac{1}{M}\sum_{i=1}^{M} z_i^f \tag{7.3}$$

and

$$P_M^f = \frac{1}{M-1}\sum_{i=1}^{M}(z_i^f - \bar{z}_M^f)(z_i^f - \bar{z}_M^f)^{\mathrm{T}} \in \mathbb{R}^{N_z \times N_z}. \tag{7.4}$$

If the likelihood function $\pi_Y(y_{\mathrm{obs}}|z)$ is also Gaussian, then the posterior is Gaussian as well with its mean and covariance matrix given by Kalman's formulas from

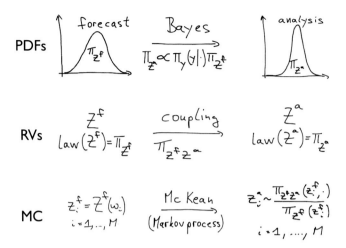

**Figure 7.1** A graphical presentation of the McKean approach to Bayesian inference in the context of Monte Carlo methods. We assume that $M$ ensemble members $z_i^f$ are available which are realisations from a generally unknown forecast/prior PDF. The first task is to estimate a statistical model in the form of a PDF $\pi_{Z^f}$ from the available ensemble members. Bayes' formula then leads to an analysis/posterior PDF $\pi_{Z^a}$. Next we need to find a coupling $\pi_{Z^f Z^a}$ between the forecast and analysis PDFs. Once such a coupling is available, an analysis ensemble $\{z_i^a\}_{i=1}^M$ can be generated following standard Monte Carlo methodologies.

Chapter 6. However, unlike the classical Kalman filter, we need to establish a coupling between the prior and posterior Gaussians in order to derive an appropriate map (7.2) for ensemble-based data assimilation algorithms. Later in this chapter we will see that the associated data assimilation algorithms give rise to the popular family of *ensemble Kalman filters*. Note that we have already discussed in Chapter 2 how to couple two Gaussian random variables. Hence we only need to put this material into the McKean data assimilation framework.

On the other hand, a non-parametric model for the forecast measure is provided by the empirical measure

$$\mu_M^f(\mathrm{d}z) = \frac{1}{M} \sum_{i=1}^M \delta(z - z_i^f)\mathrm{d}z. \tag{7.5}$$

The associated analysis measure is then

$$\mu_M^a(\mathrm{d}z) = \sum_{i=1}^M w_i \delta(z - z_i^f)\mathrm{d}z \tag{7.6}$$

with weights $w_i \propto \pi_Y(y_{\mathrm{obs}}|z_i^f)$. The problem of finding couplings for such measures has already been discussed in Chapters 2 and 5 in the context of linear transportation and a single Bayesian inference step.

The Gaussian parametric and empirical non-parametric approaches can be combined to obtain Gaussian mixture models

$$\pi_M(z) = \frac{1}{M} \sum_{i=1}^{M} \mathrm{n}(z; z_i^{\mathrm{f}}, \tau P_M^{\mathrm{f}}),$$

where $\tau > 0$ is the *bandwidth parameter* and $P_M^{\mathrm{f}}$ denotes the empirical covariance matrix (7.4) of the ensemble. In other words, the prior PDF is approximated as the sum of $M$ Gaussians with means $z_i^{\mathrm{f}}$ and identical covariance matrices equal to $\tau P_M^{\mathrm{f}}$. The empirical measure can be recovered by letting $\tau \to 0$.

One of the key findings of this chapter will be that Monte Carlo implementations of the McKean approach lead to linear ensemble transformations of the form

$$z_j^{\mathrm{a}} = \sum_{i=1}^{M} z_i^{\mathrm{f}} d_{ij}, \tag{7.7}$$

regardless of the chosen prior approximation. Data assimilation algorithms from this chapter will therefore only differ through their coefficients $d_{ij}$ in (7.7), which have some (possibly random) functional dependence on the forecast ensemble. These coefficients can be collected in an $M \times M$ matrix $D$.

**Definition 7.3** (Linear ensemble transform filters)   A particle or ensemble filter with the Bayesian inference step implemented in the form of a linear ensemble transformation (7.7) is called a *linear ensemble transform filter* (LETF).

---

**Example 7.4**   An SIR particle filter with resampling performed after each analysis step also fits into the framework of LETFs. In this case, the coefficients in (7.7) are given as realisations of a matrix-valued random variable $D: \Omega \to \mathbb{R}^{M \times M}$ whose entries satisfy

(i) $d_{ij} := D_{ij}(\omega) \in \{0, 1\}$,

(ii) $\sum_{i=1}^{M} d_{ij} = 1$, and

(iii) $\frac{1}{M} \mathbb{E} \left[ \sum_{j=1}^{M} D_{ij} \right] = w_i$.

---

So far we have discussed a single Bayesian inference step in terms of an induced Markov transition kernel $b(z^{\mathrm{a}}|z^{\mathrm{f}})$. We now combine such a kernel at each observation instance $\mathrm{t}_k$ with the Markovian model dynamics in between observations. Let us denote these kernels by $b(z^{\mathrm{a}}, \mathrm{t}_k|z^{\mathrm{f}})$ and $\pi_{N_{\mathrm{out}}}(z^{\mathrm{f}}|z^{\mathrm{a}})$, respectively. A complete transition kernel from an analysis at $\mathrm{t}_{k-1}$ to the induced analysis at $\mathrm{t}_k$ is then characterised by the marginalised transition kernel

$$\pi(z^{\mathrm{a}}(\mathrm{t}_k), \mathrm{t}_k|z^{\mathrm{a}}(\mathrm{t}_{k-1})) = \int_{\mathbb{R}^{N_z}} b(z^{\mathrm{a}}(\mathrm{t}_k), \mathrm{t}_k|z^{\mathrm{f}}) \, \pi_{N_{\mathrm{out}}}(z^{\mathrm{f}}|z^{\mathrm{a}}(\mathrm{t}_{k-1})) \, \mathrm{d}z^{\mathrm{f}}.$$

Hence, as for the Markovian model dynamics, the McKean approach to Bayesian data assimilation leads to families of analysis random variables

$$Z^{\mathrm{a}}_{\mathrm{t}_0:N_{\mathrm{obs}}} = (Z^{\mathrm{a}}(\mathrm{t}_0), Z^{\mathrm{a}}(\mathrm{t}_1), \ldots, Z^{\mathrm{a}}(\mathrm{t}_{N_{\mathrm{obs}}})),$$

with joint PDFs formally given by

$$\pi_{Z^{\mathrm{a}}_{\mathrm{t}_0:N_{\mathrm{obs}}}} (z^{\mathrm{a}}_{\mathrm{t}_0:N_{\mathrm{obs}}}) = \pi_Z(z^{\mathrm{a}}(\mathrm{t}_0), \mathrm{t}_0)\, \pi(z^{\mathrm{a}}(\mathrm{t}_1), \mathrm{t}_1 | z^{\mathrm{a}}(\mathrm{t}_0)) \cdots$$

$$\pi(z^{\mathrm{a}}(\mathrm{t}_{N_{\mathrm{obs}}}), \mathrm{t}_{N_{\mathrm{obs}}} | z^{\mathrm{a}}(\mathrm{t}_{N_{\mathrm{obs}}-1})).$$

Ensemble prediction methods for Markov processes can now be extended to sequential data assimilation problems. Two such approaches will be discussed in detail in the remainder of this chapter. More specifically, the following section discusses the McKean approach for Gaussian approximations to the forecast distribution $\pi_{Z^{\mathrm{f}}}$ in the Bayesian inference step, which gives rise to the popular class of ensemble Kalman filters. Subsequently we discuss particle filters from an optimal transportation perspective, which gives rise to another family of LETFs.

## 7.1     Ensemble Kalman filters

The classic Kalman filter formulas provide a transition from the forecast mean $\bar{z}^{\mathrm{f}}$ and covariance matrix $P^{\mathrm{f}}$ to the analysis mean $\bar{z}^{\mathrm{a}}$ and covariance matrix $P^{\mathrm{a}}$. An *ensemble Kalman filter* (EnKF) pulls this transition back onto the level of forecast ensembles $z_i^{\mathrm{f}}$, $i = 1, \ldots, M$, and analysis ensembles $z_i^{\mathrm{a}}$, $i = 1, \ldots, M$, respectively. Therefore it provides an implicit coupling between the underlying forecast and analysis random variables. The basic algorithmic steps of an EnKF can be summarised as follows.

(i) The forecast ensemble is used to define the empirical mean (7.3) and co-variance matrix (7.4).

(ii) The Kalman update formulas from Chapter 6 result in the analysis mean

$$\bar{z}^{\mathrm{a}} = \bar{z}^{\mathrm{f}}_M - K(H\bar{z}^{\mathrm{f}}_M - y_{\mathrm{obs}}), \qquad (7.8)$$

and the analysis covariance matrix

$$P^{\mathrm{a}} = P^{\mathrm{f}}_M - KHP^{\mathrm{f}}_M. \qquad (7.9)$$

Here the Kalman gain matrix is given by

$$K = P^{\mathrm{f}}_M H^{\mathrm{T}} (HP^{\mathrm{f}}_M H^{\mathrm{T}} + R)^{-1}, \qquad (7.10)$$

$H$ is the (linear) forward operator, and $R$ is the measurement error covariance matrix of an observation $y_{\mathrm{obs}}$.

(iii) Finally the analysis ensemble $\{z_i^{\mathrm{a}}\}$ is defined by a linear transformation (7.7) with the transformation matrix $D$ chosen such that

$$\frac{1}{M} \sum_{i=1}^{M} z_i^{\mathrm{a}} = \bar{z}^{\mathrm{a}}, \qquad (7.11)$$

and

$$\frac{1}{M-1}\sum_{i=1}^{M}(z_i^{\mathrm{a}} - \bar{z}^{\mathrm{a}})(z_i^{\mathrm{a}} - \bar{z}^{\mathrm{a}})^{\mathrm{T}} = P^{\mathrm{a}}. \tag{7.12}$$

If the transformation $D$ is a random matrix, we require that (7.11) and (7.12) hold in expectation.

The transformation matrix $D$ of an EnKF is not uniquely determined by the constraints (7.11) and (7.12); this allows for different implementations of an EnKF. We start with the oldest EnKF formulation, which is based on a non-deterministic coupling between the forecast and analysis ensemble.

**Definition 7.5** (EnKF with perturbed observations) Given a prior ensemble $z_i^{\mathrm{f}}$, $i = 1, \ldots, M$, with associated empirical mean (7.3) and covariance matrix (7.4), we first compute the Kalman gain matrix (7.10). The *EnKF with perturbed observations* is then based on the non-deterministic coupling

$$Z^{\mathrm{a}} = Z^{\mathrm{f}} - K(HZ^{\mathrm{f}} + \Xi - y_{\mathrm{obs}}), \tag{7.13}$$

where $\Xi$ denotes a Gaussian random variable with mean zero and covariance matrix $R$. The posterior ensemble $\{z_i^{\mathrm{a}}\}$ is obtained accordingly via

$$z_i^{\mathrm{a}} = z_i^{\mathrm{f}} - K(Hz_i^{\mathrm{f}} + \xi_i - y_{\mathrm{obs}}), \qquad i = 1, \ldots, M,$$

where the variables $\{\xi_i\}$ are realisations of $M$ i.i.d. Gaussian random variables with PDF $\mathrm{N}(0, R)$. In other words, the McKean transition kernel $b(z^{\mathrm{a}}|z^{\mathrm{f}})$ of an EnKF with perturbed observations is given by

$$b(z^{\mathrm{a}}|z^{\mathrm{f}}) = \mathrm{n}(z^{\mathrm{a}}; z^{\mathrm{f}} - K(Hz^{\mathrm{f}} - y_{\mathrm{obs}}), KRK^{\mathrm{T}}).$$

In order to ensure that

$$\sum_{i=1}^{M}\xi_i = 0, \tag{7.14}$$

it is often useful to shift a given set of samples $\{\xi_i'\}$ from $\mathrm{N}(0, R)$ by its empirical mean,

$$\bar{\xi}_M' = \frac{1}{M}\sum_{i=1}^{M}\xi_i' \in \mathbb{R}^{N_y},$$

so that $\xi_i := \xi_i' - \bar{\xi}_M'$ and (7.14) holds.

We demonstrate that (7.13) is consistent with the Kalman update formulas provided $Z^{\mathrm{f}}$ has mean $\bar{z}^{\mathrm{f}}$ and covariance matrix $P_M^{\mathrm{f}}$. We first verify that

$$\bar{z}^{\mathrm{a}} = \mathbb{E}[Z^{\mathrm{a}}] = \bar{z}_M^{\mathrm{f}} - K(H\bar{z}_M^{\mathrm{f}} - y_{\mathrm{obs}}),$$

since $\Xi$ is centred. Next, we find that

$$
\begin{aligned}
P^{a} &= \mathbb{E}[(Z^{a} - \bar{z}^{a})(Z^{a} - \bar{z}^{a})^{\mathrm{T}}] \\
&= \mathbb{E}[(Z^{f} - K(HZ^{f} + \Xi - y_{\mathrm{obs}}) - \bar{z}^{a})(Z^{f} - K(HZ^{f} + \Xi - y_{\mathrm{obs}}) - \bar{z}^{a})^{\mathrm{T}}] \\
&= \mathbb{E}[K\Xi\Xi^{\mathrm{T}}K^{\mathrm{T}}] \\
&\quad + \mathbb{E}[(Z^{f} - \bar{z}^{f}_{M} - KH(Z^{f} - \bar{z}^{f}_{M}))(Z^{f} - \bar{z}^{f}_{M} - KH(Z^{f} - \bar{z}^{f}_{M}))^{\mathrm{T}}] \\
&= KRK^{\mathrm{T}} + P^{f}_{M} - P^{f}_{M}H^{\mathrm{T}}K^{\mathrm{T}} - KHP^{f}_{M} + KHP^{f}_{M}H^{\mathrm{T}}K^{\mathrm{T}} \\
&= P^{f}_{M} - KHP^{f}_{M} .
\end{aligned}
$$

Here we have used the property that $\Xi$ and $Z^{f}$ are independent, and the identity

$$
KRK^{\mathrm{T}} + KHP^{f}_{M}H^{\mathrm{T}}K^{\mathrm{T}} = P^{f}_{M}H^{\mathrm{T}}(HP^{f}_{M}H^{\mathrm{T}} + R)^{-1}HP^{f}_{M} = P^{f}_{M}H^{\mathrm{T}}K^{\mathrm{T}}.
$$

The EnKF with perturbed observations fits into the framework of LETFs (7.7) and the associated matrix-valued random variable $D : \Omega \to \mathbb{R}^{M \times M}$ has realisations with entries

$$
d_{ij} = \delta_{ij} - \frac{1}{M-1}(z^{f}_{i} - \bar{z}^{f}_{M})^{\mathrm{T}}H^{\mathrm{T}}(HP^{f}_{M}H^{\mathrm{T}} + R)^{-1}(Hz^{f}_{j} + \xi_{j} - y_{\mathrm{obs}}), \quad (7.15)
$$

where $\delta_{ij}$ denotes the Kronecker delta, i.e., $\delta_{ii} = 1$, $\delta_{ij} = 0$ for $i \neq j$. This claim can be verified by direct calculations making use of

$$
P^{f}_{M} = \frac{1}{M-1}\sum_{i=1}^{M} z^{f}_{i}(z^{f}_{i} - \bar{z}^{f}_{M})^{\mathrm{T}}.
$$

We discuss the coupling perspective on an EnKF with perturbed observations in some more detail for the univariate case.

---

**Example 7.6**  The EnKF with perturbed observations for a scalar state variable and forward operator $H = 1$ becomes

$$
Z^{a} = Z^{f} - K(Z^{f} - y_{\mathrm{obs}} + \Xi), \qquad (7.16)
$$

with Kalman gain factor

$$
K = \frac{(\sigma^{f})^{2}}{(\sigma^{f})^{2} + R},
$$

where we have replaced the prior covariance matrix $P^{f}_{M}$ by $(\sigma^{f})^{2}$ for notational convenience. Let us interpret this update in terms of an induced coupling between $Z^{f}$ and $Z^{a}$, with $Z^{f}$ being Gaussian with mean $\bar{z}^{f}$ and variance $(\sigma^{f})^{2}$, and $Z^{a}$ being Gaussian with mean

$$
\bar{z}^{a} = \bar{z}^{f} - \frac{(\sigma^{f})^{2}}{(\sigma^{f})^{2} + R}(\bar{z}^{f} - y_{\mathrm{obs}}),
$$

and variance

$$
(\sigma^{a})^{2} = \left(1 - \frac{(\sigma^{f})^{2}}{(\sigma^{f})^{2} + R}\right)(\sigma^{f})^{2} = \frac{R}{(\sigma^{f})^{2} + R}(\sigma^{f})^{2},
$$

respectively. Any Gaussian coupling must have mean

$$(\bar{z}^{\mathrm{f}}, \bar{z}^{\mathrm{a}}) \in \mathbb{R}^2,$$

and covariance matrix

$$\Sigma = \left( \begin{array}{cc} (\sigma^{\mathrm{f}})^2 & \rho\sigma^{\mathrm{f}}\sigma^{\mathrm{a}} \\ \rho\sigma^{\mathrm{f}}\sigma^{\mathrm{a}} & (\sigma^{\mathrm{a}})^2 \end{array} \right),$$

with the correlation $\rho$ taking values between minus one and one. We have already seen in Chapter 2 that $|\rho| = 1$ leads to a deterministic coupling. In the case of the EnKF with perturbed observations, the induced coupling is not deterministic and the correlation between $Z^{\mathrm{f}}$ and $Z^{\mathrm{a}}$ is instead given by

$$\mathbb{E}[(Z^{\mathrm{f}} - \bar{z}^{\mathrm{f}})(Z^{\mathrm{a}} - \bar{z}^{\mathrm{a}})] = \mathbb{E}[(Z^{\mathrm{f}} - \bar{z}^{\mathrm{f}})(Z^{\mathrm{f}} - \bar{z}^{\mathrm{f}} - K(Z^{\mathrm{f}} - \bar{z}^{\mathrm{f}} + \Xi))]$$
$$= (\sigma^{\mathrm{f}})^2 - K(\sigma^{\mathrm{f}})^2 = (\sigma^{\mathrm{a}})^2,$$

and, therefore,

$$\Sigma = \left( \begin{array}{cc} (\sigma^{\mathrm{f}})^2 & (\sigma^{\mathrm{a}})^2 \\ (\sigma^{\mathrm{a}})^2 & (\sigma^{\mathrm{a}})^2 \end{array} \right).$$

Hence

$$\rho = \frac{\sigma^{\mathrm{a}}}{\sigma^{\mathrm{f}}} = \sqrt{\frac{R}{(\sigma^{\mathrm{f}})^2 + R}} < 1.$$

We now put the EnKF analysis step into the context of state estimation for an evolution model such as (6.28), using the notation introduced in Chapter 6.

**Algorithm 7.7** (EnKF with perturbed observations)  We draw $M$ independent realisations $z_i^0 = z_i(0)$ from a given initial distribution $\pi_Z(z, 0)$. Observations are given in intervals of $\Delta t_{\mathrm{out}} = \delta t N_{\mathrm{out}}$.

The following steps are performed recursively for $k = 1, \ldots, N_{\mathrm{obs}}$.

(i) In between observations, the initial ensemble $\{z_i(\mathsf{t}_{k-1})\}$ at $\mathsf{t}_{k-1} = (k - 1)\Delta t_{\mathrm{out}}$ is propagated under the given evolution model, such as (6.28), in order to produce a forecast ensemble $\{z_i^{\mathrm{f}}\}$ at the next observation time $\mathsf{t}_k = k\Delta t_{\mathrm{out}}$.

(ii) The forecast ensemble is transformed into an analysis ensemble $\{z_i^{\mathrm{a}}\}_{i=1}^M$ according to (7.7). The coefficients $d_{ij}$ are defined by (7.15) with observed $y_{\mathrm{obs}} = y_{\mathrm{obs}}(\mathsf{t}_k)$ and $M$ independent realisations $\xi_i$ of a Gaussian random variable with distribution $\mathrm{N}(0, R)$ satisfying (7.14). Finally, we return to (i) with new initial conditions

$$z_i(\mathsf{t}_k) := z_i^{\mathrm{a}}, \qquad i = 1, \ldots, M,$$

and the index $k$ increased by one.

We mention in passing that the EnKF with perturbed observations can be viewed as a Monte Carlo implementation of a BLUE estimator as introduced in Appendix 5.5, with the variable $X$ being replaced by the forecast state variable $Z^f$. The key observation is that $y_{obs} := Y(\omega)$, $\bar{x} := \bar{z}^f$, and $\bar{z}^a := \hat{X}(\omega)$ in (5.34). This interpretation of the EnKF with perturbed observations is appealing since it does not rely on the assumption of the prior PDF being Gaussian.

Given the theoretical results on couplings from Chapter 2, it is rather natural to look for deterministic couplings between the forecast and the analysis. Indeed, following Example 2.26 from Chapter 2, a suitable analysis ensemble could, for example, be defined by the linear transformation

$$z_i^a = \bar{z}^a + (P^a)^{1/2}(P_M^f)^{-1/2}(z_i^f - \bar{z}_M^f), \qquad i = 1, \ldots, M, \qquad (7.17)$$

with $\bar{z}^a$ given by (7.8) and $P^a$ by (7.9), respectively. This formulation requires the computation of the square root of two $N_z \times N_z$ matrices, which can be computationally demanding if $N_z$ is large.

In order to derive an alternative update formula, we write the empirical forecast covariance matrix (7.4) as

$$P_M^f = \frac{1}{M-1} A^f (A^f)^T, \qquad (7.18)$$

with the $N_z \times M$ matrix of forecast *ensemble perturbations* (also called *ensemble anomalies*)

$$A^f := \left[ \ (z_1^f - \bar{z}_M^f) \quad (z_2^f - \bar{z}_M^f) \quad \cdots \quad (z_M^f - \bar{z}_M^f) \ \right]. \qquad (7.19)$$

We next seek a matrix $S \in \mathbb{R}^{M \times M}$ such that

$$\frac{1}{M-1} A^f SS^T (A^f)^T = P^a = P_M^f - KHP_M^f. \qquad (7.20)$$

A set of analysis ensemble anomalies is then provided by

$$A^a := A^f S \in \mathbb{R}^{N_z \times M}. \qquad (7.21)$$

More specifically, Equation (7.20) together with (7.18) imply

$$P^a = \frac{1}{M-1} A^f \left\{ I - \frac{1}{M-1}(HA^f)^T \left[ HP_M^f H^T + R \right]^{-1} HA^f \right\} (A^f)^T,$$

and hence

$$S := \left\{ I - \frac{1}{M-1}(HA^f)^T \left[ HP_M^f H^T + R \right]^{-1} HA^f \right\}^{1/2}.$$

Recall that the square root of a positive semi-definite matrix $U$ is the unique symmetric matrix $U^{1/2}$ such that $U^{1/2}U^{1/2} = U$.

An application of the Sherman–Morrison–Woodbury formula (6.9) leads to the equivalent formulation

$$S = \left\{ I + \frac{1}{M-1}(HA^f)^T R^{-1} HA^f \right\}^{-1/2}. \qquad (7.22)$$

Formulation (7.22) is preferable computationally whenever the ensemble size $M$ is smaller than the number of observations $N_y$, and $R$ is diagonal. Furthermore, the equivalent Kalman update formula

$$\bar{z}^{\mathrm{a}} = \bar{z}^{\mathrm{f}}_M - P^{\mathrm{a}}H^{\mathrm{T}}R^{-1}(H\bar{z}^{\mathrm{f}}_M - y_{\mathrm{obs}})$$

$$= \bar{z}^{\mathrm{f}}_M - \frac{1}{M-1}A^{\mathrm{f}}S^2(A^{\mathrm{f}})^{\mathrm{T}}H^{\mathrm{T}}R^{-1}(H\bar{z}^{\mathrm{f}}_M - y_{\mathrm{obs}}),$$

can be used to bring (7.8) into the form

$$\bar{z}^{\mathrm{a}} = \sum_{i=1}^{M} z_i^{\mathrm{f}} w_i, \qquad (7.23)$$

with the weights $w_i$ defined as the $i$th entry of the column vector

$$w = \frac{1}{M}\mathbf{1} - \frac{1}{M-1}S^2(A^{\mathrm{f}})^{\mathrm{T}}H^{\mathrm{T}}R^{-1}\left(H\bar{z}^{\mathrm{f}}_M - y_{\mathrm{obs}}\right). \qquad (7.24)$$

Here $\mathbf{1} := (1,1,\ldots,1)^{\mathrm{T}} \in \mathbb{R}^M$. Since $S\mathbf{1} = \mathbf{1}$ and $A^{\mathrm{f}}\mathbf{1} = 0$ it follows that

$$A^{\mathrm{a}}\mathbf{1} = A^{\mathrm{f}}S\mathbf{1} = 0, \qquad (7.25)$$

and the weights $w_i$ satisfy

$$\sum_{i=1}^{M} w_i = 1.$$

The weights can therefore be interpreted as "importance" weights similar to the weights in an SIS or SIR particle filter. See Chapter 6 and the discussion later in the chapter.

A complete ensemble update is given by

$$z_j^{\mathrm{a}} = \sum_{i=1}^{M} w_i z_i^{\mathrm{f}} + \sum_{i=1}^{M}(z_i^{\mathrm{f}} - \bar{z}^{\mathrm{f}}_M)s_{ij} = \sum_{i=1}^{M} z_i^{\mathrm{f}}\left\{w_i + s_{ij} - \frac{1}{M}\right\}, \qquad (7.26)$$

where $s_{ij} = (S)_{ij}$ denotes the $(i,j)$th entry of the transform matrix $S$ which satisifies $\sum_{i=1}^{M} s_{ij} = 1$. This formula forms the basis of the popular *ensemble square root filter* (ESRF). We can bring (7.26) into the form (7.7) with coefficients

$$d_{ij} = w_i - \frac{1}{M} + s_{ij}.$$

We have already discussed in Example 2.32 of Chapter 2 that the transformation (7.17) is not optimal in the sense of the Monge–Kantorovitch transportation problem as formulated in Definition 2.27. The same applies to the ESRF update (7.26). An optimal update in the sense of Monge–Kantorovitch is

$$z_i^{\mathrm{a}} = \bar{z}^{\mathrm{a}} + \frac{1}{\sqrt{M-1}}A^{\mathrm{a}}\left[(A^{\mathrm{a}})^{\mathrm{T}}P^{\mathrm{f}}_M A^{\mathrm{a}}\right]^{-1/2}(A^{\mathrm{a}})^{\mathrm{T}}(z_i^{\mathrm{f}} - \bar{z}^{\mathrm{f}}_M), \qquad (7.27)$$

where $A^{\mathrm{a}}$ is defined by (7.21). Compare Equation (2.24) from Example 2.32. Note that (7.27) requires an additional computation of an $M \times M$ matrix square root.

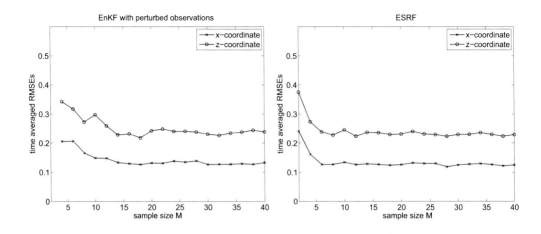

**Figure 7.2** Data assimilation results for the Lorenz-63 model over a time period $[0, 10]$ and varying ensemble sizes $M$. Filtering is performed with the EnKF with perturbed observations and the ESRF. The left (right) panel displays the time-averaged RMSEs from the EnKF (ESRF) as a function of the ensemble size $M$. When averaged over the time period, the RMSEs quickly converge as $M$ is increased; the size of the errors is comparable to those obtained from the SIR filter implementation for much larger ensemble sizes, as depicted in Figure 6.5. Also note that the ESRF is stable even for $M = 2$ while the EnKF with perturbed observations requires at least $M = 4$.

The ESRF update formulas give rise to the following algorithm for performing sequential data assimilation.

**Algorithm 7.8** (ESRF)    Given an initial distribution $\pi_Z(z, 0)$, we draw $M$ independent realisations $z_i^0 = z_i(0)$ from this distribution. Observations are given in intervals of $\Delta t_{\text{out}} = \delta t N_{\text{out}}$.

The following steps are performed recursively for $k = 1, \ldots, N_{\text{obs}}$.

(i) In between observations, the initial ensemble $\{z_i(\mathsf{t}_{k-1})\}$ at $\mathsf{t}_{k-1} = (k - 1)\Delta t_{\text{out}}$ is propagated under the given evolution model, such as (6.28), in order to produce a forecast ensemble $\{z_i^f\}$ at the next observation time $\mathsf{t}_k = k\Delta t_{\text{out}}$.

(ii) A Gaussian $\mathrm{N}(\overline{x}_M^f, P_M^f)$ is fit to the forecast ensemble $z_i^f$, $i = 1, \ldots, M$. The observation $y_{\text{obs}} = y_{\text{obs}}(\mathsf{t}_k)$ leads to a posterior Gaussian $\mathrm{N}(\overline{z}^a, P^a)$. Using either (7.26) or (7.27) together with either (7.8) or (7.23), we define a posterior ensemble $z_i^a$, $i = 1, \ldots, M$. Finally, we return to (i) with new initial conditions

$$z_i(\mathsf{t}_k) := z_i^a, \qquad i = 1, \ldots, M,$$

and the index $k$ increased by one.

**Example 7.9**    We return to the stochastically perturbed Lorenz-63 model from

Chapter 4. The EnKF with perturbed observations and the ESRF are implemented for the data assimilation setting of Example 6.9 from Chapter 6. Numerical results for the time-averaged RMSEs as a function of the ensemble size $M$ can be found for both ensemble Kalman filter implementations in Figure 7.2. The results should be compared to those obtained for the SIR filter in Example 6.11. Remarkably, the ensemble Kalman filter implementations lead to smaller time-averaged RMSEs than the SIR filter for small ensemble sizes, and to comparable errors for larger ensemble sizes. These results indicate that the forecast PDFs are nearly Gaussian under this experimental setting (frequent observations and small measurement errors).

## 7.2    Ensemble transform particle filter

The ensemble Kalman filter relies on a Gaussian approximation to the forecast PDF and an interpretation of the classical Kalman formulas in terms of an ensemble transform or coupling step. While this relatively simple parametric approach is rather robust, it becomes inconsistent whenever the forecast uncertainties are not well represented by a Gaussian distribution. We now discuss a class of LETFs that are developed using non-parametric statistical models for the forecast PDFs instead.

The forecast empirical measure (7.5) and the analysis empirical measure (7.6) provide the starting point for the derivation of the *ensemble transform particle filter* (ETPF). This step is identical to that of a classical SIS or SIR particle filter. Instead of resampling, the ETPF then follows the coupling methodology developed in Chapter 5, using the solution of the associated linear transport problem

$$T^* = \arg\min \sum_{i,j=1}^{M} t_{ij} \|z_i^{\mathrm{f}} - z_j^{\mathrm{f}}\|^2, \tag{7.28}$$

for non-negative $t_{ij}$ subject to

$$\sum_{i=1}^{M} t_{ij} = 1/M, \qquad \sum_{j=1}^{M} t_{ij} = w_i.$$

The analysis ensemble members $z_j^{\mathrm{a}}$ are defined by

$$z_j^{\mathrm{a}} = \sum_{i=1}^{M} z_i^{\mathrm{f}} p_{ij}, \qquad p_{ij} := M t_{ij}^*, \tag{7.29}$$

for $j = 1, \ldots, M$.

The ETPF formulation (7.29) can lead to the creation of identical or near-identical analysis ensemble members, which is problematic if the dynamic model is deterministic. Just as for the SIR particle filter, *particle rejuvenation* can be applied, which replaces (7.29) by

$$z_j^a = \sum_{i=1}^{M} z_i^f p_{ij} + \xi_j. \qquad (7.30)$$

for $j = 1, \ldots, M$, where the variables $\{\xi_j\}$ are independent realisations from Gaussian distributions $N(0, P_j^a)$ with some chosen covariance matrix $P_j^a$. A simple choice is $P_j^a = \tau P_M^f$ for all $j = 1, \ldots, M$ with *bandwidth parameter* $\tau \geq 0$. Note that $\tau = 0$ leads back to the linear update (7.29). We now summarise the complete ETPF as follows.

**Algorithm 7.10** (ETPF)    Given an initial distribution $\pi_Z(z, 0)$, we draw $M$ independent realisations $z_i^0 = z_i(0)$ from this distribution. Observations are given in intervals of $\Delta t_{\text{out}} = \delta t N_{\text{out}}$.

    The following steps are performed recursively for $k = 1, \ldots, N_{\text{obs}}$ for given bandwidth parameter $\tau \geq 0$.

  (i) In between observations, the initial ensemble $\{z_i(t_{k-1})\}$ at $t_{k-1} = (k - 1)\Delta t_{\text{out}}$ is propagated under the given evolution model, such as (6.28), in order to produce a forecast ensemble $\{z_i^f\}$ at the next observation time $t_k = k \Delta t_{\text{out}}$.

 (ii) The empirical measure (7.5) is fit to the forecast ensemble $z_i^f$, $i = 1, \ldots, M$. The observation $y_{\text{obs}} = y_{\text{obs}}(t_k)$ leads to the analysis empirical measure (7.6) with weights defined by

$$w_i \propto \exp\left( -\frac{1}{2}(H z_i^f - y_{\text{obs}})^{\mathrm{T}} R^{-1}(H z_i^f - y_{\text{obs}}) \right)$$

with the constant of proportionality chosen such that $\sum_i w_i = 1$. We solve the associated linear transport problem (7.28) and obtain the analysis ensemble $\{z_i^a\}$ according to (7.30) with the variables $\{\xi_j\}$ being independent realisations from the Gaussian $N(0, \tau P_M^f)$ distribution.

(iii) Finally, we return to (i) with initial conditions

$$z_i(t_k) := z_i^a, \qquad i = 1, \ldots, M,$$

and the index $k$ increased by one.

    The essential steps of an algorithm for solving the linear transport problem (7.28) are outlined in Appendix 7.4. A fast implementation, called *FastEMD*, is discussed by Pele & Werman (2009). *FastEMD* is also available as a Matlab subroutine.

    The ETPF update is substantially more computationally expensive than an EnKF update because of the need to solve a linear transport problem in each assimilation step. This shortcoming will be addressed partially in Chapter 8 when the concept of *localisation* is introduced. More specifically, the problem of solving one linear transport problem in $\mathbb{R}^{N_z}$ will be replaced by solving $N_z$ linear

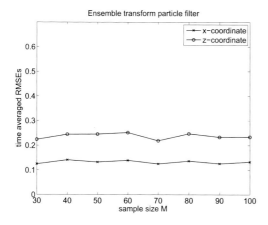

**Figure 7.3** Time-averaged RMSEs for the ETPF in the data assimilation setting of Example 7.9. The ETPF requires larger ensemble sizes than the EnKF but leads to otherwise similar time-averaged RMSEs.

transport problems in one dimension. These linear transport problems can be solved simultaneously by the efficient algorithm given in Appendix 5.8.

**Example 7.11**   The data assimilation setting of Example 7.9 is now also used for testing the performance of the ETPF in its formulation (7.29). The time-averaged RMSEs can be found in Figure 7.3. The ETPF does not improve the time-averaged RMSEs obtained for the EnKF implementations and also requires larger ensemble sizes $M$. This finding indicates again that the forecast and analysis PDFs are close to Gaussian for this data assimilation setting.

We discuss two more examples in order to explore the behaviour of the various proposed filter algorithms in a more non-Gaussian context.

**Example 7.12**   Let us consider the one-dimensional stochastic dynamical system (7.36) from Problem 7.4 with $\phi(z) = z^3$. Solutions of the associated dynamical system approach $\pm\infty$ in finite time with probability one. We shall use this as our model, but simulate "observations" at every iteration according to

$$y_{\text{obs}}^n = \xi^n, \qquad n \geq 1,$$

with the variables $\{\xi^n\}$ being realisations of independent and identically distributed $N(0,4)$ Gaussian random variables. This is an example of assimilating data with an unstable reference solution and strongly nonlinear model dynamics, providing a simple way to obtain very non-Gaussian PDFs. We will assume that the initial ensemble $z_i^0$, $i = 1, \ldots, M$, follows a Gaussian distribution $N(0,2)$. Experiments were conducted with ensemble sizes varying from $M = 100$ to $M = 10000$, using RMSEs averaged over $N_{\text{obs}} = 10000$ assimilation cycles to compare the perturbed observations EnKF to the ETPF, implemented using (7.29). The results from the EnKF can be found in Figure 7.4 while those from the ETPF can be found in Figure 7.5. The RMSEs from the EnKF are approximately equal to the standard deviation of the observations, which indicates that

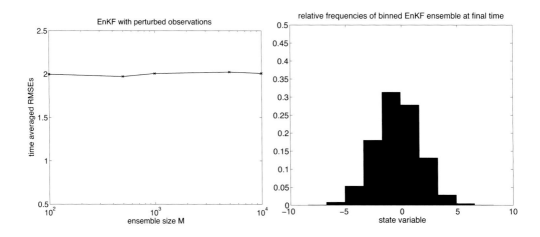

**Figure 7.4** The EnKF with perturbed observations is applied to the stochastic dynamical system from Example 7.12. The time-averaged RMSEs for ensemble sizes varying between $M = 100$ and $M = 10000$ are displayed in the left panel. Note that the standard deviation of the measurement errors is $R^{1/2} = 2$. Hence on average, the EnKF does not provide any additional information beyond what is already contained in the observations $y_{\text{obs}}^n$. The right panel shows the histogram produced from the analysis ensemble at final time and $M = 10000$.

the EnKF is not providing any additional information: we could have simply replaced the output of the dynamical system by the observed quantity. In other words, the EnKF only manages to stabilise the unstable dynamics towards the observed values. The ETPF, on the other hand, leads to significantly smaller time-averaged RMSEs. We mention that the SIR filter from Chapter 6 leads to results similar to those obtained from the ETPF filter and that the ETPF is implemented using the algorithm from Appendix 5.8.

**Example 7.13** In this example, we formulate a more nonlinear data assimilation setting by returning to the Lorenz-63 model. First, we set the time-dependent function $g(t)$ in (1.1) equal to zero. We also replace the forward Euler time-stepping by the implicit midpoint approximation

$$z^{n+1} = z^n + \delta t f(z^{n+1/2}), \qquad z^{n+1/2} = \frac{1}{2}(z^{n+1} + z^n), \qquad (7.31)$$

with step-size $\delta t = 0.01$. The state variable is $z = (x, y, z)^{\mathrm{T}} \in \mathbb{R}^3$ and right hand side of the iteration is provided by

$$f(z) = \begin{pmatrix} 10(y - x) \\ x(28 - z) - y \\ xy - 8/3z \end{pmatrix}.$$

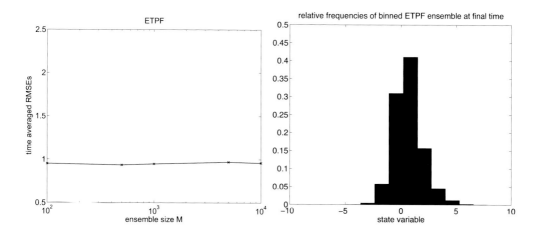

**Figure 7.5** The ETPF is applied to the stochastic dynamical system from Example 7.12. We display the same quantities as shown in Figure 7.4 for the EnKF with perturbed observations. The time-averaged RMSEs from the ETPF are significantly smaller than those displayed in Figure 7.4. The analysis ensemble at final time is also distributed rather differently.

Instead of observations of the x-variable being taken every $\Delta t_{\text{out}} = 5\delta t = 0.05$ time units, we increase the observation interval to $\Delta t_{\text{out}} = 12\delta t = 0.12$ and observe all three solution components. The measurement error variance is also increased from $R = 1/15$ to $R = 9$ and measurement errors in the three solution components are mutually independent. The reference trajectory $z_{\text{ref}}^n$, $n \geq 0$, is obtained from (7.31) with initial condition

$$x^0 = -0.587276, \quad y^0 = -0.563678, \quad z^0 = 16.8708.$$

Note that the model for generating the reference solution is identical to the model used for generating forecasts in this setting, and is autonomous and deterministic. This is, in fact, a standard setting found in the literature for testing data assimilation algorithms, referred to as an *identical twin experiment*. While identical twin experiments are clearly a strong idealisation, they allow for an easier assessment of data assimilation algorithms. Here we compare the ESRF, SIR filter, and the ETPF, using a total of 50000 of data assimilation steps in identical twin experiments.

The distribution for the initial ensemble is Gaussian with mean $z^0 = (x^0, y^0, z^0)$, covariance matrix $\sigma^2 I$, and $\sigma = 0.1$. All filter algorithms are implemented with a rejuvenation step (as outlined in Definition 6.13), by adding Gaussian $N(0, \tau P_M^{\text{f}})$ perturbations to the analysis. The bandwidth parameter $\tau$ is chosen from the interval $[0, 0.5]$. The SIR filter resamples the particles after each assimilation step using residual resampling as outlined in Chapter 3. The smallest time-averaged RMSEs for fixed ensemble sizes ranging from $M = 10$ to $M = 80$ are given for each method in Figure 7.6. We find that the ESRF settles at a time-averaged

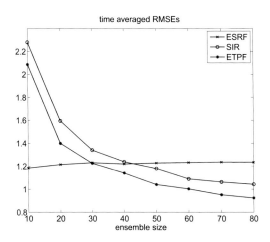

time averaged RMSEs

- ESRF
- SIR
- ETPF

ensemble size

**Figure 7.6** Time-averaged RMSEs obtained by the ESRF, the SIR particle filter, and the ETPF for the modified Lorenz-63 model of Example 7.13. The ESRF settles at an RMSE of about 1.2 for all ensemble sizes. This value is significantly smaller than the measurement error standard deviation $R^{1/2} = 3$. Both the SIR filter and the ETPF lead to more skilful results as $M$ increases. Furthermore, the ETPF outperforms the SIR filter for all values of $M$. Displayed are the smallest RMSEs for rejuvenation parameters $\tau \in [0, 0.5]$.

RMSE of about 1.2, independent from the ensemble size, while both the SIR and the ETPF keep improving their RMSEs as $M$ increases. The ETPF also performs consistently better than the SIR filter implementation.

We now compare the ESRF and the ETPF within the context of linear ensemble transform filters (7.7) in further detail. The ETPF without particle rejuvenation leads directly to a representation in the form of (7.7) with $d_{ij} = p_{ij}$. We now demonstrate that the ETPF update formula (7.29) can be decomposed into an update of the mean and the ensemble deviations, just as for the ESRF. First we note that

$$\bar{z}^{\mathrm{a}} = \frac{1}{M} \sum_{i,j=1}^{M} p_{ij} z_i^{\mathrm{f}} = \sum_{i=1}^{M} w_i z_i^{\mathrm{f}},$$

which provides a consistent estimator for the analysis mean under importance sampling from the forecast distribution. We next formulate an ETPF update formula for the ensemble deviations, i.e.,

$$z_j^{\mathrm{a}} - \bar{z}^{\mathrm{a}} = \sum_{i=1}^{M} z_i^{\mathrm{f}} p_{ij} - \bar{z}^{\mathrm{a}}$$

$$= \sum_{i=1}^{M} (z_i^{\mathrm{f}} - \bar{z}_M^{\mathrm{f}}) p_{ij} - \sum_{i=1}^{M} \left( w_i - \frac{1}{M} \right) z_i^{\mathrm{f}}$$

$$= \sum_{i=1}^{M} (z_i^{\mathrm{f}} - \bar{z}_M^{\mathrm{f}}) \left\{ p_{ij} + \frac{1}{M} - w_i \right\}. \tag{7.32}$$

Here we have used that $\sum_{i=1}^{M} p_{ij} = 1$. Hence we can compare the transform

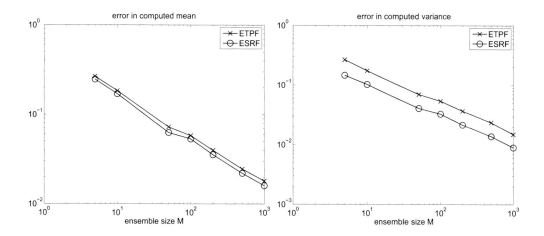

**Figure 7.7** Averaged errors in the posterior means (left panel) and the variance (right panel) from a single ESRF and ETPF assimilation step as a function of the ensemble size $M$. A convergence of both approximations as $M$ is increased can clearly be seen. The convergence rate is approximately $M^{-1/2}$. The ESRF gives slightly more accurate estimates for the mean and variance, which is not surprising given the fact that the prior ensemble is Gaussian.

matrix (7.22) of an ESRF to the transform matrix $\tilde{S}$, with entries given by

$$\tilde{s}_{ij} = p_{ij} - w_i + \frac{1}{M} \; ,$$

of the ETPF. It should be noted that the coefficients $d_{ij} = p_{ij}$ and $w_i$ of an ETPF are all non-negative while this is not the case for an ESRF. This fact is important when entries of the state vector should only take non-negative values, for example, when $z$ represents concentrations or densities. In this case, an ESRF analysis step can potentially lead to an analysis ensemble $\{z_i^a\}$ for which some of its members take negative entries. See Janjić, McLaughlin, Cohn & Verlaan (2014) for more details.

---

**Example 7.14** We compare the ESRF transformation with the ETPF transformation for a single Bayesian assimilation step for a univariate Gaussian random variable with prior mean zero and variance one. The observed value is $y_{\mathrm{obs}} = 1$, with measurement error variance $R = 1$. The posterior is then also Gaussian with mean $\bar{z}^a = 1/2$ and variance $1/2$. Given $M \in \{5, 10, \ldots, 1000\}$ realisations from the prior distribution, we compare the resulting empirical posterior means and variances under both LETFs as well as the difference between the importance weights

$$w_i^{\mathrm{ETPF}} \propto e^{-(z_i^f - 1)^2 / 2}$$

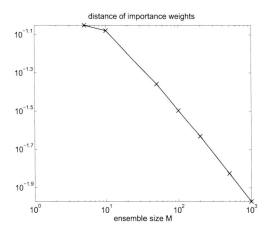

distance of importance weights

ensemble size M

**Figure 7.8** Difference between the importance weights from an importance sampling step with the weights (7.24) generated by an ESRF. The difference vanishes as $M$ increases, which indicates that the ESRF asymptotically approximates the importance weights from a Gaussian likelihood provided the prior is Gaussian.

and the weights (7.24) from the ESRF (denoted here by $w_i^{\mathrm{ESRF}}$), given by

$$\|w^{\mathrm{ETPF}} - w^{\mathrm{ESRF}}\|_2 = \left(\sum_{i=1}^M |w_i^{\mathrm{ETPF}} - w_i^{\mathrm{ESRF}}|^2\right)^{1/2}.$$

The results averaged over 200 experiments for each fixed ensemble size can be found in Figures 7.7 and 7.8, for ETPF and ESRF respectively. A convergence of all quantities as $M$ increases can clearly be seen.

This discussion leads us to consider LETFs (7.7) in their representation

$$z_j^{\mathrm{a}} = \sum_{i=1}^M z_i^{\mathrm{f}}\left\{w_i - \frac{1}{M} + s_{ij}\right\} \tag{7.33}$$

with the transformation matrix $S \in \mathbb{R}^{M \times M}$ and the weight vector $w \in \mathbb{R}^M$ suitably defined. The matrix $S$ should satisfy $\sum_{j=1}^M s_{ij} = 1$ in order to preserve the mean given by $\bar{z}^{\mathrm{a}} = \sum_i w_i z_i^{\mathrm{f}}$. For example, we could combine parts of an ESRF with parts of the ETPF filter.

Another class of transform filters, which fits into the framework (7.33), has been proposed by Anderson (2010). We explain the key idea for a univariate observable $y \in \mathbb{R}$ with forward operator $H \in \mathbb{R}^{1 \times N_z}$. The first step is to define a forecast ensemble $y_i^{\mathrm{f}} := H z_i^{\mathrm{f}}$, $i = 1, \ldots, M$, in observation space. The second step consists of defining an analysis ensemble $y_i^{\mathrm{a}}$, $i = 1, \ldots, M$, in observation space by an appropriate filter algorithm. This amounts to implementing a Bayesian inference step

$$\pi_Y(y|y_{\mathrm{obs}}) \propto \pi_Y(y_{\mathrm{obs}}|y)\pi_Y(y),$$

in observation space with likelihood

$$\pi_Y(y_{\mathrm{obs}}|y) = \frac{1}{\sqrt{2\pi R}} e^{-(y - y_{\mathrm{obs}})^2/2R},$$

and the prior PDF $\pi_Y$ representing the ensemble $\{y_i^f\}_{i=1}^M$. The analysis ensemble is then defined through an appropriate coupling of the univariate prior and posterior PDFs. The particular choice

$$\pi_Y(y)dy = \frac{1}{M} \sum_{i=1}^M \delta(y - y_i^f)dy, \tag{7.34}$$

for the prior PDF leads to an implementation of the ETPF in observation space. See Anderson (2010) for another choice for $\pi_Y$, which leads to the *rank histogram filter*.

Once the analysis ensemble $\{y_i^a\}$ has been computed, the update in state space is defined by linear regression

$$\begin{aligned}
z_i^a &= z_i^f + P_M^f H^T (H P_M^f H^T)^{-1} (y_i^a - y_i^f) \\
&= z_i^f + \frac{1}{M-1} A^f (A^f)^T H^T (H P_M^f H^T)^{-1} (y_i^a - y_i^f) \tag{7.35}
\end{aligned}$$

onto the state space $\mathcal{Z} = \mathbb{R}^{N_z}$. Hence we obtain

$$\bar{z}^a = \bar{z}_M^f + P_M^f H^T (H P_M^f H^T)^{-1} (\bar{y}^a - \bar{y}_M^f),$$

which satisfies $H\bar{z}^a = \bar{y}^a$. More generally, we have $y_i^a = H z_i^a$ and, therefore,

$$\begin{aligned}
A^a &= A^f + \frac{1}{M-1} A^f (A^f)^T H^T (H P_M^f H^T)^{-1} H (A^a - A^f) \\
&= A^f \left( I + \frac{1}{M-1} (A^f)^T H^T (H P_M^f H^T)^{-1} H (A^a - A^f) \right) \\
&= A^f S
\end{aligned}$$

with the second line implicitly defining a transform matrix $S$ for the ensemble deviations.

This algorithm can be extended to multivariate observables $y_{\text{obs}}$ either by solving the filtering problem directly in the associated observation space $\mathcal{Y} = \mathbb{R}^{N_y}$ or, in the case where the measurement error covariance matrix $R$ is diagonal, by sequentially processing each entry in the observed vector $y_{\text{obs}} \in \mathbb{R}^{N_y}$ (since the likelihood function $\pi_Y(y|z)$ factors into a product of univariate likelihood functions).

## Problems

**7.1**   Consider a forecast ensemble of four members $z_1^f = -3$, $z_2^f = -1$, $z_3^f = 1$ and $z_4^f = 3$ with equal weights $1/4$. Suppose that a particle filter importance sampling step leads to non-uniform weights

$$(w_1, w_2, w_3, w_4) = (1/16, 3/16, 5/16, 7/16),$$

and that subsequently a residual resampling step is performed (compare Example 3.29). Interpret the resulting SIR analysis step in terms of a random matrix

$D : \Omega \to \mathbb{R}^{4 \times 4}$ as outlined in Example 7.4 above. Write down all possible realisations of $D$ and their associated probabilities.

**7.2** Write the EnKF update step (7.16) for scalar state variable $z \in \mathbb{R}$ in
the form of an LETF (7.7). Assume that the forecast ensemble $\{z_i^{\mathrm{f}}\}$ consists of
independent samples from a random variable $Z^{\mathrm{f}}$ with PDF $\pi_{Z^{\mathrm{f}}}$, $H = 1$, and that
a set of realisations $\xi_i \in \mathbb{R}$, $i = 1, \ldots, M$ of $\Xi$ is given.

    (i)   Show that

$$\sum_{i=1}^{M} d_{ij} = 1.$$

    (ii)   What can be said about $w_i = \sum_{j=1}^{M} d_{ij}$ in the limit $M \to \infty$?

    (iii)   Construct an example that demonstrates that $Z^{\mathrm{f}} \geq 0$, i.e., $z_i^{\mathrm{f}} \geq 0$,
does not necessarily imply $z_i^{\mathrm{a}} \geq 0$.

    (iv)   Consider an implementation of the EnKF with perturbed observa-
tions where we replace the empirical covariance matrix $P_M^{\mathrm{f}}$ by an a
*priori* given covariance matrix $B$ in the Kalman gain matrix. Deter-
mine the resulting analysis mean $\bar{z}^{\mathrm{a}}$ and covariance matrix $P^{\mathrm{a}}$ and
discuss their dependence on $B$. We mention that such an *a priori*
choice is often found in *nudging* techniques.

**7.3** Show that the weights defined by (7.24) minimise the cost function

$$J(w) = \frac{1}{2}(\bar{z}^{\mathrm{a}} - \bar{z}_M^{\mathrm{f}})^{\mathrm{T}}(P_M^{\mathrm{f}})^{-1}(\bar{z}^{\mathrm{a}} - \bar{z}_M^{\mathrm{f}}) + \frac{1}{2}(H\bar{z}^{\mathrm{a}} - y_{\mathrm{obs}})R^{-1}(H\bar{z}^{\mathrm{a}} - y_{\mathrm{obs}}),$$

with $\bar{z}^{\mathrm{a}}$ given by (7.23). Here we have assumed for simplicity that the empirical
covariance matrix,

$$P_M^{\mathrm{f}} = \frac{1}{M-1} A^{\mathrm{f}}(A^{\mathrm{f}})^{\mathrm{T}},$$

is invertible. Hint: First demonstrate that $\bar{z}^{\mathrm{a}} - \bar{z}_M^{\mathrm{f}} = A^{\mathrm{f}}\delta w$ with the vector
$\delta w \in \mathbb{R}^M$ having entries $\delta w_i = w_i - 1/M$ and $\sum_{i=1}^{M} \delta w_i = 0$.

**7.4** Consider a scalar dynamical system

$$z^{n+1} = \phi(z^n) + \eta^n, \qquad n \geq 0, \qquad (7.36)$$

where the variables $\{\eta^n\}$ are realisations of independent and identically distributed Gaussian random variables $N(0, 1)$. We also assume that $\phi(0) = 0$ and
the desired reference solution is simply given by $z_{\mathrm{ref}}^n = 0$ and observations are
generated at every iteration according to

$$y_{\mathrm{obs}}^n = \xi^n, \qquad n \geq 1,$$

with the $\xi^n$ being independent realisations of independent and identically distributed Gaussians $N(0, 4)$. The initial distribution for the filtering problem is
Gaussian $N(0, 2)$.

    Implement the EnKF with perturbed observations and an ESRF for the special
choices $\phi(z) = -z$, $\phi(z) = z$ and $\phi(z) = z^3$ and ensemble sizes varying from $M =$

10 to $M = 1000$. Compute time-averaged RMSEs over a total of $N_{\text{obs}} = 10000$ assimilation cycles. How does the RMSE vary for the different choices of $\phi$?

**7.5** With linear observation operator $h(z) = Hz$ and scalar observations, find the functional $J(z_i^{\text{a}})$ whose minimiser produces the analysis

$$z_i^{\text{a}} = z_i^{\text{f}} - P_M^{\text{f}} H^{\text{T}} (H P_M^{\text{f}} H^{\text{T}} + R)^{-1} (H z_i^{\text{f}} + \xi_i - y_{\text{obs}})$$

for the $i$th ensemble member in an EnKF with perturbed observations (recall (5.10)). You may assume that $P_M^{\text{f}}$ is invertible.

We now consider general nonlinear observation operators $h(z)$. By replacing $Hz$ with $h(z)$ in the functional $J(z_i^{\text{a}})$ and finding the equations for the minimiser, obtain EnKF update formulas when $h$ is nonlinear.

**7.6** Implement the EnKF with perturbed observations for the problem described in Example 5.9. How does the mean value compare with the MAP estimator value computed in Chapter 5?

**7.7** We return to Problem 6.4 and replace the particle filter implementations from Problem 6.5 by the ESRF. Study the behaviour of the filter for $M = 10$ and increasing dimension $N_z \in \{1, 10, 20, \dots, 100, 200\}$ of state space. Compare your results to those from Problem 6.5. A localised particle filter was suggested in Problem 6.6. Can you suggest an extension of the concept of *localisation* to the ESRF? Implement your ideas and compare results to those from Problem 6.6.

**7.8** Return to Example 7.1 and find the associated optimal coupling matrix $T^* \in \mathbb{R}^{4 \times 4}$. Which values do the analysis ensemble members $z_i^{\text{a}} \in \mathbb{R}$, $i = 1, \dots, 4$, take?

**7.9** Implement the ETPF for the data assimilation problems described in Problem 7.4 and compare the resulting time-averaged RMSEs to those obtained for the two EnKF implementations. Use the algorithm from Appendix 5.8 in order to implement the ETPF.

## 7.3 Guide to literature

The McKean approach is discussed in the context of general Feynman–Kac models in del Moral (2004). In particular, this approach leads to an interpretation of recursive Bayesian inference as an interacting particle system; this also forms the basis for the discussion of ensemble-based data assimilation algorithms in this chapter. A discussion of ensemble Kalman filters from a linear transformation perspective can, for example, be found in Tippett, Anderson, Bishop, Hamill & Whitaker (2003), Wang, Bishop & Julier (2004), Livings, Dance & Nichols (2008), Ott, Hunt, Szunyogh, Zimin, Kostelich, Corazza, Kalnay, Patil & Yorke (2004), Hunt, Kostelich & Szunyogh (2007), and Nerger, Pfander, Schröter & Hiller (2012). A more detailed introduction to ensemble Kalman filters is given by Evensen (2006).

There are a number of algorithms which are closely related to the family of ensemble Kalman filters. The analysis step of the ensemble Kalman filter with perturbed observations is, for example, equivalent to a method proposed by Oliver (1996), which has been generalised to what is now called the *randomised maximum likelihood method* (Kitanidis 1995, Oliver, He & Reynolds 1996). The ensemble square root filter is, on the other hand, similar to the *unscented Kalman filter* and the reader is referred to Julier & Uhlmann (1997) and Särkkä (2013) for more details.

Extensions of the ensemble Kalman filter to non-Gaussian forecast PDFs and nonlinear forward operators include the rank histogram filter (RHF) by Anderson (2010), the moment matching filter by Lei & Bickel (2011), and the randomised maximum likelihood method as already mentioned.

Another broad class of methods is based on Gaussian mixture approximations to the forecast PDF. The analysis PDF is then also a Gaussian mixture provided the forward operator $h$ is linear. Compare Example 5.11 from Chapter 5. Several procedures have been proposed to adjust the forecast ensemble such that the analysis ensemble approximately follows the analysis Gaussian mixture PDF. See, for example, Smith (2007*a*), Frei & Künsch (2013), Stordal, Karlsen, Nævdal, Skaug & Vallés (2011), and Reich (2012).

The idea of using couplings to describe ensemble-based Bayesian inference and filtering can be found in the survey paper by Reich & Cotter (2013) and in Moselhy & Marzouk (2012). The ETPF was introduced in Reich (2013*b*) and was developed further in Cheng & Reich (2013). A gentle introduction to linear programming and transport problems can be found in Strang (1986). *FastEMD* has been used in our numerical implementations of the ETPF (Pele & Werman 2009).

## 7.4      Appendix: Linear transport algorithm

The ETPF requires the solution of linear transport problems of type (7.28). An algorithm for finding $T^*$ for one-dimensional ensembles has been stated in Appendix 5.8. Here we outline an extension of this algorithm to ensembles $z_i^{\mathrm{f}} \in \mathbb{R}^{N_z}$, $i = 1, \ldots, M$, with $N_z > 1$.

For notational convenience, we introduce

$$d_{ij} := \|z_i^{\mathrm{f}} - z_j^{\mathrm{f}}\|^2.$$

The proposed algorithm generates sequences of admissible $M \times M$ matrices $T$, where admissible means that

$$t_{ij} \geq 0, \quad \sum_{i=1}^{M} t_{ij} = 1/M, \quad \text{and} \quad \sum_{j=1}^{M} t_{ij} = w_i,$$

for a given set of importance weights $w_i$. We note that the algorithm from Appendix 5.8 can be used to obtain admissible matrices regardless of whether ensemble members can be sorted or not. Iterative improvements are based on the *dual formulation* in terms of variables $u_i$, $i = 1, \ldots, M$, and $v_i$, $i = 1, \ldots, M$, which satisfy the inequality constraints

$$u_i + v_j \leq d_{ij},$$

for $i, j = 1, \ldots, M$, and maximise the cost function

$$V = \sum_{i=1}^{M} (u_i w_i + v_i / M).$$

The optimal solution satisfies

$$u_i^* + v_j^* = d_{ij},$$

for all pairs $(i, j)$ for which $t_{ij}^* \neq 0$. We denote the set of such indices as the supp $(T)$. See Appendix 2.5 and Strang (1986) for more details on the primal and dual formulations of linear transport problems.

**Algorithm 7.15** (Linear transport problem)   Given an ensemble $\{z_i^f\}_{i=1}^M$, importance weights $w_i$, and distances $d_{ij}$, an initial admissible $T^{(0)}$ is found by applying the algorithm from Appendix 5.8. The cost of $T^{(0)}$ is given by

$$C^{(0)} = \sum_{i,j=1}^{M} t_{ij}^{(0)} d_{ij}.$$

A sequence of admissible matrices $\{T^{(l)}\}$ with associated costs

$$C^{(l)} = \sum_{i,j=1}^{M} t_{ij}^{(l)} d_{ij}, \quad l \geq 0,$$

is now generated by the following procedure.

(i) Choose values $\{u_i\}$ and $\{v_j\}$ such that $u_i + v_j = d_{ij}$ for pairs $(i, j) \in$ supp $(T^{(l)})$. Start with $u_1 = 0$.

(ii) If $u_i + v_j \leq d_{ij}$ for all pairs $(i, j)$ then the algorithm terminates and $T^* = T^{(l)}$. Otherwise find the pair $(i^*, j^*)$ for which $u_i + v_j - d_{ij}$ is maximised.

(iii) Set

$$t_{i^* j^*}^{(l+1)} = \varepsilon,$$

where $\varepsilon > 0$ is yet to be determined. Adjust $t_{ij}^{(l)} > 0$ to

$$t_{ij}^{(l+1)} = t_{ij}^{(l)} \pm \varepsilon,$$

for an appropriate subset $S$ of indices $(i, j) \in$ supp $(T^{(l)})$ in order to keep the new $T^{(l+1)}$ admissible. Pick $\varepsilon > 0$ such that at least one $t_{ij}^{(l+1)} = t_{ij}^{(l)} - \varepsilon$ drops to zero.

The set $\mathcal{S} \subset \{1, \ldots, M\} \times \{1, \ldots, M\}$ in step (iii) needs to be chosen such that the entries of $T^{(l+1)} - T^{(l)}$ sum to zero across all rows and columns.

We remark that the algorithm needs to be modified if fewer than $2M - 1$ entries in a $T^{(l)}$ are non-zero. In this case the sets of values $\{u_i\}$ and $\{v_j\}$ in Step (ii) are not uniquely determined. There are also more efficient algorithms available for solving linear transport problems. Their computational complexity is $\mathcal{O}(M^3 \ln M)$ with respect to the ensemble size $M$. For the computational experiments in this book we have used the *FastEMD* algorithm developed by Pele & Werman (2009). *FastEMD* is available as a Matlab subroutine.

---

**Example 7.16**   Consider the following linear transport problem for which the entries of the optimal $T^* \in \mathbb{R}^{N \times M}$ take integer values and $T$ is no longer a square matrix, i.e., $N \neq M$. We set $N = 3$ and $M = 5$. Admissible transport plans $T \in \mathbb{R}^{3 \times 5}$ are now defined by the conditions $t_{ij} \geq 0$,

$$\sum_{j=1}^{5} t_{ij} = S_i, \qquad \sum_{i=1}^{3} t_{ij} = D_j,$$

with $S_1 = 15$, $S_2 = 20$, $S_3 = 15$, $D_1 = 11$, $D_2 = 12$, $D_3 = 9$, $D_4 = 10$, and $D_5 = 8$. Note that we still have $\sum_i S_i = \sum_j D_j$ while no longer being equal to one. The transport costs $d_{ij}$ are given by the following table:

| $d_{ij}$ | 1 | 2 | 3 | 4 | 5 |
|----------|----|----|----|----|----|
| 1 | 51 | 62 | 35 | 45 | 56 |
| 2 | 59 | 68 | 50 | 39 | 46 |
| 3 | 49 | 56 | 53 | 51 | 37 |

The optimal transport plan $T^*$ is provided by

| $t_{ij}^*$ | 1 | 2 | 3 | 4 | 5 |
|----------|----|----|----|----|----|
| 1 | 6 | 0 | 9 | 0 | 0 |
| 2 | 2 | 0 | 0 | 10 | 8 |
| 3 | 3 | 12 | 0 | 0 | 0 |

You might want to derive this optimal transport plan through an appropriate adaptation of Algorithm 7.15.

---

## 7.5    Appendix: Gaussian mixture transform filter

In this appendix we discuss an alternative ETPF implementation which replaces the ensemble generated empirical measure by Gaussian mixtures of the form

$$\pi_{Z^f}(z) = \frac{1}{M} \sum_{i=1}^{M} \mathrm{n}(z; z_i^f, B). \tag{7.37}$$

Recall that $\mathrm{n}(z; \bar{z}, B)$ denotes the PDF of a Gaussian with mean $\bar{z}$ and covariance matrix $B$. The forecast ensemble members $z_i^{\mathrm{f}}$ are the centres of the Gaussian mixture components while the covariance matrix can either be set to $B = \tau I$ with $\tau > 0$ a *bandwidth* parameter or to

$$B = \tau P_M^{\mathrm{f}}. \tag{7.38}$$

Provided that an observation comes from a linear forward model

$$y_{\mathrm{obs}}(\mathrm{t}_k) = H z_{\mathrm{ref}}(\mathrm{t}_k) + \xi^k,$$

with $\xi^k$ being a realisation of a Gaussian with mean zero and covariance matrix $R$, the analysis PDF can be explicitly computed and is given by

$$\pi_Z(z|y_{\mathrm{obs}}) = \sum_{i=1}^{M} \alpha_i \mathrm{n}(z; z_i^{\mathrm{c}}, B^{\mathrm{c}}),$$

as already discussed in Example 5.10. Here the parameters entering the analysis PDF are defined as follows:

$$\alpha_i \propto \exp\left(-\frac{1}{2}(Hz_i^{\mathrm{f}} - y_{\mathrm{obs}}(\mathrm{t}_k))^{\mathrm{T}}(HBH^{\mathrm{T}} + R)^{-1}(Hz_i^{\mathrm{f}} - y_{\mathrm{obs}}(\mathrm{t}_k))\right),$$

with the constant of proportionality chosen such that $\sum \alpha_i = 1$,

$$z_i^{\mathrm{c}} = z_i^{\mathrm{f}} - K(Hz_i^{\mathrm{f}} - y_{\mathrm{obs}}(\mathrm{t}_k)), \tag{7.39}$$

and

$$B^{\mathrm{c}} = B - KHB, \tag{7.40}$$

with Kalman gain matrix $K = BH^{\mathrm{T}}(HBH^{\mathrm{T}} + R)^{-1}$.

We now construct a (non-optimal) coupling between the prior and posterior Gaussian mixtures. The first step consists in solving the linear transport problem

$$T^* = \arg\min \sum_{i,j=1}^{M} t_{ij}\|z_i^{\mathrm{c}} - z_j^{\mathrm{c}}\|^2, \tag{7.41}$$

for non-negative $t_{ij}$ subject to

$$\sum_{i=1}^{M} t_{ij} = 1/M, \qquad \sum_{j=1}^{M} t_{ij} = \alpha_i.$$

We then define new Gaussian centres by

$$\bar{z}_j^{\mathrm{c}} = \sum_{i=1}^{M} z_i^{\mathrm{c}} p_{ij}, \qquad p_{ij} := M t_{ij}^*,$$

for $j = 1, \dots, M$, and finally obtain an analysis ensemble $z_j^{\mathrm{a}}$, $j = 1, \dots, M$, by drawing a single realisation from each of the Gaussian distributions $\mathrm{N}(\bar{z}_j^{\mathrm{c}}, B^{\mathrm{c}})$, i.e.,

$$z_i^{\mathrm{a}} = Z_i^{\mathrm{a}}(\omega), \qquad Z_i^{\mathrm{a}} \sim \mathrm{N}(\bar{z}_i^{\mathrm{c}}, B^{\mathrm{c}}). \tag{7.42}$$

We call this filter the *Gaussian mixture transform filter*. The Gaussian mixture transform filter converges to the ETPF as the bandwidth $\tau$ in (7.38) approaches zero.

In practice a bandwidth $\tau$ needs to be determined. Assume that a finite set of observed or computed state estimates $\hat{z}_{\text{ref}}(t_k)$, $k = 1, \ldots, N_{\text{obs}}$, is available. These estimates can be used as a training set in order to determine an appropriate $\tau > 0$. For example, one possibility is to choose the parameter $\tau$ in the covariance matrix $B = \tau I$ or $B = \tau P_M^{\text{f}}$ such that the value of the time-averaged logarithmic scoring rule, i.e.,

$$\overline{S}_{\log}(\tau) := \frac{-1}{N_{\text{obs}}} \sum_{k=1}^{N_{\text{obs}}} \ln \left\{ \frac{1}{M} \sum_{i=1}^{M} \text{n}(\hat{z}_{\text{ref}}(t_k); z_i(t_k), B) \right\},$$

is minimised along an ensemble $\{z_i(t_k)\}$ of model predictions.

# 8  Data assimilation for spatio-temporal processes

So far we have investigated the behaviour of data assimilation algorithms for models with state space dimension $N_z \leq 3$. Furthermore, we have investigated the behaviour of ensemble-based data assimilation algorithms for ensemble sizes $M \gg N_z$. Classical theoretical results about particle filters discuss convergence to the optimal estimates for $M \to \infty$ within the perfect model scenario and with fixed dimension of state space $N_z$. While we do not cover these theoretical results in this book, in the previous two chapters we found that the particle filters did indeed converge numerically in terms of their time-averaged RMSEs as the ensemble size $M$ was increased. In fact, the same observation also applies to the ensemble Kalman filters. However, an ensemble Kalman filter does not generally converge to the optimal estimates because of a systematic bias due to the Gaussian assumption in the Bayesian inference step. Nevertheless, the ensemble Kalman filter remains a very popular method in the geosciences since it has much better control over the variance error for small ensemble sizes.

In this chapter, we will apply ensemble-based data assimilation algorithms to models which arise from spatio-temporal processes. More specifically, the models from this chapter can be viewed as spatial and temporal discretisations of *partial differential equations* (PDEs). For simplicity, we will only consider evolutionary PDEs in one spatial dimension (denoted by $x$). The dimension of state space of the arising models is inversely proportional to the spatial discretisation parameter $\Delta x$ and the limit $\Delta x \to 0$ leads to $N_z \to \infty$. While a rigorous analysis of data assimilation algorithms for $M$ fixed and $N_z \to \infty$ is beyond the scope of this book, we will demonstrate some of the practical problems that arise from such a scenario, which is often referred to as the *curse of dimensionality*.[1] We will also introduce *ensemble inflation* and *localisation*[2] as two practical techniques for making ensemble-based data assimilation techniques applicable to spatio-temporal processes.

We start this chapter with a simple example that demonstrates how finite ensemble sizes $M$ can have a systematic impact on the behaviour of an ensemble

---

[1] The difficulty with high-dimensional problems can already be appreciated from the following well-known fact: the probability of a sample drawn uniformly from a hypercube in $\mathbb{R}^{N_z}$ hitting the embedded hypersphere goes to zero as $N_z \to \infty$.

[2] We have already discussed the implementation of particle filters and EnKFs for a trivially high-dimensional problem in Problems 6.4 to 6.6 and Problem 7.7. The localisation idea, proposed in Problem 6.6 will be extended to spatio-temporal processes in this chapter.

Kalman filter. Recall that an ensemble Kalman filter is built upon the empirical forecast covariance matrix $P_M^f$ and the resulting Kalman gain matrix, $K = P_M^f H^T (H P_M^f H + R)^{-1}$, which is needed for updating the ensemble mean and for transforming $P_M^f$ into an analysis covariance $P^a$.

---

**Example 8.1**   We consider the empirical estimator for the covariance matrix

$$ P_M^f = \frac{1}{M-1} \sum_{i=1}^M (z_i^f - \bar{z}_M^f)(z_i^f - \bar{z}_M^f)^T, \qquad \bar{z}_M^f = \frac{1}{M} \sum_{i=1}^M z_i^f, \qquad (8.1) $$

for $M$ samples $z_i^f \in \mathbb{R}^{N_z}$ from a Gaussian random variable $Z^f \sim N(0, I)$. It is known that the estimator is unbiased, i.e.

$$ \mathbb{E}[P_M^f] = I. $$

However, any finite $M$ leads to a non-vanishing variance in the estimator. In this example, we will assess this variance numerically, taking $N_z = 10$ and using ensembles of size $M > 10$. We will inspect two aspects of $P_M^f$ which will be of particular relevance in this chapter. First, we consider spurious cross-correlations $p_{kl} := (P_M^f)_{kl}$, $k \neq l$, in $P_M^f$, which we quantify by averaging the quantity

$$ c = \frac{1}{N_z(N_z - 1)} \sum_{l,k=1, l \neq k}^{N_z} |p_{kl}| \qquad (8.2) $$

over one thousand ensembles $\{z_i^f\}$ of size $M$. We know that $|p_{kl}| \to 0$, $k \neq l$, as $M \to 0$. Second, we consider $|P_M^f|^{1/N_z}$ as a measure of how much the overall variance in the samples is underestimated or overestimated. Again we know *a priori* that $|P_M^f|^{1/N_z} \to 1$ as $M \to \infty$ and $|P_M^f| = 0$ for $M \leq N_z$.

The average over ensembles $\{z_i^f\}_{i=1}^M$ with $M$ ranging between 11 and 2000 can be found in Figure 8.1. Not unexpectedly, on average the empirical $P_M^f$ underestimates the true value of the determinant of the covariance matrix and significant spurious correlations arise even for moderate values of $M$. In other words, the ensemble spread is likely to be too small, implying that the true forecast uncertainties are underestimated. Furthermore, spurious correlations are introduced, which are not present in the underlying statistical reference model. Both these phenomena can have catastrophic effects on the performance of an ensemble data assimilation algorithm.

---

Note that an EnKF can be interpreted as first computing an analysis ensemble $\{y_i^a\}$ in observation space which is then mapped back onto state space by the linear regression formula

$$ z_i^a = z_i^f + P_M^f H^T (H P_M^f H^T)^{-1}(y_i^a - y_i^f) $$

with $y_i^f := H z_i^f$. Hence spurious correlations in $P_M^f$, as found in Example 8.1, imply spurious correlations in $P_M^f H^T$. These spurious correlations in turn lead to

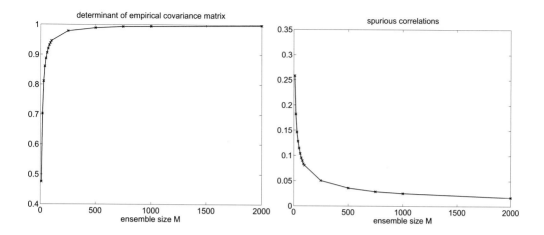

**Figure 8.1** We display values of $|P_M^f|^{1/N_z}$ (left panel) and the quantity $c$ in Equation (8.2) (right panel), for $N_z = 10$, having averaged over one thousand ensembles of size $M$, displayed as a function of the ensemble size $M$. The realisations are drawn from a Gaussian distribution with mean zero and covariance matrix $P^f = I$. Hence the analytic value for $|P^f|^{1/N_z}$ is one and the analytic values of the off-diagonal terms of $P^f$ are all zero. These values are indeed approached by $P_M^f$ as $M \to \infty$, but modest ensemble sizes lead to a significant underestimation of $|P^f|^{1/N_z}$ together with spurious non-zero cross correlations.

an erroneous transformation of the increments $\Delta y_i = y_i^a - y_i^f$ back to state space. The problem of spurious correlations between observation and state space variables becomes particularly relevant for data assimilation problems which involve spatio-temporal evolution models. In such cases the ensemble sizes are often relatively small, since each run of the spatio-temporal model can be computationally demanding. Furthermore, spurious correlations between an observation and spatial locations far from the actual measurement can clearly impact negatively on the performance of a data assimilation algorithm.

In the ensemble Kalman filter literature, *ensemble inflation* and *localisation* are two techniques for dealing with small ensemble sizes which have become popular in the context of spatio-temporal systems. Localisation reduces the impact of spurious correlations between observation and state space, whilst ensemble inflation increases the ensemble spread in order to avoid an underestimation of the reduced Kalman gain matrix

$$HK = HP_M^f H^T (HP_M^f H^T + R)^{-1},$$

in the update of the ensemble mean

$$\bar{y}^a = \bar{y}_M^f - HK(\bar{y}_M^f - y_{obs}),$$

in observation space. This correction is important, since an underestimation of $HK$ can lead to *filter divergence*, i.e., the filter is no longer able to track the reference solution.

**Definition 8.2** (Filter divergence)    Given reference values $y_{\text{ref}}(t_k)$, associated observations $y_{\text{obs}}(t_k)$, and ensemble values $y_i(t_k)$, $k = 1, \ldots, N_{\text{obs}}$, from a filter algorithm, we speak of *filter divergence* if

$$\sum_{k=1}^{N_{\text{obs}}} (y_{\text{ref}}(t_k) - \overline{y}_M(t_k))^2 \gg \sum_{k=1}^{N_{\text{obs}}} (y_{\text{ref}}(t_k) - y_{\text{obs}}(t_k))^2,$$

i.e., the ensemble means, as produced by a filter algorithm, yield a prediction for the underlying reference values which is much worse than using the observations alone.

---

**Example 8.3**    Filter divergence can arise when the ensemble spread becomes much smaller than the distance of the ensemble mean to an observation, i.e.,

$$\max_{i=1,\ldots,M} |y_i(t_k) - \overline{y}_M(t_k)| \ll |y_{\text{obs}}(t_k) - \overline{y}_M(t_k)|.$$

In an extreme case $y_1(t_k) = y_2(t_k) = \cdots = y_M(t_k)$ in which case the induced Kalman gain matrix becomes $K = 0$ and any observed $y_{\text{obs}}(t_k)$ gets completely ignored by the filter.

---

In this chapter, we will also demonstrate how localisation and inflation can be applied to particle filters and how these techniques improve the performance of particle filters for spatio-temporal dynamical systems. However, before we describe ensemble inflation and localisation in more detail, we introduce the spatio-temporal model systems which will be used throughout this chapter.

## 8.1     Spatio-temporal model systems

For simplicity, we restrict our discussion to PDEs with a single spatial variable, which we denote by $x$ and which will be restricted to a periodic domain $x \in [0, L]$ of length $L > 0$. Hence, our state space variables $z \in \mathbb{R}^{N_z}$ are replaced by functions $u(x)$ which are periodic in $x$, i.e., $u(x) = u(x + L)$.[3] Below we discuss a few specific PDEs which naturally arise in the context of geophysical fluid dynamics, together with their numerical treatment, which immediately leads back to a finite-dimensional state space with $N_z \gg 1$. All of these models are popular in the data assimilation literature as toy models for testing assimilation algorithms, since they provide an intermediate step between low-dimensional ODEs and more realistic, but complex, geophysical models.

We start with the *linear advection equation*

$$\frac{\partial u}{\partial t} = -a \frac{\partial u}{\partial x}, \tag{8.3}$$

---

[3]  The spatial domain should be viewed as a circle with circumference $L$ and serves us as a simple one-dimensional "approximation" to the two-dimensional spherical shape of the Earth.

which implicitly characterises the time evolution of the function $u$ in time, i.e., the desired $u$ is a function of space and time with its partial derivatives related by (8.3) for all $(x, t)$, $x \in [0, L]$, $t \geq 0$. The *advection velocity* $a \in \mathbb{R}$ is assumed to be constant. We are, in addition, given $u(x, t)$ at time $t = 0$, i.e., $u(x, 0) = u_0(x)$ for given $u_0$. The function $u_0$ is called the initial condition.

The task is to find the function $u(x, t)$ that simultaneously satisfies (8.3) and the initial condition. First, note that any function $u$ of the special form $u(x, t) = \rho(x - at)$ has partial derivatives

$$\frac{\partial u}{\partial t}(x, t) = -a\rho'(x - at), \qquad \frac{\partial u}{\partial x}(x, t) = \rho'(x - at),$$

and therefore satisfies (8.3). Here $\rho : \mathbb{R} \to \mathbb{R}$ is a differentiable function and $\rho'$ denotes its derivative. Second, note that $u(x, 0) = \rho(x)$ and the given initial condition implies that $\rho(x) = u_0(x)$ for $x \in [0, L]$ and $\rho(x) = u_0(x \bmod L)$ for all $x \in \mathbb{R}$ by periodic extension.[4] Hence we have deduced that

$$u(x, t) = u_0(x - at \bmod L)$$

provides a solution to (8.3) given the initial condition $u(x, 0) = u_0(x)$ (existence of a solution to the initial value problem). It could be possible that more than one solution exists (non-uniqueness of the initial value problem) but this turns out not to be the case for the linear advection equation. A closer inspection reveals that $u(x, t)$ is constant along straight lines in the $(x, t)$ plane defined by $x = x_0 + at$ for given $x_0 \in [0, L]$. These straight lines are called *characteristics* and satisfy the differential equation

$$\frac{\mathrm{d}x}{\mathrm{d}t} = a$$

with initial condition $x(0) = x_0$. This equation also explains why $a$ is called the *advection velocity*. For periodic boundary conditions we must replace $x(t) = x_0 + at$ by $x_0 + at \bmod L$.

We can generalise the linear advection equation by replacing the constant $a$ by a function which depends on $x$ (and possibly also on time $t$). Hence we obtain the differential equation

$$\frac{\mathrm{d}x}{\mathrm{d}t} = a(x) \tag{8.4}$$

for the characteristics, which we need to solve for all initial conditions $x(0) = x_0 \in [0, L]$. We denote the solutions with initial condition $x_0$ by $x(t; x_0)$. As for the linear advection equation with constant velocity, we say that the time evolution of a function $u(x, t)$ with initial condition $u(x, 0) = u_0(x)$ is characterised by

$$u(x(t; x_0), t) = u_0(x_0), \qquad t \geq 0.$$

However, the last equation says that $u(x(t; x_0), t)$ is constant in time. This implies

---

[4] Here $a \bmod b$ stands for $a$ modulo $b$, which is the remainder of the division of $a$ by $b$.

that its total derivative with respect to time has to vanish, i.e.,

$$\frac{\mathrm{d}u}{\mathrm{d}t} = \frac{\partial u}{\partial x}\frac{\mathrm{d}x}{\mathrm{d}t} + \frac{\partial u}{\partial t}$$

$$= \frac{\partial u}{\partial x}a(x) + \frac{\partial u}{\partial t} = 0. \tag{8.5}$$

Upon rearranging (8.5) we obtain the generalised *linear advection equation*

$$\frac{\partial u}{\partial t} = -a(x)\frac{\partial u}{\partial x}. \tag{8.6}$$

We have shown that solving a rather complicated looking evolutionary PDE can be reduced to solving the ODE (8.4).

We now describe a numerical discretisation method based upon this structure. We discretise the interval $[0, L]$ into $N_d$ equal intervals of length $\Delta x = L/N_d$ and introduce equally spaced initial positions $x_k^0 := k\Delta x$ for $k = 1, \ldots, N_d$. We next take the solutions of the ODE (8.4) with those initial values, i.e., $x(0) = x_k^0$, $k = 1, \ldots, N_d$, and abbreviate these solutions $x(t; x_k^0)$ by $x_k(t)$. Then

$$u(x_k(t), t) = u_0(x_k(0)).$$

Furthermore, if $x_k(t)$ falls outside the domain $[0, L]$ for some $t > 0$, then we make use of

$$u(x_k(t) \pm L, t) = u(x_k(t), t)$$

to map $x_k(t)$ back onto the domain $[0, L]$. Hence we always end up with $N_d$ points $x_k(t) \in [0, L]$ with constant function values $u_k = u_0(x_k(0))$. The pairs $(x_k(t), u_k)$ can be linearly interpolated in order to get a continuous function $\tilde{u}(x, t)$ which serves as a numerical approximation to the analytic $u(x, t)$. This is called the *method of characteristics*. Note that $\tilde{u}(x_k(t), t) = u(x_k(t), t)$ along all computed characteristics and we anticipate convergence of $\tilde{u}(x, t)$ to $u(x, t)$ for fixed $t > 0$ and all $x \in [0, L]$ as $\Delta x \to 0$ ($N_d \to \infty$).

---

**Example 8.4**   Consider advection under the spatially- and temporally-periodic velocity field

$$a(x, t) = \sin(2\pi x)\cos(\pi t) \tag{8.7}$$

with periodic boundary conditions over the domain $x \in [0, 1]$, i.e., $L = 1$. The initial field is $u_0(x) = \sin(2\pi x)$. We implement the method of characteristics by subdividing the interval $[0, 1]$ into $N_d = 100$ subintervals of length $\Delta x = 0.01$. The initial positions of the characteristics are $x_k^0 = k\Delta x$, $k = 1, \ldots, 100$, with constant solution values $u_k = \sin(2\pi k\Delta x)$. The positions evolve in time under the forward Euler discretisation

$$x_k^{n+1} = x_k^n + \Delta t \sin(2\pi x_k^n)\cos(\pi t_n), \qquad t_n = n\Delta t,$$

with step-size $\Delta t = 0.001$. Periodic boundary conditions are used to map $x_k^{n+1}$ back onto $[0, 1]$ if necessary. The numerical results are displayed in Figure 8.2.

---

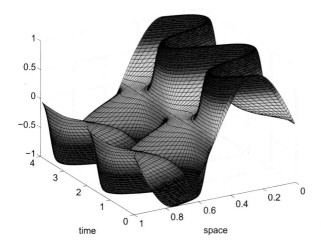

**Figure 8.2** Numerical results from the method of characteristics applied to the linear advection equation with advecting velocity field given by (8.7).

The method of characteristics works very well in one spatial dimension but it becomes more complicated in more than one spatial dimension. An alternative discretisation method is based on the idea of *finite differences*, which can be directly applied to the PDE (8.6) and more easily generalises to higher spatial dimensions. In addition to the temporal grid $t_n = n\Delta t$ we now introduce a fixed spatial grid $x_k = k\Delta x$. An approximation of $u$ at the fixed spatio-temporal location $(x_k, t_n)$ is denoted by $u_k^n$ and we replace partial derivatives by finite difference approximations such as

$$\frac{\partial u}{\partial t}(x_k, t_n) \approx \frac{u(x_k, t_n + \Delta t) - u(x_k, t_n)}{\Delta t} \approx \frac{u_k^{n+1} - u_k^n}{\Delta t}$$

for the first-order temporal derivative and

$$\frac{\partial u}{\partial x}(x_k, t_n) \approx \frac{u(x_k, t_n) - u(x_k - \Delta x, t_n)}{\Delta x} \approx \frac{u_k^n - u_{k-1}^n}{\Delta x},$$

or

$$\frac{\partial u}{\partial x}(x_k, t_n) \approx \frac{u(x_k + \Delta x, t_n) - u(x_k, t_n)}{\Delta x} \approx \frac{u_{k+1}^n - u_k^n}{\Delta x}.$$

for the first-order spatial derivative. Plugging these finite difference approximations into (8.6) and rearranging terms into an explicit iteration in the temporal iteration index $n$, we obtain two examples of possible discretisations,

$$u_k^{n+1} = u_k^n - \frac{a(x_k)\Delta t}{\Delta x}(u_{k+1}^n - u_k^n) \qquad \text{(right differencing)}, \qquad (8.8)$$

and

$$u_k^{n+1} = u_k^n - \frac{a(x_k)\Delta t}{\Delta x}(u_k^n - u_{k-1}^n) \qquad \text{(left differencing)}, \qquad (8.9)$$

respectively. Without going into technical details, we state that for stable results, the spatial mesh-size $\Delta x$ and the time-step-size $\Delta t$ needs to be chosen such that

$$|a(x_k)|\frac{\Delta t}{\Delta x} \leq 1,$$

and that the right differencing scheme (8.8) is used whenever $a(x_k) \leq 0$ and the left differencing scheme is used if $a(x_k) > 0$ (this is called the *upwind method*, since the spatial difference is evaluating in the upwind direction). The numerical approximation scheme is now completed by setting $u_k^0 = u_0(x_k)$ and by cycling through all $x_k$, $k = 1, \ldots, N_d$, for each $n \geq 0$. Once again we make use of periodicity in the spatial domain, i.e., $u_k^n = u_{k \pm N_d}^n$, in order to define spatial finite difference approximations near the boundaries at $x = 0$ and $x = L$.

---

**Example 8.5**   We apply the upwind method to the advection equations with advecting velocity field (8.7). We compare numerical results for a spatial mesh of $\Delta x = 0.01$ and time-step $\Delta t = 0.01$ to those for $\Delta x = 0.001$ and $\Delta t = 0.001$ in Figure 8.3. We observe that the coarser resolution leads to a significant numerical damping of the advected solution while $\Delta x = 0.001$ leads to results closer to those obtained from the method of characteristics in Example 8.6. Compare Figure 8.3. This numerical example demonstrates that discretisations of partial differential equations can lead to significant systematic errors unless the discretisation parameters are chosen sufficiently small. Further problems can arise from unstable discretisations (such as interchanging left differencing with right differencing and vice versa). We will not discuss these numerical issues further in this book, but they must be taken into account when applying data assimilation algorithms to real world problems. This renders the perfect model scenario often used in theoretical studies rather unrealistic from a practical perspective.

---

Let us now complicate matters further by replacing the predefined advection velocity $a(x, t)$ by the unknown function $u(x, t)$ itself. This leads us to the *nonlinear advection equation*

$$\frac{\partial u}{\partial t} = -u \frac{\partial u}{\partial x} = -\frac{1}{2} \frac{\partial (u)^2}{\partial x}.$$

The solution theory for this PDE is rather more complicated than the equations considered so far. To avoid the technical discussion of *shocks and rarefactions*, we immediately move on to *Burgers' equation*

$$\frac{\partial u}{\partial t} = -\frac{1}{2} \frac{\partial (u)^2}{\partial x} + \mu \frac{\partial^2 u}{\partial x^2} \tag{8.10}$$

with *viscosity coefficient* $\mu > 0$ and initial velocity field $u_0(x)$. A finite difference approximation is provided by

$$\frac{u_k^{n+1} - u_k^n}{\Delta t} = -\frac{(u_{k+1}^n)^2 - (u_{k-1}^n)^2}{4\Delta x} + \mu \frac{u_{k+1}^n - 2u_k^n + u_{k-1}^n}{\Delta x^2} \tag{8.11}$$

with the step-size chosen such that

$$\Delta t < \min\{\Delta x^2/\mu, u_{\max}\Delta x/2\}, \qquad u_{\max} := \max_{x \in [0,L]} |u_0(x)|.$$

It turns out that the time evolution of $u(x, t)$ under Burgers' equation leads

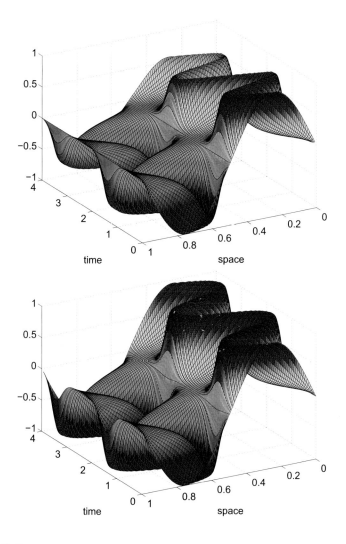

**Figure 8.3** Numerical results from the upwind method applied to the advection equation with advecting velocity field (8.7). The top panel has been obtained for spatial mesh-size $\Delta x = 0.01$ while the bottom panel is for $\Delta x = 0.001$. These results should be compared to those from the method of characteristics (Figure 8.2). It is obvious that $\Delta x = 0.01$ leads to a severe artificial damping of the advected sine wave.

to a constant function as $t \to \infty$, regardless of the initial velocity field $u_0(x)$; this is due to the non-vanishing viscosity. This makes prediction of the solution at long times insufficiently challenging, and hence we need to make alterations in order to obtain a good model for assessing data assimilation algorithms. We do this by adding random additive forcing to obtain

$$\frac{\partial u}{\partial t} = -\frac{1}{2}\frac{\partial(u)^2}{\partial x} + \mu\frac{\partial^2 u}{\partial x^2} + \sum_{l=1}^{N_f} \zeta_l(t)\sin\left(\frac{2\pi l}{L}x\right), \qquad (8.12)$$

where the time-dependent coefficients $\zeta_l$ satisfy the following SDEs,

$$d\zeta_l = -l^2\zeta_l dt + dW_l, \qquad l = 1,\ldots,N_f, \qquad (8.13)$$

and the variables $\{W_l(t)\}$ denote mutually independent standard Brownian motions. The model description is completed by setting the length of the domain to $L = 1$, the viscosity coefficient to $\mu = 0.0005$, and the number of stochastic modes to $N_f = 20$.

---

**Example 8.6** We describe a computational implementation of the model (8.12)–(8.13). In a first step only the spatial domain $[0, 1]$ is subdivided into 100 intervals of length $\Delta x = 0.01$. Numerical approximations at the grid points $x_k = k\Delta x$ are denoted by $u_k(t)$. Using basic finite-difference approximations for the spatial partial derivatives in (8.12) we obtain the spatially discretised system of stochastic differential equations

$$\frac{du_k}{dt} = -\frac{(u_{k+1})^2 - (u_{k-1})^2}{4\Delta x} + \mu\frac{u_{k+1} - 2u_k + u_{k-1}}{\Delta x^2}$$
$$+ \sum_{l=1}^{20} \zeta_l(t)\sin(2\pi l x_k), \qquad (8.14)$$

where the evolution of the variables $\{\zeta_l\}$ is determined by (8.13).

We next apply the forward Euler method to discretise (8.13) and (8.14) in time with step-size $\Delta t$ resulting in

$$u_k^{n+1} = u_k^n - \Delta t\frac{(u_{k+1}^n)^2 - (u_{k-1}^n)^2}{4\Delta x} + \mu\Delta t\frac{u_{k+1}^n - 2u_k^n + u_{k-1}^n}{\Delta x^2}$$
$$+ \Delta t\sum_{l=1}^{20} \zeta_l^n \sin(2\pi l x_k) , \qquad (8.15)$$
$$\zeta_l^{n+1} = \zeta_l^n - l^2\Delta t\zeta_l^n + \Delta t^{1/2}\xi_l^n, \qquad (8.16)$$

with the variables $\{\xi_l^n\}$ denoting mutually independent realisations of standard Gaussian random variables with mean zero and variance one. The step-size is set equal to $\Delta t = 0.001$. We collect the complete set of state variables $\{u_k^n\}$ and $\{\zeta_l^n\}$ into the state vector $z^n \in \mathbb{R}^{N_d + N_f}$ with $N_d + N_f = 120$.

Simulations are started from the trivial initial conditions $u_0(x) = 0$, $\zeta_l(0) = 0$, and ensemble prediction is performed by applying different realisations of the noise terms $\{\xi_l^n\}$ to each ensemble member. The ensemble sizes range from $M = 5$ to $M = 1000$ and ensemble members at $t_n = n\Delta t$ are denoted by $z_i^n$.

We monitor the time evolution of the empirical covariance matrices

$$P_M^n = \frac{1}{M-1} \sum_{i=1}^{M} Q_u (z_i^n - \bar{z}_M^n)(z_i^n - \bar{z}_M^n)^\mathrm{T} Q_u^\mathrm{T},$$

where $Q_u : \mathbb{R}^{N_\mathrm{d}+N_\mathrm{f}} \to \mathbb{R}^{N_\mathrm{d}}$ projects $z^n$ onto its $\{u_k^n\}$ components. Example 8.1 provided a demonstration that finite ensemble sizes lead to an underestimation of $|P_M^n|$. Instead, in this example we monitor the time evolution of the leading singular value of $P_M^n$ and its dependence on the ensemble size $M$. The result is shown in Figure 8.4. Small ensemble sizes of $M = 5, 10$ lead to large fluctuations in the leading singular value of the system, but the results with $M = 100$ agree extremely well with the results for $M = 1000$ and so it appears that the numerical results have converged. We also conclude that the leading singular value approaches an asymptotic value close to 10 for this system. A typical spatio-temporal structure of the $u(x,t)$ solution fields is also displayed in Figure 8.4.

In addition to the stochastically forced PDE model we will use the dynamical system

$$\frac{\mathrm{d}u_k}{\mathrm{d}t} = -\frac{u_{k-1}u_{k+1} - u_{k-2}u_{k-1}}{3\Delta x} - u_k + F, \qquad k = 1, \ldots, 40, \qquad (8.17)$$

known as the Lorenz-96 model, as a model for testing data assimilation algorithms. This system can be seen as a coarse spatial approximation to the forced-dissipative PDE

$$\frac{\partial u}{\partial t} = -\frac{1}{2}\frac{\partial (u)^2}{\partial x} - u + F,$$

with a particular spatial discretisation of the nonlinear advection term, mesh-size $\Delta x = 1/3$, $N_\mathrm{d} = 40$ grid points and domain length $L = 40/3$. Here $F > 0$ is a constant forcing term and periodic boundary conditions are assumed, i.e., $u_{k\pm 40}(t) = u_k(t)$. Furthermore, the viscosity term $\mu u_{xx}$ in Burgers' equation has been replaced by the Newtonian damping term $-u$.

**Example 8.7** We now repeat the numerical experiments conducted in Example 8.6 with the model (8.12)–(8.13) being replaced by the Lorenz-96 model (8.17). The differential equations (8.17) are discretised in time by the forward Euler method with step-size $\Delta t = 0.001$. The initial conditions are drawn from the Gaussian $\mathrm{N}(0, I)$ distribution. We compare results obtained with two different values $F = 2$ and $F = 8$ for the forcing term. We again display typical spatio-temporal solution fields and the time-evolved leading singular value of ensemble generated covariance matrices in Figures 8.5 and 8.6, respectively. Note that the randomly generated initial ensembles already lead to an increased leading singular value for small ensemble sizes. Furthermore, $F = 8$ leads to a dramatic increase in the the leading singular value of the Lorenz-96 model and the spatial structure of the solution fields is highly irregular in both cases. It can be expected

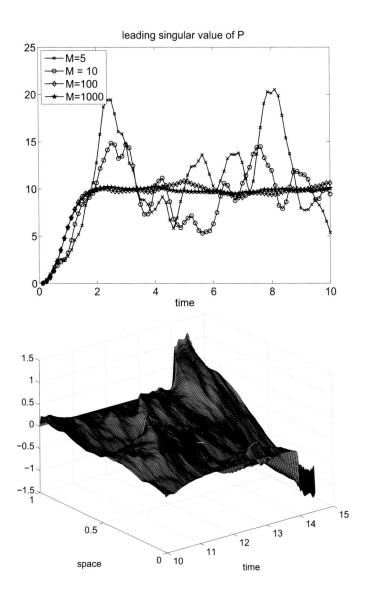

**Figure 8.4** Ensemble prediction for the model system (8.12)–(8.13). The numerical implementation is described in Example 8.6. We display a typical $u(x,t)$ field in the bottom panel while the top panel shows the time evolution of the leading singular value of the ensemble generated empirical covariance matrices for four different ensemble sizes. Small ensemble sizes lead to large fluctuations in the leading singular value of the system while $M = 100$ and $M = 1000$ lead to essentially identical results.

that (8.17) with $F = 8$ will provide a tough test case for any data assimilation scheme.

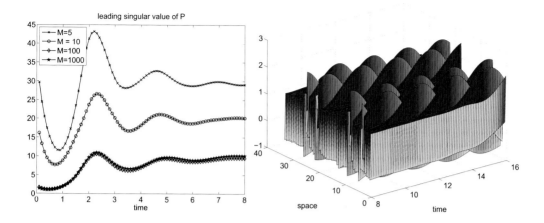

**Figure 8.5** Ensemble prediction for the Lorenz-96 model (8.17) with $F = 2$. We display a typical $u(x, t)$ field in the right panel while the left panel shows the time evolution of the leading singular value of the ensemble generated empirical covariance matrices for four different ensemble sizes. Small ensemble sizes lead to an overestimation of the leading singular value of the system while $M = 100$ and $M = 1000$ lead to essentially identical results. We conclude that the leading singular value approaches an asymptotic value close to 10 for this system.

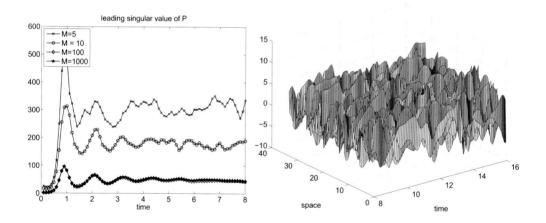

**Figure 8.6** Lorenz-96 model (8.17) with $F = 8$. The spatio-temporal fields (right panel) become much more irregular (compare Figure 8.5) and the asymptotic value of the leading singular value increases to about 40.

We finally specify the process of generating observations for the purpose of testing assimilation algorithms. Throughout this chapter we will concentrate on the simplified *identical twin experiment/perfect model setting* in which the reference solution and model forecasts are generated from the same numerical model. Systematic biases between forecast models and reference solutions and their impact on data assimilation will be explored in Chapter 9. The reference solution will be denoted by $u_{\text{ref}}(x,t)$, which has been extended from computed grid values $u^n_{k,\text{ref}}$ by bilinear interpolation to arbitrary values of $(x,t) \in [0,L] \times [0,t_{\text{end}}]$. We observe grid point values of $u_{\text{ref}}(x,t)$ subject to measurement errors, i.e.,

$$y^n_{\text{obs}}(\mathfrak{x}_k) = u_{\text{ref}}(\mathfrak{x}_k, \mathfrak{t}_n) + \xi^n_k,$$

with observations taken in spatial intervals of $\Delta x_{\text{out}}$ and in temporal intervals of $\Delta t_{\text{out}}$, i.e.,

$$\mathfrak{x}_k = k\Delta x_{\text{out}}, \qquad \mathfrak{t}_n = n\Delta t_{\text{out}}.$$

The measurement errors $\xi^n_k$ are mutually independent and Gaussian distributed with mean zero and variance $R$. In general, the observation grid $\{(\mathfrak{x}_k, \mathfrak{t}_n)\}$ will be coarser than the computational grid $\{(x_k, t_n)\}$.

Therefore, in the context of *Laplace's demon*, we are considering the situation where our model is a perfect replica of "reality". In the case of the Lorenz-96 model (8.17), it is also directly computable (up to round-off errors due to finite machine precision). Hence forecast/analysis uncertainties only arise from uncertain initial conditions as well as partial and noisy observations of the current model states. The situation is slightly more complex for the stochastic model (8.15)–(8.16), where the unknown stochastic forcing terms represent an additional source of uncertainty.

In the remainder of this chapter we discuss the application of the ensemble transform filters of Chapter 7 to the Lorenz-96 model (8.17) and the model (8.13)–(8.14). Two additional techniques need to be introduced in order to obtain acceptable results when applying these filters to spatio-temporal processes. These are *ensemble inflation* and *localisation*. We start with the concept of ensemble inflation.

We continue using the notation $z \in \mathbb{R}^{N_z}$ with $N_z = N_d + N_f$ and $N_z = N_d$, respectively, for the state variables of our spatially discretised spatio-temporal models (8.13)–(8.14) and (8.17), respectively, unless stated otherwise. We will also use the notation $z(x_k)$ in order to denote the value of $z$ at the spatial location $x_k$, for example $z(x_k) = u_k$, and to emphasise the spatial dependence of the entries in the state vector $z$.

## 8.2      Ensemble inflation

The simple idea behind ensemble inflation is to increase the spread of a forecast ensemble $\{z^f_i\}$ about its mean $\bar{z}^f_M$. In other words, we artificially increase the forecast uncertainty in order to make an ensemble Kalman filter implementation more robust against the finite ensemble size effects, as discussed at the beginning of this chapter, and deviations from the assumed Gaussian behaviour of the forecast ensemble.

**Definition 8.8** (Ensemble inflation)   Given a forecast ensemble $z_i^{\mathrm{f}} \in \mathbb{R}^{N_z}$, $i = 1, \ldots, M$, we first compute its empirical mean $\bar{z}_M^{\mathrm{f}}$ and the ensemble anomalies $\Delta z_i := z_i^{\mathrm{f}} - \bar{z}_M^{\mathrm{f}}$. An *inflated ensemble* is defined by

$$z_i^{\mathrm{f}} := \bar{z}_M^{\mathrm{f}} + \alpha\, \Delta z_i^{\mathrm{f}} \tag{8.18}$$

with inflation factor $\alpha > 1$.

The approach (8.18) is called *multiplicative ensemble inflation*. Alternatively, we could apply particle rejuvenation, following Definition 6.13, in order to replace the forecast ensemble by $z_i^{\mathrm{f}} + \xi_i$, where the variables $\{\xi_i\}$ are independent realisations of some chosen random variable $\Xi$ with zero mean. Such an *additive ensemble inflation* strategy is often associated with stochastic model errors, but multiplicative inflation has been found to be more effective in the context of ensemble Kalman filter implementations. Note that multiplicative ensemble inflation is typically applied prior to an assimilation step.

We apply the ensemble Kalman filter with inflation to the model system (8.12)–(8.13) as described in Example 8.6 and to the Lorenz-96 model (8.17) as described in Example 8.7. We have already found that (8.12)–(8.13) leads to solutions which are much more spatially regular than those of (8.17). Furthermore, (8.17) is deterministic with a large leading singular value of the ensemble covariance matrix while (8.12)–(8.13) are stochastically driven with a smaller leading singular value of the associated time-evolved ensemble covariance matrices.

---

**Example 8.9**   Consider (8.12)–(8.13) over a spatially-periodic domain of length $L = 1$ as outlined in Example 8.6. The computational grid has grid-spacing $\Delta x = 0.01$, and the $u$ variable is observed every fourth grid-point (implying that $\Delta x_{\mathrm{out}} = 0.04$). Measurement errors are mutually uncorrelated with variance $R = 0.01$, and the forward model at an observation time $t_n$ is

$$y_{\mathrm{obs}}^n(\mathfrak{x}_k) = u_{\mathrm{ref}}(\mathfrak{x}_k, t_n) + \xi_k^n, \qquad \mathfrak{x}_k = k\Delta x_{\mathrm{out}},\ t_n = n\Delta t_{\mathrm{out}}.$$

The step-size is $\Delta t = 0.001$ and observations are taken every 125 time-steps, i.e., $\Delta t_{\mathrm{out}} = 0.125$. A total of 5100 data assimilation cycles are performed, with the first 100 cycles being used for equilibration of the algorithm.

We compare the performance of the EnKF with perturbed observations (i) without inflation and (ii) with multiplicative inflation using an inflation factor $\alpha$ from the range $\{1.05, 1.1, \ldots, 1.2\}$. The comparison is made using the spatially- and temporally-averaged RMSE:

$$\mathrm{RMSE} = \sqrt{\frac{1}{N_{\mathrm{obs}}N_{\mathrm{d}}} \sum_{k=1}^{N_{\mathrm{d}}} \sum_{n=1}^{N_{\mathrm{obs}}} |u_{\mathrm{ref}}(x_k, t_n) - \bar{u}_M^{\mathrm{a}}(x_k, t_n)|^2}.$$

Here $\bar{u}_M^{\mathrm{a}}(x_k, t_n) := Q_u \bar{z}_M^{\mathrm{a}}(x_k, t_n)$ and $\bar{z}_M^{\mathrm{a}}(x_k, t_n)$ denotes the ensemble mean of the analysis ensemble at grid point $x_k = k\Delta x$ and observation time

$$t_n = n\Delta t_{\mathrm{out}} = 125\, n\, \Delta t = 0.125\, n.$$

**Table 8.1** Spatially- and temporally-averaged RMSEs for the EnKF with perturbed observations, applied to the model system (8.12)–(8.13), as a function of the ensemble size $M \in \{5, 10, 20, 40, 100\}$. The table also states the inflation factors which lead to the smallest time-averaged RMSEs. If the stated inflation factor is 1.0 then using no inflation is optimal. It can be concluded that the effect of ensemble inflation is significant only at the smallest ensemble size of $M = 5$.

| RMSE/inflation factor | No inflation | Optimal inflation |
|---|---|---|
| $M = 5$ | 0.1064 | 0.0680/1.15 |
| $M = 10$ | 0.0483 | 0.0457/1.15 |
| $M = 20$ | 0.0429 | 0.0390/1.10 |
| $M = 40$ | 0.0388 | 0.0382/1.05 |
| $M = 100$ | 0.0374 | 0.0374/1.00 |

Ensemble inflation is applied prior to an analysis step. As shown in Table 8.1, we find that an ensemble size of $M = 10$ is required in order to obtain skilful results, i.e. to RMSEs which are smaller than $R^{1/2} = 0.1$, without inflation, and that the time-averaged RMSE can be improved by applying ensemble inflation for small ensemble sizes.

**Example 8.10**   In this example, multiplicative ensemble inflation is tested on the Lorenz-96 model (8.17) with $F = 8$. Every grid point is observed every $\Delta t_{\text{out}} = 0.1$ time units. The measurement covariance matrix $R$ is diagonal with variances equal to 1. The numerical implementation of the Lorenz-96 model is as described in Example 8.7, with the initial ensemble now drawn from the Gaussian $\mathrm{N}(\bar{z}^0, R)$ distribution with $\bar{z}^0 \in \mathbb{R}^{40}$ given by

$$\bar{z}^0 = (-1.76, -0.66, -2.11, 2.02, -2.26, 4.57, -0.38, 4.35, 1.58, 2.31,$$
$$1.89, 0.13, 0.55, 2.61, 0.22, 7.25, 0.74, 1.89, 4.29, -2.47,$$
$$4.61, 0.57, 1.90, 0.28, -0.12, 5.25, -0.81, 3.70, 2.62, 0.36,$$
$$-0.84, 2.25, 0.74, 7.27, 3.15, -0.14, 4.91, 0.58, 0.89, 1.15).$$

The reference trajectory has initial value $\bar{z}^0$, and is generated by the same numerical implementation of the Lorenz-96 model. We compare the spatially- and temporally-averaged RMSEs for the EnKF with perturbed observations for ensemble sizes $M = 20, 22, 24, 26$ and inflation factors from the range $\alpha \in \{1.05, 1.10, \ldots, 1.35, 1.40\}$. A total of 20000 assimilation cycles is performed. Again inflation is applied prior to each analysis step. The smallest spatially- and temporally-averaged RMSEs and the corresponding optimal inflation factors can be found in Figure 8.7. Contrary to Example 8.9, ensemble inflation is now essential to the success of the EnKF, i.e., in order to avoid filter divergence. It should be kept in mind that we conducted identical twin experiments al-

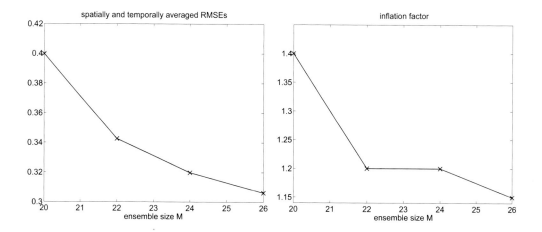

**Figure 8.7** Optimal ensemble inflation for the EnKF with perturbed observations applied to the Lorenz-96 model. The left panel shows the spatially- and temporally-averaged RMSEs while the right panel shows the corresponding optimised inflation factors from the range $\alpha \in \{1.05, 1.10, \ldots, 1.35, 1.40\}$.

lowing us to directly assess RMSEs. The computation of an optimal choice of inflation factors is impossible in most practical applications since the true reference solution is not available. Methods for the practical estimation of inflation factors are discussed in the references at the end of this chapter.

Recall that the particle rejuvenation step was introduced in Definition 6.13 to avoid the creation of identical analysis ensemble members $z_i^a$ under a particle resampling/transformation step, whether in the form of the SIR filter or the ETPF. We now discuss the effect of particle rejuvenation on the ETPF in the context of additive ensemble inflation. We first note that the ETPF update formula (7.30) with $P_j^a = \tau P_M^f$ can be viewed as producing balanced samples (i.e., an equal number of samples are drawn from each mixture component) from the Gaussian mixture PDF

$$\pi_{Z^a}(z) = \frac{1}{M} \sum_{j=1}^{M} \mathrm{n}(z; \bar{z}_j^a, \tau P_M^f), \qquad \bar{z}_j^a = \sum_{i=1}^{M} z_i^f p_{ij} \qquad (8.19)$$

and the ETPF update without particle rejuvenation corresponds to a balanced sample from the empirical measure

$$\mu_{Z^a}(\mathrm{d}z) = \frac{1}{M} \sum_{j=1}^{M} \delta(z - \bar{z}_j^a)\mathrm{d}z. \qquad (8.20)$$

Although the same mean value

$$\bar{z}^{\mathrm{a}} = \frac{1}{M} \sum_{j=1}^{M} \bar{z}_j^{\mathrm{a}},$$

is obtained for both PDFs (8.19) and (8.20), the covariance matrices satisfy

$$P^{\mathrm{a}} = \frac{1}{M-1} \sum_{j=1}^{M} (\bar{z}_j^{\mathrm{a}} - \bar{z}^{\mathrm{a}})(\bar{z}_j^{\mathrm{a}} - \bar{z}^{\mathrm{a}})^{\mathrm{T}} + \tau P_M^{\mathrm{f}}$$

and

$$P^{\mathrm{a}} = \frac{1}{M-1} \sum_{j=1}^{M} (\bar{z}_j^{\mathrm{a}} - \bar{z}^{\mathrm{a}})(\bar{z}_j^{\mathrm{a}} - \bar{z}^{\mathrm{a}})^{\mathrm{T}}, \qquad (8.21)$$

respectively. Hence we may conclude that particle rejuvenation has a similar effect as ensemble inflation: it increases the ensemble spread while preserving the ensemble mean.

We now discuss why particle rejuvenation is necessary for the ETPF when used with small ensemble sizes. In Chapter 5 we have already seen that the analysis ensemble $\{z_i^{\mathrm{a}}\}$ exactly reproduces the posterior mean $\bar{z}^{\mathrm{a}} = \sum_i w_i z_i^{\mathrm{f}}$. We have also shown that empirical expectation of a function $g(z)$ converges to the analytical expectation as $M \to \infty$. However, we also find that, for finite ensemble sizes, the empirical covariance matrix (8.21) of the analysis ensemble underestimates the posterior covariance matrix

$$\hat{P}^{\mathrm{a}} = \frac{M}{M-1} \sum_{i=1}^{M} (z_i^{\mathrm{f}} - \bar{z}^{\mathrm{a}}) w_i (z_i^{\mathrm{f}} - \bar{z}^{\mathrm{a}})^{\mathrm{T}}$$

defined through the importance weights $\{w_i\}$.

---

**Example 8.11**   Consider a univariate forecast ensemble $\{z_i^{\mathrm{f}}\}$ with importance weights $\{w_i\}$. The posterior variance is given by

$$(\hat{\sigma}^{\mathrm{a}})^2 = \frac{M}{M-1} \sum_{i=1}^{M} w_i (z_i^{\mathrm{f}} - \bar{z}^{\mathrm{a}})^2,$$

while the variance of the analysis ensemble

$$z_j^{\mathrm{a}} = \sum_{i=1}^{M} z_i^{\mathrm{f}} p_{ij}$$

is equal to

$$(\sigma^{\mathrm{a}})^2 = \frac{1}{M-1} \sum_{i=1}^{M} (z_i^{\mathrm{a}} - \bar{z}^{\mathrm{a}})^2.$$

**Table 8.2** Spatially- and temporally-averaged RMSEs obtained by the SIR filter and the ETPF applied to the model system (8.12)–(8.13) as a function of the ensemble size $M \in \{5, 10, 20, 40, 100\}$. We also state the bandwidths $\tau$ for the rejuvenation step. Overall the RMSEs are substantially larger than those displayed in Table 8.1 for the EnKF with perturbed observations. This gap in performance closes as the ensemble size increases.

| RMSE/bandwidth | SIR | ETPF |
|---|---|---|
| $M = 5$ | 0.1363/0.15 | 0.1358/0.15 |
| $M = 10$ | 0.0844/0.20 | 0.0914/0.20 |
| $M = 20$ | 0.0630/0.20 | 0.0687/0.20 |
| $M = 40$ | 0.0520/0.15 | 0.0527/0.20 |
| $M = 100$ | 0.0438/0.15 | 0.0481/0.15 |

We find that $\sigma^{\mathrm{a}}$ and $\hat{\sigma}^{\mathrm{a}}$ satisfy

$$(\hat{\sigma}^{\mathrm{a}})^2 = (\sigma^{\mathrm{a}})^2 + \frac{1}{M-1} \sum_{j=1}^{M} \sum_{i=1}^{M} p_{ij} (z_i^{\mathrm{f}} - z_j^{\mathrm{a}})^2. \qquad (8.22)$$

Although the convergence result from Chapter 5 implies that $\sigma^{\mathrm{a}} \to \hat{\sigma}^{\mathrm{a}}$ as $M \to \infty$, we have $\sigma^{\mathrm{a}} < \hat{\sigma}^{\mathrm{a}}$ for all ensemble sizes $M$ (unless the optimal coupling $T^*$ happens to be a permutation matrix) and particle rejuvenation can be used to compensate for the implied reduction in ensemble spread. Related expressions hold for multivariate state variables.

---

**Example 8.12**    We apply the SIR particle filter and the ETPF from Chapter 7 to the model (8.12)–(8.13) in the data assimilation setting of Example 8.9. Both filters are implemented with particle rejuvenation, i.e., analysis ensembles are drawn as balanced samples from (8.19). Spatially- and temporally-averaged RMSEs as a function of ensemble size for an optimised bandwidth in the range $\tau \in \{0.05, 0.1, 0.15, 0.2\}$ are collected in Table 8.2; these should be compared to those from the EnKF displayed in Table 8.1.

---

**Example 8.13**    We turn to the Lorenz-96 model (8.17) with $F = 8$ in the data assimilation setting of Example 8.10. We find that neither particle filter implementation is able to track the reference solution, i.e., both filters result in filter divergence, unless the ensemble size is increased to $M = 100$. The SIR filter with $M = 100$ and bandwidth $\tau = 0.8$ yields a spatially- and temporally-averaged RMSE of 0.3673 while the ETPF results in an RMSE of 0.3381 for the same setting.

---

The performance gap between the ensemble Kalman filters and particle filters for the Lorenz-96 model in terms of achievable ensemble sizes is striking. It is exactly this robustness of the ensemble Kalman filters which has made them so popular for large-scale geophysical applications. The next section will introduce a technique which further improves the behaviour of ensemble data assimilation algorithms in the setting of relatively small ensemble sizes.

## 8.3      Localisation

While ensemble inflation does not take the spatial structure of solutions into account directly, we will now discuss a method, called *localisation*, which exploits the spatial decay of correlations in the solutions $u(x, t)$ of a PDE. Let us therefore consider an ensemble $\{z_i^n\}$ of numerical solutions to a PDE at a time $t_n$. If the PDE under consideration is a scalar evolution equation with periodic boundary conditions discretised by $N_d$ grid points, then $z_i^n \in \mathbb{R}^{N_z}$ with $N_z = N_d$ and the $k$th entry of $z_i^n$ is an approximation to the solution $u(x, t)$ at $(x_k, l_n)$. We use the abbreviation $z_i^n(x_k)$ for these approximations, i.e.

$$z_i^n = (z_i^n(x_1), z_i^n(x_2), \dots, z_i^n(x_{N_d}))^{\mathrm{T}}. \tag{8.23}$$

Similarly we can define forecast values $z_i^f(x_k)$ and analysis values $z_i^a(x_k)$, which are collected in state vectors $z_i^f$ and $z_i^a$ respectively. Formally, we also introduce periodic extensions of, for example, $z_i^n(x_{k\pm N_d}) = z_i^n(x_k)$ for given $z_i^n(x_k)$, $k = 1, \dots, N_d$. Also recall that observations are taken in spatial intervals of $\Delta x_{\mathrm{out}}$ and that the corresponding grid values are denoted by $\mathfrak{x}_k = k\Delta x_{\mathrm{out}}$.

**Definition 8.14** (Spatial correlation coefficients)   Given numerically generated approximations $z_i^n(x_k)$ for a time index $n \geq 0$, spatial indices $k = 1, \dots, N_d$, and ensemble indices $i = 1, \dots, M$, we define *spatial correlation* coefficients $C^n(l\Delta x)$ at $t_n$ by

$$C^n(l\Delta x) = \frac{1}{C_0^n} \sum_{i=1}^{M} \sum_{k=1}^{N_d} (z_i^n(x_k) - \bar{z}_M^n(x_k))(z_i^n(x_{k+l}) - \bar{z}_M^n(x_{k+l})), \tag{8.24}$$

for $0 \leq l \leq N_d/2$ with spatial mesh-size $\Delta x = L/N_d$, normalisation constant

$$C_0^n = \sum_{i=1}^{M} \sum_{k=1}^{N_d} (z_i^n(x_k) - \bar{z}_M^n(x_k))^2,$$

and grid-point empirical means

$$\bar{z}_M^n(x_k) = \frac{1}{M} \sum_{i=1}^{M} z_i^n(x_k).$$

By definition, we have $C^n(0) = 1$.

---

**Example 8.15**   We compute (8.24) for the Lorenz-96 model (8.17) and the model (8.12)–(8.13) for $n = 1, \dots, 5000$ and ensemble size $M = 10$ . In the case

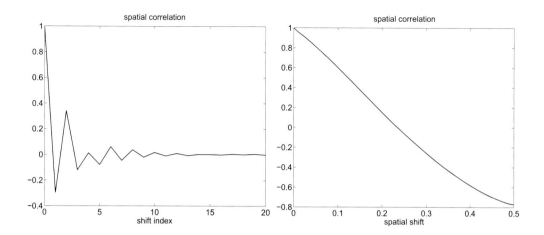

**Figure 8.8** Time-averaged spatial correlation coefficients, as defined by (8.25), for the Lorenz-96 model (left panel) and the model (8.12)–(8.13) (right panel). The spatial shift $l\Delta x$ (shift index $l$) is restricted to half of the domain $[0, L]$ ($0 \leq l \leq N_d/2$) because of the assumed periodic boundary conditions, which also implies a periodic behaviour of the spatial correlation coefficients. While the time-averaged spatial correlations for the Lorenz-96 model decay quickly in $l$, the model (8.12)–(8.13) leads to a significant correlation across the whole domain.

of (8.12)–(8.13) we only compute spatial correlation coefficients for the $u$ field. The spatial correlation coefficients are then averaged in time, i.e.,

$$C(l\Delta x) = \frac{1}{5000} \sum_{n=1}^{5000} C^n(l\Delta x).$$ 

$$(8.25)$$

The numerical results can be found in Figure 8.8. While the Lorenz-96 model leads to a rapid decay of spatial correlation, the stochastic Burgers' model (8.12)–(8.13) leads to correlations which are significant across the whole domain $x \in [0, 1]$. This different behaviour of the spatial correlation factors is a manifestation of the different spatial regularity of individual solutions as displayed in Figures 8.4 and 8.5, respectively.

Spatial correlation structures have important ramifications for data assimilation algorithms since the forecast ensemble $\{z_i^f\}$ must reproduce those spatial correlations in order to correctly distribute increments in observation space across the computational domain. We discuss this aspect in more detail for a single observation $y_{obs}$ at a grid point $\mathfrak{x}_k$ for simplicity. If the state vector is of the form (8.23), then the associated forward model is simply

$$Y = z_{ref}(\mathfrak{x}_k) + \Xi,$$

where $\Xi \sim N(0, R)$. An ensemble Kalman filter implementation can be decomposed into the following three steps. First, define forecasts $y_i^f = z_i^f(\mathfrak{x}_k)$ and their empirical mean $\overline{y}_M^f = \overline{z}_M^f(\mathfrak{x}_k)$ in observation space. Second, an analysis ensemble $y_i^a \in \mathbb{R}$ is produced, together with the associated ensemble increments $\Delta y_i := y_i^a - y_i^f$ in observation space. Third, these increments are mapped back onto state space via

$$z_i^a = z_i^f + \frac{\sum_{j=1}^M (z_j^f - \overline{z}_M^f)(z_j^f(\mathfrak{x}_k) - \overline{z}_M^f(\mathfrak{x}_k))}{\sum_{j=1}^M (z_j^f(\mathfrak{x}_k) - \overline{z}_M^f(\mathfrak{x}_k))^2} \Delta y_i. \tag{8.26}$$

Let us now assume that the spatial correlation coefficients $C^n(l\Delta x)$, as defined by (8.24), are close to zero for $l \geq l_*$ for the model under consideration. The associated correlation coefficients in (8.26) should then also be close to zero, i.e.,

$$\frac{\sum_{j=1}^M (z_j^f(\mathfrak{x}_k + l\Delta x) - \overline{z}_M^f(\mathfrak{x}_k + l\Delta x))(z_j^f(\mathfrak{x}_k) - \overline{z}_M^f(\mathfrak{x}_k))}{\sum_{j=1}^M (z_j^f(\mathfrak{x}_k) - \overline{z}_M^f(\mathfrak{x}_k))^2} \approx 0 \tag{8.27}$$

for all $|l| \geq l_*$. One way to enforce this statistical constraint is to bring these correlations to zero, regardless of whether a forecast ensemble $\{z_i^f\}$ is correctly reproducing (8.27) or not. This is called *localisation*.

In order to reformulate (8.26) with localisation we introduce $r_{k,k'} = |x_k - x_{k'}|$ as the spatial distance between grid points $x_k$ and $x_{k'}$ and define weight factors $\rho(r_{k,k'}/r_{\text{loc}})$ for some appropriate *filter function* $\rho$ as well as a chosen *localisation radius* $r_{\text{loc}} \geq 0$. Note that periodicity needs to be taken into account in defining $r_{k,k'}$ in the case of a spatially-periodic domain, i.e.,

$$r_{k,k'} = |x_k - x_{k'}|_L := \min\{|x_k - x_{k'} - L|, |x_k - x_{k'}|, |x_k - x_{k'} + L|\}.$$

We introduce the abbreviation

$$s := \frac{r_{k,k'}}{r_{\text{loc}}} \geq 0$$

and state two possible filter functions. The filter function could be as simple as

$$\rho(s) = \begin{cases} 1 - \frac{1}{2}s & \text{for } s \leq 2, \\ 0 & \text{otherwise}. \end{cases} \tag{8.28}$$

Alternatively, a higher-order piecewise polynomial such as

$$\rho(s) = \begin{cases} 1 - \frac{5}{3}s^2 + \frac{5}{8}s^3 + \frac{1}{2}s^4 - \frac{1}{4}s^5 & \text{for } s \leq 1, \\ -\frac{2}{3}s^{-1} + 4 - 5s + \frac{5}{3}s^2 + \frac{5}{8}s^3 - \frac{1}{2}s^4 + \frac{1}{12}s^5 & \text{for } 1 \leq s \leq 2, \\ 0 & \text{otherwise}, \end{cases} \tag{8.29}$$

could be used. Given an observation at grid point $\mathfrak{x}_k = k\Delta x_{\text{out}}$, we define the vector $c_k \in \mathbb{R}^{N_d}$ with entries

$$(c_k)_l = \rho_{kl} := \rho\left(\frac{|x_l - \mathfrak{x}_k|_L}{r_{\text{loc}}}\right)$$

for $l = 1, \ldots, N_d$. We also introduce the *Schur product* $A \circ B$ of two matrices (or vectors) $A$ and $B$ of equal size, defined in terms of their matrix entries by

$$(A \circ B)_{kl} = (A)_{kl}(B)_{kl}.$$

The localised version of the update (8.26) is now given by

$$z_i^a = z_i^f + (c_k \circ (P_M^f H^T))(HP_M^f H^T)^{-1} \Delta y_i, \tag{8.30}$$

where the index $k$ refers to the index of the grid point $\mathfrak{x}_k$ at which the observation $y_{obs}$ has been taken and $H \in \mathbb{R}^{1 \times N_z}$ is the forward operator defined by

$$Hz = z(\mathfrak{x}_k). \tag{8.31}$$

The localised update (8.30) can be reformulated more abstractly by introducing the localisation matrix $C \in \mathbb{R}^{N_d \times N_d}$ with entries

$$(C)_{kl} = \rho\left(\frac{|x_k - x_l|_L}{r_{loc}}\right). \tag{8.32}$$

The matrix $C$ becomes circulant on a one-dimensional periodic domain.

---

**Example 8.16**   We give a simple example of a localisation matrix for a spatially-periodic domain of length $L = 1$ discretised into $N_d = 10$ grid points with grid spacing $\Delta x = 0.1$. We use the filter function $\rho$ defined in (8.28) with the localisation radius set to $r_{loc} = \Delta x$. The resulting localisation matrix $C \in \mathbb{R}^{10 \times 10}$ is given by

$$C = \begin{pmatrix}
1 & 1/2 & 0 & 0 & 0 & 0 & 0 & 0 & 0 & 1/2 \\
1/2 & 1 & 1/2 & 0 & 0 & 0 & 0 & 0 & 0 & 0 \\
0 & 1/2 & 1 & 1/2 & 0 & 0 & 0 & 0 & 0 & 0 \\
0 & 0 & 1/2 & 1 & 1/2 & 0 & 0 & 0 & 0 & 0 \\
0 & 0 & 0 & 1/2 & 1 & 1/2 & 0 & 0 & 0 & 0 \\
0 & 0 & 0 & 0 & 1/2 & 1 & 1/2 & 0 & 0 & 0 \\
0 & 0 & 0 & 0 & 0 & 1/2 & 1 & 1/2 & 0 & 0 \\
0 & 0 & 0 & 0 & 0 & 0 & 1/2 & 1 & 1/2 & 0 \\
0 & 0 & 0 & 0 & 0 & 0 & 0 & 1/2 & 1 & 1/2 \\
1/2 & 0 & 0 & 0 & 0 & 0 & 0 & 0 & 1/2 & 1
\end{pmatrix}.$$

---

With the localisation matrix $C$ defined as above, note that $(C)_{kk} = 1$, i.e., the diagonal entries of $C$ are equal to one and therefore

$$H(C \circ P_M^f)H^T = HP_M^f H^T$$

for the forward operator $H$ defined in (8.31). It is then easy to verify that (8.30) becomes equivalent to

$$z_i^a = z_i^f + (C \circ P_M^f)H^T \frac{\Delta y_i}{H(C \circ P_M^f)H^T}. \tag{8.33}$$

We now extend the concept of localisation to multivariate observations. If the measurement errors of all observations are mutually independent, i.e., the error covariance matrix $R$ is diagonal, then observations can be processed sequentially one after another, following the procedure we have just discussed for the single observation case. However, more efficient approaches can be followed. We will focus here on two alternatives which allow the simultaneous assimilation of multivariate observations $y_{\text{obs}}$. We start with the concept of *B-localisation*. We continue considering evolution equations with a single spatial dimension and periodic boundary conditions. Hence $N_z = N_{\text{d}}$.

For simplicity of exposition we assume that observations are taken at grid points and hence the forward operator $H$ has exactly one entry equal to one in each row with all other entries being identically zero.

**Definition 8.17** (B-localisation for EnKF with perturbed observations)    Given a filter function $\rho$ such as (8.28) or (8.29), a localisation radius $r_{\text{loc}}$, and an associated localisation matrix $\mathrm{C} \in \mathbb{R}^{N_{\text{d}} \times N_{\text{d}}}$ with entries defined by (8.32), *B-localisation* for the EnKF with perturbed observations is defined by

$$z_i^{\text{a}} = z_i^{\text{f}} - K_{\text{loc}}(Hz_i^{\text{f}} - y_{\text{obs}} + \xi_i)$$

with localised Kalman gain matrix

$$K_{\text{loc}} = (\mathrm{C} \circ P_M^{\text{f}})H^{\text{T}}(H(\mathrm{C} \circ P_M^{\text{f}})H^{\text{T}} + R)^{-1}. \tag{8.34}$$

All other quantities are defined as before for the EnKF with perturbed observations. Here the forward operator $H \in \mathbb{R}^{N_y \times N_{\text{d}}}$ collects now all observations of the state vector $z$ at the $N_y$ grid points $\mathfrak{x}_k = k\Delta x_{\text{out}}$.

Note that because of the assumed structure of the forward operator $H$ we can also define a localisation operator

$$\hat{\mathrm{C}} = HCH^{\text{T}} \in \mathbb{R}^{N_y \times N_y}$$

in observation space. It holds that

$$(\hat{\mathrm{C}})_{kl} = \rho\left(\frac{|\mathfrak{x}_k - \mathfrak{x}_l|_L}{r_{\text{loc}}}\right)$$

and

$$H(\mathrm{C} \circ P_M^{\text{f}})H^{\text{T}} = \hat{\mathrm{C}} \circ (HP_M^{\text{f}}H^{\text{T}}).$$

Similar considerations apply to $(\mathrm{C} \circ P_M^{\text{f}})H^{\text{T}}$ and help to reduce the computational expenses of a localised EnKF implementation.

Localisation is slightly more difficult to implement for the family of ESRFs. Here we discuss the use of *R-localisation*, a popular localisation technique in ensemble Kalman filtering that has given rise to the *local ensemble transform Kalman filter* (LETKF) (Ott et al. 2004, Hunt et al. 2007). First recall that an ESRF can be written as a LETF which in our context amounts to

$$z_j^{\text{a}}(x_k) = \sum_{i=1}^{M} z_i^{\text{f}}(x_k)d_{ij}, \qquad k = 1, \ldots, N_{\text{d}}.$$

R-localisation replaces this global spatial update by separate updates for each grid point $x_k$, $k = 1, \ldots, N_d$, in the form

$$z_i^{\mathrm{a}}(x_k) = \sum_{i=1}^{M} z_i^{\mathrm{f}}(x_k) d_{ij}(x_k).$$

The associated transformation matrices $D = \{d_{ij}(x_k)\}$ now depend on the grid point $x_k$.

Next, for each grid point $x_k$ we introduce the diagonal matrix $\tilde{C}_k \in \mathbb{R}^{N_y \times N_y}$ in observation space with diagonal entries

$$(\tilde{C}_k)_{ll} = \rho\left(\frac{|x_k - \mathfrak{x}_l|_L}{r_{\mathrm{loc}}}\right), \tag{8.35}$$

for $l = 1, \ldots, N_y$ and $\mathfrak{x}_l = l \Delta x_{\mathrm{out}}$. Also recall the definition of the matrix

$$A^{\mathrm{f}} = \left(z_1^{\mathrm{f}} - \bar{z}_M^{\mathrm{f}}, z_2^{\mathrm{f}} - \bar{z}_M^{\mathrm{f}}, \ldots, z_M^{\mathrm{f}} - \bar{z}_M^{\mathrm{f}}\right) \in \mathbb{R}^{N_d \times M}$$

of ensemble anomalies. In order to implement R-localisation for the ensemble anomalies $A^{\mathrm{f}}$, we need to introduce the ensemble anomalies

$$A^{\mathrm{f}}(x_k) := \left[(z_1^{\mathrm{f}}(x_k) - \bar{z}_M^{\mathrm{f}}(x_k)), \ldots, (z_M^{\mathrm{f}}(x_k) - \bar{z}_M^{\mathrm{f}}(x_k))\right] \in \mathbb{R}^{1 \times M}$$

at each grid point $x_k$ with their updates being individually defined by a linear transform approach of type (7.21).

**Definition 8.18** (R-localisation for ESRF/LETKF)   The matrix $A^{\mathrm{f}}$ of forecast ensemble anomalies is updated at grid point $x_k$ by

$$A^{\mathrm{a}}(x_k) = A^{\mathrm{f}}(x_k) S(x_k) \in \mathbb{R}^{1 \times M}$$

with the transformation matrix $S(x_k) \in \mathbb{R}^{M \times M}$ given by[5]

$$S(x_k) = \left(I + \frac{1}{M-1}(HA^{\mathrm{f}})^{\mathrm{T}}(\tilde{C}_k R^{-1})HA^{\mathrm{f}}\right)^{-1/2}.$$

The complete set of analysis ensemble anomalies is collected in

$$A^{\mathrm{a}} = \begin{bmatrix} A^{\mathrm{a}}(x_1) \\ A^{\mathrm{a}}(x_2) \\ \vdots \\ A^{\mathrm{a}}(x_{N_d}) \end{bmatrix} \in \mathbb{R}^{N_d \times M}.$$

The localised update for the forecast ensemble mean $\bar{z}_M^{\mathrm{f}} \in \mathbb{R}^{N_d}$ can be written as

$$\bar{z}^{\mathrm{a}}(x_k) = \sum_{i=1}^{M} z_i^{\mathrm{f}}(x_k) w_i(x_k), \qquad k = 1, \ldots, N_d, \tag{8.36}$$

---

[5] This formula is the localised version of the update formula (7.22) derived previously in Chapter 7. The only difference is that the inverse error covariance matrix $R^{-1}$ is replaced by $\tilde{C}_k R^{-1}$.

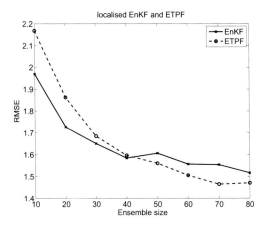

localised EnKF and ETPF

**Figure 8.9** Spatially- and temporally-averaged RMSEs for the localised EnKF with perturbed observations and the localised ETPF for ensemble sizes $M \in \{10, 20, \ldots, 80\}$. We only display the smallest RMSEs over a range of localisation radii and inflation/rejuvenation factors.

with the vectors $w(x_k) \in \mathbb{R}^M$ given by

$$w(x_k) = \frac{1}{M}\mathbf{1} - \frac{1}{M-1}S(x_k)^2 (A^{\mathrm{f}})^{\mathrm{T}} H^{\mathrm{T}} (\tilde{C}_k R^{-1}) \left( H\bar{z}_M^{\mathrm{f}} - y_{\mathrm{obs}} \right).$$

(Compare (7.23) and (7.24) from Chapter 7.)

We note that it is possible to replace the update (8.36) for the ensemble mean by

$$\bar{z}^{\mathrm{a}} = \bar{z}_M^{\mathrm{f}} - K_{\mathrm{loc}}(H\bar{z}_M^{\mathrm{f}} - y_{\mathrm{obs}}).$$

However, the formulation (8.36) is to be preferred if $M \ll N_y$, since the computation of $K_{\mathrm{loc}}$ requires the inversion of a non-diagonal $N_y \times N_y$ matrix.

---

**Example 8.19**  We return to the Lorenz-96 model (8.17) in the setting of Example 8.10 and investigate the impact of localisation on the behaviour of ensemble-based filtering algorithms. To make the problem even more challenging, we observe only every second grid point in time intervals of $\Delta t_{\mathrm{out}} = 0.11$ with the variance of the independent measurement errors increased to 8.0. A total of 10000 assimilation steps are performed. We implement B-localisation for the EnKF with perturbed observations with multiplicative inflation $\alpha \in \{1.0, 1.02, \ldots, 1.12\}$ and for localisation radii $r_{\mathrm{loc}} \in \{1/3, 2/3, \ldots, 10/3\}$ and localisation function (8.29). Recall that $\Delta x = 1/3$ for the Lorenz-96 model. The results can be found in Figure 8.9 where the smallest averaged RMSE is displayed.

---

We now extend the idea of R-localisation to the ETPF from Chapter 7. Since the ensemble Kalman filters and the ETPF both rely on a linear transformation of type (7.7), an application of R-localisation to a ETPF is rather straightforward. The ETPF Algorithm 7.10 uses a transformation

$$z_j^{\mathrm{a}} = \sum_{i'=1}^{M} z_i^{\mathrm{f}} p_{ij}$$

of the forecast into the analysis ensemble with the transform matrix $P = MT^*$ being determined by importance sampling and an associated linear transport problem. To implement R-localisation for the ETPF we proceed essentially as for the LETKF, i.e., we define separate transformation matrices $P(x_k)$ for each grid point $x_k$, $k = 1, \ldots, N_d$. We summarise the resulting filter algorithm in the following definition.

**Definition 8.20** (R-localisation for ETPF) We define a localised/weighted distance between two ensemble members $z_{i_1}^f, z_{i_2}^f \in \mathbb{R}^{N_d}$ at a grid point $x_k$ as follows:

$$\|z_{i_1}^f - z_{i_2}^f\|_k^2 = \sum_{l=1}^{N_d} \rho \left( \frac{|x_k - x_l|_L}{r_{\text{loc}}} \right) (z_{i_1}^f(x_l) - z_{i_2}^f(x_l))^2. \tag{8.37}$$

This distance represents a weighted averaged difference between the two ensemble members over neighbouring gridpoints.

We also localise the impact of observations by modifying the likelihood of $z_i^f$ with respect to a set of observations to

$$w_i(x_k) \propto \exp \left( -\frac{1}{2} (y_{\text{obs}} - Hz_i^f)^{\text{T}} (\tilde{C}_k R^{-1}) (y_{\text{obs}} - Hz_i^f) \right), \tag{8.38}$$

for $i = 1, \ldots, M$ with the diagonal matrix $\tilde{C}_k$ defined by (8.35). Again we have assumed that only grid values of $u(x, t)$ are being observed and that the measurement error covariance matrix $R$ is diagonal. The optimal coupling matrix $T^*(x_k) \in \mathbb{R}^{M \times M}$ at grid point $x_k$ is obtained as the solution to the linear transport problem coupling the two probability vectors $w(x_k)$ and $1/M$ under the distance $\| \cdot \|_k$. Finally the analysis ensemble at grid point $x_k$ is given by

$$z_j^a(x_k) = \sum_{i=1}^M z_i^f(x_k) p_{ij}(x_k), \qquad j = 1, \ldots, M,$$

where $p_{ij}(x_k) = Mt_{ij}^*(x_k)$.

We note that different localisation radii can be used in (8.37) and (8.38). Computationally it is most efficient to set $r_{\text{loc}} = 0$ in (8.37) since it reduces the associated distance to

$$\|z_{i_1}^f - z_{i_2}^f\|_k^2 = (z_{i_1}^f(x_k) - z_{i_2}^f(x_k))^2 \tag{8.39}$$

and the linear transport problem to an univariate transport problem which can be solved very efficiently using the algorithm from Appendix 5.8.

Alternatively, we could process observations sequentially which would lead to a separate linear transport problem for each observation with "localised" cost function defined by the distance $\|z_{i_1}^f - z_{i_2}^f\|_k^2$, where the index $k$ now refers to the location $\mathfrak{r}_k$ of the $k$th observation. Furthermore, the impact of the resulting coupling matrix $T^*(\mathfrak{r}_k)$ on the forecast ensemble would be limited to grid points in the vicinity of $\mathfrak{r}_k$ as done in B-localisation.

We have seen in Example 8.16 that particle filters are unable to track reference solutions of the Lorenz-96 model unless the ensemble size is increased to the order of $10^2$. We now demonstrate that this situation can be rectified with the localised ETPF.

---

**Example 8.21**   We repeat the experiment set out in Example 8.19 with the localised EnKF being replaced by the localised ETPF implementation of Algorithm 7.10. The spatially- and temporally-averaged RMSEs for ensemble sizes $M \in \{10, 20 \ldots, 80\}$ can be found in Figure 8.9. The localised ETPF outperforms the localised EnKF for ensemble sizes $M \geq 50$. The computational costs of a localised ETPF update are, however, significantly higher than those for ensemble Kalman filter implementations. See Cheng & Reich (2013) for more details.

---

## Problems

**8.1**   Consider a Gaussian random variable $X$ in $N_x \gg 1$ dimensions with mean zero and covariance matrix $P = \sigma^2 I$. We set $\sigma^2 = N_x^{-1}$ and consider the associated univariate random variable

$$Y := \|X\| = \sqrt{\sum_{i=1}^{N_x} X_i^2}$$

with PDF

$$\pi_Y(y) \propto r^{N_x - 1} e^{-\frac{r^2}{2}}, \qquad r := N_x^{1/2} y \geq 0.$$

Plot $\pi_Y$ as a function of $y \in [0, 2]$ for $N_x = 1$, $N_x = 10$, $N_x = 100$, and $N_x = 200$. Discuss the implications of your results on the behaviour of the multivariate random variable $X$ as $N_x$ increases.

**8.2**   Repeat the numerical experiment from Example 8.4 with the advecting velocity field (8.7) replaced by the time-independent field $a(x) = \sin(2\pi x)$. Compare the resulting approximation at $t = 1$ for $N_d = 100$ grid points with those for $N_d = 20$. Find the analytic solution to the differential equation

$$\frac{dx}{dt} = \sin(2\pi x)$$

for initial conditions $x(0) \in [0, 1]$. Compare the exact solution for initial $x(0) = 1/4$ at $t = 1$ with the approximations from Euler's method for step-sizes $\Delta t = 0.001$, $\Delta t = 0.01$, and $\Delta t = 0.1$. Which rate of convergence to the true solution is observed as $\Delta t$ is decreased?

**8.3**   Repeat the numerical experiment from Example 8.5 after replacing the advecting velocity field (8.7) with the time-independent field $a(x) = \sin(2\pi x)$. Compare the results to those obtained in Problem 8.2 for $N_d = 100$ and $N_d = 20$.

**8.4**   Implement the Lorenz-96 model with $F = 8$ in the setting of Example 8.15 and integrate the equations using the forward Euler method with step-size $\Delta t = 0.001$ over a time interval $[0, 8]$. The initial ensemble is drawn from a Gaussian distribution with mean $\overline{u}^0 = 0$ and covariance matrix $P = I$. Compare the time evolution of the leading eigenvalue of the empirical covariance matrix for ensemble sizes $M = 10, 20, 40, 80$ and $M = 100$ with those displayed in Figure 8.6. Repeat the experiment for different realisations of the initial ensemble drawn from the Gaussian $N(0, I)$ distribution.

**8.5** Implement the EnKF with perturbed observations with fixed ensemble inflation parameter $\alpha = 1.15$ for the Lorenz-96 model. Follow the implementation details from Example 8.10. Note that ensemble inflation is applied prior to the EnKF analysis step. Compute spatially- and temporally-averaged RMSEs for ensembles of size $M = 20$ and $M = 26$. Compare your results to those from Figure 8.7.

**8.6** Verify formula (8.22).

**8.7** Recompute the localisation matrix C from Example 8.16, with the filter function (8.28) replaced by (8.29).

**8.8** Verify that $H(C \circ P_M^f)H^T = \hat{C} \circ (HP_M^f H^T)$, given that the entries $h_{ij}$ of the linear forward operator $H$ satisfy $h_{ij} \in \{0, 1\}$ and $\sum_{j=1}^{N_d} h_{ij} = 1$ for all $i = 1, \ldots, N_y$.

**8.9** Implement B-localisation for the EnKF with perturbed observations and apply your implementation to the Lorenz-96 model as outlined in Example 8.19. Use ensemble sizes of $M \in \{10, 20, \ldots, 80\}$ with associated localisation radii given by[6]

| $M$ | 10 | 20 | 30 | 40 | 50 | 60 | 70 | 80 |
|---|---|---|---|---|---|---|---|---|
| $r_{\text{loc}}$ | 2/3 | 4/3 | 6/3 | 6/3 | 7/3 | 7/3 | 8/3 | 8/3 |

and inflation parameters $\alpha \in \{1.0, 1.02, \ldots, 1.12\}$.

## 8.4 Guide to literature

An excellent textbook on PDEs is Evans (1998). A deeper dynamical systems perspective on PDEs is given in Robinson (2001). A solid introduction to the numerics of evolution equations such as those considered in this chapter can be found in Ascher (2008).

Standard ensemble inflation and localisation techniques for ensemble Kalman filters are covered in Evensen (2006).

The estimation of optimal inflation factor $\alpha$ has been investigated in a number of publications. Anderson (2007) suggested treating the unknown $\alpha$ as part of the state estimation problem, then applying data assimilation to the combined state-parameter estimation problem. Alternatively, a hierarchical Bayesian approach to the estimation of the prior distribution for the Bayesian assimilation step was suggested by Bocquet & Sakov (2012), putting a Jeffreys prior on the covariance matrix to be estimated. A third option is provided by a Gaussian approach to covariance inflation proposed by Miyoshi (2011).

[6] Recall that $\Delta x = 1/3$ for the Lorenz-96 model. Hence $r_{\text{loc}} = 2/3 = 2\Delta x$, for example.

A recent comparison between R- and B-localisation can be found in Nerger et al. (2012) and references cited therein. An adaptive localisation algorithm was proposed by Anderson (2012). See also Majda & Harlim (2012) for further discussions on the application of ensemble-based filter techniques to spatially extended systems. Majda & Harlim (2012) introduce, in particular, the idea of localisation for linear PDEs in spectral space.

The failure of standard particle filters in high dimensions is studied and explained in Bengtsson et al. (2008). Extending particle filters to spatio-temporal Markov processes is a very active area of research. Several authors have introduced alternative proposal steps into the particle filter which lead to forecast ensemble members $z_i^{\mathrm{f}}$ with high and nearly uniform likelihoods $\pi_Y(z_i^{\mathrm{f}}|y_{\mathrm{obs}})$. For example, a combined particle and Kalman filter is proposed in van Leeuwen (2010) and van Leeuwen & Ades (2013) (see also the discussion in Bocquet, Pires & Wu (2010)), while in Chorin, Morzfeld & Tu (2010), Morzfeld, Tu, Atkins & Chorin (2012), and Morzfeld & Chorin (2012), forecast ensemble members $z_i^{\mathrm{f}}$ are defined by means of implicit equations. See also Reich (2013a).

More details on the localised ETPF, including numerical results for the Lorenz-96 model, can be found in Cheng & Reich (2013). The idea of localised particle filters also appears in Rebeschini & van Handel (2013).

# 9 Dealing with imperfect models

Recall from our discussion in the Preface that Laplace's demon possessed (i) a perfect mathematical model of the physical process under consideration, (ii) a snapshot of the state of that process at an arbitrary point in the past or the present, and (iii) infinite computational resources to unravel explicit solutions of the mathematical model. In Chapter 1 we discussed these aspects in a very simplified mathematical setting where physical processes were reduced to one set of mathematical equations (the surrogate physical process) and the mathematical model was represented by a system of difference equations. We also discussed partial and noisy observations of state space as presentations of our knowledge about the surrogate physical process, and briefly touched upon the issue of numerical approximation errors, which arise from putting a mathematical model into algorithmic form amenable to computer implementations. However, contrary to these general considerations made in Chapter 1, we have mostly limited the discussion of data assimilation algorithms in Chapters 6 to 8 to an even more simplified setting where the mathematical model is assumed to be a perfect replica of the surrogate physical process. In other words, the same model has been used both for generating the surrogate physical process and for making predictions about this process. We also generally assumed that the mathematical models come in algorithmic form and discretisation errors were discarded. This setting is called an *ideal twin experiment*. Within a perfect model setting, uncertainty only arises from incomplete knowledge of the model's initial state. A slight generalisation of this perfect model scenario arises when the surrogate physical process is a particular realisation of the stochastic difference equation which is used for producing forecasts. In that case, forecast uncertainties are caused by the unknown distribution of initial conditions and the unknown realisations of the stochastic contributions to the evolution equation.

In this chapter, we will discuss how to deal with imperfect models and parameter dependent families of imperfect models from a Bayesian perspective. Again our situation will be simplified by the assumption that the underlying reference solution is generated by a known computational model. However, different computational models will be used for making forecasts and for producing observations.

A key problem with an imperfect model setting is that computed forecast ensemble distributions might not be fully representative of actual forecast uncertainties. This is particularly worrisome if the forecast ensemble spread is too small relative to an ensemble spread from a perfect model setting. One solution is to use ensemble inflation, as introduced in Chapter 8, in order to artificially increase ensemble spreads. At the same time we are often faced with the problem of having to evaluate the performance of several imperfect models. This leads us to the topic of *model comparison*. In this chapter, we start with comparing models based on their *evidence* with respect to the available observations. This discussion will then be extended to adapting model parameters using observations. Here we will focus on ensemble-based parameter estimation techniques instead of the more classical maximum likelihood estimators. Ensemble-based methods have the advantage that they not only provide a "best" fit estimate of the parameter, but also a characterisation of the uncertainty in this value.

In the second part of this chapter we will discuss mollified formulations of sequential data assimilation algorithms. These formulations allow us to view data assimilation algorithms as *nudging* terms added to a model in order to "steer" model states towards closer agreement with the unknown reference solution. Nudging is often used in the presence of strong model errors and unreliable quantification of forecast uncertanties. We will also discuss the treatment of nonlinear forward operators in the context of ensemble Kalman filters.

## 9.1        Model selection

Recall the importance sampling approach to Bayesian inference: given an ensemble $z_i^f$ of $M$ realisations with weights $w_i^f \geq 0$ from a forecast PDF $\pi_{Z^f}$, the analysis ensemble is characterised by new weights

$$w_i^a \propto w_i^f \pi_Y(y_{\mathrm{obs}}|z_i^f),$$

where the constant of proportionality is chosen such that

$$\sum_{i=1}^{M} w_i^a = 1.$$

The constant of proportionality is explicitly given by

$$E(y_{\mathrm{obs}}) := \sum_{i=1}^{M} w_i^f \pi_Y(y_{\mathrm{obs}}|z_i^f)$$

and provides a Monte Carlo approximation to the marginal PDF

$$\pi_Y(y) = \int_{\mathbb{R}^N} \pi_Y(y|z)\pi_{Z^f}(z)\mathrm{d}z$$

evaluated at $y = y_{\mathrm{obs}}$. The normalisation factor $\pi_Y(y_{\mathrm{obs}})$, and its numerical approximation by $E(y_{\mathrm{obs}})$, play a key role in this section.

More specifically, we compare different models based on their fit to given observations. Here a model, denoted by $\mathcal{M}$, consists of an initial PDF $\pi_Z(z, t_0)$

and evolution equations for evolving ensemble members $z_i(t_n)$, $i = 1, \ldots, M$, with initial conditions drawn from $\pi_Z(0, t_0)$. Let us assume that we are given $L$ such models, which we denote by $\mathcal{M}_l$. These models may differ by their initial PDFs, the evolution equations or both. Identical sets of observations are then applied to each of the models in order to perform sequential data assimilation using any of the assimilation methods from Chapter 7. The novel aspect is that, in addition to performing the assimilation steps, we also compute the ensemble-based *evidence* or *likelihood* for each model.

**Definition 9.1** (Model evidence/likelihood)  Let

$$Y_{t_{1:N_{\text{obs}}}} = (Y(t_1), \ldots, Y(t_{N_{\text{obs}}})) : \Omega \to \mathbb{R}^{N_y \times N_{\text{obs}}},$$

be the random variable describing observations at times $t_1 < t_2 < \cdots < t_{N_{\text{obs}}}$. Given a model $\mathcal{M}$ that provides a joint distribution for a discrete stochastic process $\{Z(t_k)\}_{k=0}^{N_{\text{obs}}}$, which for notational convenience is now abbreviated as

$$Z_{t_{0:N_{\text{obs}}}} = (Z(t_0), Z(t_1), \ldots, Z(t_{N_{\text{obs}}})) : \Omega \to \mathbb{R}^{N_z \times (N_{\text{obs}}+1)},$$

we write the marginal distribution (recall Lemma 2.16) for $Y_{t_{1:N_{\text{obs}}}}$ as

$$\pi_{Y_{t_{1:N_{\text{obs}}}}}(y_{t_{1:N_{\text{obs}}}} | \mathcal{M}) = \mathbb{E}\left[\pi_{Y_{t_{1:N_{\text{obs}}}}}\left(y_{t_{1:N_{\text{obs}}}} | Z_{t_{0:N_{\text{obs}}}}\right)\right], \tag{9.1}$$

for all

$$y_{t_{1:N_{\text{obs}}}} = (y(t_1), \ldots, y(t_{N_{\text{obs}}})) \in \mathbb{R}^{N_y \times N_{\text{obs}}}.$$

Here the expectation is taken over all possible trajectories $z_{t_{0:N_{\text{obs}}}} = Z_{t_{0:N_{\text{obs}}}}(\omega)$ of the model $\mathcal{M}$.

Given a sequence of actual observations

$$y_{t_{1:N_{\text{obs}}}}^{\text{obs}} = (y_{\text{obs}}(t_1), \ldots, y_{\text{obs}}(t_{N_{\text{obs}}})) \in \mathbb{R}^{N_y \times N_{\text{obs}}},$$

the *evidence* or *likelihood* of the data $y_{t_{1:N_{\text{obs}}}}^{\text{obs}}$ under the model $\mathcal{M}$, is then defined as $\pi_{Y_{t_{1:N_{\text{obs}}}}}(y_{t_{1:N_{\text{obs}}}}^{\text{obs}} | \mathcal{M})$.

A higher value evidence suggests that a model fits better with the available data. Of course, it is feasible that a certain model might provide a better fit to certain data sets, while another model might be better for others. We could alternatively use any of the scoring rules from Chapter 4, which can be used to assess sequences of analysis ensembles as well as the forecast ensembles as they were introduced in that chapter. However, we will concentrate on the calculation of evidence in this chapter since it makes a link to posterior probability distributions via Bayes' theorem.

We now make the usual assumption that given a realisation of the model $\mathcal{M}$, the observations are mutually independent, and $y_{\text{obs}}(t_k)$ has a PDF that only has conditional dependence on $z(t_k)$, for $1 \le k \le N_{\text{obs}}$. This means that we may write

$$\pi_{Y_{t_{1:N_{\mathrm{obs}}}}}\left(y_{t_{1:N_{\mathrm{obs}}}}^{\mathrm{obs}} | \mathcal{M}\right) = \mathbb{E}\left[\prod_{k=1}^{N_{\mathrm{obs}}} \pi_Y(y_{\mathrm{obs}}(t_k) | Z(t_k))\right]. \tag{9.2}$$

A Monte Carlo approximation to the formulation in Equation (9.2) would involve obtaining an ensemble of $M$ realisations of the model $\mathcal{M}$,

$$(z_i(t_0), z_i(t_1), z_i(t_2), \ldots, z_i(t_{N_{\mathrm{obs}}})), \quad i = 1, \ldots, M,$$

and then computing the ensemble average

$$E(y_{t_{1:N_{\mathrm{obs}}}}^{\mathrm{obs}}) = \frac{1}{M} \sum_{i=1}^{M} \prod_{k=1}^{N_{\mathrm{obs}}} \pi_Y(y_{\mathrm{obs}}(t_k) | z_i(t_k)), \tag{9.3}$$

where $\pi_Y(y|z)$ denotes the standard likelihood function for a state $z$ given an observation $y$. This Monte Carlo approximation will suffer from the same problems as the particle filter without resampling, i.e., the distribution of weights

$$w_i = \prod_{k=1}^{N_{\mathrm{obs}}} \pi_Y(y_{\mathrm{obs}}(t_k) | z_i(t_k)) \tag{9.4}$$

will be highly non-uniform. This is because it is very unlikely that any of the realisations $Z_{t_{0:N_{\mathrm{obs}}}}(\omega)$ will be close to the data: a huge number of trajectories are required to obtain an accurate approximation of the evidence. We would prefer to use an adaptive resampling approach that only computes weights for trajectories sufficiently close to the data.

To facilitate a resampling approach, we rewrite Equation (9.2) using the disintegration formula (see Definition 2.15) applied to a conditional probability to obtain

$$\pi_{Y_{t_{1:N_{\mathrm{obs}}}}}\left(y_{t_{1:N_{\mathrm{obs}}}} | \mathcal{M}\right) = \mathbb{E}\left[\pi_{Y_{t_{1:N_{\mathrm{obs}}}}}\left(y_{t_{1:N_{\mathrm{obs}}}} | Z_{t_{0:N_{\mathrm{obs}}}}\right)\right]$$

$$= \mathbb{E}\left[\prod_{k=1}^{N_{\mathrm{obs}}} \pi_Y\left(y(t_k) | y_{t_{1:k-1}}, Z_{t_{0:k}}\right)\right]$$

$$= \mathbb{E}\left[\prod_{k=1}^{N_{\mathrm{obs}}} \pi_Y(y(t_k) | Z_{t_k}^{\mathrm{f}})\right]$$

$$= \prod_{k=1}^{N_{\mathrm{obs}}}\left(\int_{\mathcal{Z}} \pi_Y(y(t_k) | z) \pi_Z(z, t_k | y_{t_{1:k-1}}) \, \mathrm{d}z\right), \tag{9.5}$$

where (as in previous chapters) $\pi_Z(z, t_k | y_{t_{1:k-1}})$ denotes the PDF for the forecast $Z^{\mathrm{f}}$ at $t_k$ which is conditional on all observations up to and including $t_{k-1}$. Approximations of (9.5) can be based on an SIR or ETPF filter, recursively generating equally weighted forecast ensembles from the forecast PDFs $\pi_Z(z, t_k | y_{t_{1:k-1}})$. The evidence can thus be computed by calculating with stochastic processes that stay sufficiently close to the data. This leads to the following algorithmic implementation of (9.5).

**Algorithm 9.2** (Computing model evidence)   Given a set of observations $y_{\text{obs}}(t_k)$, $k = 1 \ldots, N_{\text{obs}}$, at observation times $t_k = k\Delta t_{\text{out}}$, a dynamic model $\mathcal{M}$, and an initial ensemble $\{z_i^a(t_0)\}$, the model evidence (9.5) can be recursively approximated using

$$E_k = E_{k-1} \left\{ \frac{1}{M} \sum_{i=1}^{M} \pi_Y(y_{\text{obs}}(t_k)|z_i^f(t_k)) \right\} \tag{9.6}$$

with initial value $E_0 = 1$. Then

$$E(y_{t_{1:N_{\text{obs}}}}^{\text{obs}} | \mathcal{M}) := E_{N_{\text{obs}}}$$

provides a Monte Carlo approximation to $\pi_{Y_{t_{1:N_{\text{obs}}}}}(y_{t_{1:N_{\text{obs}}}}^{\text{obs}} | \mathcal{M})$. Here $\{z_i^f(t_k)\}$ denotes the model generated forecast ensemble at observation time $t_k$ which is based on an equally weighted analysis ensemble $\{z_i^a(t_{k-1})\}$ at time $t_{k-1}$. The desired ensembles can be computed using either the SIR particle filter or the ETPF from Chapter 7, with resampling after each assimilation step.

---

**Example 9.3**   We return to the imperfect model setting from Chapter 1. Recall that a reference solution $z_{\text{ref}}(t) = (x_{\text{ref}}(t), y_{\text{ref}}(t), z_{\text{ref}}(t))^{\text{T}} \in \mathbb{R}^3$ is generated in Example 1.1 from a perturbed Lorenz-63 model. Given this reference solution, observations $x_{\text{obs}}(t_k)$ for $t_k = k\Delta t_{\text{out}}$ of the x-component are then generated in intervals of $\Delta t_{\text{out}} = 0.05$, using the computational procedure described in Example 1.2. Furthermore, we have defined a forward model for this observation process in Example 2.20 of the form

$$x_{\text{obs}}(t_k) = x_{\text{ref}}(t_k) + \xi_k,$$

where $\{\xi_k\}$ are independent realisations of Gaussian random variables with mean zero and variance $R = 1/15$. Finally we have also constructed a stochastic model (4.18)–(4.20) in Chapter 4 with the stochastic forcing terms being Gaussian with mean zero and variance $\sigma^2 = 0.0838$ in each solution component. We now assess the fit of this stochastic model by computing its evidence with respect to the available observational data. We do this to compare the variance value $\sigma^2 = 0.0838$ to other values from the range $\{0.02, 0.05, 0.1, 0.2\}$. Hence we have $L = 5$ models $\mathcal{M}_l$, which we can compare against each other in terms of their evidence. The computations are performed for ensembles of size $M - 1000$ with the initial ensemble drawn from a Gaussian with mean equal to the value of the reference solution at $t = 0$ and covariance matrix $P^0 = 1/15I$. The computed evidence along 200 observations is then averaged over 100 independent draws of the initial ensemble from $N(z_{\text{ref}}(0), P^0)$. The results from an SIR particle filter implementation without particle rejuvenation can be found in Figure 9.1. The numerical results confirm that $\sigma^2 = 0.0838$ is a good choice for the stochastic forcing term. We also found that slightly larger or smaller values of $\sigma^2$ lead to similar values for the averaged evidence.

---

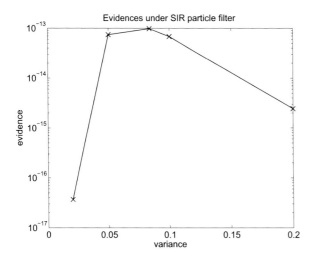

**Figure 9.1** Evidence of the stochastic Lorenz-63 model along observations $x_{\rm obs}(t_k)$, $k = 1, \ldots, 200$, for different values of the variance $\sigma^2$ of the stochastic forcing terms. Results from an SIR particle filter are averaged over 100 initial ensembles drawn from $N(z_{\rm ref}(0), P^0)$. In each case the ensemble size is $M = 1000$. The evidence for the SIR filter is largest for $\sigma^2 \in \{0.05, 0.0838, 0.1\}$. Outside this range the evidence quickly falls off, indicating a poorer match between the resulting stochastic model and the underlying reference model from which the observations are generated.

**Example 9.4**  Let us discuss Equation (9.2) for deterministic model dynamics in some more detail. Since

$$Z(t_k) = \psi^k(Z(t_0))$$

for an appropriate map $\psi$, we obtain

$$\pi_{Y_{t_{1:N_{\rm obs}}}}(y_{t_{1:N_{\rm obs}}}|z(t_0), \mathcal{M}) = \prod_{k=1}^{N_{\rm obs}} \pi_Y(y(t_k)|\psi^k(z(t_0))) \qquad (9.7)$$

and

$$\pi_{Y_{t_{1:N_{\rm obs}}}}(y_{t_{1:N_{\rm obs}}}|\mathcal{M}) = \mathbb{E}\left[ \prod_{k=1}^{N_{\rm obs}} \pi_Y(y(t_k)|\psi^k(Z(t_0))) \right]$$

$$= \int_{\mathcal{Z}} \prod_{k=1}^{N_{\rm obs}} \pi_Y(y(t_k)|\psi^k(z)) \, \pi_Z(z, t_0) dz.$$

If a large number of accurate observations $\{y_{\rm obs}(t_k)\}$ are available then it makes sense to approximate the evidence $\pi_{Y_{t_{1:N_{\rm obs}}}}(y_{t_{1:N_{\rm obs}}}^{\rm obs}|\mathcal{M})$ using *Laplace's method* from Chapter 3. More precisely, define

$$g(z) := -\ln\left\{ \prod_{k=1}^{N_{\rm obs}} \pi_Y(y_{\rm obs}(t_k)|\psi^k(z)) \, \pi_Z(z, t_0) \right\}$$

and let $\hat{z}$ denote the MAP estimate,

$$\hat{z} = \arg\min g(z).$$

Here we have suppressed an explicit dependence of $g$ on the model $\mathcal{M}$ and the data $y^{\text{obs}}_{t_1:N_{\text{obs}}}$. An application of Laplace's method is now based on the quadratic approximation

$$g(z) \approx g(\hat{z}) + \frac{1}{2}(z - \hat{z})^{\text{T}} D^2 g(\hat{z})(z - \hat{z}), \tag{9.8}$$

i.e.,

$$\pi_{Y_{t_1:N_{\text{obs}}}}(y_{t_1:N_{\text{obs}}}|\mathcal{M}) \approx e^{-g(\hat{z})} \int_{\mathcal{Z}} e^{-\frac{1}{2}(z-\hat{z})^{\text{T}} D^2 g(\hat{z})(z-\hat{z})} \mathrm{d}z$$

$$= e^{-g(\hat{z})}(2\pi)^{N_z/2}|D^2 g(\hat{z})|^{-1/2} .$$

See Chapter 3 for further details. Here $D^2 g(\hat{z}) \in \mathbb{R}^{N_z \times N_z}$ denotes the Hessian matrix of second-order partial derivatives of $g$.

We mention in passing that further approximations to the quadratic contribution in (9.8) lead to the *Bayesian information criterion* (BIC) for model comparison (Hastie et al. 2009).

In the Bayesian setting, it may be the case that we have also developed some prior experience of which of the models is more appropriate. Each model $\mathcal{M}_l$ would then be given a prior probability $\mathbb{P}(\mathcal{M}_l)$, in order to make a *Bayesian model comparison*. For simplicity, consider the case of two models $\mathcal{M}_1$ and $\mathcal{M}_2$ with evidence $\pi_{Y_{t_1:N_{\text{obs}}}}\left(y^{\text{obs}}_{t_1:N_{\text{obs}}}|\mathcal{M}_1\right)$ and $\pi_{Y_{t_1:N_{\text{obs}}}}\left(y^{\text{obs}}_{t_1:N_{\text{obs}}}|\mathcal{M}_2\right)$, respectively. The posterior model probabilities are then simply defined by

$$\mathcal{P}(\mathcal{M}_1|y^{\text{obs}}_{t_1:N_{\text{obs}}}) = \frac{\pi_{Y_{t_1:N_{\text{obs}}}}(y^{\text{obs}}_{t_1:N_{\text{obs}}}|\mathcal{M}_1)\mathbb{P}(\mathcal{M}_1)}{\pi_{Y_{t_1:N_{\text{obs}}}}(y^{\text{obs}}_{t_1:N_{\text{obs}}}|\mathcal{M}_1)\mathbb{P}(\mathcal{M}_1) + \pi_{Y_{t_1:N_{\text{obs}}}}(y^{\text{obs}}_{t_1:N_{\text{obs}}}|\mathcal{M}_2)\mathbb{P}(\mathcal{M}_2)}$$

and

$$\mathcal{P}(\mathcal{M}_2|y^{\text{obs}}_{t_1:N_{\text{obs}}}) = \frac{\pi_{Y_{t_1:N_{\text{obs}}}}(y^{\text{obs}}_{t_1:N_{\text{obs}}}|\mathcal{M}_2)\mathbb{P}(\mathcal{M}_2)}{\pi_{Y_{t_1:N_{\text{obs}}}}(y^{\text{obs}}_{t_1:N_{\text{obs}}}|\mathcal{M}_1)\mathbb{P}(\mathcal{M}_1) + \pi_{Y_{t_1:N_{\text{obs}}}}(y^{\text{obs}}_{t_1:N_{\text{obs}}}|\mathcal{M}_2)\mathbb{P}(\mathcal{M}_2)},$$

respectively. If there is no initial preference for one or the other model then we would choose

$$\mathbb{P}(\mathcal{M}_2) = \mathbb{P}(\mathcal{M}_1) - 1/2$$

as the prior probabilities. However, past experience with the models might suggest different relative probabilities; the Bayesian model comparison framework allows us to take this into account.

The extent to which observations support $\mathcal{M}_1$ over $\mathcal{M}_2$, characterised by the ratio

$$\frac{\mathcal{P}(\mathcal{M}_1|y^{\text{obs}}_{t_1:N_{\text{obs}}})}{\mathcal{P}(\mathcal{M}_2|y^{\text{obs}}_{t_1:N_{\text{obs}}})} = \frac{\pi_{Y_{t_1:N_{\text{obs}}}}(y^{\text{obs}}_{t_1:N_{\text{obs}}}|\mathcal{M}_1)}{\pi_{Y_{t_1:N_{\text{obs}}}}(y^{\text{obs}}_{t_1:N_{\text{obs}}}|\mathcal{M}_2)} \times \frac{\mathbb{P}(\mathcal{M}_1)}{\mathbb{P}(\mathcal{M}_2)},$$

is called the *posterior odds* for $\mathcal{M}_1$ against $\mathcal{M}_2$.

## 9.2      Parameter estimation

If the forecast model involves free parameters (such as the parameters $\sigma$, $\rho$ and $\beta$ in the Lorenz model (1.4)) then it is clearly useful to compare the outcome of different parameter choices, as discussed in the previous section. However, it is much more useful to go beyond that, and adaptively select parameters to increase the fit between model forecasts and measurements. This task falls into the broad field of parameter estimation; here we will consider two parameter estimation approaches which fit particularly well with the data assimilation algorithms developed in this book.

To outline the basic ideas let us assume that the forecast model comes in the form of a recursion

$$z^{n+1} = z^n + \delta t f(z^n, \lambda), \qquad (9.9)$$

where the right hand term $f$ now also depends on the parameters $\lambda \in \mathbb{R}^{N_\lambda}$ and $\delta t > 0$ is the step-size such that $t_n = n\delta t$, $n \geq 0$. For simplicity, we restrict the discussion to univariate parameters, i.e., $N_\lambda = 1$. Following the Bayesian perspective taken throughout this book, we treat $\lambda$ as a random variable with a specified prior distribution $\pi_\Lambda$. One way to deal with this is to incorporate $\lambda$ into the state. We rewrite (9.9) in the augmented state-space form

$$z^{n+1} = z^n + \delta t f(z^n, \lambda^n), \qquad (9.10)$$
$$\lambda^{n+1} = \lambda^n, \qquad (9.11)$$

placing the parameter $\lambda$ on equal footing with the state variable $z \in \mathbb{R}^{N_z}$, despite its trivial dynamics. Given an extended ensemble $\{z_i, \lambda_i\}$, $i = 1, \ldots, M$, from the product PDF $\pi_Z(z, t_0)\pi_\Lambda(\lambda)$ for the initial conditions, we can now apply any ensemble-based data assimilation algorithm to recursively update both the state and the parameter upon receiving incoming observations.

**Definition 9.5** (Sequential state parameter estimation with stochastic perturbations)    Given initial (or prior) distributions for the model state $z$ at time $t_0$ and the parameter $\lambda$ and an associated initial ensemble $(z_i^0, \lambda_i^0)$, $i = 1, \ldots, M$, combined *sequential state parameter estimation* is performed by applying an ensemble-based assimilation algorithm to the augmented model

$$z_i^{n+1} = z_i^n + \delta t f(z_i^n, \lambda_i^n), \qquad (9.12)$$
$$\lambda_i^{n+1} = \lambda_i^n + \sqrt{\delta t} \epsilon_i^n \qquad (9.13)$$

for given observations $y_{\text{obs}}(t_k)$ at times $t_k = k\Delta t_{\text{out}}$ and $k = 1, \ldots, N_{\text{obs}}$. Here $\{\epsilon_i^n\}$ are independent realisations of a univariate Gaussian random variable with mean zero and variance $\sigma^2$.

The role of the noise term in the evolution equation for $\lambda$ is to spread out the marginal PDF for $\lambda$ as time progresses, i.e., to increase the spread of the ensemble in $\lambda$. The choice of $\sigma$ is crucial for a good performance of a sequential state parameter estimation algorithm: smaller values for $\sigma$ make the outcome more dependent on the initial distribution $\pi_\Lambda$, while larger values of $\sigma$ can lead to excessive spreading of ensembles. As an alternative to the stochastic perturbations in (9.13) we could also apply ensemble inflation, as introduced for ensemble Kalman filter algorithms. In this case, the strength of the ensemble inflation has a similar impact on the quality of the parameter estimation as the size of $\sigma$.

---

**Example 9.6**   We consider the Lorenz-63 equations in the setting of Example 7.13 from Chapter 7. Recall that the Lorenz-63 model comes in the form of an ordinary differential equation with right hand side given by

$$f(z) = \begin{pmatrix} 10(y - x) \\ x(28 - z) - y \\ xy - 8/3z \end{pmatrix} . \tag{9.14}$$

The state variable is $z = (x, y, z)^{\mathrm{T}} \in \mathbb{R}^3$ and the forward Euler method (9.10) with step-size $\delta t = 0.001$ is used to numerically approximate the reference trajectory $z_{\mathrm{ref}}(t)$. The initial condition for the reference solution is

$$\bar{z}^0 = (-0.587276, -0563678, 16.8708)^{\mathrm{T}}.$$

Let us now assume that the first component in $f$ is replaced by

$$f_{\mathrm{x}}(z) = \lambda(y - x) , \tag{9.15}$$

where $\lambda$ is treated as an unknown parameter with uniform prior distribution $U[7, 11]$ and the initial conditions are distributed according to $N(\bar{z}^0, I)$. We implement the ESRF with $M = 20$ ensemble members and inflation factor $\alpha = 1.005$, over the extended phase space $(z^{\mathrm{T}}, \lambda)^{\mathrm{T}} \in \mathbb{R}^4$ in order to estimate the parameter $\lambda$. Ensemble members are propagated under the forward Euler method (9.12) and observations of $z_{\mathrm{ref}}(t) \in \mathbb{R}^3$ are assimilated in intervals of $\Delta t_{\mathrm{out}} = 0.10$. All three components of the state vector $z$ are observed with a measurement error variance of $R = 8$. Since ensemble inflation is used, the random perturbations $\epsilon_i^n$ in (9.13) are set to zero. The time evolution of the ensemble mean

$$\bar{\lambda}_M = \frac{1}{M} \sum_{i=1}^{M} \lambda_i$$

can be found in Figure 9.2. For comparison we also present results for an increased inflation factor of $\alpha = 1.02$.

---

The sequential parameter adaptation approach is designed to improve the estimate of the parameter $\lambda$ sequentially, as data are received. A more robust alternative is to try to sample directly from the marginalised posterior distribution for $\lambda$, using either importance or rejection sampling. Standard Markov

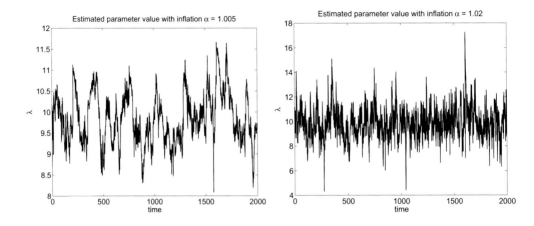

**Figure 9.2** Parameter estimation for the Lorenz-63 model. The ESRF is applied in extended phase space $(z, \lambda)$ in order to estimate the $\lambda$ parameter from noisy observations of the state vector $z$. An ensemble inflation factor of $\alpha = 1.005$ and $\alpha = 1.02$, respectively, is applied and the ensemble size is $M = 20$. The time evolution of the ensemble mean $\bar{\lambda}_M$ is displayed over a time interval $[0, 2000]$. Ensemble inflation leads to a fluctuation of the estimated parameter value about its correct value $\lambda = 10$. The strength of these fluctuations depends on the inflation factor $\alpha$.

chain Monte Carlo methods would produce samples from the joint posterior distribution,

$$\pi_{Z_{t_{0:N_{obs}}}\Lambda}\big(z_{t_{0:N_{obs}}}, \lambda | y^{obs}_{t_{1:N_{obs}}}\big),$$

but we wish to sample from the marginalised posterior distribution

$$\pi_\Lambda(\lambda | y^{obs}_{t_{1:N_{obs}}}) = \int_{\mathcal{Z}^{N_{obs}+1}} \pi_{Z_{t_{0:N_{obs}}}\Lambda}\big(z_{t_{0:N_{obs}}}, \lambda | y^{obs}_{t_{1:N_{obs}}}\big) \mathrm{d}z_{t_{0:N_{obs}}}.$$

Hence, in order to compute the importance weight (or to determine whether to accept or reject the sample in the case of rejection sampling) we need to evaluate this marginalised posterior distribution for particular values of parameters $\lambda$ and observations $y^{obs}_{t_{1:N_{obs}}}$. In other words, we define a particular model $\mathcal{M}_\lambda$ for each proposed $\lambda$ value and compute the evidence for the model $\mathcal{M}_\lambda$. The corresponding evidence formula (9.2) can be approximated by an SIS particle filter.

More specifically, the following Markov chain Monte Carlo algorithm samples from the posterior distribution in the model parameter $\lambda$ given an initial PDF $\pi_Z(\cdot, t_0)$ for the state variable $z \in \mathbb{R}^{N_z}$, a prior PDF $\pi_\Lambda$ for the parameter $\lambda \in \mathbb{R}$, and a fixed set of observations $y_{obs}(t_k)$, $k = 1, \ldots, N_{obs}$, with conditional PDF $\pi_Y(y|z)$.

**Algorithm 9.7** (Pseudo-marginal Markov chain Monte Carlo method)   A sequence of parameters $\lambda_l$, $l = 1, \ldots, L$, from its posterior PDF is obtained by the following Markov chain Monte Carlo method.

Draw a realisation $\lambda_1$ from the distribution $\pi_\Lambda$ and formally set $E_1 = 0$. For $l = 1, \ldots, L$ perform the following steps.

(i) Using the previous accepted parameter $\lambda_l$ with evidence $E_l$, draw an initial ensemble $\{z_i^0\}_{i=1}^M$ from $\pi_Z(\cdot, t_0)$ and a new proposal

$$\lambda^* = \lambda_l + \xi, \tag{9.16}$$

where $\xi$ is a realisation of a random variable with PDF $\pi_\Xi$. This proposal distribution needs to satisfy $\pi_\Xi(\xi) = \pi_\Xi(-\xi)$.

(ii) Compute an ensemble of $M$ trajectories $\{z_i(t_k)\}$ of the model with parameter value $\lambda = \lambda^*$ and initial values $z_i(t_0) = z_i^0$. Determine the associated evidence according to

$$E(y_{t_{1:N_{\mathrm{obs}}}}^{\mathrm{obs}} | \mathcal{M}_{\lambda^*}) := \frac{1}{M} \sum_{i=1}^{M} \prod_{k=1}^{N_{\mathrm{obs}}} \pi_Y(y_{\mathrm{obs}}(t_k) | z_i(t_k)). \tag{9.17}$$

(iii) Accept the proposed $\lambda^*$ with probability

$$p = \min\left\{1, \frac{E^* \, \pi_\Lambda(\lambda^*)}{E_l \, \pi_\Lambda(\lambda_l)}\right\},$$

where the abbreviation $E^* = E(y_{t_{1:N_{\mathrm{obs}}}}^{\mathrm{obs}} | \mathcal{M}_{\lambda^*})$ has been used. If accepted, set $\lambda_{l+1} = \lambda^*$ and $E_{l+1} = E^*$, otherwise continue with $\lambda_{l+1} = \lambda_l$ and $E_{l+1} = E_l$. Increase the index $l$ by one and return to (i) unless $l = L + 1$.

The sequence $\{\lambda_l\}_{l=1}^L$, $L \gg 1$, provides (correlated) samples from the posterior distribution

$$\pi_\Lambda(\lambda | y_{t_{1:N_{\mathrm{obs}}}}^{\mathrm{obs}}) \propto \pi_{Y_{t_{1:N_{\mathrm{obs}}}}}(y_{t_{1:N_{\mathrm{obs}}}}^{\mathrm{obs}} | \lambda) \, \pi_\Lambda(\lambda).$$

Note that this conditional PDF also depends on the choice of $\pi_Z(\cdot, t_0)$. For notational convenience we have suppressed this dependence. The above algorithm is a special instance of the *grouped independence Metropolis–Hastings (GIMH)* Monte Carlo method proposed by Beaumont (2003). The GIMH method does not fit the standard Markov chain Monte Carlo setting since it does not directly evaluate the required marginal PDF, but instead approximates the marginalisation as an ensemble average. However, it can be shown that the algorithm asymptotically samples the posterior PDF as $L \to \infty$ since the computed evidences $E_l$ provides an unbiased approximation to $\pi_{Y_{t_{1:N_{\mathrm{obs}}}}}(y_{t_{1:N_{\mathrm{obs}}}}^{\mathrm{obs}} | \lambda)$ for any finite ensemble size $M$ (Andrieu & Roberts 2009). The GIMH method is also referred to as the *pseudo-marginal Monte Carlo method* which is the term that we use in this book.

The proposal step (9.16) can be replaced by alternative proposals such as directly sampling from the prior distribution $\pi_\Lambda$ in which case the acceptance probability simplifies to

$$p = \min\left\{1, \frac{E^*}{E_l}\right\}.$$

Furthermore, in order to avoid a degeneracy of weights (9.4), we could replace (9.17) by the alternative approximation provided by Algorithm 9.2.

---

**Example 9.8**  We return to the imperfect model setting from Example 9.3, in order to evaluate the evidence for different strength of the stochastic forcing terms in the model (4.18)–(4.20) from Chapter 4. In this example we fix the true variance of the stochastic forcing term to 0.08383 and treat the parameter $\lambda$ in (9.15) as random with uniform prior distribution U[7, 11]. Recall that the value used in the reference model from Example 1.1 is $\lambda = 10$.

We apply Algorithm 9.7 to this problem with proposals $\lambda^*$ directly drawn from U[7, 11]. The distribution of the initial ensemble $z_i^0$, $i = 1, \ldots, M$, $M = 20$, is Gaussian with mean $\bar{z}^0 = (-0.587, -0.563, 16.870)^T$ and diagonal covariance matrix with diagonal entries $1/15$. The estimated evidence $E(y_{t_1:N_{\mathrm{obs}}}^{\mathrm{obs}} | \mathcal{M}_{\lambda^*})$ for each proposed $\lambda^*$ is computed using Algorithm 9.2. The observations of the x component of the state variable as generated in Example 1.2 are used and the likelihood $\pi_Y(y|z)$ is assumed to be Gaussian with variance $R = 1/15$. However we limit the number of assimilated data points to $N_{\mathrm{obs}} = 20$ and $N_{\mathrm{obs}} = 100$, respectively, and investigate its impact on the posterior distribution of the parameter. A total of $L = 10,000$ samples is generated and the resulting histograms for the parameter $\lambda$ are displayed in Figure 9.3.

---

It should be noted that while Algorithm 9.7 allows for mathematically rigorous sampling from the posterior parameter distribution, the sequential approach of Algorithm 9.5 is much easier to implement, in particular when combined with an ensemble Kalman filter. Therefore the later approach is often preferable when considering large systems and parameter distributions that can be assumed to be close to Gaussian.

## 9.3        Mollified data assimilation

In the previous section we described how model errors can be compared and minimised during the data assimilation process. In this section, we describe how model errors can lead to unrealistic dynamics when combined with Bayesian data assimilation. We then introduce techniques that attempt to apply the Bayesian update in a less impulsive manner, with the aim of reducing this effect.

We start with a discussion of model errors in terms of dynamical systems and their attractors. Assume that the underlying surrogate physical process $\{z_{\mathrm{ref}}^n\}_{n \geq 0}$ satisfies a dynamical system

$$z_{\mathrm{ref}}^{n+1} = \psi_{\mathrm{ref}}(z_{\mathrm{ref}}^n),$$

for some appropriate map $\psi_{\mathrm{ref}} : \mathbb{R}^{N_z} \to \mathbb{R}^{N_z}$. On the other hand, assume that

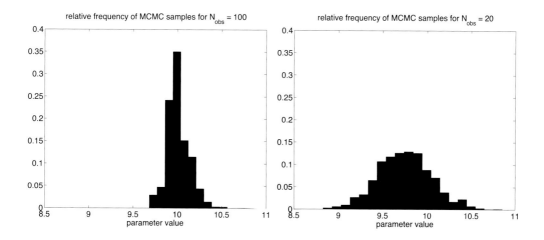

**Figure 9.3** Parameter estimation using the pseudo-marginal Markov chain Monte Carlo method. Samples $\lambda_l$ from the posterior distribution of the $\lambda$ parameter in (9.15) are generated using a total of $N_{\text{obs}} = 100$ (left panel) and $N_{\text{obs}} = 20$ (right panel), respectively, observations. Each histogram is based on 10,000 samples. The proposal step of the pseudo-marginal Markov chain Monte Carlo method uses the SIR particle filter implementation of the underlying data assimilation problem. It can be seen that the larger $N_{\text{obs}}$ value leads to a more focused posterior distribution and the imprint of the prior parameter distribution $U[7,11]$ is reduced.

our forecast model is given by the dynamical system

$$z^{n+1} = \psi(z^n).$$

We assume that both dynamical systems possess unique global attractors $\mathcal{A}_{\text{ref}}$ and $\mathcal{A}$, respectively. We also assume that $z^n \in \mathcal{A}$ and $z^n_{\text{ref}} \in \mathcal{A}_{\text{ref}}$ for $n$ sufficiently large.

Partial observations of $z^n_{\text{ref}}$, $n \geq 0$, are generated according to

$$y^n_{\text{obs}} = h(z^n_{\text{ref}}) + \xi^n,$$

where the variables $\{\xi^n\}$ are independent realisations of a Gaussian $N(0, R)$ random variable. Even if $z^n_{\text{ref}} \in \mathcal{A}_{\text{ref}}$, measurement errors lead to observations that are not consistent with data on the attractor, i.e.,

$$y^n_{\text{obs}} \notin h(\mathcal{A}_{\text{ref}}).$$

To quantify this discrepency, we introduce the distance

$$d(y, \mathcal{B}) = \inf_{y' \in \mathcal{B}} \|y - y'\|$$

between a point $y \in \mathbb{R}^{N_y}$ and a set $\mathcal{B} \subset \mathbb{R}^{N_y}$ in observation space. We see that relatively small measurement errors and large model errors can lead to a situation where

$$d(h(z^n), h(\mathcal{A}_{\text{ref}})) \gg d(y^n_{\text{obs}}, h(\mathcal{A}_{\text{ref}})).$$

If this situation occurs, and $z^n$ is then used as the forecast value $z^f$ in a data assimilation cycle, we can expect that the analysis $z^a$ will be pulled off the attractor $\mathcal{A}$ towards $\mathcal{A}_{\text{ref}}$, i.e.

$$d(h(z^a), h(\mathcal{A})) \gg 0,$$

even though $z^f \in \mathcal{A}$. As a consequence, data assimilation can create analysis states that will trigger the forecast model to readjust rapidly towards its attractor $\mathcal{A}$. These rapid data driven model adjustments are untypical of real trajectories, and we will introduce *mollification* and *nudging* as techniques to reduce them. Furthermore, model generated ensembles might lead to a severe misrepresentation of forecast errors, which puts the Bayesian perspective of data assimilation into question.

Most dynamical systems considered throughout this book have been derived as forward Euler discretisations of an underlying ODE. However, in the current context it is easier to discuss algorithms based on the underlying continuous time ODE formulation. In particular, we reformulate sequential data assimilation for an ensemble prediction model

$$\frac{dz_i}{dt} = f(z_i), \qquad i = 1, \dots, M,$$

in terms of an additional driving or nudging term to the model, i.e.,

$$\frac{dz_i}{dt} = f(z_i) + \sum_{k=1}^{N_{\text{obs}}} \delta(t - t_k) g_i(\{z_j\}_{j=1}^{M}, y_{\text{obs}}(t_k)), \qquad (9.18)$$

where the functions $g_i$, $i = 1, \dots, M$, depend on the whole ensemble and the observations $y_{\text{obs}}(t_k)$. Here, as before, $\delta(s)$ denotes the Dirac delta function. In other words, assimilation of data effectively leads to an *interacting particle system*. We see that each ensemble member propagates independently of the rest of the ensemble, except at observation times $t = t_k$, when it undergoes an impulsive "kick" from the nudging term, designed to keep the overall ensemble close to the observations.

In order to understand the implied mathematical structure, the Dirac delta function should be replaced by a family of approximations $\delta_\varepsilon(s) \geq 0$, $\varepsilon > 0$, with the properties that

$$\int_{\mathbb{R}} \delta_\varepsilon(s) ds = 1,$$

and

$$\lim_{\varepsilon \to 0} \int_{\mathbb{R}} h(s) \delta_\varepsilon(s) ds = h(0),$$

for all smooth functions $h$. Consider, for example, the step-function approximation

$$\delta_\varepsilon(s) = \begin{cases} 0 & \text{for } |s| \geq \varepsilon/2, \\ 1/\varepsilon & \text{otherwise.} \end{cases} \qquad (9.19)$$

Upon replacing the Dirac delta function in (9.18) by $\delta_\varepsilon(s)$ and taking the limit $\varepsilon \to 0$ we find that (9.18) is equivalent to:

(i) integrating the model equations up to time $t_k$, denoting the resulting ensemble by $\{z_i^f\}$, then

(ii) solving the system

$$\frac{dz_i}{ds} = g_i(\{z_j\}_{j=1}^M, y_{obs}(t_k)) \tag{9.20}$$

over a unit time interval in the fictitious time $s \in [0, 1]$ with initial conditions $z_i(0) = z_i^f$, and finally

(iii) using the solutions at $s = 1$ of Equation (9.20) to provide the analysed ensemble $\{z_i^a\}$, which is used as input to the model equations at $t_k$ to advance the ensemble beyond $t_k$ up to the next observation point $t_{k+1}$.

Hence (9.18) is indeed equivalent to sequential ensemble data assimilation, as discussed throughout this book, provided the fictitious dynamics (9.20) can be chosen such that they induce a (possibly only approximate) transformation from the prior to the posterior distribution.

We put the ensemble-based framework aside for a moment, and consider a simple deterministic nudging approach given by

$$\frac{dz}{dt} = f(z) - \sum_{k \geq 1} \delta(t - t_k) B H^T R^{-1}(Hz - y_{obs}(t_k)), \tag{9.21}$$

where $B \in \mathbb{R}^{N_z \times N_z}$ is a positive-definite matrix.[1] This equation is for a single trajectory $z(t)$ that follows the model dynamics until an observation is taken, in which case it is nudged towards the observation. As we have already discussed, this leads to unphysical dynamics for $z$ if it is pulled away from the model attractor $\mathcal{A}$, so we would like to nudge the system in a more "gentle" manner. This can be done by replacing the Dirac delta function with a regularised Dirac delta function,

$$\frac{dz}{dt} = f(z) - \sum_{k \geq 1} \delta_\varepsilon(t - t_k) B H^T R^{-1}(Hz - y_{obs}(t_k)), \tag{9.22}$$

with the parameter $\varepsilon > 0$ chosen appropriately. In particular, the regularised Dirac delta function $\delta_\varepsilon$ needs to be chosen such that solutions $z(t)$ are pulled smoothly towards $z_{ref}(t) \in \mathcal{A}_{ref}$. Hence we replace (9.19) by the continuous function

$$\delta_\varepsilon(s) = \begin{cases} 0 & \text{for } |s| \geq \varepsilon, \\ \varepsilon^{-2}(\varepsilon - |s|) & \text{otherwise.} \end{cases}$$

The system (9.22) can be integrated in time by a standard time-stepping method such as the explicit Euler method or the implicit midpoint rule. The regularised

[1] In the case where $B$ is constant in time, this type of system is closely related to a data assimilation technique called *3DVar*, where the matrix $B$ is called the *background covariance matrix*. See Kalnay (2002) and Evensen (2006) for more details.

function $\delta_\varepsilon$ is referred to as a *mollified* Dirac delta function, and so we call this system *mollified nudging*.

We would like to generalise this mollified approach to arbitrary data assimilation algorithms in the McKean setting. This is done by first writing the transformation from prior to posterior distributions in the form of Equation (9.20). This then defines the form of the functions $\{g_i\}$ in Equation (9.18). Finally, the Dirac delta function in that equation can be replaced by a mollified Dirac delta function $\delta_\epsilon$.

Having established this approach, we will spend the rest of this section describing how to write our various prior-to-posterior transformations in the form of Equation (9.20). We start with the case in which all of the PDFs are Gaussian and the observation operator is linear, i.e. the Kalman update step.

**Proposition 9.9** (Kalman–Bucy equations)  The standard Kalman update step for the mean and covariance matrix can be formulated as a differential equation in artificial time $s \in [0,1]$. The Kalman–Bucy equations are

$$\frac{\mathrm{d}\bar{z}}{\mathrm{d}s} = -PH^{\mathrm{T}}R^{-1}(H\bar{z} - y_{\mathrm{obs}}) \tag{9.23}$$

and

$$\frac{\mathrm{d}P}{\mathrm{d}s} = -PH^{\mathrm{T}}R^{-1}HP. \tag{9.24}$$

The initial conditions are $\bar{z}(0) = \bar{z}^{\mathrm{f}}$ and $P(0) = P^{\mathrm{f}}$ and the Kalman update is obtained from the final conditions $\bar{z}^{\mathrm{a}} = \bar{z}(1)$ and $P^{\mathrm{a}} = P(1)$.

*Proof*  We present the proof for $N_z = 1$ (one-dimensional state space), $N_y = 1$ (a single observation), and $H = 1$. Under these assumptions, the standard Kalman analysis step gives rise to

$$P^{\mathrm{a}} = \frac{P^{\mathrm{f}}R}{P^{\mathrm{f}} + R}, \qquad \bar{z}^{\mathrm{a}} = \frac{\bar{z}^{\mathrm{f}}R + y_{\mathrm{obs}}P^{\mathrm{f}}}{P^{\mathrm{f}} + R},$$

for a given observation value $y_{\mathrm{obs}}$.

We now demonstrate that one single Kalman analysis step is equivalent to the succesive application of two Kalman analysis steps with $R$ replaced by $2R$. Specifically, we obtain

$$\hat{P}^{\mathrm{a}} = \frac{2P_{\mathrm{m}}R}{P_{\mathrm{m}} + 2R}, \qquad P_{\mathrm{m}} = \frac{2P^{\mathrm{f}}R}{P^{\mathrm{f}} + 2R},$$

for the variance $\hat{P}^{\mathrm{a}}$ with intermediate value $\{P_{\mathrm{m}}\}$. The analysis mean $\hat{z}^{\mathrm{a}}$ is provided by

$$\hat{z}^{\mathrm{a}} = \frac{2\bar{z}_{\mathrm{m}}R + y_{\mathrm{obs}}P_{\mathrm{m}}}{P_{\mathrm{m}} + 2R}, \qquad \bar{z}_{\mathrm{m}} = \frac{2\bar{z}^{\mathrm{f}}R + y_{\mathrm{obs}}P^{\mathrm{f}}}{P^{\mathrm{f}} + 2R}.$$

We need to demonstrate that $P^{\mathrm{a}} = \hat{P}^{\mathrm{a}}$ and $\bar{z}^{\mathrm{a}} = \hat{z}^{\mathrm{a}}$. We start with the variance and obtain

$$\hat{P}^{\mathrm{a}} = \frac{\frac{4P^{\mathrm{f}}R}{P^{\mathrm{f}}+2R}R}{\frac{2P^{\mathrm{f}}R}{P^{\mathrm{f}}+2R}+2R} = \frac{4P^{\mathrm{f}}R^2}{4P^{\mathrm{f}}R+4R^2} = \frac{P^{\mathrm{f}}R}{P^{\mathrm{f}}+R} = P^{\mathrm{a}}.$$

A similar calculation for $\hat{z}^{\mathrm{a}}$ yields

$$\hat{z}^{\mathrm{a}} = \frac{2\frac{2\bar{z}^{\mathrm{f}}R+y_{\mathrm{obs}}P^{\mathrm{f}}}{P^{\mathrm{f}}+2R}R + y_{\mathrm{obs}}\frac{2P^{\mathrm{f}}R}{P^{\mathrm{f}}+2R}}{2R + \frac{2P^{\mathrm{f}}R}{P^{\mathrm{f}}+2R}} = \frac{4\bar{z}^{\mathrm{f}}R^2 + 4y_{\mathrm{obs}}P^{\mathrm{f}}R}{4R^2 + 4RP^{\mathrm{f}}} = \bar{z}^{\mathrm{a}}.$$

Hence, by induction, we can replace the standard Kalman analysis step by $D > 2$ iterative applications of a Kalman analysis with $R$ replaced by $DR$. We set $P_0 = P^{\mathrm{f}}$, $\bar{z}_0 = \bar{z}^{\mathrm{f}}$, and iteratively compute $P_{j+1}$ and $\bar{z}_{j+1}$ from

$$P_{j+1} = \frac{DP_jR}{P_j+DR}, \qquad \bar{z}_{j+1} = \frac{DR\bar{z}_j + P_jy_{\mathrm{obs}}}{P_j+DR}$$

for $j = 0,\dots,D-1$. We finally set $P^{\mathrm{a}} = P_D$ and $\bar{z}^{\mathrm{a}} = \bar{z}_D$. Next we introduce a step-size $\delta s = 1/D$ and assume $D \gg 1$. Then

$$\bar{z}_{j+1} = \frac{R\bar{z}_j + \delta s P_j y_{\mathrm{obs}}}{R + \delta s P_j} = \bar{z}_j - \delta s P_j R^{-1}\left(\bar{z}_j - y_{\mathrm{obs}}\right) + \mathcal{O}(\delta s^2)$$

as well as

$$P_{j+1} = \frac{P_jR}{R + \delta s P_j} = P_j - \delta s P_j R^{-1}P_j + \mathcal{O}(\delta s^2).$$

Taking the limit $\delta s \to 0$, we obtain the two differential equations

$$\frac{\mathrm{d}P}{\mathrm{d}s} = -PR^{-1}P, \qquad \frac{\mathrm{d}\bar{z}}{\mathrm{d}s} = -PR^{-1}\left(\bar{z} - y_{\mathrm{obs}}\right)$$

for the variance and mean, respectively. The equation for $P$ can be rewritten in terms of its square root $P^{1/2}$ as

$$\frac{\mathrm{d}P^{1/2}}{\mathrm{d}s} = -\frac{1}{2}PR^{-1}P^{1/2}. \tag{9.25}$$

□

Next we recall the definition (7.19) of the ensemble anomalies matrix $A$ from Chapter 7, which satisfies $P - 1/(M-1)AA^{\mathrm{T}}$. It is easy to verify that the square root $P^{1/2}$ can be replaced by the matrix of ensemble anomalies $A$ in (9.25) and we obtain the ensemble transform Kalman–Bucy filter equations of Bergemann & Reich (2010), Bergemann & Reich (2012) and Amezcua, Kalnay, Ide & Reich (2014).

**Definition 9.10** (Ensemble transform Kalman–Bucy filter equations)  The *ensemble transform Kalman–Bucy filter* equations for the assimilation of an observation $y_{\mathrm{obs}} = y_{\mathrm{obs}}(\mathsf{t}_k)$ at $\mathsf{t}_k$ are given by

$$\frac{\mathrm{d}z_i}{\mathrm{d}s} = -\frac{1}{2}P_M H^{\mathrm{T}}R^{-1}(Hz_i + H\bar{z}_M - 2y_{\mathrm{obs}})$$

in terms of the ensemble members $z_i$, $i = 1, \ldots, M$, and are solved over a unit time interval in artificial time $s \in [0,1]$ with initial conditions $z_i(0) = z_i^{\mathrm{f}}$. Here

$$P_M(s) = \frac{1}{M-1} \sum_{i=1}^{M} (z_i(s) - \bar{z}_M(s))(z_i(s) - \bar{z}_M(s))^{\mathrm{T}}$$

denotes the empirical covariance matrix, $\bar{z}_M(s)$ the empirical mean of the ensemble, and the analysis ensemble is given at $s = 1$ by $z_i^{\mathrm{a}} = z_i(1)$. The nudging formulation of an ESRF is therefore given by the coupled system of ODEs

$$\frac{\mathrm{d}z_i}{\mathrm{d}t} = f(z_i) - \frac{1}{2} \sum_{k \geq 1} \delta_\varepsilon(t - t_k) P_M H^{\mathrm{T}} R^{-1}(H z_i + H \bar{z}_M - 2 y_{\mathrm{obs}}(t_k)), \quad (9.26)$$

$i = 1, \ldots, M$, and replaces (9.22).

Note that (9.26) leads to the evolution equation

$$\frac{\mathrm{d}\bar{z}_M}{\mathrm{d}t} = \frac{1}{M} \sum_{i=1}^{M} f(z_i) - \sum_{k \geq 1} \delta_\varepsilon(t - t_k) P_M H^{\mathrm{T}} R^{-1}(H \bar{z}_M - y_{\mathrm{obs}}(t_k))$$

for the ensemble mean. After making the approximation

$$\frac{1}{M} \sum_{i=1}^{M} f(z_i) \to f(\bar{z}_M)$$

we obtain

$$\frac{\mathrm{d}\bar{z}_M}{\mathrm{d}t} = f(\bar{z}_M) - \sum_{k \geq 1} \delta_\varepsilon(t - t_k) P_M H^{\mathrm{T}} R^{-1}(H \bar{z}_M - y_{\mathrm{obs}}(t_k)),$$

which can be compared to (9.21). In fact we can consider hybrid data assimilation techniques in which the ensemble generated covariance matrix $P_M$ is replaced by a linear combination $\alpha P_M + (1 - \alpha) B$ in (9.26) with $\alpha \in (0, 1)$.

The ensemble transform Kalman–Bucy equations are an approximation to the differential equation

$$\frac{\mathrm{d}Z}{\mathrm{d}s} = -\frac{1}{2} P H^{\mathrm{T}} R^{-1}(H Z + H \bar{z} - 2 y_{\mathrm{obs}}) \quad (9.27)$$

in the random variable $Z$ with mean

$$\bar{z} = \mathbb{E}[Z] = \int_{\mathbb{R}^{N_z}} z \pi_Z \mathrm{d}z$$

and covariance matrix

$$P = \mathbb{E}[(Z - \bar{z})(Z - \bar{z})^{\mathrm{T}}].$$

The associated evolution of the PDF $\pi_Z(z, s)$ (here assumed to be absolutely continuous) is given by Liouville's equation

$$\frac{\partial \pi_Z}{\partial s} = -\nabla_z \cdot (\pi_Z v) \quad (9.28)$$

with velocity field

$$v(z) = -\frac{1}{2}PH^{\mathrm{T}}R^{-1}(Hz + H\bar{z} - 2y_{\mathrm{obs}}).\tag{9.29}$$

Recalling the earlier discussion of the Fokker–Planck equation in Chapter 5, we note that (9.28) with velocity field (9.29) also has an interesting geometric structure.

**Proposition 9.11** (Ensemble transform Kalman–Bucy equations as a gradient flow)
The velocity field (9.29) is equivalent to

$$v(z) = -P\nabla_z \frac{\delta F}{\delta \pi_Z}$$

with potential

$$F(\pi_Z) = \frac{1}{4}\int_{\mathbb{R}^{N_z}} (Hz - y_{\mathrm{obs}})^{\mathrm{T}}R^{-1}(Hz - y_{\mathrm{obs}})\pi_Z \mathrm{d}z$$
$$+ \frac{1}{4}(H\bar{z} - y_{\mathrm{obs}})^{\mathrm{T}}R^{-1}(H\bar{z} - y_{\mathrm{obs}}).\tag{9.30}$$

Liouville's equation can be stated as

$$\frac{\partial \pi_Z}{\partial s} = -\nabla_z \cdot (\pi_Z v) = -\mathrm{grad}_{\pi_Z}F(\pi_Z).$$

*Proof* The result can be verified by direct calculation using the definitions from Appendix 5.6 with $\mathrm{M} = P$. □

Nonlinear forward operators can be treated in this framework by replacing the potential (9.30) by, for example,

$$F(\pi_Z) = \frac{1}{4}\int_{\mathbb{R}^{N_z}} (h(z) - y_{\mathrm{obs}})^{\mathrm{T}}R^{-1}(h(z) - y_{\mathrm{obs}})\pi_Z \mathrm{d}z$$
$$+ \frac{1}{4}(h(\bar{z}) - y_{\mathrm{obs}})^{\mathrm{T}}R^{-1}(h(\bar{z}) - y_{\mathrm{obs}}).$$

Further, efficient time-stepping methods for the ensemble transform Kalman–Bucy filter equations are discussed in Amezcua et al. (2014); an application to continuous data assimilation can be found in Bergemann & Reich (2012).

In the regime of strong model errors and relatively accurate measurements, it might also be helpful to increase the ensemble spread artificially with ensemble inflation and, at the same time, nudge the ensemble mean more closely towards the observations. This can be achieved by modifying (9.29) to

$$v(z) = -\frac{1}{2}PH^{\mathrm{T}}R^{-1}(\alpha Hz + \beta H\bar{z} - (\alpha + \beta)y_{\mathrm{obs}})$$

with the two non-negative parameters $\alpha < 1$ and $\beta > 1$ chosen such that $\alpha + \beta > 2$.

So far we have discussed a continuous formulation of the ESRF. The corresponding equation for the EnKF with perturbed observations is given by

$$\mathrm{d}Z = -PH^{\mathrm{T}}R^{-1}(HZ - y_{\mathrm{obs}})\mathrm{d}s + PH^{\mathrm{T}}R^{-1/2}\mathrm{d}W,\tag{9.31}$$

where $W(s)$ denotes standard Brownian motion. Indeed an Euler–Maruyama discretisation of (9.31) with step-size $\delta s$ leads to

$$Z^{n+1} = Z^n - \delta s P^n H^\mathrm{T} R^{-1}(HZ^n - y_{\mathrm{obs}}) + \sqrt{\delta s} P^n H^\mathrm{T} R^{-1/2} \Xi^n$$

with $\Xi^n \sim \mathrm{N}(0, I)$. We can immediately extract the associated evolution for the mean $\bar{z}$ which is

$$\bar{z}^{n+1} = \bar{z}^n - \delta s P^n H^\mathrm{T} R^{-1}(H\bar{z}^n - y_{\mathrm{obs}}).$$

The update for the covariance matrix is a bit more involved. We introduce the shorthand $\delta Z^n = Z^n - \bar{z}^n$ and use the independence of $\Xi^n$ and $Z^n$ in order to obtain

$$\begin{aligned}
P^{n+1} &= \mathbb{E}\left[(Z^{n+1} - \bar{z}^{n+1})(Z^{n+1} - \bar{z}^{n+1})^\mathrm{T}\right] \\
&= \mathbb{E}\left[(\delta Z^n - \delta s P^n H^\mathrm{T} R^{-1} H \delta Z^n + \sqrt{\delta s} P^n H^\mathrm{T} R^{-1/2} \Xi^n)\right. \\
&\qquad \left.(\delta Z^n - \delta s P^n H^\mathrm{T} R^{-1} H \delta Z^n + \sqrt{\delta s} P^n H^\mathrm{T} R^{-1/2} \Xi^n)^\mathrm{T}\right] \\
&= P^n - 2\delta s P^n H^\mathrm{T} R^{-1} H P^n \\
&\quad + \delta s^2 P^n H^\mathrm{T} R^{-1} H P^n H^\mathrm{T} R^{-1} H P^n + \delta s P^n H^\mathrm{T} R^{-1} H P^n \\
&= P^n - \delta s P^n H^\mathrm{T} R^{-1} H P^n + \delta s^2 P^n H^\mathrm{T} R^{-1} H P^n H^\mathrm{T} R^{-1} H P^n.
\end{aligned}$$

Upon taking the limit $\delta s \to 0$ we conclude that (9.31) is consistent with the continuous Kalman–Bucy equations (9.23)–(9.24).

The continuous EnKF formulation (9.31) also reveals another interesting option for extending the EnKF to nonlinear forward operators $h(z)$. We simply replace $PH^\mathrm{T}$ in (9.31) by

$$P_{zh} = \mathbb{E}[(Z - \bar{z})(h(Z) - \bar{h})^\mathrm{T}] \tag{9.32}$$

in order to obtain

$$\mathrm{d}Z = -P_{zh} R^{-1}(h(Z) - y_{\mathrm{obs}})\mathrm{d}s + P_{zh} R^{-1/2} \mathrm{d}W. \tag{9.33}$$

Equation (9.33) can be thought of as providing a stochastic linearisation by directly utilising the correlation between state and observation space.

---

**Example 9.12**    We consider a single Bayesian analysis step with the EnKF with perturbed observations applied to an ensemble of size $M = 2000$ from a Gaussian prior with mean $\bar{z}^\mathrm{f} = -2$ and variance $\sigma^2 = 1/2$. The forward model is given by

$$Y = \frac{7}{12}z^3 - \frac{7}{2}z^2 + 8z + \Xi$$

with $\Xi \sim \mathrm{N}(0, 1)$. The observed value is $y_{\mathrm{obs}} = 2.0$. This example has already been investigated in Example 5.9. The resulting posterior PDF and ensemble histograms from the single-step standard EnKF with perturbed observations as well as its continuous counterpart can be found in Figure 9.4. The continuous

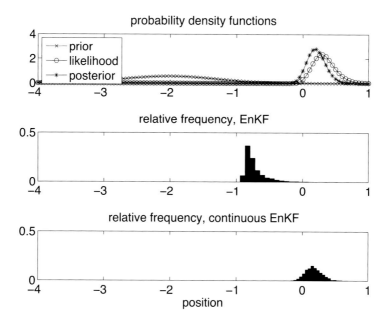

**Figure 9.4** Comparison between the standard EnKF with perturbed observations and its continuous formulation for a Gaussian prior but strongly nonlinear forward operator. Displayed are the analytic prior and posterior PDFs as well as relative frequencies from an ensembles of size $M = 2000$ for each of the two methods. The continuous formulation clearly leads to a closer agreement with the analytic posterior PDF.

EnKF formulation (9.33) obviously leads to a better agreement with the posterior PDF than the standard EnKF with perturbed observations based on a single evaluation of the covariance matrix $P_{zh}$ over the prior ensemble. The continuous formulation is discretised by the forward Euler–Maruyama method with step-size $\delta s = 1/2000$.

We now summarise a continuous formulation of Bayes' formula which generalises the continuous EnKF formulation from above, addressing the question of how to define $g_i$ in (9.18) for non-Gaussian prior distributions within a Bayesian framework. However, it should be kept in mind that the Bayesian framework might not be appropriate in the case of strong and systematic model errors which might lead to an inappropriate ensemble distribution relative to the underlying reference solution $z_{\text{ref}}(t)$ from which the observations $y_{\text{obs}}(t_k)$ are drawn. In fact, the robustness of the ensemble Kalman filter techniques with respect to unavoidable model errors has contributed much to the popularity of the method.

We first note that a single application of Bayes' formula can be replaced by a

$D$-fold recursive application of the incremental likelihood $\widehat{\pi}_Y$:

$$\widehat{\pi}_Y(y|z) = \frac{1}{(2\pi D)^{N_y/2}|R|^{1/2}} \exp\left(-\frac{1}{2D}(h(z)-y)^{\mathrm{T}} R^{-1}(h(z)-y)\right), \quad (9.34)$$

i.e., we first write Bayes' formula as

$$\pi_Z(z|y_{\mathrm{obs}}) \propto \pi_Z(z) \prod_{j=1}^{D} \widehat{\pi}_Y(y_{\mathrm{obs}}|z),$$

where the constant of proportionality depends only on $y_{\mathrm{obs}}$, and then consider the implied iteration

$$\pi_{j+1}(z) = \frac{\pi_j(z)\,\widehat{\pi}_Y(y_{\mathrm{obs}}|z)}{\int_{\mathbb{R}^{N_z}} \widehat{\pi}_Y(y_{\mathrm{obs}}|z)\,\pi_j(z)\,dz} \quad (9.35)$$

with $\pi_0 = \pi_Z$ and $\pi_Z(\cdot|y_{\mathrm{obs}}) = \pi_D$. We write (9.35) more compactly as

$$\pi_{j+1}(z) = \pi_j(z)\frac{\exp(-\delta s L)}{\mathbb{E}[\exp(-\delta s L)]}, \quad (9.36)$$

where $\delta s = 1/D$ and $L$ denotes the negative log likelihood function

$$L(z; y_{\mathrm{obs}}) = \frac{1}{2}(h(z) - y_{\mathrm{obs}})^{\mathrm{T}} R^{-1}(h(z) - y_{\mathrm{obs}}). \quad (9.37)$$

We now expand the exponential functions in (9.36) in the small parameter $\delta s$, and obtain

$$\frac{\exp(-\delta s L)}{\mathbb{E}[\exp(-\delta s L)]} \approx \frac{1 - \delta s L}{1 - \delta s \overline{L}} \approx 1 - \delta s(L - \overline{L}), \quad (9.38)$$

which implies

$$\frac{\pi_{j+1}(z) - \pi_j(z)}{\delta s} \approx -\pi_j(z)(L(z) - \overline{L})$$

with $\overline{L} = \mathbb{E}[L(Z; y_{\mathrm{obs}})]$. Finally, upon taking the limit $\delta s \to 0$, we derive the evolution equation

$$\frac{\partial \pi_Z}{\partial s} = -\pi_Z\left(L - \overline{L}\right) \quad (9.39)$$

in the fictitious time $s \in [0, 1]$. We set $\pi_Z(z, 0) = \pi_Z(z)$ at $s = 0$ and obtain $\pi_Z(z|y_{\mathrm{obs}}) = \pi(z, 1)$ at $s = 1$.

It should be noted that the continuous embedding defined by (9.39) is not unique. Moser (1965), for example, used the linear interpolation

$$\pi_Z(z, s) = (1 - s)\pi_Z(z) + s\pi_Z(z|y_{\mathrm{obs}}),$$

which results in

$$\frac{\partial \pi_Z}{\partial s} = \pi_Z(z|y_{\mathrm{obs}}) - \pi_Z(z). \quad (9.40)$$

Equation (9.39) (or, alternatively, (9.40)) defines the change (or transport) of the PDF $\pi_Z$ in fictitious time $s \in [0, 1]$. Alternatively, following Moser (1965) and Villani (2003), we can view this change as being induced by a continuity (Liouville) equation

$$\frac{\partial \pi_Z}{\partial s} = -\nabla_z \cdot (\pi_Z g) \qquad (9.41)$$

for an appropriate vector field $g(z, s) \in \mathbb{R}^{N_z}$.

At any time $s \in [0, 1]$ the vector field $g(\cdot, s)$ is not uniquely determined by (9.39) and (9.41), unless we also require that it is the minimiser of the kinetic energy

$$\mathcal{T}(v) = \frac{1}{2} \int_{\mathbb{R}^{N_z}} \pi_Z v^{\mathrm{T}} \mathrm{M}^{-1} v \, \mathrm{d}z$$

over all admissible vector fields $v : \mathbb{R}^{N_z} \to \mathbb{R}^{N_z}$, where $\mathrm{M} \in \mathbb{R}^{N_z \times N_z}$ is a symmetric, positive definite matrix. Here admissible means that the vector field satisfies (9.41) for given $\pi_Z$ and $\partial \pi_Z / \partial s$. Under these assumptions, minimisation of the functional

$$\mathcal{L}[v, \psi] = \frac{1}{2} \int_{\mathbb{R}^{N_z}} \pi_Z v^{\mathrm{T}} \mathrm{M}^{-1} v \, \mathrm{d}z + \int_{\mathbb{R}^{N_z}} \psi \left\{ \frac{\partial \pi_Z}{\partial s} + \nabla_z \cdot (\pi_Z v) \right\} \mathrm{d}z$$

for given $\pi_Z$ and $\partial \pi_Z / \partial s$ leads to the Euler–Lagrange equations

$$\pi_Z \mathrm{M}^{-1} g - \pi_Z \nabla_z \psi = 0, \qquad \frac{\partial \pi_Z}{\partial s} + \nabla_z \cdot (\pi_Z g) = 0$$

in the velocity field $g = v$ and the potential $\psi$. Hence, provided that $\pi_Z(z, s) > 0$, the desired vector field is given by $g = \mathrm{M} \nabla_z \psi$, and we have shown the following result.

**Proposition 9.13** (Transport map from gradient flow)   If the potential $\psi(z, s)$ is the solution of the elliptic PDE

$$\nabla_z \cdot (\pi_Z \mathrm{M} \nabla_z \psi) = \pi_Z \left( L - \overline{L} \right), \qquad (9.42)$$

then the desired transport map $z' = T(z)$ for the random variable $Z$ with PDF $\pi(z, s)$ is defined by the time-one-flow map of the differential equation

$$\frac{\mathrm{d}z}{\mathrm{d}s} = -\mathrm{M} \nabla_z \psi. \qquad (9.43)$$

If the PDF $\pi_Z(z, s)$ is approximated by a Gaussian, then the elliptic PDE (9.42) can be solved analytically, and the resulting differential equations are equivalent to the ensemble transform Kalman–Bucy equations (9.27). Appropriate analytic expressions can also be found if $\pi_Z(z, s)$ is approximated by a Gaussian mixture and the forward map $h(z)$ is linear (see Reich (2012) for details).

## Problems

**9.1**   Verify Equation (9.5) for $N_{\mathrm{obs}} = 2$ and under the assumption that the transition kernel $\pi(z'|z)$ describes the Markovian model dynamics in between observations. Hint: note that

$$\mathbb{E}\left[\pi_{Y_{t_{1:2}}}(y_{t_{1:2}}|Z_{t_{0:2}})\right] =$$

$$\int_{\mathcal{Z}}\int_{\mathcal{Z}}\int_{\mathcal{Z}} \pi_Y(y(t_2)|z^2)\pi(z^2|z^1)\pi_Y(y(t_1)|z^1)\pi(z^1|z^0)\pi_Z(z^0,0)dz^0dz^1dz^2.$$

**9.2**    Use the experimental setting from Example 9.3 and ensemble prediction in order to approximate the evidence (9.2) as a function of the variance $\sigma^2$ in the stochastic driving terms of the modified Lorenz-63 model (4.18)–(4.20). Instead of one hundred ensembles of size $M = 1000$, use a single ensemble of size $M = 10000$ and assimilate only the first 50 observations, i.e., set $N_{\text{obs}} = 50$. Compare your findings with those displayed in Figure 9.1.

**9.3**    Repeat the numerical experiment from Example 9.6 with a prior distribution of $U[6, 10]$ in $\lambda$. Compare your findings with those from Figure 9.2.

**9.4**    Derive explicit solution formulas for the differential equation

$$\frac{dz}{dt} = -az + \delta_\varepsilon(t-1)bz$$

over the time interval $t \in [0, 2]$ with initial condition $z(0) = 1$, $a$, $b$ given parameters, and the mollified Dirac delta function given by (9.19). Discuss the limit $\varepsilon \to 0$.

**9.5**    Repeat Example 9.12 with $y_{\text{obs}} = 0$ and $\delta s = 1/200$. What do you observe for $\delta s = 1/100$? In order to explain your findings you may wish to consult the paper by Amezcua et al. (2014).

**9.6**    Verify that the continuous Kalman–Bucy filter equations are a special case of (9.43) with $M = P$ and $\psi = \delta F/\delta \pi_Z$ with the functional $F$ given by (9.30).

**9.7**    Consider the sequence of univariate random variables

$$\delta Y_j := h\delta s + \sqrt{\delta s}\Xi_j, \qquad j = 1, \ldots, D,$$

where the random variables $\{\Xi_j\}$ are Gaussian and identically distributed with mean zero and variance one, $h$ is a given constant, $\delta s = t/D$ is the step-size and $D$ the number of steps. We are interested in the properties of the sum of squares

$$S_D = \sum_{j=1}^{D}(\delta Y_j)^2$$

in the limit $D \to \infty$.

(i)    Show that

$$\lim_{D\to\infty} \mathbb{E}[S_D] = t.$$

(ii)    What do you obtain for var $(S_D)$ as $D \to \infty$? *Remark*: The results of this problem can be used to justify (9.49) from Appendix 9.5.

## 9.4 Guide to literature

A stimulating discussion of chaos, imperfect models and predictions is given by Smith (2007b). Data assimilation for imperfect models and parameter estimation are also discussed in Majda & Harlim (2012). Raftery (1995) provides an introduction to Bayesian model selection. Classical variational techniques for parameter estimation are, for example, covered in Tarantola (2005), and the textbook by Särkkä (2013) discusses parameter estimation techniques based on Monte Carlo methods.

A discussion of general Markov chain Monte Carlo methods can be found in Liu (2001) and Robert & Casella (2004). The pseudo-marginal Markov chain Monte Carlo method is described by Beaumont (2003) and Andrieu & Roberts (2009).

The use of nudging to initialise forecast models goes back to Hoke & Anthes (1976). Incremental or mollified data analysis was first proposed by Bloom, Takacs, Silva & Ledvina (1996). Mollified ensemble Kalman filter implementations are implemented in Bergemann & Reich (2010) in the context of a Lorenz-96 model coupled to a linear wave equation, where the generation of spurious unbalanced waves through intermittent assimilation of data is studied.

The idea of a continuous reformulation of the ensemble Kalman analysis step is also closely related to iterative approaches to data assimilation for strongly nonlinear forward operators as proposed, for example, by Sakov, Oliver & Bertino (2012), Chen & Oliver (2013), and Emerik & Reynolds (2012). These iterative algorithms can also be viewed as derivative-free implementations of a regularised Levenberg–Marquardt algorithm for ill-posed inverse problems (Engl, Hanke & Neubauer 2000).

See Daum & Huang (2011) and Reich & Cotter (2013) for further discussions on the implementation of (9.42)–(9.43) in the context of nonlinear filters.

Theoretical results on the ability of filtering algorithms of type (9.22) to track a partially observed reference solution for hyperbolic systems, such as the Lorenz-63 model, over infinite time intervals can be found, for example, in González-Tokman & Hunt (2013) and Law, Shukia & Stuart (2014).

## 9.5 Appendix: Continuous-time filtering

Throughout this book we have considered measurements taken at discrete times $t_k$. However, it is also possible to consider continuous measurements with forward model

$$dY = h(Z)dt + R^{1/2}dW ,  \qquad (9.44)$$

where $W(t)$ denotes $N_y$-dimensional Brownian motion. While discrete-time observations are more common from a practical point of view, the continuous data model (9.44) can often be found in mathematical textbooks on filtering because of its mathematical elegance. Without proof we state the associated ensemble Kalman–Bucy filter formulation with perturbed observations

$$\mathrm{d}Z = f(Z)\mathrm{d}t - P_{zh}R^{-1}(h(Z)\mathrm{d}t - \mathrm{d}y_{\mathrm{obs}}(t) + R^{1/2}\mathrm{d}W) \qquad (9.45)$$

and we see that the original dynamics, given by

$$\mathrm{d}Z = f(Z)\mathrm{d}t , \qquad (9.46)$$

is now constantly nudged towards the observed $\mathrm{d}y_{\mathrm{obs}}(t)$. Here the cross-correlation covariance matrix $P_{zh}$ is defined by (9.32). The equation (9.45) can be discretised in time by the Euler–Maruyama method. In fact, a derivation of (9.45) starts from such a discrete-time formulation together with a discretised forward model

$$\delta Y = h(Z)\delta t + (\delta t R)^{1/2}\Xi,$$

$\Xi \sim \mathrm{N}(0, I)$, and subsequent limit $\delta t \to 0$.

---

**Example 9.14**   We consider the discretised Lorenz-63 system (9.9) from Example 9.6 with right hand side given by (9.14). However, instead of intermittent observations and misspecified parameter values, we now consider the forward observation model

$$\delta y_{\mathrm{obs}}^n = e_1^{\mathrm{T}} f(z_{\mathrm{ref}}^n)\delta t + \sqrt{\delta t}\xi^n$$

with $e_1 = (1, 0, 0)^{\mathrm{T}}$ and $\xi^n$ a realisation of $\mathrm{N}(0, 1)$, i.e., $h(z) = e_1^{\mathrm{T}} f(z)$ and we observe a noisy version of the increments in the x-component of the reference solution. The computational data assimilation model is given by an Euler–Maruyama discretisation of the continuous EnKF formulation (9.45), i.e.,

$$z_i^{n+1} = z_i^n + \delta t f(z^n) - P_{zh}R^{-1}\left(e_1^{\mathrm{T}} f(z^n)\delta t - \delta y_{\mathrm{obs}}^n + \sqrt{\delta t}R^{1/2}\zeta^n\right), \qquad (9.47)$$

where $R = 1$ in our setting, the variables $\{\zeta^n\}$ are independent realisations of $\mathrm{N}(0, 1)$, and the empirical correlation matrix between state and observation variables is given by

$$P_{zh} = \frac{1}{M-1}\sum_{i=1}^{M} (z_i^n - \bar{z}^n)\left(e_1^{\mathrm{T}} f(z_i^n) - \frac{1}{M}\sum_{i=1}^{M} e_1^{\mathrm{T}} f(z_i^n)\right).$$

In this example, the ensemble size is set to $M = 20$, the step-size is $\delta t = 0.0025$, and the initial ensemble is generated as outlined in Example 9.6. The time-averaged RMSE along the whole trajectory and averaged over all three solution components is found to be 0.1890. See Figure 9.5 for numerical results.

---

We end this appendix with a brief discussion of the general continuous data assimilation problem in terms of an evolution equation for the marginal PDF $\pi_Z(z, t)$. In order to derive this evolution equation we consider continuous measurements of type (9.44) and apply a discretisation with an outer step-size $\delta t$ and

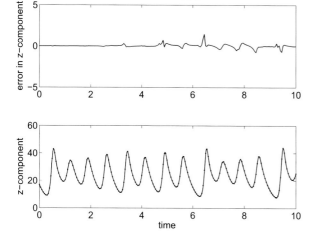

**Figure 9.5** Continuous EnKF applied to the Lorenz-63 model. Displayed are the z-component of the filtered solution and its error with respect to the reference solution.

an inner step-size $\delta s = \delta t/D$, $D \gg 1$. The Euler–Maruyama method is applied at the inner time-step resulting in

$$\delta y_j = h(z_{\mathrm{ref}}(t))\delta s + \sqrt{\delta s}R^{1/2}\xi_j,$$

where $\{\xi_j\}$ are independent realisations from the $\mathrm{N}(0, I)$ distribution. The outer approximation is then given by

$$\delta y_{\mathrm{obs}} = \sum_{j=1}^{D} \delta y_j \ . \tag{9.48}$$

We now proceed along the lines of (9.35) with conditional PDFs

$$\pi(\delta y_j | z) \propto e^{-L_j}$$

and negative log likelihood functions

$$L_j(z; \delta y_j) = \frac{1}{2} \left( h(z)\delta s^{1/2} - \delta s^{-1/2}\delta y_j \right)^{\mathrm{T}} R^{-1} \left( h(z)\delta s^{1/2} - \delta s^{-1/2}\delta y_j \right).$$

Following the previous discussion on the continuous Bayesian formalism, we consider the iteration

$$\pi_{j+1}(z) = \pi_j(z)\frac{\exp(-L_j)}{\mathbb{E}[\exp(-L_j)]}.$$

Due to the presence of the $\delta s^{-1/2}$ term in $L_j$, the exponential function needs to be expanded more carefully in order to keep all terms of order $\mathcal{O}(\delta s)$. In order to simplify the notation, we continue the discussion for a scalar observation, set $R = 1$, and drop the argument in the forward map $h$. We also immediately drop all terms that give rise to contributions of order $\mathcal{O}(\delta s^{3/2})$. This leads to the following approximations:

$$\frac{\exp(-L_j)}{\mathbb{E}[\exp(-L_j)]} = \frac{\exp\left(-\frac{1}{2}h^2\delta s + h\delta y_j\right)}{\mathbb{E}[\exp\left(-\frac{1}{2}h^2\delta s + h\delta y_j\right)]}$$

$$\approx \frac{1 - \frac{1}{2}h^2\delta s + h\delta y_j + \frac{1}{2}h^2\delta y_j^2}{1 - \frac{1}{2}\overline{h^2}\delta s + \overline{h}\delta y_j + \frac{1}{2}\overline{h^2}\delta y_j^2}$$

$$\approx \left(1 - \frac{1}{2}h^2\delta s + h\delta y_j + \frac{1}{2}h^2\delta y_j^2\right)$$

$$\times \left(1 + \frac{1}{2}\overline{h^2}\delta s - \overline{h}\delta y_j - \frac{1}{2}\overline{h^2}\delta y_j^2 + \overline{h}^2\delta y_j^2\right)$$

$$\approx 1 - \frac{1}{2}(h^2 - \overline{h^2})\delta s + \frac{1}{2}(h^2 - 2h\overline{h} + 2\overline{h}^2 - \overline{h^2})\delta y_j^2 + (h - \overline{h})\delta y_j.$$

Since $\delta t = D\delta s$ and (9.48) the $D$-fold product can be approximated as

$$\prod_{j=1}^{D}\frac{\exp(-L_j)}{\mathbb{E}[\exp(-L_j)]} \approx 1 - \frac{1}{2}\sum_{j=1}^{D}(h^2 - \overline{h^2})\delta s$$

$$+ \sum_{j=1}^{D}\left\{(h - \overline{h})\delta y_j + \frac{1}{2}(h^2 - 2h\overline{h} + 2\overline{h}^2 - \overline{h^2})\delta y_j^2\right\}$$

$$\approx 1 - \frac{1}{2}(h^2 - \overline{h^2})\delta t + (h - \overline{h})\delta y_{\text{obs}}$$

$$+ \sum_{j=1}^{D}\delta y_j^2\left\{\frac{1}{2}(h^2 - \overline{h^2}) - (h - \overline{h})\overline{h}\right\}.$$

Note that (compare Problem 9.7)

$$\lim_{D\to\infty}\sum_{j=1}^{D}\delta y_j^2 \approx \delta t \tag{9.49}$$

and the evolution of the marginal PDF $\pi_Z(z, t)$ under a continuous observation over a time increment $\delta t$ can be approximated by

$$\pi_Z(z, t + \delta t) \approx \pi_Z(z, t) + \pi_Z(z, t)\left\{(h(z) - \overline{h})^{\text{T}}R^{-1}(\delta y_{\text{obs}} - \overline{h}\delta t)\right\}.$$

We finally take the limit $\delta t \to 0$, return to the general observation model with covariance matrix $R$, and obtain the evolution equation

$$d\pi_Z = \pi_Z\left(h - \mathbb{E}[h(Z)]\right)^{\text{T}}R^{-1}(dy_{\text{obs}} - \mathbb{E}[h(Z)]dt), \tag{9.50}$$

which provides the "nudging" part of the Kushner–Stratonovitch filter equation

$$d\pi_Z = -\nabla_z \cdot (\pi_Z f)dt + \pi_Z\left(h - \mathbb{E}[h(Z)]\right)^{\text{T}}R^{-1}(dy_{\text{obs}} - \mathbb{E}[h(Z)]dt), \tag{9.51}$$

under an observed process $y_{\text{obs}}(t)$. See Jazwinski (1970) for a related derivation and more details.

The Kushner–Stratonovitch equation (9.51) generalises the Liouville (or more generally Fokker–Planck) equation for the marginal PDFs under the dynamic model to the continuous time observation case. The theory of continuous time filtering is covered, for example, in Jazwinski (1970) and Øksendal (2000).

As for the evolution equation (9.39) for the marginal PDF $\pi_Z$ under a discrete-time observation, the contribution (9.50) can be given an interpretation as providing additional driving terms to the model equation (9.46). However, the derivation of these driving terms and McKean-type continuous time filtering techniques are beyond the mathematical machinery developed in this book and we refer the interested reader to Crisan & Xiong (2010) and Yang, Mehta & Meyn (2013). We mention that the additional driving terms reduce to the Kalman–Bucy terms considered earlier in this section in the case of a Gaussian $\pi_Z$ and linear forward operator (Bergemann & Reich 2012).

# A postscript

We have come to the end of our introduction to ensemble-based forecasting and data assimilation algorithms. The field is rapidly developing and key challenges come from imperfect model scenarios and the high dimensionality of models. While certain particle filters are asymptotically optimal within a perfect model scenario, this picture is much less clear for "real world" data assimilation problems. Here the ensemble Kalman filter has been shown to be both robust and sufficiently accurate for many practical problems. However, it should be kept in mind that most successful applications of the ensemble Kalman filter have arisen against a background of relatively advanced mechanistic models and for problems for which the forecast uncertainties can be approximated by Gaussian distributions. Further challenges arise when, in the absence of accepted mechanistic design principles, only crude empirical models are available and model parameters as well as model states need to be estimated. Ideally, in such cases one might wish to convert empirical models into mechanistic design principles by extracting causalities from data using data assimilation algorithms. These topics are beyond our introductory textbook and we end by inviting the reader to become an active participant in the exciting enterprise called *probabilistic forecasting* and *data assimilation*.

# References

Amezcua, J., Kalnay, E., Ide, K. & Reich, S. (2014), 'Ensemble transform Kalman–Bucy filters', *Q.J.R. Meteor. Soc.* **140**, 995–1004.

Anderson, J. (2007), 'An adaptive covariance inflation error correction algorithm for ensemble filters', *Tellus* **59A**, 210–224.

Anderson, J. (2010), 'A non-Gaussian ensemble filter update for data assimilation', *Mon. Wea. Rev.* **138**, 4186–4198.

Anderson, J. (2012), 'Localization and sampling error correction in ensemble Kalman filter data assimilation', *Mon. Wea. Rev.* **140**, 2359–2371.

Andrieu, C. & Roberts, G. (2009), 'The pseudo-marginal approach for efficient Monte-Carlo computations', *Ann. Statist.* **37**, 697–725.

Arnold, V. (1989), *Mathematical Methods of Classical Mechanics*, 2nd edn, Springer-Verlag, New York.

Arulampalam, M., Maskell, S., Gordon, N. & Clapp, T. (2002), 'A tutorial on particle filters for online nonlinear/non-Gaussian Bayesian tracking', *IEEE Trans. Sign. Process.* **50**, 174–188.

Ascher, U. (2008), *Numerical Methods for Evolutionary Differential Equations*, SIAM, Philadelphia, PA.

Bain, A. & Crisan, D. (2009), *Fundamentals of Stochastic Filtering*, Vol. 60 of *Stochastic Modelling and Applied Probability*, Springer-Verlag, New York.

Beaumont, M. (2003), 'Estimation of population growth or decline in genetically monitored populations', *Genetics* **164**, 1139–1160.

Benamou, J. & Brenier, Y. (2000), 'A computational fluid mechanics solution to the Monge–Kantorovitch mass transfer problem', *Numer. Math.* **84**, 375–393.

Bengtsson, T., Bickel, P. & Li, B. (2008), 'Curse of dimensionality revisited: Collapse of the particle filter in very large scale systems'. In *IMS Collections, Probability and Statistics: Essays in Honor of David F. Freedman*, **2**, 316–334.

Bergemann, K. & Reich, S. (2010), 'A mollified ensemble Kalman filter', *Q.J.R. Meteorolog. Soc.* **136**, 1636–1643.

Bergemann, K. & Reich, S. (2012), 'An ensemble Kalman–Bucy filter for continuous data assimilation', *Meteorolog. Zeitschrift* **21**, 213–219.

Bloom, S., Takacs, L., Silva, A.D. & Ledvina, D. (1996), 'Data assimilation using incremental analysis updates', *Q.J.R. Meteorolog. Soc.* **124**, 1256–1271.

Bocquet, M. & Sakov, P. (2012), 'Combining inflation-free and iterative ensemble Kalman filters for strongly nonlinear systems', *Nonlin. Processes Geophys.* **19**, 383–399.

Bocquet, M., Pires, C. & Wu, L. (2010), 'Beyond Gaussian statistical modeling in geophysical data assimilaition', *Mon. Wea. Rev.* **138**, 2997–3022.

Breźniak, Z. & Zastawniak, T. (1999), *Basic Stochastic Processes*, Springer-Verlag, London.

Bröcker, J. (2012), 'Evaluating raw ensembles with the continuous ranked probability score', *Q.J.R. Meteorolog. Soc.* **138**, 1611–1617.

Bungartz, H.-J. & Griebel, M. (2004), 'Sparse grids', *Acta Numerica* **13**, 147–269.

Caflisch, R. (1998), 'Monte Carlo and Quasi-Monte Carlo methods', *Acta Numerica* **7**, 1–49.

Chen, Y. & Oliver, D. (2013), 'Levenberg–Marquardt forms of the iterative ensemble smoother for efficient history matching and uncertainty quantification', *Computational Geoscience* **17**, 689–703.

Cheng, Y. & Reich, S. (2013), 'A McKean optimal transportation perspective on Feynman–Kac formulae with application to data assimilation'., arXiv:1311.6300. To appear in *Frontiers in Applied Dynamical Systems*, Vol. 1, Springer-Verlag, New York.

Chorin, A. & Hald, O. (2009), *Stochastic Tools in Mathematics and Science*, 2nd edn, Springer-Verlag, Berlin.

Chorin, A., Morzfeld, M. & Tu, X. (2010), 'Implicit filters for data assimilation', *Comm. Appl. Math. Comp. Sc.* **5**, 221–240.

Coles, S. (2001), *An Introduction to Statistical Modeling of Extreme Values*, Springer-Verlag, New York.

Collet, P. & Eckmann, J.-P. (2006), *Concepts and Results in Chaotic Dynamics*, Springer-Verlag, Berlin.

Crisan, D. & Xiong, J. (2010), 'Approximate McKean–Vlasov representation for a class of SPDEs', *Stochastics* **82**, 53–68.

Daley, R. (1993), *Atmospheric Data Analysis*, Cambridge University Press, Cambridge.

Daum, F. & Huang, J. (2011), 'Particle filter for nonlinear filters'. In *Acoustics, Speech and Signal Processing (ICASSP), 2011 IEEE International Conference*, IEEE, New York, 5920–5923.

del Moral, P. (2004), *Feynman–Kac Formulae: Genealogical and Interacting Particle Systems with Applications*, Springer-Verlag, New York.

Doucet, A., de Freitas, N. & Gordon, N., editors (2001), *Sequential Monte Carlo Methods in Practice*, Springer-Verlag, Berlin.

Emerik, A. & Reynolds, A. (2012), 'Ensemble smoother with multiple data assimilation', *Computers & Geosciences* **55**, 3–15.

Engl, H., Hanke, M. & Neubauer, A. (2000), *Regularization of Inverse Problems*, Kluwer Academic Publishers, Dordrecht.

Evans, L. (1998), *Partial Differential Equations*, American Mathematical Society, Providence, RI.

Evans, L. (2013), *An Introduction to Stochastic Differential Equations*, American Mathematical Society, Providence, RI.

Evensen, G. (2006), *Data Assimilation. The Ensemble Kalman Filter*, Springer-Verlag, New York.

Frei, M. & Künsch, H. (2013), 'Mixture ensemble Kalman filters', *Computational Statistics and Data Analysis* **58**, 127–138.

Gardiner, C. (2004), *Handbook of Stochastic Methods*, 3rd edn, Springer-Verlag.

Gneiting, T., Balabdaoui, F. & Raftery, A. (2007), 'Probabilistic forecasts, calibration and sharpness', *J. R. Statist. Soc. B* **69**, 243–268.

Golub, G. & Loan, C.V. (1996), *Matrix Computations*, 3rd edn, Johns Hopkins University Press, Baltimore, MD.

González-Tokman, C. & Hunt, B. (2013), 'Ensemble data assimilation for hyperbolic systems', *Physica D* **243**, 128–142.

Hand, D. (2008), *Statistics: A Very Short Introduction*, Oxford University Press, Oxford.

Hastie, T., Tibshirani, R. & Friedman, J. (2009), *The Elements of Statistical Learning*, 2nd edn, Springer-Verlag, New York.

Higham, D. (2001), 'An algorithmic introduction to numerical simulation of stochastic differential equations', *SIAM Review* **43**, 525–546.

Hoke, J. & Anthes, R. (1976), 'The initialization of numerical models by a dynamic relaxation technique', *Mon. Wea. Rev.* **104**, 1551–1556.

Holtz, M. (2011), *Sparse Grid Quadrature in High Dimensions with Applications in Finance and Insurance*, Springer-Verlag, Berlin.

Hunt, B., Kostelich, E. & Szunyogh, I. (2007), 'Efficient data assimilation for spatial-temporal chaos: A local ensemble transform Kalman filter', *Physica D* **230**, 112–137.

Janjić, T., McLaughlin, D., Cohn, S. & Verlaan, M. (2014), 'Convervation of mass and preservation of positivity with ensemble-type Kalman filter algorithms', *Mon. Wea. Rev.* **142**, 755–773.

Jazwinski, A. (1970), *Stochastic Processes and Filtering Theory*, Academic Press, New York.

Julier, S.J. & Uhlmann, J.K. (1997), 'A new extension of the Kalman filter to nonlinear systems'. In *Proc. AeroSense: 11th Int. Symp. Aerospace/Defense Sensing, Simulation and Controls*, pp. 182–193.

Kaipio, J. & Somersalo, E. (2005), *Statistical and Computational Inverse Problems*, Springer-Verlag, New York.

Kalnay, E. (2002), *Atmospheric Modeling, Data Assimilation and Predictability*, Cambridge University Press, Cambridge.

Katok, A. & Hasselblatt, B. (1995), *Introduction to the Modern Theory of Dynamical Systems*, Cambridge University Press, Cambridge.

Kitanidis, P. (1995), 'Quasi-linear geostatistical theory for inverting', *Water Resources Research* **31**, 2411–2419.

Kloeden, P. & Platen, E. (1992), *Numerical Solution of Stochastic Differential Equations*, Springer-Verlag, Berlin.

Künsch, H. (2005), 'Recursive Monte Carlo filter: Algorithms and theoretical analysis', *Ann. Statist.* **33**, 1983–2021.

Lasota, A. & Mackey, M. (1994), *Chaos, Fractals, and Noise*, 2nd edn, Springer-Verlag, New York.

Law, K., Shukia, A. & Stuart, A. (2014), 'Analysis of the 3DVAR filter for the partially observed Lorenz '63 model', *Discrete and Continuous Dynamical Systems A* **34**, 1061–1078.

Lei, J. & Bickel, P. (2011), 'A moment matching ensemble filter for nonlinear and non-Gaussian data assimilation', *Mon. Wea. Rev.* **139**, 3964–3973.

Lewis, J., Lakshmivarahan, S. & Dhall, S. (2006), *Dynamic Data Assimilation: A Least Squares Approach*, Cambridge University Press, Cambridge.

Liu, J. (2001), *Monte Carlo Strategies in Scientific Computing*, Springer-Verlag, New York.

Livings, D., Dance, S. & Nichols, N. (2008), 'Unbiased ensemble square root filters', *Physica D* **237**, 1021–1028.

Lorenz, E. (1963), 'Deterministic non-periodic flows', *J. Atmos. Sci.* **20**, 130–141.

Majda, A. & Harlim, J. (2012), *Filtering Complex Turbulent Systems*, Cambridge University Press, Cambridge.

McCann, R. (1995), 'Existence and uniqueness of monotone measure-preserving maps', *Duke Math. J.* **80**, 309–323.

McKean, H. (1966), 'A class of Markov processes associated with nonlinear parabolic equations', *Proc. Natl. Acad. Sci. USA* **56**, 1907–1911.

Meyn, S. & Tweedie, R. (1993), *Markov Chains and Stochastic Stability*, Springer-Verlag, London.

Miyoshi, T. (2011), 'The Gaussian approach to adaptive covariance inflation and its implementation with the local ensemble transform Kalman filter', *Mon. Wea. Rev.* **139**, 1519–1535.

Morzfeld, M. & Chorin, A. (2012), 'Implicit particle filtering for models with partial noise and an application to geomagnetic data assimilation', *Nonlinear Processes in Geophysics* **19**, 365–382.

Morzfeld, M., Tu, X., Atkins, E. & Chorin, A. (2012), 'A random map implementation of implicit filters', *J. Comput. Phys.* **231**, 2049–2066.

Moselhy, T.E. & Marzouk, Y. (2012), 'Bayesian inference with optimal maps', *J. Comput. Phys.* **231**, 7815–7850.

Moser, J. (1965), 'On the volume elements on a manifold', *Trans. Amer. Math. Soc.* **120**, 286–294.

Neal, R. (1996), *Bayesian Learning for Neural Networks*, Springer-Verlag, New York.

Nerger, L., Pfander, T.J., Schröter, J. & Hiller, W. (2012), 'A regulated localization scheme for ensemble-based Kalman filters', *Q.J.R. Meteorolog. Soc.* **138**, 802–812.

Nocedal, J. & Wright, S. (2006), *Numerical Optimization*, 2nd edn, Springer-Verlag, New York.

Øksendal, B. (2000), *Stochastic Differential Equations*, 5th edn, Springer-Verlag, Berlin.

Oliver, D. (1996), 'On conditional simulation to inaccurate data', *Math. Geology* **28**, 811–817.

Oliver, D., He, N. & Reynolds, A. (1996), 'Conditioning permeability fields on pressure data. *Technical Report*: presented at the 5th European Conference on the Mathematics of Oil Recovery, Leoben, Austria.

Olkin, I. & Pukelsheim, F. (1982), 'The distance between two random vectors with given dispersion matrices', *Lin. Alg. and its Applns.* **48**, 257–263.

Ott, E., Hunt, B., Szunyogh, I., Zimin, A., Kostelich, E., Corazza, M., Kalnay, E., Patil, D. & Yorke, J.A. (2004), 'A local ensemble Kalman filter for atmospheric data assimilation', *Tellus* **A 56**, 415–428.

Otto, F. (2001), 'The geometry of dissipative evolution equations: the porous medium equation', *Comm. Part. Diff. Eqs.* **26**, 101–174.

Pavliotis, G. (2014), *Stochastic Processes and Applications*, Springer-Verlag, New York.

Pele, O. & Werman, M. (2009), 'Fast and robust earth mover's distances'. In *12th IEEE International Conference on Computer Vision*, IEEE New York, pp. 460–467.

Raftery, A. (1995), 'Bayesian model selection in social research', *Sociological Methodology* **25**, 111–163.

Rebeschini, P. & van Handel, R. (2013), 'Can local particle filters beat the curse of dimensionality?', arXiv:1301.6585.

Reich, S. (2011), 'A dynamical systems framework for intermittent data assimilation', *BIT Numer Math* **51**, 235–249.

Reich, S. (2012), 'A Gaussian mixture ensemble transform filter', *Q.J.R. Meteorolog. Soc.* **138**, 222–233.

Reich, S. (2013*a*), 'A guided sequential Monte Carlo method for the assimilation of data into stochastic dynamical systems'. In *Recent Trends in Dynamical Systems*, Proceedings in Mathematics and Statistics, **35**, Springer-Verlag, Basel, pp. 205–220.

Reich, S. (2013*b*), 'A nonparametric ensemble transform method for Bayesian inference', *SIAM J. Sci. Comput.* **35**, A2013–A2024.

Reich, S. & Cotter, C. (2013), 'Ensemble filter techniques for intermittent data assimilation'. In *Large Scale Inverse Problems. Computational Methods and Applications in the Earth Sciences*, M. Cullen, M.A. Freitag, S. Kindermann & R. Scheichl, eds, Radon Ser. Comput. Appl. Math., **13**, de Gruyter, Berlin, pp. 91–134.

Robert, C. (2001), *The Bayesian Choice: From Decision-Theoretic Motivations to Computational Implementations*, 2nd edn, Springer-Verlag, New York.

Robert, C. & Casella, G. (2004), *Monte Carlo Statistical Methods*, 2nd edn, Springer-Verlag, New York.

Robinson, J. (2001), *Infinite-Dimensional Dynamical Systems*, Cambridge University Press, Cambridge.

Sakov, P., Oliver, D. & Bertino, L. (2012), 'An iterative EnKF for strongly nonlinear systems', *Mon. Wea. Rev.* **140**, 1988–2004.

Särkkä, S. (2013), *Bayesian Filtering and Smoothing*, Cambridge University Press, Cambridge.

Simon, D. (2006), *Optimal State Estimation*, Wiley, New York.

Smith, K. (2007*a*), 'Cluster ensemble Kalman filter', *Tellus* **59A**, 749–757.

Smith, L. (2007*b*), *Chaos: A Very Short Introduction*, Oxford University Press, Oxford.

Smith, R. (2014), *Uncertainty Quantification*, SIAM, Philadelphia, PA.

Stordal, A., Karlsen, H., Nævdal, G., Skaug, H. & Vallés, B. (2011), 'Bridging the ensemble Kalman filter and particle filters: the adaptive Gaussian mixture filter', *Comput. Geosci.* **15**, 293–305.

Strang, G. (1986), *Introduction to Applied Mathematics*, 2nd edn, Wellesley-Cambridge Press, Wellesley, MA.

Stuart, A. (2010), 'Inverse problems: a Bayesian perspective', *Acta Numerica* **17**, 451–559.

Süli, E. & Mayers, D. (2006), *An Introduction to Numerical Analysis*, Cambridge University Press, Cambridge.

Takens, F. (1981), 'Detecting strange attractors in turbulence'. In *Dynamical Systems and Turbulence*. Lecture Notes in Mathematics, **898**, Springer-Verlag, Berlin, pp. 366–381.

Tarantola, A. (2005), *Inverse Problem Theory and Methods for Model Parameter Estimation*, SIAM, Philadelphia, PA.

Tijms, H. (2012), *Understanding Probability*, 3rd edn, Cambridge University Press, Cambridge.

Tippett, M., Anderson, J., Bishop, G., Hamill, T. & Whitaker, J. (2003), 'Ensemble square root filters', *Mon. Wea. Rev.* **131**, 1485–1490.

van Leeuwen, P. (2010), 'Nonlinear data assimilation in the geosciences: an extremely efficient particle filter', *Q.J.R. Meteorolog. Soc.* **136**, 1991–1996.

van Leeuwen, P. & Ades, M. (2013), 'Efficient fully nonlinear data assimilation for geophysical fluid dynamics', *Computers & Geosciences* **55**, 16–27.

Verhulst, F. (2000), *Nonlinear Differential Equations and Dynamical Systems*, 2nd edn, Springer-Verlag, Berlin.

Villani, C. (2003), *Topics in Optimal Transportation*, American Mathematical Society, Providence, RI.

Villani, C. (2009), *Optimal Transportation: Old and New*, Springer-Verlag, Berlin.

Wang, X., Bishop, C. & Julier, S. (2004), 'Which is better, an ensemble of positive-negative pairs or a centered spherical simplex ensemble?', *Mon. Wea. Rev.* **132**, 1590–1505.

Yang, T., Mehta, P. & Meyn, S. (2013), 'Feedback particle filter', *IEEE Trans. Automatic Control* **58**, 2465–2480.

# Index

Printed in the United States
By Bookmasters